Personality at work

Personality at Work examines the increasingly controversial role of individual differences in predicting and determining behaviour at work. It asks whether psychological tests measuring personality traits can predict behaviour at work, such as job satisfaction, productivity, as well as absenteeism and turnover. Importantly, it is a critical and comprehensive review of that literature from psychology, sociology and management science which lies at the interface of personality theory, occupational psychology and organizational behaviour.

Drawing on a vast body of published material, Adrian Furnham describes for the first time the current state of knowledge in this area. The result is a volume which will be an enormously useful resource to the researcher and practitioner, as well as students of psychology, management science and sociology. *Personality at Work* is the only exhaustive and incisive multi-disciplinary work to assess the role of psychological testing in the management of the workplace.

Adrian Furnham is Reader in Psychology at University College London. His previous books include *Young People's Understanding of Society* (with Barrie Stacey), *Culture Shock* (with Stephen Bochner) and *The Protestant Work Ethic*.

ALSO BY ADRIAN FURNHAM

Social Situations (1981) (with Michael Argyle and Jean Graham)

The Psychology of Social Situations (1981) (Edited with Michael Argyle)

Social Behaviour in Context (1986) (Edited)

The Economic Mind (1986) (with Alan Lewis)

Culture Shock (1986) (with Stephen Bochner)

Personality Psychology in Europe (1986) (Edited with Alois Angleitner and Guus van Heck)

Lay Theories (1988)

The Anatomy of Adolescence (1989) (with Barrie Gunter)

The Protestant Work Ethic (1990)

Young People's Understanding of Society (1991) (with Barrie Stacey)

Consumer Profiles: An Introduction to Psychographics (1992) (with Barrie Gunter)

Personality at work

The role of individual differences in the workplace

Adrian Furnham

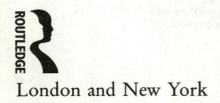

London and New York

For my friend David Pendleton who probably taught me more than I ever taught him.

First published in 1992
by Routledge
11 New Fetter Lane, London EC4P 4EE

Simultaneously published in the USA and Canada
by Routledge
a division of Routledge, Chapman and Hall Inc.
29 West 35th Street, New York, NY 10001

Typeset by Falcon Typographic Art Ltd, Fife, Scotland
Printed and bound in Great Britain by Mackays of Chatham PLC, Kent

British Library Cataloguing in Publication Data
A catalogue record for this book is available from the British Library.

Library of Congress Cataloging in Publication Data
Furnham, Adrian.
Personality at work: the role of individual differences in the workplace / Adrian Furnham.
p. cm.
Includes bibliographical references and index.
1. Personality tests. 2. Prediction of occupational success. 3. Work –
Psychological aspects – Testing. 4. Industrial psychology.
I. Title.
BF698.9.03F87 1992
158.7–dc20
91–43286
CIP

ISBN 0–415–03547–3

Contents

Figures and tables

FIGURES

TABLES

Foreword

Despite overall similarities, all human beings are unique; they differ in intelligence, personality and special abilities, as well as in height, weight, beauty, and all sorts of other mental and physical variables. They also differ, as a consequence, in their ability to do satisfactory work in any of the many jobs, professions and callings which are provided in our society. Some are good at the job, some are not; taking quite simple occupations, it is usually found that the good do twice as much work as the bad. While a number of bottoms scoured by a good worker might amount to 500 or so a day, others only average 150 or thereabouts. In the weaving industry, when the total number of yards of cloth produced from the warp was measured for different workers, variations ranged from the rate of 62 picks per minute to 130 picks per minute. The same ratio has been found for hourly piece-work earnings of hosiery workers, pounds of women's hose produced per hour by knitting-machine operators, and earnings of taxicab drivers working under similar conditions. As the work becomes more complex and demanding, the ratio becomes even greater, so that a good physicist produces work many times better than the bad physicist, and the outstanding entrepreneur exceeds many times the success rate of those less talented.

As a consequence, people have always tried to select those likely to succeed, and to reject those likely to fail, using many different types of method to establish such a likelihood. Perhaps one of the oldest examples is to be found in the Bible, where Gideon is reported to have used a two-stage selection procedure in his war against the Midianites.

Even earlier than Gideon, the ancient Chinese used selection tests, not very dissimilar to our own, in the selection of clerics and other civil servants, as we now call them. The method worked well in producing highly intelligent, diligent and literate people to run the civil service, and the stability of the Chinese Empire owed much to the people so selected.

Nowadays, business and government use many different selection devices, some good, some bad and some indifferent. For the selection of high-level businessmen, the French apparently put much stress on astrology and graphology, two pseudo-sciences which are hardly in a position to bear the burden of selecting good candidates! Even more widely used are interviews, which have usually been found by empirical investigations to have little reliability and less validity. Different interviewers differ profoundly in their conclusions and when the selected candidates are followed up, their actual careers show little agreement with the interviewer's predictions. In many cases, interviewers have in fact been found to have negative validity, i.e. to select the less successful over the more successful workers, as judged by their final achievements.

Psychologists have made a genuine contribution by perfecting tests of ability and personality which are objective, and which have been found to make much better predictions than are possible in any other way. Ability tests measure general intelligence, as well as special abilities, such as verbal, numerical, visual–spatial, memory and other types of ability. Personality tests measure different traits, such as impulsivity, persistence, sociability, anxiety proneness, depression etc, as well as higher-order concepts like introversion, extraversion, emotional stability versus instability, etc, but more important perhaps than the making up of tests have been proved to be the other contributions of psychology.

The first of these has been the insistence on the scientific measurement of the efficacy of a given procedure. People advocating astrology, graphology or interviewing usually simply state that they have been successful in the past, and that their record speaks for itself. The only evidence usually given is anecdotal; a graphologist may point to a particular person who he recommended, and who was outstandingly successful. All this of course could simply be due to chance, and is not scientific evidence of any kind.

I remember on one occasion giving a lecture on the interview, pointing out its deficiencies to a group of matrons and nursing sisters who were actively engaged in the process of appointing new nurses. One of them, a highly intelligent woman working as matron at a leading London teaching hospital, came up to me afterwards and said: '92 per cent of all the nurses I have interviewed and engaged have proved to be very successful; does that not prove that the interview works?' I answered: 'I imagine that practically all the nurses who come to your very prestigious hospital have already shown themselves to be excellent nurses, otherwise they wouldn't dare to come. If you selected them on a random basis, you would probably find much the same percentage of successes, so that your 92 per cent doesn't really prove anything at all, because you have no control group.' She went away and for the next wave of applicants, took everyone who applied. The final success rate was 94 per cent! This finding can be generalized to most senior jobs; only good candidates would be interviewed, or sent to the graphologist, or have their horoscopes read by an astrologer; the rest would have been eliminated on the basis of inadequate qualifications at an earlier stage. As a consequence, the great majority of candidates would probably do reasonably well, so that without a control group we cannot really say anything about the adequacy of the selection device. Hence, the necessity of doing controlled experiments to find out the adequacy, or otherwise, of the given selection procedure. It is of course small wonder that practitioners of interviewing, astrological star-gazing or graphological analysis have been very hostile to psychology, fearing the negative outcome of such experiments. The results have proved their fears to be only too justified.

The second great contribution that psychology has made has been the use of theories out of the laboratory, and which can be applied to selection procedures. A great deal is known from experimental and clinical studies about such personality variables as extraversion–introversion, and neuroticism as opposed to emotional stability. The theory would suggest that people who are extraverted (i.e. who are lively, somewhat impulsive, sensation-seeking etc) and people who are emotionally unstable (i.e. suffering from anxieties, over-acting emotionally to dangerous situations, and who tend to be very tense) would be more likely than others to be involved in traffic accidents. This has indeed been found to be so. Accident categories were established on the basis of a person's history classifying him as a good, fair, poor or bad driver. Of the good drivers, 80 per cent had a good personality test rating (i.e. stable and introverted). Of the bad drivers, only 3 per cent had such a personality rating. Conversely, of the bad drivers, 80 per cent had a bad personality test rating (extraverted and unstable), whereas of the good drivers only 2 per cent had such a rating. When selection procedures were applied in a company running buses all over Johannesburg, the accident rate was reduced very markedly, making the business financially successful for the first time.

Similarly, it has been predicted, and found, that successful scientists tend to be overwhelmingly introverted and stable. There are of course a few exceptions, but there is no doubt that the rule holds in general. Prediction can be quite specific. Thus, for instance, in looking at the personality of successful shooters, it was found that the prone rifle-shooters with a fixed target and virtually no movement of the weapon were the most introverted; they had all the time in the world to adjust to circumstances, wait for the right moment and then shoot. On the other hand, the rapid-fire pistol group had very little time to fire five shots, and also had to cope very rapidly with changes in position to move the pistol from target to target. They emerged as very extraverted. Other groups of shooters are intermediate, but there is a general tendency for good shooters to be stable rather than unstable emotionally.

To pick out the right test to use requires a good theory, as well as practical experience. Such theories are now available, making the task of correct selection very much easier. This is an important point. Critics sometimes look at the overall success rate of all the studies reported in the literature, and come to the conclusion that the overall size of the correlation between test and success is not very high. There are several reasons for this which require consideration. In the first place, even fairly small correlations would make a good deal of difference to the actual success rate achieved. In the second place, such overall comparisons are based on a mixture of good, poor and indifferent investigations; the existence of poor ones, where inappropriate tests are chosen, should not be used to downgrade the achievement of the good ones, where appropriate tests are used. It is here that theory is so important; many psychologists do not use any theory at all, but select the test almost on a random basis, or because it is popular at the time (the Minnesota Multi-phasic Personality Inventory (MMPI) is an example in point). Such studies are inherently worthless, and do not take away anything from the effectiveness of studies using a good theory, and an appropriate tool.

But most important of all is probably the fact that the relationship found between test and success rate is limited by the reliability of the measure of success. Good criteria are often difficult to find, and they severely reduce the apparent success rate of testing procedures. Consider selection procedures which were used during the war to find proficient pilots. Many tests were devised for the purpose, and tested against the performance of the pilots after training. This was being judged by two experienced Air Force sergeants before whom the pilots went through a series of standard manoeuvres. The final results were devastating; there was no relationship between the test predictions, and the performance as judged by the sergeants! However, a closer look demonstrated that there was no correlation between the judgements made by the two sergeants – in other words, the criterion was completely unreliable and worthless. It took a long time to improve the criterion, until finally cameras were fixed in the aeroplane to film the actual movements of the pointers on the dials installed in the cockpit. When an objective criterion was thus obtained, the test turned out to give surprisingly good predictions!

Criteria were not only difficult to obtain; in many cases, there is an actual reluctance on the part of companies to furnish such criteria. On one occasion, I was asked by a large firm of motor-car manufacturers to test applicants for the position of apprentices in the firm, positions which were widely sought after because of the high wages and security enjoyed by workers in that industry at the time. I devised such a battery, and it was used for quite a number of years to the satisfaction of the company. However, when I suggested that the success of the battery should be tested against the actual performance of the apprentices, the company politely refused. They said that they were quite satisfied and didn't see any need for such validation. I pointed out that surely some apprentices would do better work than others, and that it would be worthwhile to correlate these differences in performance against the selection tests. They said: 'No, all the apprentices are doing equally well', which obviously makes no sense at all. However, there was nothing to be done; I still believe that our battery of tests was a good predictor, but company policy made it impossible to prove that hypothesis! There is widespread dislike in many companies of the need to assess performance, and when it is done, it is usually done so poorly and subjectively that the results are practically worthless. Hence, it is often difficult to prove the efficacy of the selection procedure, not because the procedure itself is not objective and valid, but because the criterion is poor or absent.

Another problem that often occurs is the unrealistic nature of the requirements stated by a company. When I first engaged in selection procedures in the United States, I asked the Chairman of the company about the kind of people he wanted me to select. 'Well, I certainly don't want "yes" men; I want people who are independent, creative and original in their work.' When I devised a battery that would procure such people, together with the type of personality that is associated with creativity and novelty-producing temperament, he was highly displeased and finally returned to a retinue of 'yes' men! Bosses don't always know what they really want, and what they have to say is more often motivated by stereotypes that have no basis in fact.

This problem is related to another one, which besets the psychologist engaged in selection. What a given company needs, and what it wants, may be two quite different things. I remember being asked to look at the selection procedures used for the Civil Service, and to comment about their adequacy. I had to say that they were well designed to produce the same kind of person who was already running the Civil Service, so that my report was very favourable. It was not part of my brief to say that possibly the kind of person who was running the Foreign Office was in fact unlikely to make the right decisions, and had certain generalized attitudes and beliefs which made his decisions unlikely to meet the needs of modern society. The psychologist-selector usually works to a brief, and it is not part of his business to dispute that brief! For many companies, that is what is most urgently needed.

Another problem for the selector is the fact that most bosses believe that they know as much about psychology, or more, than the people they employ as psychologists. One of my students was once asked to discover why the products of a certain manufacturer concerned with the production of mints were relatively unsuccessful, particularly when comparing his sales with those of Polo Mints (Lifesavers to our American friends!). My student interviewed customers and sales people and came back with a very simple answer – people got more for their money buying Polo Mints than buying his products! He exploded with fury. 'It's obvious what they are responding to – it's the sexual symbolism of the Polo Mint with the hole in the middle!' He fired my student, and hired a psychoanalyst instead. He went into liquidation a year later. There is a general tendency for leading business people to accept psychological advice only when it agrees with their prejudices, whatever these may be.

Adrian Furnham has written an important, much-needed book. In this comprehensive and scholarly book, he has collected, ordered, criticized and thought about individual differences as they apply to the world of work. It will, I am sure, remain a reference work in the area for many years to come.

H.J. Eysenck, PhD, DSc
Professor Emeritus of Psychology
University of London
March 1990

Preface

My primary interest in the topic of this book arose from two quite different experiences: the one 'applied', the other 'academic'.

My applied experience was the result of being called in as a consultant to a number of organizations interested in applying psychological principles and research findings to such things as recruitment, training and selection. It is not always easy for an academic to be faced by the questions of 'real-world professionals', who require, it seems, certain, succinct and immediate answers to complicated questions. Academics are trained to be cautious; their theories and findings are filled with caveats and warnings about over-generalization and over-simplification. The words 'towards', 'perhaps' and 'notwithstanding' pepper their writings, and the gestation period for theories, experiments and reports is fairly lengthy. They are primarily interested in getting the theory right; in replicating results; in designing and executing elegant experiments to disprove (or provide evidence for) hypotheses; and attempt to expound strong, powerful yet parsimonious theories.

Despite its undoubted progress this century, academic psychology is no match for the 'hard', 'pure' sciences like physics or even the applied discipline of medicine. Whatever the reason for this comparative lack of progress (and very many have been advanced), academic psychologists are therefore cautious and conservative about psychological findings and knowledge. Some laws, models and theories exist, but are highly specific. Other well-known, replicated (and occasionally counter-intuitive) findings have trickled down into 'common sense' and hence seem less interesting. But there are numerous grand, even imperialistic, theories in psychology that purport to give an accurate, complete, veridical (and radical) insight into the whole working of the human psyche. Like other grand theories (e.g. communism or catholicism), there are psychological theories that can 'explain' practically everything. Unfortunately, it is these grand theories which often invoke difficult and ambiguous concepts like the unconscious or conscience, that are most frequently popularized. It seems to some psychologists that the more encompassing and disprovable a psychological concept or theory is, the more it is eagerly embraced by the lay person. As a result, the lay view of psychology is frequently lamentably misconceived.

It seems self-evident to the lay person – educated or not – that psychologists know all about personality and individual differences; that the processes and structures concerning individual behaviour are agreed and understood; that psychologists can, for instance, spot lying, and have considerable insight into a person's motives, desires and needs. Thus, it is, in the eyes of academics, that many people have somewhat unrealistic expectations as to what psychologists can do without uncertainty, or margin of error. Psychological diagnosis may not be very different from medical diagnosis in its reliability and behavioural measurement and may be even more sophisticated than many of the other social sciences (such as economics and criminology).

Always conscious of the limitations and shortcomings of theory and measurement, the cautious, critical, hesitant don is frequently unhappy in the role of consultant to an action-oriented, problem-solving, real-world professional. Over the past 20 years, personnel managers and human-resource experts have turned to psychologists to help them in their decision-making. Academic psychologists have been hesitant and critical, and as a result have not always provided the sort of answers their enquirers wished to hear. To fill this void, however, a substantial number of 'psychological consultants' have appeared, to service the growing need of people who have interests in appraisal, development, counselling, selection and training. Some astute 'business-oriented' psychologists offer their clients precisely what they are looking for. They offer certain, clear answers to complex behavioural issues.

In what sense do academic researchers differ from psychological consultants? With David Pendleton, I considered some of the major differences between the two worlds, which are set out in Figure 1 (over page).

For the academic, research may have a 'blue-skies' air about it. Its aim is to achieve insight, understanding, or knowledge that may not be useful, applicable or saleable. The aim is to know the cause of things and to have a comprehensive understanding of the issue under investigation. While for many academics, 'pure' research is the major aim, for the business executive, research is nearly always 'applied'. Research is action-oriented, problem-solving, operation-intended. In this sense, the aim is much clearer and probably short-term. Academics start with a puzzle, consultants with a problem, and the former are satisfied to know and understand, while the latter want to use the knowledge and sell it.

Consultants are time-conscious, high-urgency people, driven by deadlines. They want the answer *now* and are perplexed by the apparent sluggish, procrastinatory ways of academics who resist the immediate fix-it nature

	Academics	Consultants
Major aims	Insight and knowledge	Action and operation
Speed of solution	Low urgency	High urgency
Type of solution valued	Elegant and critical	Applicable and comprehensible
Source of data	Direct empirical base	Second-hand empirical base
Level of complexity	Frequently complex	Frequently simple
Dealing with uncertainty	Dealt with statistically	Dealt with personally
Preferred medium or presentation	Written documents/ tables	Face to face
Self-presentation	Irrelevant, often shabby	Crucial, fashionably smart
Means of persuasion	Empirical data	Rhetoricl
Cost-benefit analysis	Irrelevant	Crucial
Type of personality valued	Introvert	Extrovert

Figure 1. Characteristics which separate the two worlds – academics and consultants

of consultancy jobs. Consultants certainly adhere to Benjamin Franklin's maxims: 'Lost time is never found again; remember that time is money'. Expectations about time and its use are remarkably different in the two worlds, and this is a source of considerable frustration, particularly for consultants dealing with academics.

To a large extent, academics and consultants look for different things in solutions to problems. Whereas academics value elegance, parsimony, scope, precision and testability, consultants often value applicability, comprehensibility and feasibility. Academics like theories and solutions that are reliable, testable, logically consistent, explicit, verifiable and systematic. Although the consultant might admire these characteristics, unless the theory or solution is usable, or at least insightful, it is near worthless.

Most academics rely on original, empirical data to support their advice or theories. While the database can be of many kinds, it is important that it is representative, comprehensive, correctly sampled and measured, and free of 'noise' and errors. Some consultants are happy with a second-hand empirical base, non-original sources and particularly illustrative case-histories to make a point. Whereas the source of the data may be all-important for academics, it is not as crucial for people in business who do not have to persuade others on the basis of their data. In this sense, the two are probably epistemologically divided as well, the former being empiricists, the latter rationalists.

The levels of complexity of theory, or model, often differ in the two worlds. Academics' level of analysis is frequently complex and they expect the audience, whoever that is, to deal with the complexity. Consultants strive to simplify and clarify, in order to help the audience or the client to comprehend. Academics are often scathing about the simple-minded solutions of consultants, while the consultant sees the academic as needlessly obfuscating an issue that can be presented much more clearly.

The way in which uncertainty, or the unknown, is dealt with is very different in the two worlds. Among academics, the issue is usually dealt with statistically by offering probabilities on the likelihood of various outcomes. Academics, then, expect people to be able to interpret the application of results themselves. Consultants often find that they have to deal with the uncertainty issue personally, by reassurance or interpretation. In some senses, consultants feel that they need to 'own the problem', while academics take a more distant, uninvolved approach.

Consultants like to sell ideas, solutions and 'theories', and they usually prefer to do so face to face. As polished presenters, consultants might have slick slides, memorable mnemonics and helpful hand-outs, but their preference is for the live medium. Academics prefer documents, tables and charts, and seem happiest giving and receiving information in this form. Not even skilled at chalk-and-talk, most academics feel most secure communicating by writing; hence, their love of word processors but not car phones or, worse, video phones.

For academics, self-presentation, in terms of dress and equipment, is irrelevant because they value what is being said, and the quality of ideas, over packaging. Often shabby, nearly always unfashionable and frequently something of an eyesore, the academic is easy to spot, even in a crowd. For consultants, the opposite is true. They know that their clients will be acutely aware of the messages that are sent by such small things as the type of watch, size of briefcase and elegance of technology used. Consultants never underestimate the packaging of services because they have come to learn the extent to which impression-management can influence customer satisfaction. In this sense, academics are ragged individualists and consultants smart mimics.

Academics rely on their ability to persuade, often by the quality of their data. The numbers do the talking. Consultants, on the other hand, often use rhetoric – and with some success. This is not to suggest that there are not some extremely skilled rhetoricians among academics, or that consultants are empirically naïve, but that, when looking at their reports and presentations, academics prefer the disinterested nature of empirical data and consultants the power of persuasive words.

Whereas for consultants and their clients, value for money has always been important, academics are only recently having to argue the potential benefits of their work in relation to its costs. For most academics, cost-benefit analyses are impossible to calculate: they will cite many examples of chance discoveries which have followed from blue-skies research. Consultants have to demonstrate value in the short term.

Finally, it seems that academics and consultants not only have different personalities but they value certain characteristics differently. Academics tend to be phlegmatic, stable introverts, respecting others, thoughtful, controlled, reliable, reserved, calm, even-tempered types. Consultants, on the other hand, tend to be sanguine, stable extraverts – active, impulsive, optimistic, responsive, easygoing and sociable. These differences occur partly out of necessity – consultants have to get on with people, to socialize and to persuade. Academics, meanwhile, have to spend long periods alone in libraries and laboratories collecting data very carefully.

There are, no doubt, hundreds of exceptions to the rules listed here – instances where the differences either do not occur or occur in the opposite way to that described. Certainly, there are academics who can deal well with the commercial world, and consultants whose training and methods are rigorous. The problem remains, however, that academics and business people still do not fully understand one another. They come from different cultures, share different values and expectations, and have different aims and strategies of communication. Although they are both interested in personality differences at work, they frequently have different agendas.

Two things struck me when I first seriously began to consider writing this book. The first was that surely it had already been written – there must be a book that covered in a comprehensive and critical manner the role of individual differences in the workplace. True, there were many books on occupational psychology, which dedicated a frequently brief, under-referenced and somewhat simplistic chapter to personality and individual differences, but rarely did textbooks in personality theory consider how these individual differences manifest themselves in the workplace. There are many books on personality assessment and organizational behaviour but few which consider the topic of this book. If indeed I was correct, and it is very unwise to be dogmatic about which books are in existence, the question remained, why was this area at the interface of personality and occupational psychology so badly neglected? Of course, one could put forward a number of hypotheses for this state of affairs.

What I did discover, however, was that although there is a fairly substantial literature in this field, it is highly scattered in terms of the journals it was published in, and by inference the disciplines from which it emanated. Hence, the quality is very patchy. Despite the fact that many disciplines shelter under the umbrella term 'social science', they emphasize, stress and value rather different types of research. Typically, this involves favouring one methodology or theory over others and being either hostile to, ignorant about or, more likely, naïve concerning opposite approaches. More interestingly, however, it seemed to me that some business disciplines seemed, in their theories and methods, almost totally derivative from more established social sciences, which render them unlikely to throw up many new ideas, but in an ideal position to test old ones.

A second thought about the proposed book that immediately occurred to me was that it should be very easy to structure. If I could decide on a limited number of personality dimensions, the *independent* variable, these could provide the *within* chapter structure, while the occupational behaviours, the *dependent* variable, would provide the chapter topics. I even envisaged a rather grand summary grid at the end, the columns being personality dimensions and the rows being occupational behaviours. A simplistic version of this grid appears in Table 1 (over page). However good that idea and how neat, parsimonious and orderly the plan to carve nature at her joints so clearly, I had not taken into account that the extant literature had not been planned that way. Some of my 'cells' were empty (I could find little or no research), others were over-full (representing a popular research topic), while I had other salient and important topics with good research which did not easily fit into the matrix. The best compromise was to attempt to keep some structure, but be less rigid and let in other sections where necessary.

Various major and fundamental controversies surround personality theories, all of which are highly germane to the topic of this book. The controversies are not new, nor are they easily solvable, although there is perhaps more consensus on each than first seems apparent. Essentially, some of the issues are these:

- What are the fundamental dimensions of personality?
- Do personality factors predict occupational behaviour?
- Is personality stable over time, or variable?
- Is personality inherited or learnt?
- Can personality be changed?
- How can personality be reliably and variously measured?
- What other individual differences, apart from personality, predict occupational behaviours?
- How are the relevant traits related to one another?
- Are traits the same as types?
- How can one use information about personality type to make decisions about job selection, developmental needs in the workplace etc?

We shall encounter all of the above throughout the pages of this volume.

Overall, I have enjoyed writing this book. Two hours (05.30–07.30) every morning at the desk, before going to work, gives one a sense of achievement, and before the real workday has begun. Every so often I was in a position to take my rather tatty script, chapter by chapter, to Lee Drew, who transformed it into beautifully clear word-processed clarity. She has been quite invaluable to me, and I am more than happy to acknowledge her cheerfulness and occasional editing of my clumsy phrasing.

Adrian Furnham
Bloomsbury, London 1991

Table 1 Initial speculations about the relationship between individual differences and work-related behaviour

	Vocational Choice	Motivation	Satisfaction	Productivity	'Problems' e.g. Absenteeism	Leisure
Extraversion Impulsivity Sociability Sensation-seeking Screening Augmenting/Reducing	*	**	**	**	*	***
Neuroticism Obsessionality Trait anxiety Defence mechanism Coping strategies Depression	*	**	***	***	***	*
Intelligence Thinking styles Education	*	**	*	**	*	**
Expectancies Locus of control Self-efficacy Attributional style	**	***	**		***	*
Values/attitudes Conservative Protestant ethic Just world beliefs	***	**	*	*	***	***

The asterisks denote the strength rather than the directionality of the relationship

Chapter 1

Modelling personality at work

The difference in companies is people. I would rather have a first-class manager running a second-rate business than a second-class manager running a first-rate business.

J.E. Reichert

Everyone loves success, but they hate successful people.

John McEnroe

Competence, like truth, beauty and contact lenses, is in the eye of the beholder.

L.J. Peter

Success is that old ABC – ability, breaks and courage.

C. Luckman

There is no success without hardship.

Sophocles

People are always blaming their circumstances for what they are. I don't believe in circumstances. The people who get on in the world are the people who get up and look for the circumstances they want, and, if they can't find them, make them.

G.B. Shaw

1.1 INTRODUCTION

This book is an attempt to provide a critical, comprehensive and contemporary review of the management science, psychological and sociological literature at the interface of personality theory and occupational psychology/organizational behaviour (OP/OB). The focus of the book, as the subtitle suggests, concerns the role of individual differences in predicting, and determining, behaviour at work.

It might come as a surprise to any reader that, just as occupational

psychologists, organizational behaviour theorists and management scientists
have neglected to examine individual differences in any systematic way, so
personality theorists have failed to take occupational behaviour seriously as
a correlate of individual differences. A cursory glance at the many textbooks
from these two subdisciplines shows clearly their ignorance of one another.
While textbooks on occupational pyschology/organizational behaviour may
even have a chapter (or part chapter) labelled personality, it is frequently dealt
with in a cursory and tangential manner. Any personality theorist would
be amazed at the datedness and ignorance that occupational/organizational
researchers have of this area. The latter's interest is faddish, eccentric
and capricious. Some personality dimensions such as machiavellianism,
self-monitoring or A-type behaviour frequently excite temporary interest,
but are soon forgotten. Major debates in personality theory, such as the
person–situation debate, the issue of the basic super-factors describing
personality or the biological/genetic determinants of behaviour, are often
not considered worthy of attention. Although occupational/organizational
theorists may occasionally admit the importance of individual differences,
they seem unable to deal with it appropriately. On the other hand, there
are those with a more sociological than psychological training, who tend to
underplay individual differences for various politico-philosophical reasons
and believe that individual differences play a very small role, in comparison
with socio-structural and organizational factors, in determining behaviour
at work.

However, the paucity of literature at the interface between personality and occupational psychology/organizational behaviour cannot all be
blamed on the ignorance of one party. Surprisingly, while personality
theorists have been eager to examine clinical, educational, medical and social
correlates of individual differences/personality dimensions, they have consistently ignored occupational/organizational correlates. Hence, one finds
the journals examining the links between personality and social behaviour,
personality and clinical behaviour, but none dedicated to personality at work.
Where personality researchers have examined occupational/organizational
correlates, it has nearly always been to test their theories rather than actually
to examine the latter in depth. It should be pointed out, however, that this is
not true of the East European literature – the Russians and Poles have always
stressed the relationship between personality dimensions (particularly those
derived from the Pavlovian model) and work-related behaviours (Strelau,
1981). It is not clear why Western personality theorists are so unconcerned
with occupational/organizational correlates of personality, save perhaps that
many of them are originally trained as either clinical or social psychologists
and naturally examine abnormal behaviours and beliefs as the primary
dependent variable.

Another way to understand the extant literature on personality at work
is to note that, whereas personality theorists have usually conceived of

personality as the independent variable and work behaviour as the dependent variable, occupational/organizational psychologists have done the precise opposite. On the one hand, it could be argued that it does not fundamentally matter which is the dependent and which the independent variable as any relationship will be manifest in the results. But it is critical to scientific method and the notion of causality which is cause and which effect. It does seem that researchers are frequently more skilled and knowledgeable about independent variables, which they systematically and sensitively manipulate, compared to the dependent variable. That is, their knowledge of the dependent variable is less comprehensive because it is often seen as only a way of cheating the validity of the theory about the independent variable.

1.2 SIX APPROACHES TO PERSONALITY AT WORK

An examination of the highly diverse, dispersed and divergent literature concerning personality at work has highlighted six rather different approaches to the topic.

Classic Personality Theory

This approach starts with a theory of personality and relates empirically assessed measures (as the independent variable) to various work-related behaviours. The personality variable chosen may vary on a number of dimensions:

- Single or multiple traits are measured. A single trait might be considered, e.g. self-monitoring (Snyder, 1974), or locus of control (Rotter, 1966), or alternatively a trait system, bound up in an elaborate theory like that of Eysenck (1967a) or Cattell (1971). It is frequently the case that multiple traits are used, as single trait theories are usually not as rich a source of hypotheses.
- Cognitive or biologically based traits are measured. For instance, some 'traits' or personality dimensions are quite clearly conceived of in cognitive terms, e.g. belief systems such as conservatism (Wilson, 1973) or attributional styles (Brewin, 1988). These cognitive traits refer to the way that people perceive the world, or attribute the cause of their own or others' behaviour. On the other hand, some traits, e.g. extraversion (Eysenck, 1967a) or sensation-seeking (Zuckerman, 1979), are conceived of in biological terms such that the person's behaviour is a function of biological differences. Both approaches seem equally popular.
- 'Normal' and 'abnormal' traits can be measured. For instance, some traits are clearly conceived of in terms of abnormal behaviour, like

depression, psychopathy or hypochondriasis which measure some aspect of 'abnormal' behaviour. Although valid and indeed at times quite relevant to work-related behaviours, those seem less useful than 'normal' traits, because many working people do not exhibit these traits to any degree. This is, however, not true of neuroticism which is very common.

- Dynamic vs stylistic traits. This is the distinction made between Freudian/ neo-Freudian ideas (such as the oral or anal personality which supposedly measures deep-seated, possibly unconscious, needs and fears) and stylistic traits which do not presume the same aetiology (in childhood) or processes. To date, however, very few Freudian personality tests have been applied to the workplace, save perhaps Kline's (1978) work on the oral and anal personality.

The basic tenet of this 'classic personality theory' approach is to measure personality as the independent variable and to see how it correlates with some (often rather arbitrarily chosen) work-related behaviour. In criticism of this approach, it should be pointed out that:

- So far, the approach has been piecemeal and there is very little evidence of a concerted, systematic and programmatic research effort, which is perhaps not that unusual.
- Sometimes this research has been laboratory based and hence it frequently has poor ecological validity.
- The selection of work-related variables is somewhat random and based on convenience, because researchers are either unable to get better measures or, indeed, are not sure what to look for.
- Essentially, studies such as these are nearly always seen by personality researchers simply as supporting evidence for their ideas.

Compared to the extensive research on the relationship between personality and, say, learning, mental health or social behaviour, the extant research from classic personality theory on occupational/organizational variables has been disappointing.

Classic Occupational Psychology/Organizational Behaviour

This approach starts with some work-related variable, be it conceived at the individual, group or organizational level, and examines its personality correlates. Again, the independent variables may be conceived of, or measured, quite differently:

- Self-report vs behavioural. Some variables are measured by questionnaire ratings or interviews, others by actual behaviour, such as absenteeism, produce made or sold, or number of promotions. Both self-report and behavioural measures are subject to different forms of systematic error.

- Single vs aggregate measures. The work-related behaviour may be a single, one-off assessment, or an aggregate measure made up either from different parts (i.e. combining superior, subordinate, self and colleague assessments) or measurements conducted over time. Clearly, in terms of reliability and representativeness, aggregate measures are more preferable.
- Within vs between organizations. Sometimes variables are examined only within an organization while others are compared between different organizations. The clear advantage of the latter approach is that one can control for organizational variables which are quite likely to have major effects.

Researchers in this tradition are usually interested in examining personality correlates of specific work behaviours which might help personnel and human–resource professionals select, appraise, promote or train individuals. But this research has a number of limitations:

- The choice of personality variables has been arbitrary and uninformed. Some personality tests have been favoured mainly because they have been commercially exploited rather than because they are reliable and valid. Some outdated tests, largely forgotten and condemned by psycho-metricians, remain a popular choice and hence seriously threaten the nature of the results.
- Similarly, statistical analyses have been simple and naïve. As a rule, simple correlations have been computed rather than partial correlations, or even more preferably multi-variate statistics to prevent type II errors (finding more significant differences than actually occur). Given that both independent and dependent variables are multi-factorial, it is essential that sufficiently robust and sensitive multi-variate statistics are used to analyse results.
- Studies in this area are frequently exploratory and a-theoretical rather than based on a sound theory or programmatic research endeavour. As a result, interesting results are rarely followed up and the theoretical implications rarely exploited.
- Often, researchers ignore possible organizational and societal factors that either directly or indirectly affect the dependent variable. That is, work-related behaviours are rarely solely under the control of the individual and may be moderated by powerful organizational factors which need to be taken into account.

The occupational psychology/organizational behaviour literature is diverse, often poor but sometimes very good. Alas, good research and theorizing is difficult to find and limited in both quantity and scope.

The Development of a Work-specific Individual Difference Measure

A third approach is to develop a personality measure aimed at predicting exclusively a specific work-related behaviour (like absenteeism) and to use this measure to predict that behaviour. This is not necessarily tautological, although at first it may seem so. A fairly large number of these measures already exist. But they are highly varied and may be:

- Narrow vs wide in conceptualization. For instance, the personality measures might attempt to predict a specific (narrow) form of occupational behaviour, such as absenteeism, or a much wider range of occupational behaviours, such as satisfaction or productivity. It is probably true that the former is a much more common approach than the latter (Cook *et al.*, 1981; Furnham, 1990b).
- Single vs multiple traits. That is, the measure (usually a questionnaire) could be multi-dimensional, supposedly measuring many different behaviours/beliefs at work, or a single trait measure, which only measures one dimension.
- Self-report vs behaviour. There is no reason why the individual difference measure need necessarily be self-report based. It could well be biographical, behavioural or physiological; indeed, all have been used at one time or another to try to predict work-related behaviour.
- Attitudinal vs attributional. Most of these measures are of the self-report kind, but some are attitudinal, systematically examining work-related attitudes and beliefs (Buchholz, 1976), while others are quite specifically concerned with attributional styles.

The approach of the development of a work-specific individual difference measure has been taken by those from both personality and occupational psychology traditions. However, there are a number of self-evident drawbacks. These include:

- Rarely, if ever, do researchers pay much attention to the aetiology of the trait or dimension being measured. This could be an important feature in understanding developmental features associated with the trait.
- Almost by definition the measures have limited applicability, as they are designed specifically for the workplace and are therefore presumably restricted to it in terms of predictability.
- Frequently, but not always, the background theoretical work on the processes, mechanisms and phenomena associated with the trait (that explains how and why the trait determines behaviour) is not done sufficiently or sufficiently well, no doubt because the task is seen primarily as an applied one.
- As mentioned earlier, there is frequently a confounding or overlap between the independent and dependent variable such that it is very circular and tautological. Thus, some measures ask with whom a person communicates

at work and then proceed to determine through sociometric analysis that person's communication patterns. Tautological research can be a waste of time.

There is clearly still much scope for this approach to personality at work. The current literature shows sporadic rather than sustained effort and some evidence of faddishness regarding the choice of both independent and dependent variable. Nevertheless, there is some considerable evidence that this approach may prove very fruitful, e.g. the work on occupationally salient attributional style (Furnham, Sadka and Brewin, 1992).

The Concept of 'Fit' and 'Misfit' at Work

Probably because of its intuitive appeal, this approach has a fairly long history (Pervin, 1967). The idea is quite simple: based on personality predispositions, some jobs are more suitable for the individual than others. Based on a comparable analysis of both the person and the job, it may be possible to measure accurately the degree of fit (which is desirable) or misfit (undesirable). The work of Holland (1973) (see Chapter 3) is most relevant here. Variations on this theme include:

• Whether the analysis is based more on jobs or individuals. Clearly, to obtain a measure of fit, both people and jobs need to be analysed and measured. However, the measurement of one is nearly always based on the concepts/language developed by the other. In most cases, and for obvious reasons, the conceptual language of fit is based on personality or individual differences rather than jobs.
• Impressionistic vs 'geometric'. A second crucial feature is whether the concept of 'fit' is simply subjectively impressionistic or objective, measurable and 'geometric'. Few would argue that the former approach is the more desirable, but there are certain difficulties associated with the latter approach, notably the complexity of the multi-dimensional geometric model.
• Similarity vs complementarity. There is extensive, if somewhat equivocal, literature on similarity and attraction between individuals which offers three hypotheses: similar people are attracted; the attraction of opposites; and the concept of complementarity. Although there is no evidence for the attraction of opposites concept (which in the context of Pervin's work becomes the misfit hypothesis), it remains uncertain whether the similarity or complementarity hypothesis is to be supported.

This approach, like the others, is not without its problems:

• Pattern vs formulae. One approach to this area is to devise a limited number of types (of people and/or job) and to show their relationships in some mosaic or pattern. This allows for some nice geometric (Euclidean) calculations. On the other hand, it may be possible to write a formula that expresses fit in the form of simultaneous equations.

- 'Fit' studies are, by definition, correlational and not causal; hence, it is not possible to infer directionality, such as the idea that misfit *leads to* absenteeism. Indeed, it is quite possible and feasible to derive hypotheses and explanations with fit as the dependent, not the independent, variable.
- Everything in this approach is based on the veridical nature, sensitivity, comprehensiveness and clarity of conceptualization of the variables that make up the fit. Where these are, for instance, conceived too vaguely or widely, the resultant fit measures are practically worthless.

This remains one of the most promising areas of research, notwithstanding these problems, because of its predictive power. Predictably, the concept of fit has been particularly popular in such research areas as vocational choice (see Chapter 2) and 'problems' at work – for instance, stress and health. However, the real promise of the fit–misfit literature lies in predicting motivation and satisfaction at work, an area still currently neglected.

Longitudinal Studies of People in Work

It is almost universally recognized that longitudinal research is invaluable in examining how a multitude of variables (personality, psychographic, demographic) change over time, relate to one another at different periods, and *predict* behaviour. That is, the concept of cause is best examined longitudinally. However, it is also widely recognized that longitudinal research is fiendishly difficult, expensive and problematic. Nevertheless, some studies have examined personality at work over time. Again, studies come in many different forms:

- Short, medium vs long time spans. It is not always clear what comprises a 'longitudinal' time span – a year, five years, ten years? Studies of less than a couple of years, although longitudinal, cannot reveal substantial differences which operate over longer periods such as decades. On the other hand, studies carried out over very long periods (20 years or more) have difficulties in accounting for drop-outs etc.
- Within or between organizations. Some organizations have sponsored or allowed research to be conducted within their, albeit very large, organization. Within-organization studies, by definition, seriously restrict the range and type of variable that can be examined. On the other hand, between-organizational studies (following individuals over time) frequently do not allow for sufficient comparisons.
- Retrospective vs prospective. Some longitudinal studies are done by archival research, where past records are compared to current data. Given that these records exist, such studies are robust, useful and sensitive. Alternatively, one can begin a study now and plan it into

the future. The latter approach is clearly more preferable because one has more control over what is measured, how and when.

Longitudinal research only has problems if it is done badly or discontinued for one reason or another. Scarcity of resources frequently means that good research is not done. The most common problems are:

- Too few subjects, or not knowing whether 'drop-outs' occur for systematic reasons. Tracing people's behaviour at work over lengthy periods is difficult, but restricting numbers because of costs only limits the generalizability of the research.
- Poor measurement of the variables. Either because one is limited to the organization's own records (such as application and assessment forms), or because measurement techniques have substantially improved over the years, early measures may be psychometrically unsound, thus threatening the quality of the results.
- Restricted range of variables. Studies done on particular individuals (a class of students), or of employees from a particular organization, by definition, are restricted and thus may not be reliable. In addition, between-organization variables cannot be considered. Clearly, this is only important if these unmeasured variables are significant, but one can only know this if they are examined.

A few good longitudinal studies of this sort exist, but they too have their limitations. It is highly desirable, if we are to understand personality differences at work, that more research of this sort be done.

Biographical or Case-History Research

This approach, akin to the 'great-man' theory of history, examines in detail the life of one individual to see what clues it provides as to which biographical factors predict job success. There are not many examples of this approach, but those that exist do differ on various criteria:

- Individuals vs groups. Some approaches consider only the lives of particular individuals, while others consider a whole family (a dynasty), or people who have attended a particular institution and done well later in life.
- Monetary vs 'other' success criteria. It is rather difficult to decide which criteria of success (or failure) are appropriate to use in order to select the 'successful' people to examine.
- Impressionistic vs scholarly. Some studies on successful entrepreneurs are in the 'best seller' tradition, where the 'readability' of the story is more important than obtaining or understanding the facts. On the other hand,

scholarly biographies are rarely sweepingly interpretative as to how, when and why biographical factors predict occupational success.

The biographical approach is intuitively appealing, and often most interesting to the general public, but it is very uncertain to what extent it can and does highlight personality determinants of work success. Major problems include:

- Only highly successful people are considered. Thus, there is a very serious sampling problem, because there appears to be no theoretical reason why particular people are chosen for analysis. This means that the data available is highly unrepresentative.
- There is almost never a control group. That is, there is no person or group against which to compare those studied in detail. It is therefore impossible to understand precisely which factors do, or do not, relate to occupational success.
- A-theoretical research means no systematic testing of hypotheses. Rarely, if ever, do biographers attempt to seek out particular facts to test hypotheses.

1.3 A RESEARCH MODEL

As has been noted, much of the research literature in the field of personality and behaviour at work is theoretically naïve and methodologically weak. How, then, might one conceive a model to derive theoretically based hypotheses which may be tested empirically? A major problem at present appears to be that practitioners (and some researchers) hope to find personality correlates of occupational behaviour without understanding how or why.

The research model set out here attempts to describe some of the major factors that affect the relationship between personality and occupational variables.

Figure 1.1 shows a simple model which may help to explain some of the variables that affect the relationship between personality variables and work-related behaviour.

1. The primary interest of practitioners such as personnel and human-resource professionals is the simple relationship between personality and work-related behaviour. Two features need to be mentioned, which can be seen from Figure 1.1. The first is that the line between personality characteristics and occupational variables is discontinuous, emphasizing the important point that this relationship is moderated by a whole range of other, significantly important, variables. The second feature is that the relationship between the two variables is bi-directional.

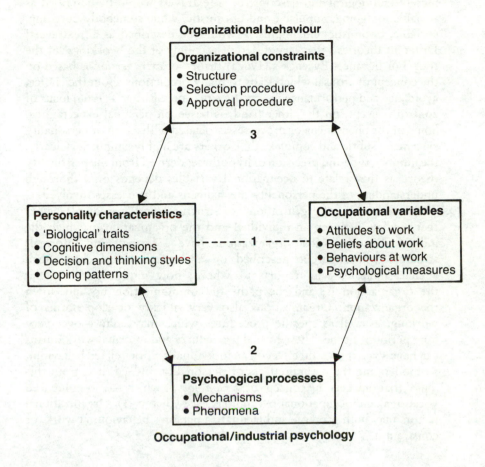

Figure 1.1 A research model for examining the relationship between personality and work

That is, personality factors determine (in part) work-related behaviours (the predispositional model), while organizational/occupational variables shape and selectively reward personality functioning (the socialization model). Thus, the relationship between personality and work-related outcomes is *neither* direct *nor* uni-causal.

2. The second 'path' in this model is the traditional occupational/industrial psychology model that is well informed about personality theory. Nearly all reputable theories describe some phenomenon, mechanism or process

which causes the trait. Indeed, if they did not, the theories would be merely tautological and descriptive: an extravert would be described as sociable, outgoing, impulsive and optimistic, while somebody outgoing, sociable, optimistic and impulsive would be described as an extravert! Different theories offer very different accounts of the 'workings' of the trait. For instance, Eysenck's (1967a) theory of *extraversion* is based on the concept of arousal which leads to many predictions about the choice, avoidance and performance in specific situations. Rotter's (1966) locus of control concept, on the other hand, is based on personal expectations. Some of the phenomena or processes associated with a trait or personality system are subtle and complex while others are highly simplistic. Clearly, the number, type and precision of hypotheses derived from the personality theory as they relate to occupational variables depends on a thorough understanding of the personality mechanisms and processes involved.

3. The third 'path' is of organizational or structural (and procedural) factors that mediate between an individual and the organization in which the individual works. Most organizations have a formal (and informal) structure which can be described on an organizational chart. Such a chart indicates who reports to whom; how multi-layered or flat the organization is; and the paths of communication up and down the organization. Organizations also very quickly develop norms of working, as well as specific procedures which may endure over very long periods of time. These formal procedures and informal work norms can have a very powerful effect on an individual's work-related behaviour, so moderating the natural effects of personality. Indeed, it is from this 'path' that one gets the concept of *person–job fit* which has so influenced vocational and occupational psychology (see Chapter 3). Organizational factors may both promote and facilitate a person's behaviour at work, or constrain it.

1.4 ELEMENTS IN THE MODEL

One of the features that frustrates any reviewer in this area is the loose use of terminology. Hence, it becomes difficult to specify the basic factors in the model and how they are related, to one another.

Figure 1.2 shows five basic factors and how they relate to occupational behaviour:

1 *Ability*. This refers to the extent to which a person can *efficiently* carry out multiple processes in co-ordination to achieve a specified goal. These range from relatively simple, dextrous, hand–eye co-ordination tasks to complex, intellectual decision processes, and are thus related to intelligence but distinguished from it.

2 *Demographic factors*. These refer to background factors such as sex, age,

class and education. Demographic factors usually relate to biographic factors in the life of a particular person – e.g. birth-order, occupation of parents, type of school attended – and are distinguishable from psychographic factors which refer to beliefs and values.

3 *Intelligence.* This refers to an individual's capacity for abstract and critical thinking. A large number of controversies surround this concept – for instance, whether it is uni- or multi-dimensional; to what extent it is inherited or learnt; and how it should be measured. Despite all of the concerns of investigators, few doubt the effect of intelligence on organizational behaviour.

4 *Motivation.* This, like intelligence, is a multi-dimensional, abstract concept that refers to the tendency to attend to some stimuli rather than others with accompanying emotion, and the drive to cause some actions rather than others. Hence, one talks of the strength of particular motivations, such as the weak need for achievement (low nAch).

5 *Personality.* This refers to all of those fundamental traits or characteristics of the person (or of people generally) that endure over time and account for consistent patterns of responses to everyday situations. Personality traits supposedly account for the what, why and how of human functioning.

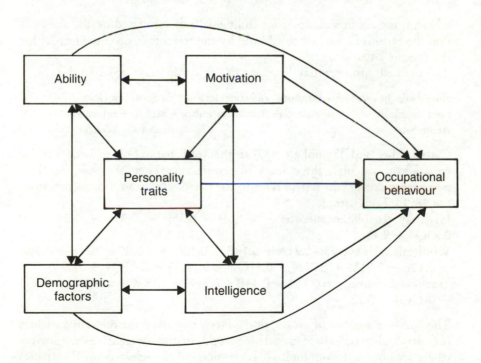

Figure 1.2 Some of the main factors predicting occupational behaviour

The model presented in Figure 1.2 is important for four reasons. First, it separates the five features distinguished above. Second, the bi-directionality of the arrows suggests that all of these factors are reciprocally influential. Third, the concept of personality is placed at the centre of the model to suggest its precedence in explanatory terms over the others. Finally, it is suggested that *each* of these factors reciprocally influences occupational behaviour both on its own and in combination.

1.5 BASIC EQUATIONS

The basic assumption of this model is that any act or behaviour pattern of a specific individual can be accurately predicted from the *linear addition* of scores on various factors like personality (e.g. extraversion), abilities (i.e. numerical or verbal) and temporary states (e.g. mood), together with some measure of situational or environmental conditions (e.g. noise or temperature), all weighted in accordance with their importance for the specific criterion behaviour (like performance ratings) that is being predicted. Mathematically, this looks as follows:

$$a_{ij} = b_j 1F1_i + b_j 2F2_i + b_j 3F3_i \ldots - + b_j NFN_i$$

where a, the act in situation j for individual i, is estimated by the status of i on the various factors F1 to FN and by the weights b_j on these factors for the specific situation.

Translated into everyday language the equation may look like this:

annual sales figures for J. Smith in Acme Sales		his extreme extraversion	his considerable numerical ability	a good health	a clean driver's licence
	=	+	+	+	

Cattell, Eber and Tatsuoka (1970) in the 16PF handbook provide various equations to calculate the efficacy of people at various jobs based on their personality scores (the letters refer to the personality trait dimensions from the 16PF). For example:

Highway patrolman success: $- 0.47A - 0.35F - 0.35L + 0.23Q2 + 0.23Q3 + 9.41$

Wholesale sales success: $0.21A + 0.10B + 0.10C + 0.10E + 0.21F + 0.10E - 0.10L - 0.31M + 0.21N - 0.31Q2 + 0.21Q3 - 0.21Q4 + 3.80$

Teaching effectiveness: $0.34A + 0.34B + 0.34C + 0.68M + 0.34N + 0.17Q3 - 0.17Q4 - 5.72$

This makes a number of assumptions. First, that all of the relevant variables (i.e. personality traits) are specified. Second, that the weightings are correct (these are obtained from multiple regressions of the selected 16PF variables to a specific measure of occupational behaviour). Third, the model has no situational modifiers which would specify how people behave in particular social encounters, although, of course, given appropriate research, they could be included. Fourth, the model assumes linearity (as opposed to additivity).

Kline (1983) has noted:

> If the model works to any extent at all, this is evidence of the importance of traits in the prediction of human behaviour . . . If, on the other hand, the psychometric model fails and no juggling with variables and specification equations produces results, then either trait psychology is worthless, or factor analysis cannot yield the fundamental variables and the fields wherein it is used, as we have argued, or alternatively both implications are correct. Whether positive or negative in outcome, therefore, testing the psychometric model will produce useful psychological knowledge (p.107).

1.6 PERSONALITY AND ORGANIZATIONAL BEHAVIOUR

Interestingly, although lay people view individual differences and personality as the most central, crucial, salient and interesting of psychologists' many missions, academic psychologists, particularly industrial/organizational (I/O) psychologists, tend to take the opposite view. Despite the fact that I/O psychologists usually proclaim that personality testing is neither useful in selection nor for the prediction of productivity, many human-resource personnel as well as negotiators and economic columnists stress the importance of understanding individual differences. Of course, the word 'personality' is used differently: lay people usually mean public reputation while psychologists usually mean structure and dynamic inner processes, which are private. 'Personality' refers to stylistic consistencies in social behaviour which are a reflection of an inner structure and process.

Most lay people are type rather than trait theorists. Types are categories, syndromes, trait summaries. They are the oldest and simplest way to classify people, hence their abiding popularity, and still find a role in modern psychology. Traits refer to single dimensions made up of related components. Thus, the trait of neuroticism, isolated by many researchers as a fundamental and unique trait, includes behaviours and cognitions associated with guilt, low self-esteem, depression, phobia, anxiety, and psychosomatic illnesses. Both trait and type theories provide useful heuristics with which to describe people. However, lay people shy away from using 'negative' traits like neuroticism, preferring more 'positive' traits such as insightful. While lay people prefer to look for positive correlates of occupational success, many psychologists are interested in (equally predictive) negative correlates of success. It seems as if lay people infer failure from success while psychologists infer success variables, processes, structures and criteria from failure.

The ease of construction and the apparent fame (and money) that may be associated with the development of an eponymous personality test means that thousands have been published. Many are awful, with little or no theoretical (or even clear) conceptualization, psychometric properties or, worse, external validity. A review by Guion and Gottier (1965) was highly influential in this rejection of standard personality measures for personnel selection, no doubt because of the quality of so many tests used. However, a major criticism of this review was that they did not group studies according to the tests used, the constructs upon which they were based, or the organizational criteria needed. Recent meta-analysis has been much more positive, but the last 20 years have shown a major crisis in the world of personality psychology.

The 1970s and 1980s showed evidence of a crisis in personality theory which may account, in part, for the paucity of good research over the period. The issues that seemed most important were as follows:

- *Situation* – the idea that in many (work) situations inter-individual variability in behaviour is low and personality differences are likely to have little predictive power. This theory, which has been largely disproved, suggested that personality traits were both unreliable and invalid, because the major determinants of behaviour were not inside individuals but rather external, situational factors. Spurious and dubious arguments have now been settled and personality theory thrives.
- *Paradigm uncertainty* – rather than form some consensus about the nature, structure and processes involved in personality, the field appears to have been further subdivided, with the latest onslaught being from constructionists who argue that personality is a construct of the observer. However, there is more and more evidence that mainstream personality theorists are accepting the evidence of both the fundamental (five) dimensions of personality and the biological structures determining them.
- *Personality (and criterion) measurement* – few measures *aggregate* multiple-act criteria or observations to provide more robust measures which reduce error variance. Once this error has been reduced, the relationship between personality measures and occupational behaviour becomes much more apparent. Previously weak findings may be simply due to measurement error rather than actual weak relationships.
- *Performance consistency* – not all behaviour is as consistent as others and so performance distributions should be considered before predictions are made. That is, neither individual difference variables nor occupational behaviour can be assured to be consistent in occurrence, because both are shaped (reinforced and inhibited) by other external and structural factors. Presumably, it is possible to document when, where and why behavioural consistency does and does not exist.
- *Time* – different types of criteria are more or less valid as predictors of occupational behaviour depending on *when* the criterion is measured.

Thus, for a person new in a job, ability will be more predictive than personality, but their role is likely to be reversed later in the same job.

A number of reviewers have pointed out the poor regard with which personality theory is held in I/O psychology: Bernardin and Beatty (1987):

> The research on individual difference variables has not borne much fruit. Rating accuracy appears to be more related to situation-specific variables than to individual characteristics (p.246).

Staw, Bell and Clausen (1986):

> The field is no longer interested in what the individual brings to the work-setting in terms of behavioural tendencies, traits, and personality (p.57).

As has been pointed out previously, organizational, occupational and industrial psychologists have historically not had much time for personality theories, constructs and measures. Certainly, the only really powerful approach to receive any attention in this area is the trait approach, within a nomothetic framework, as opposed to cognitive or 'self' approaches, conceived in an idiographic framework. Idiographic, or case-study, methods have usually been seen by psychologists in this area to be too unscientific to yield data of sufficient generalizability.

According to Weiss and Adler (1984), personality variables have taken two major roles in organizational behaviour research. To some extent, individual difference variables have had a central role in theory. Variables such as self-esteem, self-actualization, expectancy–valence, need for achievement and fear of failure are individual difference personality factors that 'drive' various theories of job motivation and performance. Other individual difference variables are seen more as moderator variables, explaining the link between job (dis)satisfaction and absenteeism. A second role has been in the design of studies, where individual differences are seen as independent, dependent or moderator variables, or a combination of all three. Naturally, 'cognitive' and 'motivational' factors have been concentrated on most.

Weiss and Adler (1984) describe four representative areas in occupational psychology where personality constructs have been used:

- *Job scope* – where motivational variables have been used extensively, e.g. locus of control and higher – order needs.
- *Leadership* – researchers have long sought personality traits linked to leadership, a concept which has been shown to have statistically significant (but not strong) direct and interactive effects on work behaviour.
- *Employee withdrawal* – the scattered and diverse literature has looked at personality correlates of turnover, absenteeism and lateness.
- *Goal setting* – the idea that personality relates to level of aspiration is only comparatively recent.

Weiss and Adler (1984) have been critical of previous research, particularly the lack of longitudinal studies and reciprocal effects research design. They also note the 'superficial thought' and 'substantially less theoretical specification' found in this area. They conclude that researchers need to put *theory before research design*, and consider *which* personality factors influence *which* occupational behaviours and in *what* way. Furthermore, they believe *theory should precede measurement* and the choice of measures should be more carefully considered.

In a later review, Adler and Weiss (1988) seem more optimistic as a result of I/O researchers' 'consideration of contextual variables and specification of criterion constructs that might relate to the personality variables of interest' (p.311). They reviewed a dozen or so studies on topics such as goal setting, charismatic leadership and job attitudes, published over the years 1986–7. They make three telling points about job attitudes:

- The fact that job attitudes are consistent over time and across situations is in accordance with a dispositional explanation.
- Unstable attitudes do not necessarily imply a situational explanation or rule out a dispositional one.
- The fact that dispositional traits might not account for more of the variance than situational factors does not mean that they are not worthy of investigation.

Adler and Weiss (1988) noted various developments occurring in the area. For instance, cognitive individual constructs (i.e. locus of control, expectancies) appear to be replacing trait measures; the development (and application) of work-specific, multi-faceted traits and other measures; and a sensitivity to the nature of the work-related predictor criteria. Three types of criteria measure have been used: type of behaviour (i.e. preferred mode or style), level of behaviour and time.

More importantly perhaps, they note the (organizational) context in which personality criteria relationships are examined. They quote an excellent illustrative study where subjects played a 24-week-long computer game. Subjects could request (at some cost) feedback (always negative) on the efficacy of their strategy, which of course made them consider changing it. Interestingly, those high in self-confidence requested feedback less often and hence adhered to failing strategies longer than those low in self-confidence. An understanding of the context, the task and the individual difference dimension clearly leads to more creative (possibly counter-intuitive) hypotheses and significant findings.

Hogan (1991) concluded his review of individual differences and personality in the I/O literature thus:

- The criticism of personality, popular in the 1970s and 1980s, is no longer valid.

- Much of early personality theory had a clinical bias and hence many measures are not really appropriate for predicting occupational behaviour.
- Factor-analytic research suggests five major independent traits relevant to social behaviour: neuroticism (adjustment), extraversion (sociability), conscientiousness (responsibility), agreeableness (warmth) and culture (imaginativeness).
- The relevance of accuracy of social perception for interviewing, selection and performance appraisal links personality and occupational psychology.
- Meta-analysis of 25 years of literature suggests that personality inventories can make valid contributions to personnel selection and assessment.
- One cannot forget the importance of measures, people, criteria and situations as moderator variables.

Recent reviewers and critics are much more optimistic and positive about the possibility of finding powerful relationships between personality (individual) difference variances and occupational behaviour. However, much work remains to be done, both theoretical and empirical.

1.7 THE DIRECTION OF CAUSALITY

The relationship between any two variables or factors can take many forms: it may be correlational or causal, and if it is causal, different directions of causality are possible. Thus, any of the following relationships between personality and occupational behaviour (OB) may occur:

1. *OB ⅄ P (no relationship between personality and OB)*. This possibility would assume that there is no systematic relationship between any major personality factor and any dimension of OB. This may only appear to be so because the relationship which actually exists is too subtle to be measured, too unstable, or is frequently 'washed out' or moderated by other more powerful and salient variables. Alternatively, it may be that there simply is no relationship at all.
2. *P → OB (personality 'determines' OB)*. This position assumes that some (but not all) personality traits determine, in some sense, various features of OB. People who adopt this position may well argue that various traits relate to, influence and determine various features of OB, or that some traits relate to all major OBs, or that most traits relate to one particular OB feature. The crucial axiom of this position is that personality traits 'causally' determine OB, along with perhaps other related variables (e.g. non-verbal behaviour).
3. *OB → P (OB 'determines' personality)*. This more unusual position assumes that personality traits are, in some sense, a function of OB variables. In a sense, this position could be seen as a manifestation of

the structurist – determinist position, in that organizational structure shapes ways of thinking and behaving which become set in behaviourally replicable traits. Precisely how this occurs, or which aspects of personality are shaped by which features of organizational structures and processes, is not clear, but what does appear to be at the core of this position is that personality traits and cognitive styles are primarily a function of external facets of the organization.

4. $P \rightarrow OB$ *(personality and OB are reciprocally determined).* This somewhat more realistic cybernetic view suggests that personality is a function of OB and vice versa; that is, there is bi-directional causality between personality and OB. This position allows for one direction of causality to be primary and the other secondary, so long as each has influence on the other. There may also be differences within the position as to which aspects of personality and which of OB are singled out for reciprocal determinism.

5. $P \rightarrow {}_1OB; P_2 \rightarrow OB; S_3 \rightarrow OB; P_4 \approx OB$ *(mixed relationships).* Some theorists may argue that, as both personality and OB are multi-faceted, it is possible that all of the previous four relationships occur *simultaneously*; that is, some personality variables reciprocally determine some OB variables; some personality variables uni-directionally determine some OB variables and vice versa; and, finally, some personality traits are not determined by, nor determine, OB, and some OB variables are not determined by, nor determine, personality.

6. $P \times OB$ *(personality and OB are moderated by other variables).* This approach suggests that both personality and organizational behaviour are determined by another variable or group of variables. This moderator variable approach can take many forms, varying in the complexity of pathways and number of variables. Given the complexity of both OB and personality, it is hard to see how most theorists would opt for this 'path-analysis' moderator variable approach. In a sense, this approach encapsulates all of the other models as well. Although it might well be true, there is certainly no agreement on the salient personality, occupational behaviour or moderator variables that are important, or on the precise causal links. Thus, while agreeing that the relationship is complex, multi-faceted and multi-causal, there are few explicit models of this process.

1.8 LONGITUDINAL STUDIES

Most researchers agree that longitudinal studies (well designed, planned and executed) are by far the best type of research as they are the best naturalistic studies able to sort out cause and correlation. However, they are difficult, expensive and, by definition, time consuming.

There are various studies which have examined the relationships between personality and work over time. Harrell and Harrell (1984) looked at personality differences between people who reached general management early, in contrast to those who held more specialized jobs. MBA students were tested five years after graduation. Over 90% (N=434) responded, who by that time were in a variety of jobs. Four scales of the MMPI showed significant differences. General managers were higher than consultants on *Pd* (psychopathic deviate). This presumably reflected a need for autonomy or independence. General managers were higher than marketeers, consultants and engineers on *Pa* (paranoia), all at the 0.05 level. This presumably reflected intensity and sincerity. General managers were higher at the 0.05 level than accountants on *Ma* (hypomania), which probably meant energy level. General managers were lower on *Si* (social introversion) than accountants (0.01 level) and those in production (0.05 level), meaning that general managers were more socially extraverted.

Later, Harrell *et al.* (1977) tested 266 graduates, five and ten years after graduating. A regression analysis was performed, aiming to regress a battery of personality data (with 31 different scales), a 'high earner's scale' which measured leadership, energy, sociability and dominance; age of entrance to university; and graduation grade-point average. Age, grade-point average and the 'higher earner's scale' correlated significantly with five-year earnings. Whereas the Strong Vocational Interest Blank (SVIB) managerial orientation correlated positively with five-year earnings, the SVIB engineer correlated negatively. The results were repeated on the ten-year group and the results were much the same. Overall, the personality data from the Minnesota Multi-phasic Personality Inventory (MMPI) did not prove significant.

Anderson (1977) tracked 90 entrepreneurs over a two-and-a-half-year period, following the debilitating effects of a natural disaster. He looked at their locus of control (as measured by the Rotter scale), their perceived stress, their various coping behaviours and their performance in the organization. Those with the more healthy and adaptive internal locus of control tended to experience low stress and employed more task-centred and less emotion-centred coping behaviours than externals. Interestingly, successful internals became more interested while unsuccessful externals became more external over this period. The cross-lagged correlation coefficients suggested that locus of control influences performance, which in turn operates as a feedback mechanism and influences locus of control.

Hinrichs's (1978) study followed 47 people who had been assessed on various dimensions over an eight-year period. Ratings of aggressiveness, persuasiveness, oral communication and self-confidence, and test ratings on ascendency and self-assurance were most strongly related to performance eight years later. The two simple ratings – overall rating and general management evaluation – correlated 0.58 with the ratings eight years later. The Gordon personal profile and various value ratings used in this study seemed excellent predictors eight years on.

Brousseau (1978) followed 116 engineers, scientists and managers employed by a large petroleum company over 5.9 years. They were given the Guilford–Zimmerman temperament survey which was used to derive four characteristics:

- *Active orientation*: outgoing, optimistic, lively and risky.
- *Philosophical orientation*: serious minded and liking self-analysis.
- *Freedom from depression*: energetic, seldom tired, vigorous and non-neurotic.
- *Self-confidence*: seldom hurt or disappointed.

These scores were related to five characteristics of the person's job: skill variety, task identity, task significance, autonomy and feedback. The results showed that active orientation (extraversion) and freedom from depression (non-neuroticism) were related to task identity, task significance and job summary. The results provide some support for the overall theory which proposes that an individual's life orientation and level of emotional well-being are influenced by the stimulus complexity of the job experience.

Schneidman (1984) interviewed 11 lawyers in the 1980s who had been interviewed by Terman in the 1920s. Occupational success seemed related to contentment, self-confidence, openness, spontaneity, and freedom from feelings of hostility, irritability and dissatisfaction. But, of course, in studies such as this it is not easy to separate cause and effect.

Kohn and Schooler (1982) examined data collected in 1964 from 3101 men (a representative male sample) and from a follow-up of a quarter of that number (who were still under 65 years of age) ten years later. They were particularly interested in the reciprocal effects of job conditions and personality. Using well over a dozen job conditions, and a similar number of subject background factors and interview questions, they devised three major dimensions of personality. These were:

- *Ideational flexibility* – intellectual activity.
- *Self-directed orientation* – conservatism, anxiety, trust, self-confidence.
- *Sense of distress* – psychologically unhappy.

Various analyses showed evidence of reciprocal effects:

Ideationally more flexible men are more likely to achieve, in time, self-directed positions. A self-directed orientation results, over time, in being less closely supervised, having greater income, and doing physically lighter work, in short, in more advantageous jobs. Psychic distress results in working under greater time pressure and in a greater likelihood of being held responsible for things outside one's control (p.1278).

They consistently found evidence of the reciprocal effects of job conditions on personality and vice versa.

They note:

Jobs that facilitate occupational self-direction increase mens's ideational flexibility, and promote a self-directed orientation to self and to society; jobs that limit occupational self-direction decrease men's ideational flexibility and promote a conformist orientation to self and to society. The analysis further demonstrates that opportunities for exercising occupational self-direction, especially for doing substantively complex work, are to a substantial extent determined by the job's location in the organizational structure with ownership, bureaucratization, and a high position in the supervisory hierarchy all facilitating the exercise of occupational self-direction. Those findings provide strong empirical support for the interpretation that class-associated conditions of work actually do affect personality. The longitudinal analysis also provides evidence of other job-to-personality effects, the most important being that oppressive working conditions produce a sense of distress ... In short, occupational self-direction, ideational flexibility, and a self-directed orientation are intertwined in a dynamic process through which the individual's place in the stratification system both affects and is affected by his personality (p.1281-3).

More recently, Inwald (1988) did a five-year, follow-up study of 219 correction officers who were hired in a one-year period. He was particularly interested in whether test results, as well as psychological interpretations and interviews, could predict 28 officers who were 'terminated'. Test results proved to be the best predictors. But, although they could identify up to 75% of those sacked, 'false hits' were scored in as many as a third of the cases. The Inwald personality inventory proved particularly useful at predicting subsequent sackings, and was, of course, much cheaper and more efficient than interviews. The author recognizes that termination does not represent the only or the best assessment criteria, but is impressed that personality inventory scores can predict so well into the future.

In an extensive longitudinal study, Mortimer, Lorence and Kumka (1986) followed 512 young men to see how social, family and personality factors affected their occupational attainments. The study aimed to address a number of quite specific questions. These included:

• Are individual psychological attributes mainly formed by the end of adolescence, or do they continue to change over time in response to major life experiences encountered in adulthood?

- What is the effect of social structure, particularly non-occupational location, on occupational attainment?
- How does family life affect work and vice versa, and what is the effect of both on personality?

Through path analysis they sought answers to both psychological and sociological questions, such as whether socio-economic origins or psychological/personality factors, together or individually, determine occupational success. The results showed a pervasive impact of the father–son relationship on such things as achievement-related attitudes, but early assistance and support was highly rated. The two measures of family influence – socio-economic status and paternal support – appeared to have both short- and long-term effects.

Because this study examined attitudes, values and experiences *before* people joined the labour market, it was possible to examine self-selection and self-fulfilling characteristics. Results showed that self-confidence indirectly influenced work autonomy a decade later through its influence on intrinsic skills.

Their data seem to suggest that the 'psychological' variables which they measured, namely self-competence, work involvement, people-oriented values, intrinsic values and extrinsic values, were fairly stable over time. The authors therefore concluded that an individual's sense of identity and values are largely formed by the end of adolescence. However, the results also indicate that experiences of autonomy in the work environment do, and can, influence self-competence. There is therefore evidence of a reciprocal effects model operating. They note:

In spite of the relatively high stability of the attitudes and values under consideration during the decade following college, work autonomy directly strengthened the individual's sense of competence, work involvement, and intrinsic reward values. It further enhanced the extrinsic and people-oriented values through its influence on the level of personal involvement in work. Income, our sole indicator of extrinsic reward and socio-economic achievement, had less pervasive psychological importance. It enhanced emphasis on extrinsic rewards, and diminished the people-oriented values. However, the positive correlations of income with competence and work involvement were shown to be spurious, either dependent on prior selection processes or on the covariance of income and work autonomy. The career pattern, a third measure of work experience, was important for psychological development mainly because of its effects on work autonomy and income. Because the degree of stability in the early career was a substantial determinant of these attainments, the career pattern indirectly affected the whole range of psychological orientations. Yet an unstable career, perhaps because of the uncertainties which occupational change and employment problems entail, was found to heighten evaluations of extrinsic as well as intrinsic occupational rewards, independently of the occupational attainments.

These findings demonstrate that psychological orientations that are relevant to work, though quite stable over time, should hardly be considered fixed from late adolescence through early adulthood. As discussed earlier in this chapter, this assumption has been the basis of many studies of the effects of attitudes on occupational choice, career change, and subjective reactions to work (such as job satisfaction). But this study shows that the relationships between work experiences and psychological attributes are instead highly reciprocal. Earlier attitudes and values influence subsequent work experiences, which, in turn, become significant determinants of psychological development at a later point in time.

A second set of findings concern the level of psychological stability over time. The generally high degree of stability in these work-related attitudes and values accentuates the need for longitudinal investigations of development through the life course. High stability, coupled with the tendency of persons to select later life situations on the basis of their earlier predispositions, could, in many instances, fully account for psychological differences among persons with varying life experiences. This possibility makes the deficiency of cross-sectional research exceedingly apparent: with cross-sectional data, the effects of selection and subsequent adult socialization are entirely confounded. Moreover, longitudinal data are necessary to ascertain the significance of changes that are apparently induced by environmental circumstances. As pointed out earlier, it is plausible to assume that even a small change in a highly stable attribute will have important implications for the developing adult personality ...

However, persistence in the other psychological constructs – work involvement, intrinsic values, and people-oriented values – seemed to be substantially dependent on adult experiences, particularly the degree of autonomy encountered in the work environment. The stability of intrinsic work values, for example, was clearly conditional on career stability and autonomy on the job. These patterns indicate that the respondents have maintained their work-related attitudes and values over time partially by creating the very circumstances and achievements that foster constancy of their original orientations. Senior work values thus influence subsequent value development directly as well as by an indirect process – operating in a previous period to select or otherwise contribute to those subsequent experiences that have significant implications for psychological stability during the transition to adulthood (p.137–8).

By far the most interesting and unique study, however, was that of Howard and Bray (1988), who followed managers for 20 years: when they attended assessment centres at joining, eight years later, and 20 years after that. The sample consisted of over 422 men who joined Bell in the 1950s. In the 1950s, they were assessed according to the following:

- Family and educational background;
- Lifestyles (nine categories were devised back as parental–familial; religious–humanism);
- Work interests;
- Work history;
- Expectations and work preferences;
- Work attitudes (ten areas were considered such as supervision, satisfaction and salary);
- Personality and motivation (various standard questionnaires yielded seven measures: self-esteem, leadership, motivation, positiveness, impulsivity, affability and ambition);
- Abilities (administrative, interpersonal and cognitive);
- Overall assessment evaluations (seven dimensions were evaluated: administrative skills, interpersonal skills, intellectual ability, advancement motivation, work involvement, stability of performance and independence).

The authors were, of course, interested in the harbingers of career advancement, the seeds of personal adjustment, and how changing times and lifestyles affected the work force. Most pertinent for this book is how personality changed over time.

The most dramatic change was in ambition, which dropped steeply in the first eight years, and then again by the 20th. Graduates, more ambitious to begin with, actually dropped more steeply.

Self-esteem remained much the same, as did impulsivity. Affability did not drop much over time. Yet achievement orientation (having a challenging job or a difficult assignment) increased over time. Aggression and autonomy went up over the years, while deference, abasement and endurance tended to drop.

Ability measures, on the other hand, tended to change less dramatically, although there were numerous and noticeable differences between college and non-college graduates. Thus, administrative skills and work involvement tended to increase for graduates over the 20-year period while they decreased for non-graduates. This may or may not be explained by intelligence.

This extremely rich and detailed account considered, among other things, the effects of career advancement. For instance, Howard and Bray examined how attitudes changed from time 1 (MPS:0) to time 20 (MPS:20). These

Table 1.1 The effects of career advancement
(a) Summary of changes over time in management questionnaire scales by
MPS:20 level

Scale	Attitudes over time
General management attitude	Higher levels consistently higher
Supervision	–
Personal satisfaction	Higher levels consistently higher
Job satisfaction	–
Pride	Higher levels consistently higher
Impersonal communications	Higher levels consistently higher
Personal communications	–
Identification	Changes varied by level (higher levels higher)
Authority	Higher levels consistently higher
Salary	Higher levels consistently higher

(b) Summary of changes over time in personality and motivation factors by
MPS:20 level

Factor	Changes over time
Self-esteem	–
Leadership motivation	Changes varied by level (higher levels higher)
Positiveness	Higher levels consistently higher
Impulsivity	Higher levels consistently higher
Affability	Changes varied by level (lower levels higher)
Ambition	Changes varied by level (higher levels higher)

(c) Summary of changes over time in personality and motivation factors by
MPS:20 adjustment

Factor	Major changes over time
Self-esteem	Poorly adjusted declined
Leadership motivation	–
Positiveness	Well-adjusted increased; poorly adjusted declined
Impulsivity	Well-adjusted consistently lower
Affability	Difference diminished with time (well-adjusted remained higher)
Ambition	Poorly adjusted declined most

Source: Howard and Bray (1988)

are shown in Table 1.1. The results showed that, over time, attitudes
changed such that low scorers got lower and high scorers got higher. In
six of the ten cases where differences were noticeable, this 'lens' effect
occurred. Similarly, personality and motivational changes were noted (see
Table 1.2). Self-esteem did not change much but other changes were
noteworthy:

- Ambition continued to differentiate workers most sharply, with the disparity growing slightly larger over time (i.e. lack of ambition led to less advancement which self-fulfilled the lack of ambition).
- Leadership motivation clearly distinguished the job level groups over time, but the higher-level men increased in this desire while the lower-level men decreased.
- Affability declined for all groups, particularly those at the top, but interestingly increased for the very bottom group.

Table 1.2 Correlations of personality and motivation factors with management potential, MPS:0 and MCS:0

Factor	MPS college (N = 274)	MPS total (N = 344)
Factors derived from MPS sample		
Leadership motivation	0.24**	0.28**
Positiveness	0.15*	0.26**
Impulsivity	0.14*	0.20**
Affability	−0.09	−0.06
Ambition	0.25**	0.27**
Factors derived from MCS sample		
Submissiveness		−0.11*
Positiveness		0.26*
Impulsivity		0.04*
Affability		−0.14*
Ambition		0.33*
Adjusted conformity		0.18**
Poise		0.36**
Flexibility		0.24**
Unconventionality		0.02
Masculinity		−0.02

MPS: Management Progress Study, MCS: Management Continuity Study
 * $p < 0.05$
** $p < 0.005$
Source: Howard and Bray (1988)

Howard and Bray 'cut' the data yet another way by looking at how the various measures related to personal adjustment 20 years on. They found that five of the six personality and motivation factors were related to adjustment ratings (see Table 1.3). Findings showed the following:

- The poorly adjusted gave up readily on career aspirations while the very opposite was true of the well adjusted.
- Positiveness and self-esteem became even more pronounced, over time, in their relatedness to adjustment.
- The relationship between affability and adjustment, while initially very strong, reduced over time.

Table 1.3 Correlations of personality and motivation factors with adjustment, MPS:0 and MCS:0

Factor	MPS college (N = 274)	MPS total (N = 344)
Factors derived from MPS sample		
Leadership motivation	0.24*†	0.04
Positiveness	0.75*	0.62*
Impulsivity	0.11	0.00
Affability	−0.04	0.08
Ambition	0.41*†	0.24*
Factors derived from MCS sample		
Submissiveness		0.21*
Positiveness		0.61*
Impulsivity		−0.07
Affability		−0.08
Ambition		0.31*
Adjusted conformity		0.52*
Poise		0.36*
Flexibility		0.08
Unconventionality		−0.09
Masculinity		0.04

† Significant difference between MPS and MCS correlations at $p < 0.05$
* $p < 0.005$
Source: Howard and Bray (1988)

This remarkable study enabled the correlates of managerial potential to be examined. At the time of joining the company, employees were rated on a five-point potential scale – that is, the potential that the person would reach a fairly high position in the company. As Table 1.4 indicates, this rating was fairly consistently related to personality factors. The higher-potential managers were characterized by a strong desire to achieve as leaders and professionals: they had a greater ambition to advance. In contrast, the lower-rated potential managers indicated in their interviews that job security was most valued. The relationship of the adjusted conformity and poise factors to potential was consistent with the relationship of potential to the positiveness factor. The positiveness factor indicated that the higher-potential managers had higher general adjustment, optimism and self-confidence as rated from the projective exercise.

Similarly, personality and motivation factors were logically, and frequently, strongly correlated with ratings of adjustment. Ambition and positivity were equally related to management potential and adjustment, while positiveness and adjusted conformity were predominantly related to adjustment. Equally, the self-esteem factor correlated significantly with adjustment, but not with management potential. Howard and Bray concluded:

A large number of variables in the table relate in similar ways to both criteria. A primary reason is that those advanced the most and those best adjusted were more involved in and satisfied with their work. They responded more positively on such management questionnaire scales as general management attitude, pride, personal satisfaction, impersonal communication, authority, and identification. The management level

Table 1.4 Summary of variables differentiating MPS advancement and adjustment subgroups across time

	Advancement	*Adjustment*
Relating to one criterion	Lower locale-residential involvement	Higher religious–humanism involvement and satisfaction[b]
	Higher service involvement	Higher supervision score (MQ)[b]
	Higher salary score (MQ)	Higher job satisfaction score (MQ)
	Higher leadership motivation[a]	Higher personal communications score (MQ)
	Higher ego-functional involvement	Higher self-esteem[b]
		Less independence
Relating to both criteria	Higher ego-functional satisfaction	
	Higher occupational involvement and satisfaction[b]	
	Higher pride score (MQ)	
	Better general management attitude (MQ)[b]	
	Higher personal satisfaction score (MQ)[b]	
	Higher impersonal communications score (MQ)[b]	
	Higher identification score (MQ)[a, b]	
	Higher authority score (MQ)[b]	
	Greater positiveness[b]	
	Greater ambition[a, b]	
	Better general effectiveness[a, b]	
	Better administrative skills[a, b]	
	Better interpersonal skills[a, b]	
	Better stability of performance[a, b]	
Relating to criteria oppositely	Lower marital–familial involvement	Higher marital–familial satisfaction
	Lower parental–familial involvement	Higher parental–familial satisfaction
	Higher impulsivity	Lower impulsivity
	Lower affability[a]	Higher affability
	Higher verbal ability	Lower verbal ability

MQ: Management Questionnaire
All variables not marked by superscript letters showed a consistent relationship over time
[a] Developed over time for advancement
[b] Developed over time for adjustment
Source: Howard and Bray (1988)

groups were rather consistently differentiated on these attitude scales over time, while the adjustment groups showed increasing dissimilarity as the maladjusted men rapidly declined in favourableness. Greater general positiveness (the personality factor) was consistently characteristic of both the higher-level managers and the better-adjusted ones.

Rapidly deteriorating attitudes for the maladjusted men also took place on scales that did not differentiate the level groups, including supervision, job satisfaction, and personal communications on the management questionnaire. The higher-level men showed more satisfaction with their salaries, which would be expected since they were paid more.

Some important management abilities also differentiated the advancement and adjustment groups. The 'rich get richer and the poor get poorer' phenomenon was prevalent for the groups by management level on the dimension factors of general effectiveness, administrative skills, and stability of performance. The higher-level groups held their own and the lower-level groups declined in interpersonal skills. In the case of the adjustment groups, there was no particular increase in these important managerial qualities on the part of either the well-adjusted or the moderately adjusted, but the poorly adjusted declined markedly. The higher-level men and the best-adjusted also showed less decline in ambition over time, while the lower-level men and the maladjusted experienced sharp drops . . .

The general decline in interpersonal skills was strongly related to management level eventually attained. Decreases were very large for those skills, the lower-level managers over the 20-year period, while the fifth and sixth level managers rose a full point on a 5-point scale (from 3 to 4!). This great gain was not because of experience in top-level assignments, since somewhat more than half of it had been achieved by the time of reassessment at MPS:8.

We thus get a picture of those who failed to advance very far in management deteriorating in management skills along with, or at least partly due to, a loss of managerial motivation. At the same time, those who wound up at the highest levels held onto their motivation and increased in job involvement as they improved their management skills.

Some personality and motivation characteristics pointed in different directions for the advancement and adjustment subgroups, sometimes because they related to the different criteria in opposite directions. The higher-level men showed an increase in leadership and motivation while the well-adjusted men had greater self-esteem and somewhat less independence. While the higher-level men demonstrated more impulsivity and less affability, the well-adjusted men showed just the opposite pattern.

There was a striking difference in the evolution of personality between the highest- and lowest-level men, in that those at the higher levels, though nonauthoritarian and (one hopes) objective, became more uninvolved in personal relationships – 'cool at the top'. The lower-level men retained their need for friendships and increased in interest in helping and sympathizing with others. This is the group, then, that was most likely to show the kind of generativity that was involved in developing others, while the majority of men were more concerned with productive outputs (p.413–14).

The importance of these longitudinal studies cannot be underestimated, because unlike most cross-sectional studies they are able to disentangle cause and effect. What most of these careful studies have demonstrated is that, firstly, personality traits do not change much over time and, secondly, that they relate directly and systematically to occupational, behavioural variables like position, promotion history and salary.

1.9 THE INDEPENDENT AND DEPENDENT VARIABLE

The Independent Variable

For nearly all of the work in this field, the independent variable is a personality test score (or profile of scores). But what does this score (scores) measure? Hogan *et al.* (1985) have suggested that theoreticians have taken one of four positions:

- Scores are veridical self-reports of internal states and external behaviour (honest, objective reporting).
- Scores do not correspond exactly to the trait, but because the trait influences how one responds to the test and how one behaves generally, there are substantive overlaps.
- Scores represent a self-presentational style, hence, the scores represent individuals' attempts to manage or control the impressions that others form of them.
- Scores can only be defined in terms of how each item functions – that is, what they predict. They don't have theoretical meaning, just predictability.

Most psychologists appear to take a position somewhere between the first two positions, although many in fact recognize that there are systematic errors involved in self-report.

Of course, the independent variable is not always a self-report score from a personality inventory. It could be an ability score, a biographical fact, a demographic classification or an organizational position. Usually, however, it is an individual difference dimension that does not have perfect reliability. Cynics, and some sceptics, reject all self-report measures, which is rather like throwing out the baby with the bath water, because if they were worthless, tests would have no validity. However, it is quite apparent that many are concurrently and predictively valid (see Chapter 2).

The Dependent Variable

The quality of research in this area depends very heavily on the dependent variable measured – i.e. the quality and quantity of work performance.

There are numerous ways of describing jobs or job characteristics, frequently the dependent variable in this area. For instance, Hackman and Lawler (1971) suggested that jobs could be described on four basic (orthogonal) dimensions: variety, autonomy, task identity and feedback. They found (as predicted) that when jobs are high on these dimensions, people with needs for accomplishment and personal growth tend to be more satisfied, less absent and rated higher by their superiors.

There are many conceptual and operational approaches to the measurement of work performance. Smith (1976) has developed a three-dimensional framework that is useful for classifying different forms of performance measures. The three dimensions are the time span covered by the measure, the specificity of the measure, and the closeness of the measure to organized goals.

The time span covered by the measure refers to the fact that performance measures can be obtained shortly after the actual on-the-job behaviour has occurred or following a delay of a few hours up to many years. Clearly, the more delayed the index, the more likely it is that one can have a cumulative and aggregated measure.

The second dimension along which performance measures may vary is specificity–generality. A particular measure may refer to a specific aspect of job performance or to some index of overall performance. An overall score can be made up of individual scores, or simply be an overall rating.

The most important dimension in Smith's classification framework is that of closeness to organizational goals. This dimension has three levels: behaviours, results and organizational effectiveness. The behaviours level refers to the direct observation of work behaviour, such as the timing of the movement elements required in the assembly of some product. The results level refers to a summary measure of the effectiveness of work behaviours of an individual. Observations from several points in time are combined to yield an inference about the work performance of the individual. These results measures may be objective (e.g. absence rate, production rate) or subjective (e.g. supervisory rating). Finally, the organizational effectiveness level consists of measures that result from another inferential step. The measures at the results level are combined or aggregated to indicate how well the organization is functioning *vis-à-vis* its goals.

The Moderator Variable

For many researchers, personality is a moderator variable between individual difference measures and occupational outcomes (Hobert and Dunnette,

1967). From a definitional point of view, these moderator variables pose the same definitional and operational problems as the independent variable.

Both personality and occupational psychology have been dogged by post-measurement. Not only are measurement tools often weak and under-refined, but the sort of data that has been collected to test hypotheses is flawed.

The following lists give examples of 'soft' vs 'hard' data. It is frequently and erroneously assumed that hard data is better because it's easier to measure reliably and less prone to human error. It may, indeed, be more reliable but it is not at all clear that it is more valid. Hard data may be influenced by different sources of noise and on occasion less reliable (see Chapters 4, 5 and 8).

SOFT DATA

Work habits
Absenteeism
Tardiness
Visits to the sick bay
Violations of safety rules
Excessive breaks

Work climate
Number of grievances
Number of discrimination charges
Employee complaints
Employee turnover

Feelings/attitudes
Attitude changes
Perceptions of job responsibilities
Perceived changes in performance
Employee loyalty

New skills
Decisions made
Problems solved
Conflicts avoided
Grievances resolved
Discrimination charges resolved
Intention to use new skills
Frequency of use of new skills

Development/advancement
Number of promotions

Number of pay increases
Number of training programs attended
Requests for transfer
Performance appraisal ratings

Initiative
Implementation of new ideas
Successful completion of projects
Number of suggestions submitted
Number of suggestions implemented

HARD DATA

Output
Units produced
Tons manufactured
Items assembled
Money collected
Items sold
Forms processed
Loans approved
Inventory turnover
Patients visited
Applications processed
Students graduated
Work backlog
Incentive bonus
Shipments delivered

Costs
Budget variances
Unit costs
Cost by account
Variable costs
Fixed costs
Overhead costs
Operating costs
Number of cost reductions
Project cost savings
Sales expenses

Time
Equipment downtime
Overtime
On-time shipments
Time to project completion

Processing time
Supervisory time
Break-in time for new employees
Training time
Repair time
Work stoppages
Late reporting
Lost time days

Quality
Scrap
Waste
Rejects
Error rates
Rework
Shortages
Product defects
Deviation from standard
Product failures
Inventory adjustments
Time card corrections
Per cent of tasks completed properly
Number of accidents

1.10 CONCLUSION

This chapter described six rather different approaches to studying individual differences as they relate to occupational behaviour. Each method has its strengths and weaknesses, and through each tradition, it may be possible to build up a picture of which, how and when individual differences affect work-related behaviour. A research model was proposed which looked at some of the moderating variables and constraints which reflect the relationship between personality and work variables. The trait model was considered as was the concept of competences, which is currently much used but little understood. Quite how occupationally relevant traits are identified was also considered rather sceptically, as it was suggested that some researchers in this field might sacrifice veridical findings for profit! However, there has been something of a renaissance of research in this area of personality and occupational behaviour, and a wealth of longitudinal studies attest to the importance of personality factors in predicting work-related behaviour.

Chapter 2

Personality testing in the workplace

Research is a bit like praying: it's private, respectable but pointless.
Roger Holmes

The greatest American superstition is a belief in fact.
Herman Keyserling

All generalizations are dangerous, even this one.
Alexander Dumas

He is no wise man that will quit a certainty for an uncertainty.
Samuel Johnson

Some of our weaknesses are born in us, others are the result of education, it is a question which of the two gives us most trouble.
Goethe

I always pass on good advice. It is the only thing to do with it. It is never of any use to oneself.
Oscar Wilde

2.1 INTRODUCTION

One obvious way to understand the relationship of individual differences to work-related behaviour is to examine the applied literature on personality testing in the workplace. Psychological tests, attempting to measure individual differences related to occupational behaviours, have been used for over 60 years, and there now exist nearly 80,000 occupational-related tests. Both world wars, particularly the second, were particularly important for the 'testing business' and most armed services are still active users of psychological tests for selection and training.

In 1869, Galton expressed an interest in intelligence testing with his book *Hereditary Genius*, which presented a classification scheme based on abilities. Wundt in the 1870s began using reaction time measures and tests of visual and auditory acuity as indexes of intelligence. This effort was greatly advanced by Binet at the turn of the century, because he reconceptualized intelligence as consisting of more complex mental processes than had Wundt and, accordingly, developed tests of memory, attention, comprehension and imagination. Munsterberg in 1913 brought this fledgling movement into the industrial context in general, and employee selection in particular, by using a battery of tests available at the time to help select motormen for the Boston Railway Company. Psychological testing has blossomed fully since that early era, to gain a place not only in industry, but also educational, clinical and counselling settings. Its greatest boost for selection purposes came during World War I. Under the leadership of many of these early pioneers, 1,726,966 men were tested (for selection and classification purposes) as a part of the war effort.

In the period since these beginnings, the numbers and types of psychological tests employed in industry have expanded greatly. In a large, national survey done by the American Society for Personnel Administration in 1975, it was reported that approximately 60% of employers with over 25,000 employees and 40% of those with less than 100 employees used psychological tests. Recent work shows that nearly 20% of French and 10% of British companies use psychological tests (Shackleton and Newell, 1991).

Personality tests and, to a lesser extent, ability tests have both their critics and enthusiasts. The former dismiss them as useless while the latter embrace them as of crucial importance.

2.2 THE ADVANTAGES AND DISADVANTAGES OF TESTING

Advantages

- Tests provide numeric information, which means that individuals can be more easily compared on the same criteria. In interviews, different questions are asked of different candidates, and the answers often forgotten. Tests provide comparable profiles.
- With data-based records, one can trace a person's development over time. In fact, by going back to test results kept in a person's file one can actually see if, and by how much, the tests were predictive of occupational success (see Chapter 1).
- Tests give explicit and specific results on temperament and ability rather than vague, ambiguous, coded platitudes that are so often found in references. A percentage or a sten score (provided of course that it is valid) makes for much clearer thinking about personal characteristics than terms like satisfactory, sufficient or high-flyer. Good norms demonstrate a candidate's relative scores.

- Tests are fair because they eliminate corruption, favouritism, old-boy, Mason – or Oxbridge – networks from self-perpetuating. That is, if a person does not have the ability or a 'dangerous' profile, they will not be chosen irrespective of their other 'assets'.
- Tests are comprehensive in that they cover all of the basic dimensions of personality and ability from which other occupational behaviour patterns derive. A good test battery can give a complete picture of individual functioning.
- Tests are scientific in that they are soundly empirically based on proven theoretical foundations – that is, they are reliable, valid and able to discriminate the good from the mediocre, and the average from the bad.
- Tests increase the behavioural conceptual language of those that use them. This gives those who are not trained in personality theory a very useful set of concepts that they can use to identify and distinguish human characteristics in the workplace.
- Empirical data resulting from the tests can be used to settle empirical arguments. That is, objective numbers provide the sort of clear evidence to justify decisions.
- Tests give testers and testees alike, interesting and powerful insights into their own beliefs and behaviours. They might also be used to explain to candidates why they have been rejected.

Disadvantages

- Many of these tests are fakeable – that is, people like to describe themselves in a positive light and receive a 'desirable' score so that they may be accepted. Yet this faking in a way reflects their 'real' personality. Some tests have lie scores to attempt to overcome this. The effects of this distortion are, however, not major (Hough *et al.*, 1990).
- Some people do not have sufficient self-insight to report on their own feelings and behaviour – that is, it is not that people lie but that they cannot, rather than *will not*, give accurate answers about themselves (some tests only look for simple behavioural data to overcome this).
- Tests are unreliable in that all sorts of temporary factors – test anxiety, boredom, weariness, a headache, period pains – lead people to give different answers on different occasions. Although this is partly true, this factor only makes a small difference.
- Most importantly, tests are invalid – they do not measure what they say they are measuring and these scores do not predict behaviour over time. For many tests, this is indeed the Achilles heel and they are lamentably short of robust proof of their validity. It is supremely important that tests have predictive and construct validity.
- They might be able to measure all sorts of dimensions of behaviour but not

the crucial ones to the organization, like trustworthiness and likelihood of absenteeism. Buying personality tests is like having a set menu, but what many managers want is an à-la-carte menu where they can select only what they want.

- People have to be sufficiently literate or articulate to do these tests, not to mention sufficiently familiar with North American jargon. Many organizations therefore believe that their work force could not do them properly, they would take up too much time, or they would cause needless embarrassment.

- There are no good norms, at least for the populations they want to test, and comparing them to American students (Caucasian sopho-mores) is dangerously misleading (this is certainly true, but not in all instances).

- The tests are unfair, and biased to White Anglo–Saxon Protestants (WASPS), hence white males tend to do better or get a more attractive profile, and therefore get selected, than say black females. They therefore fly in the face of antidiscriminatory legislation.

- Freedom of information legislation may mean that candidates would be able to see and hence challenge the scores themselves, their interpretation or the decisions made on them. The less objective the recorded data the better for those unprepared to give negative feedback.

- As (ability and personality) tests become well known, people could buy copies and practise so that they know the correct or most desirable answers. This happens extensively with General Measure Aptitude Tests (GMATs), and results could be seen to do more with preparation and practise than actual ability.

2.3 DEVELOPING A SELECTION OR APPRAISAL PROCEDURE

Frequently, personality tests are used for selection and appraisal because of the high number of applicants (particularly in times of unemployment); the high costs (man hours/reimbursement) of interviewing; the poor reliability of interviewing (specifically choosing weak candidates); the necessity for objective, comparative data (chosen vs not chosen); allegations about nepotism and favouritism (in the selection process).

There are at least four types of question that potential test users should ask themselves.

What Are the Test Results to be Used for?

Are they to be used to select people in or select them out? That is, are they best at spotting high-flyers, or those considered too dangerous or risky to employ? Quite different tests (or at least dimensions) should be used for these rather different questions. Are the results to be used in counselling or predicting work performance? The necessity that a test be reliable and valid is less important in counselling where the aim of the test might be to encourage a person to talk about particular areas of strength or weakness. The latter is much more difficult to achieve (see Chapter 10). Are the results intended to be correlated with other measures or stand alone? How reliant is one on these test results? That is, are tests used to help make decisions or are they the only or major criteria of selection?

What Dimensions of Personality or Individual Differences are Crucial?

Should one buy an off-the-shelf general test which measures the whole person? This may be interesting but does it provide the data one wants? If managers are most concerned with people being careful, scrupulous and correct, it is important to measure impulsivity, obsessionality and the need for arousal, not unrelated aspects of personality. Should one choose set menu or à la carte? Rather than buy a set menu of an already developed multi-dimensional scale, why not choose the à-la-carte menu and make up a small battery of tests specifically for the organization's needs? It is more time consuming but ultimately more useful and cost effective for each particular organization.

What is to be Done with the Results after Initial Use?

Many organizations are amnesic, forgetting the very useful data that they have on employees tested earlier. Test results gathered in selection interviews or annual appraisals can be extremely useful in checking the validity of the test for each specific organization. They also provide extremely useful data on how people change over time.

Questions to Ask when Choosing Tests

What is the object of the test? How is this objective the same or different from existing tests designed to measure the same thing? How will the objective(s) be met? Is there really a need for this test? Are there other tests that purport to measure the same thing? In what ways will the proposed test be better than existing tests? Will it be more reliable? More valid? More comprehensive? How might this not be better than the other tests? Who would use this test and why? Who would need to take this test? Who would need the data derived from an administration of it? Why? What control area should the test cover? How will the test be administered? Will the test be administered individually, or should it be amenable for both individual and group administration? What difference will exist between the individually administered version and the group-administered version? How might differences between the two versions be reflected in test scores? What is the ideal format for this test? Why? Should the test be amenable to computerized administration, scoring and/or interpretation? Should more than one form of test be developed?

What special training will be required of test users in terms of administering or interpreting the test? What background and qualifications will a prospective user of data derived from administration of this test need to have? What restrictions, if any, should be placed on distributors of the test and the test's usage?

What type of responses will be required by test takers? What 'real-world' behaviours would be anticipated to correlate these responses? Why will scores on this test be important?

Attention needs to be given to *all* of these questions before tests are employed.

2.4 EARLY STUDIES CONCERNED WITH INDUSTRIAL TESTING

The United States Employment Service provided free aptitude testing which provided a rich data bank just after the war. The 12 tests measured nine of the aptitudes thought to be related to the requirements in the performance of many jobs. The General Aptitude Test Battery (GATB), as it was known, was intended to be used in two ways:

1. As an integral part of counselling where a measure is needed of the applicant's abilities in relation to the various fields of work in which the person may have interest but no practical experience.
2. As an approach to the problem of developing specific batteries for the countless occupations for which selection tests may be needed. Those tests in the GATB which measure abilities significant to the successful performance of a given job could be administered as a specific aptitude test battery, and the other tests omitted.

Certain of the tests and their cut-off or minimum scores were recommended for use in the selection of applicants for a wide variety of occupations. For example, the job of all-round mechanical repairing would include testing for intelligence, numerical and spatial aptitudes, and finger dexterity. Plumbing would include tests for numerical and spatial aptitudes, and motor dexterity. Typewriting requires verbal aptitude, clerical perception etc.

The battery was administered to a large number of persons employed in a wide range of occupations. Over 500 employers and many schools and colleges co-operated in the development of occupational norms. While the GATB demonstrated its validity with a variety of situations and jobs, it was probably used in many situations where its value as a predictor was highly questionable.

Traditionally, industrial testing was oriented toward blue-collar (i.e. manual), sales and clerical workers, since it was felt that this was where the largest increase in efficiency could be achieved. These individuals usually presented the bulk of the labour force employed by a company, and by improving the average quality (as defined by one or more criterion dimensions), large benefits should accrue to that company. In the 1950s, the emphasis shifted to an intensified concern for selection of individuals higher up in the managerial hierarchy.

The major problem in predicting executive success is in establishing a valid multi-dimensional and sensitive criterion. Attempts to use tests to predict success, once success has been arbitrarily defined for research purposes, have been less successful – particularly tests of ability. Gaudet and Carli (1957) have estimated that seven times as many executives fail due to personality problems than for lack of technical competence. Taylor and Nevis (1957) noted that this is not really too surprising; the executive job is a very complex one. Thus, to isolate specific abilities may not be sufficient; the abilities required are generally cognitive rather than physical; intelligence measures are probably not good predictors because to get into management requires a fairly bright person in the first place.

An example of the use of tests with supervisory level personnel was given by Neel and Dunn (1960) who used the *How Supervise* test, the *F Scale* measure of authoritarian personality, and the *Wonderlic* test to predict the degree of success that 32 supervisors would have in a supervisory training program. The results are given in Table 2.1.

Table 2.1 Correlations of the tests with training success

		(1)	*(2)*	*(3)*	*Criterion*[a]
(1)	How Supervise		0.08	0.33	0.69
(2)	F Scale			−0.23	0.39
(3)	Wonderlic				0.25
	(Multiple correlation = 0.77)				

[a] The criterion was grade at end of course

Wagner (1960) attempted to predict ratings of on-the-job success of 150 executives using a total of 31 different variables. These variables included measures of both intelligence and personality. The only correlation which was found to be high enough to be of any value was the correlation between ratings and amount of education ($r = 0.39$). However, the pure chance likelihood of this correlation is substantial.

In all of this research, the criterion problem immediately raises its ugly head. What is a 'successful' scientist, sales person, manager? How does one measure success? How efficient are tests in separating good scientists from poor scientists? One of the more elaborate research projects has been conducted by Taylor *et al*. (1961), who carried out extensive interviews with over 200 physical scientists concerning the nature of scientific productivity and the characteristics of effective scientists. Using the interview suggestions as a base, data was obtained on 52 different criteria. These measures were then factored into 14 relatively independent dimensions by which the performance of scientists could be evaluated. A number of tests were then used to predict how well a scientist would score on each of the 14 dimensions. In addition to the 14 dimensions obtained in the factor analysis, three other criteria based on supervisor and peer judgements were included, since these were the most often used methods of performance evaluation. Thus, the criteria used were:

1. Productivity in written work (effectiveness in completing paper work).
2. Recent quantity of research reports (number of articles and research reports, in a two-year period).
3. Quality (without originality) of research reports.
4. Originality of written work.
5. Scientific and professional society membership.
6. Actual quantity of work output as judged by peers, supervisors and laboratory chiefs (higher-level supervisors).
7. Creativity rating by laboratory chiefs (higher-level supervisors).
8. Overall performance (quality ratings by supervisors on ten different scales).
9. Likableness as an effective member of the research group.
10. Visibility of the scientist (well known by person or by name).
11. Recognition for organization contributions (organizational awards).
12. Status-seeking, 'organizational-man' tendencies.
13. Current organizational status.
14. Contract monitoring load (number of research contracts supervised).
15. Peer ranking on productivity as a scientist.
16. Supervisory rating of drive resourcefulness.
17. Supervisory rating of creativity.

A total of 130 different predictors were validated against *each* of the 17 different criteria. Many of these predictors were simply different a priori scores which could be applied to the same questionnaire or test instrument. For example, the Personality Research Inventory was given to all scientists in the validation sample for purposes of prediction. However, this single test yielded a total of 23 subscores, each of which was separately validated. The validation sample consisted of 197 scientists.

By relating the 130 predictors to the 17 criteria, 2210 validity coefficients were obtained – a testimony to the computer technology of time! Of these, 568 were significant.

Table 2.2 The percentage of valid scores obtained from each of the major categories of predictor information

Type of test	Per cent of scores valid
Biographical information (BIB) (with empirically keyed scores)	47
Biographical Information Blank (BIB) (a priori keyed scores only)	34
Self-ratings (SR)	33
Grade-point average	24
Minimum Satisfactory Level (MSL)	22
Profile matching	20
Motivated Analysis Test (MAT)	8
Personality Research Inventory (PRI)	8
Creative process check list	6
Aptitude tests	4

The different predictors varied considerably in their efficiency as Table 2.2 shows. This result certainly would suggest the importance of biographical factors (see Chapter 9) as predictors of occupational success.

Earlier, Ghiselli and Barthol (1953) reviewed 113 studies dealing with the validity of personality inventories in employee selection. The results are summarized in Table 2.3. They conclude that, under certain circumstances, scores on personality inventories correlate better with proficiency on a wider variety of jobs than might have been expected. The authors recognize both the potential value of personality testing in industry and the need for a vast increase and improvement in research and development.

Table 2.3 Weighted mean validity coefficients of personality inventories for various occupation groups

Mean (r)	Total number of cases	Total number of r's	Occupation
0.14	518	8	General supervisors
0.18	6433	44	Foremen
0.25	1069	22	Clerks
0.36	1069	8	Sales clerks
0.36	927	12	Salesmen
0.24	536	5	Protective workers
0.16	385	6	Service workers
0.29	511	8	Trade and crafts workers

Ghiselli (1955) reported on the efficiency of testing for various types of industrial job. He examined large numbers of validation studies and classified them in terms of the type of test being used and the type of criterion involved. All validities within a particular category were then averaged to give the figures shown in Table 2.4. Note that only three of the values in Table 2.4 exceed 0.40 in size, and that two variables are *not* tests but are personal history items. While the process of averaging used by Ghiselli definitely masks some very substantial validities, it should be sufficiently clear that testing is not a complete solution to the selection problem.

Table 2.4 Average validity coefficients for various types of test

Type of test	Type of criterion	
	Training	Job proficiency
Intellectual abilities		
Intelligence	38	19
Immediate memory	29	19
Substitution	26	21
Arithmetic	41	21
Spatial abilities		
Spatial relations	31	14
Location	24	15
Perception of details		
Number comparison	26	21
Name comparison	25	21
Cancellation	29	20
Pursuit	19	17
Perceptual speed	39	27
Mechanical comprehension		
Mechanical principles	34	26
Motor abilities		
Tracing	16	16
Tapping	12	14
Dotting	14	15
Finger dexterity	22	19
Hand dexterity	38[a]	14
Arm dexterity	30[b]	17
Personality traits		
Personality	16[a]	21
Interest	14[a]	27
Personal data	44	41

All tests had $N > 1000$ unless indicated
[a] 100 to 499 cases
[b] 500 to 999 cases

The work of Ghiselli and Barthol (1953) and Ghiselli and Brown (1955) is among the most celebrated in 'the literature'. They examined intelligence, interests and personality, and looked at how these related to job performance in a variety of occupations. A summary of their work is given in Figures 2.1 to 2.3. Their work is critical, comprehensive and their conclusions cautious.

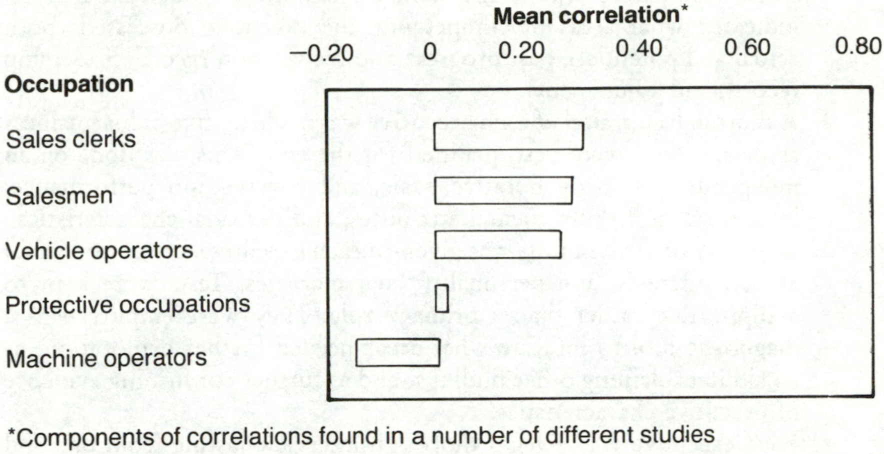

Mean correlation*

| | −0.20 | 0 | 0.20 | 0.40 | 0.60 | 0.80 |

Occupation

Sales clerks

Salesmen

Vehicle operators

Protective occupations

Machine operators

*Components of correlations found in a number of different studies

Figure 2.1 Average correlations between interest test scores and job performance for selected occupations
Source: Hollenbeck and Whitener (1988)

Ghiselli and Brown (1955) showed that intelligence tests are more likely to be helpful in selecting skilled workers, supervisors, clerical workers and sales people but of little value in selecting unskilled workers and sales clerks. One early study of the selection of clerical workers in a life insurance company showed a tendency for applicants scoring high on intelligence tests to leave the job after a few months (Kriedt and Gadel, 1953). However, the authors stated that, irrespective of the results of their study, they felt it desirable to hire some applicants demonstrating a high level of intelligence in order to have individuals on hand that could be promoted to supervisory positions.

In general, the greater the amount of preparation and training required for a job and the more complex the job, the more likely it is that intelligence is the factor in job success. Indeed, one of the most defensible arguments in favour of including intelligence tests in selection batteries is that the longer and more complex the training required for the job, the more likely intelligence is to be an important factor.

Randle (1956) provided another excellent illustration of the use of the method of the period. This study involved 1427 executives from 25 different companies. It involved four phases.

Phase I. Very extensive appraisals were carried out on each executive to provide a complete dossier on each person. This was achieved by several methods:

1. Each executive's background and experience was analysed in detail. This covered age, education; professional, social, and civic activities; work experience; health; and family relationships. Such an analysis indicated what areas of competency the executive possessed (both actual and potential), past progress and recognition record, leadership record, and adjustments.
2. A thorough appraisal of each executive was made by five of his business associates who were best qualified for the task. This was done on an independent, noncollaborative basis, and covered job performance, human relation skills, mental attributes, and personal characteristics.
3. A battery of written tests was given to each executive, covering mental ability, interests, and personality characteristics. Tests were kept to a supporting rather than a primary role. They were employed as a diagnostic tool to indicate what areas needed further exploration, as an aid in explaining other findings, and as further confirming evidence of executive characteristics.
4. Each executive was given a thorough interview lasting from one and one half to three hours. This interview was conducted only after a

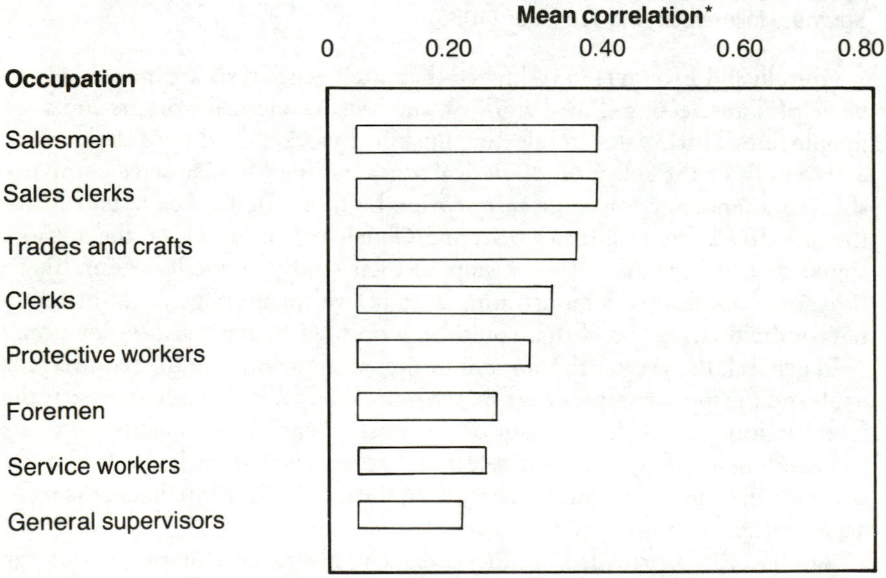

*Components of correlations found in a number of different studies

Figure 2.2 Average correlations between personality test scores and job performance for selected occupations

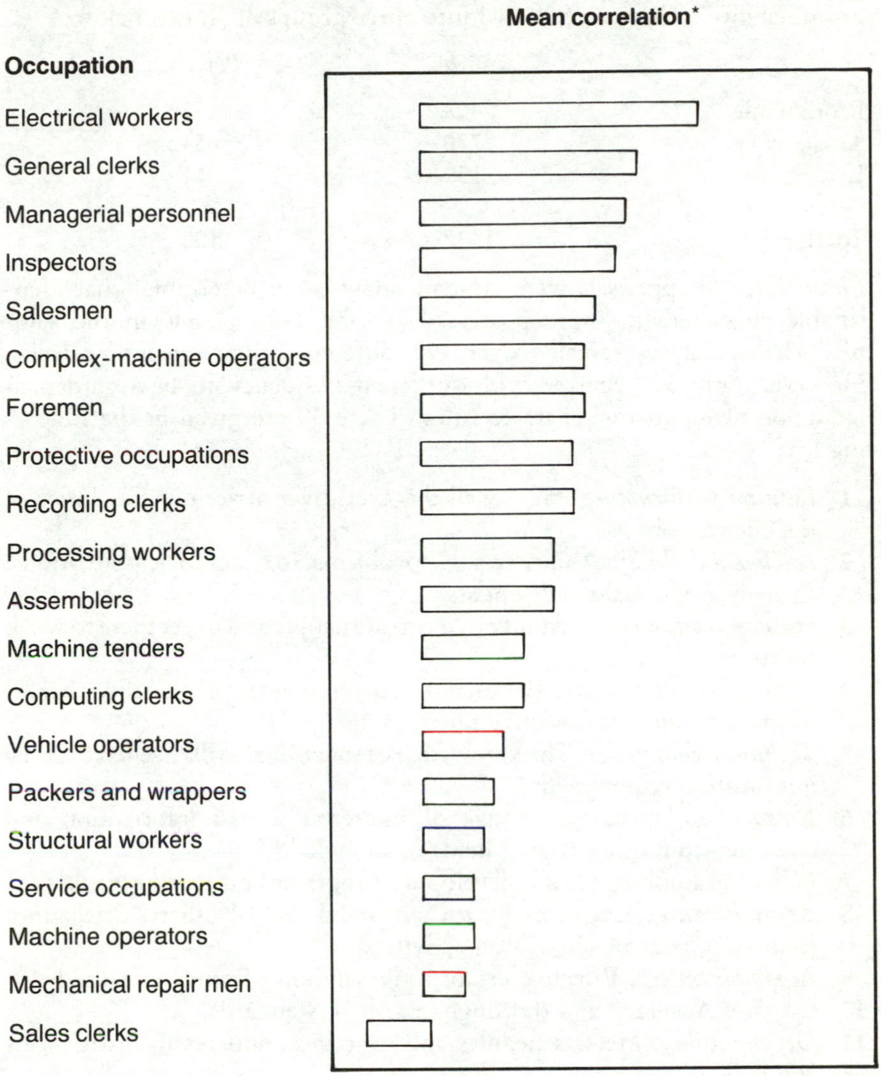

Mean correlation*

Occupation

Occupation	
Electrical workers	
General clerks	
Managerial personnel	
Inspectors	
Salesmen	
Complex-machine operators	
Foremen	
Protective occupations	
Recording clerks	
Processing workers	
Assemblers	
Machine tenders	
Computing clerks	
Vehicle operators	
Packers and wrappers	
Structural workers	
Service occupations	
Machine operators	
Mechanical repair men	
Sales clerks	

*Composites of correlations found in a number of different studies

Figure 2.3 Average correlations between intelligence test scores and job performance for selected occupations

complete review of all other appraisal results. It was employed to clear up areas of question, to verify other appraisal findings and to gain firsthand impressions of the executive such as were not available from the other techniques (p.64).

Phase II. Each executive's dossier was examined to determine the 'degree of promotability'. They were classed into three groups as shown below:

	Number	Percent
Promotable	498	35
Satisfactory	770	54
Inadequate	159	11
Total	1427	100

Phase III. All appraisals were content analysed to determine what identifiable characteristics were possessed by the 1427 people in the sample. These analyses revealed over 100 different characteristics or traits. However, only 30 occurred with sufficient frequency to be regarded as 'common denominator' characteristics. These 30 are given in the following list:

1. *Position performance.* How well the executive carries out the duties of the current job.
2. *Intellectual ability.* Ability to solve problems, to adapt to new situations, to analyse and make judgements.
3. *Human relations skill.* Ability to motivate people and to get them to work together.
4. *Personal characteristics.* The total of temperament or personality characteristics bearing on executive functioning.
5. *Technical knowledge.* The knowledge of functional skills needed to carry out position requirements.
6. *Breadth of knowledge.* Range of interests; use of information and concepts from other related fields of knowledge.
7. *Planning.* Looking ahead; developing programs and work schedules.
8. *Administration.* Organizing own work and that of others; delegation, follow-up, control of position activities.
9. *Accomplishment.* Effective use of time; amount of work produced.
10. *Quality.* Accuracy and thoroughness; high standards.
11. *Dependability.* Meets schedules and deadlines; adheres to instructions and policy.
12. *Acuteness.* Mentally alert; understands instructions, explanations, unusual situations and circumstances quickly.
13. *Capacity.* Mental depth and breadth; reservoir of mental ability.
14. *Flexibility.* Adaptable; adjusts rapidly to changing conditions; copes with the unexpected.
15. *Analysis and judgement.* Critical observer; breaks problem into components, weighs and relates; arrives at sound conclusions.

16. *Creativeness*. Original ideas; inquiring mind; fresh approaches to problems.
17. *Verbal facility*. Articulate, communicative; generally understood by persons at all levels.
18. *Socialness*. Makes friends easily; works 'comfortably' with others; has sincere interest in people.
19. *Acceptance*. Gains confidence of others; earns respect.
20. *Sensitivity*. Has a 'feel' for people, recognizes their problems; quick to pick up 'the way the wind is blowing'; is considerate of others.
21. *Leadership*. Receives loyalty and co-operation from others; manages and motivates others to full effectiveness.
22. *Developing others*. Develops competent successors and replacements.
23. *Motivation*. Has well-planned goals; willingly assumes greater responsibilities; realistically ambitious.
24. *Attitude*. Enthusiastic, constructive, optimistic; loyal; good orientation to company, position and associates.
25. *Vision*. Has foresight, sees new opportunities; appreciates, but not bound by, tradition or custom.
26. *Self-control*. Calm and poised under pressure.
27. *Initiative*. Self-starting; prompt to take hold of a problem; sees and acts on new opportunities.
28. *Drive*. Works with energy; not easily discouraged; basic urge to get things done.
29. *Self-confidence*. Assured bearing; inner security; self-reliant; takes new developments in stride.
30. *Objectivity*. Has an open mind; keeps emotional or personal interests from influencing decisions.

Phase IV. The final phase was to determine which of these 30 characteristics were related to promotability. To be considered a predictor of promotability, a characteristic had to be either significantly more or significantly less present in those judged promotable than in those judged inadequate. The results indicated that the 'composite executive' was a person who was distinguished by the eight qualities shown in Table 2.5.

In addition to these general 'traits' for successful executives, Randle also found that there was a tendency for certain traits to gain in importance as one goes up in the managerial hierarchy. This was particularly true of the *motivation* characteristic, which was judged outstanding in 84% of top executives considered promotable and in only 14% of top executives considered inadequate.

But how susceptible to bias were these early studies? Some of the early tests used in this period showed up the important issue of response bias. In another study, Borislow (1958) gave a group of students the Edwards Personal

Table 2.5 Qualities of the 'composite executive'

	Percentage present	
Characteristics	Promotable executives	Inadequate executives
Position performance	50	5
Drive	47	14
Intellectual ability	44	8
Leadership	41	6
Administration	40	6
Initiative	38	7
Motivation	34	8
Creativeness	30	6

Preference Schedule (EPPS) under standard self-assessment conditions. They were then divided into three matched groups for a retest two weeks later. Group A took the EPPS a second time under conditions identical to the initial testing session. Group B received the instructions to respond as a 'perfect' person would respond. Group C was told to respond in terms of what they would 'like to be' rather than in terms of what they actually were. Test–retest correlations ranged from 0.65 to 0.91 for the people in Group A, from 0.03 to 0.68 for those in Group B, and from −0.03 to 0.68 for those in Group C. These values indicated that the people in groups B and C responded under the new instructions a great deal less like their original performance than did the controls, indicating that the EPPS is susceptible to deliberate falsification.

Bridgman and Hollenbeck (1961) asked four groups to fill out the Kuder Preference Record and each group received a different set of instructions:

Group   *Instructions*

A   As if applying for the job of sanitary supply salesperson
B   As if applying for the job of industrial psychologist
C   As if applying for an unspecified job in industry
D   As if tests were being taken for purposes of vocational counselling

All inventories were then scored using a scale developed for the sanitary supply salesperson and the Kuder industrial psychologist scale.

The results were quite interesting. As Table 2.6 shows, the scores of groups A and B did not differ significantly from the norm groups they were impersonating. Also, the highest scores on each key were obtained by that group which had been instructed to assume a particular set of responses. The verification scores for all fake groups were higher than the control, indicating that they might be of use in identifying biased test results, although their actual magnitude was of questionable practical value in all cases except with the salesperson group.

Table 2.6 Main occupational interest scales for each of the four groups

Instructions	Sales person key	Psychologist key	Verification key
Sales person	71.5	48.7	46.8
Psychologist	61.4	53.2	45.5
Typical job	64.8	48.9	48.9
Vocational counselling	61.8	44.6	51.1
Actual sales person (norm)	73.1	–	–
Actual psychologist (norm)	–	54.5	–

Both of the foregoing studies indicate that faking can take place in a *laboratory* setting. Kirchner (1961, 1962) has reported two instances in which clear evidence for response faking was found in an actual selection situation. In his first study, responses made on the Strong Vocational Interest Blank (SVIB) for 92 retail and 64 industrial sales assistants (later hired) as part of the selection procedure were compared with responses made by 68 retail and 49 industrial salespeople who had been employed at least five years and who had completed the SVIB voluntarily as part of a concurrent validity study. Of 96 mean differences on the 48 scales, 32 were significant at the 0.05 level. Both the retail and industrial applicants tended to score higher in social service and business occupations, and lower in technical–scientific and, surprisingly, sales. In general, applicants indicated a greater liking for things than did employed salespeople, which suggests that they were completing the SVIB in the most socially acceptable fashion: liking much, disliking little.

In a second study, the EPPS scores for 97 retail sales applicants and 66 industrial sales applicants (all later hired) were compared to those of 69 retail and 49 industrial salespeople (all tested on the job). Results showed that retail applicants tended to score significantly higher than retail salespeople on the orderliness, intraception and dominance scales, and lower on the heterosexuality scale. There was no significant difference, however, between industrial applicants and industrial salespeople. Kirchner suggested that people more oriented towards selling in terms of interests and personality (thus, retail sales applicants) are more likely to distort answers to the EPPS.

There have also been a number of early studies on job satisfaction. One of the early community-wide surveys was conducted by Hoppock (1935) where 351 employed adults answered the lengthy questionnaire. The results indicate that 15% of the sample had negative attitudes, or job dissatisfaction.

This early finding is quite similar to the evidence that has since been reported. Robinson and Hoppock (1952) have collated the data on 191 assorted studies reporting percentages of job dissatisfaction.

Hoppock asked 36 nationally prominent personnel officers to estimate percentages of workers who were dissatisfied. The answers ranged from 0 to 80%, the average being 49%. As Hoppock points out, if numbers from 0 to 100 were put in a hat, the average of the numbers drawn would be 50. Hence, it may well be that the 49% is as void of meaning as chance itself. The view that is clearly taken is that the majority of the gainfully employed tend to have job satisfaction, or are at least neutral. Only a small percentage have job dissatisfaction.

An index of job satisfaction was computed and a breakdown according to occupational classification indicates that the average index is lower for the unskilled category and highest for the professional category.

Hoppock also conducted a survey on people in one occupation, namely teaching. Five hundred teachers from 51 urban and rural communities in the northeastern United States estimated their job satisfaction on four attitude scales. By combining these scales, a measure of job satisfaction was obtained. Of this group, the 100 most satisfied and 100 least satisfied were asked about 200 questions. A comparison of their answers differentiated the satisfied from the dissatisfied teachers in the following areas:

1. The satisfied showed fewer indications of emotional maladjustment.
2. The satisfied were more religious.
3. The satisfied enjoyed better human relationships with superiors and associates.
4. The satisfied were teaching in cities of over 10,000 population.
5. The satisfied felt more successful.
6. Family influence and social status were more favourable among the satisfied.
7. The satisfied 'selected' their vocation.
8. Monotony and fatigue were reported more frequently by the dissatisfied.
9. The satisfied averaged 7.5 years older.

One interesting finding is that the difference in average salaries between the two groups was not statistically significant. Apart from problems of faking, these sorts of studies cannot separate cause and effect. Thus, it may well be that satisfaction causes some of the above, just as much as it is caused by them.

Most of the foregoing studies were conducted by academics interested in occupational behaviour before the mid 1960s (i.e. 25 years ago). But there have been studies by practitioners – human relations and personnel officers – in which they have tested the validity of personality tests in their organization. Miller (1975a) has edited a useful volume in which personnel managers write about their experiences of tests. For instance, Wilson (1975) used tests – the 16PF and AH6 (a British intelligence test) – along with an interview, case-study and peer rating for judging graduate recruitment. In order to determine the efficiency of the 16PF, they (at United Biscuits) compared high- and low-rated managers on the 16PF. The results are shown in Table 2.7. High-rated managers were more intelligent, relaxed, outgoing, self-assured, sensitive, group oriented, less rule bound, concerned over procedure, and shrewd. Twelve of the 16 factors showed significant differences, suggesting the usefulness of the test on selection and promotion decisions.

Table 2.7 16PF and AH6 results for 59 middle managers attending company assessment centres (average age 35)

Test		Raw score means and standard deviations					
16PFL	Maximum score	Low-rated managers (N = 20)		Middle-rated managers (N = 14)		High-rated managers (N = 16)	
		$\bar{x}$	SD	$\bar{x}$	SD	$\bar{x}$	SD
A	(20)	10.9	3.7	10.5	2.4	12.4	3.3
B	(13)	9.0	1.5	10.3	2.4	12.4	3.3
C	(26)	16.7	3.5	18.9	3.5	18.1	3.2
E	(26)	14.8	5.9	14.2	4.8	16.1	3.6
F	(26)	13.1	3.0	13.7	4.1	15.4	4.6
G	(20)	14.9	3.3	13.7	4.4	11.6	3.7
H	(26)	16.2	5.2	15.4	4.1	16.6	5.7
I	(20)	7.3	3.7	11.1	3.0	8.6	3.9
L	(20)	5.9	3.5	7.1	2.8	6.9	3.3
M	(26)	15.2	3.3	15.3	3.6	16.6	3.6
N	(20)	9.9	3.2	9.3	3.3	8.3	3.3
O	(26)	7.5	4.6	6.9	3.3	7.1	3.3
Q1	(20)	10.5	3.3	10.4	3.0	11.7	2.8
Q2	(20)	10.8	3.2	10.8	4.2	9.4	2.8
Q3	(20)	15.0	3.3	13.7	2.2	12.5	2.8
Q4	(26)	11.1	5.6	9.4	3.0	8.2	4.5
AH6							
PT1		14.4	3.6	18.1	4.4	19.5	3.6
PT2		13.6	4.2	14.7	6.7	18.5	4.5
Total		28.0	7.1	32.8	6.7	38.1	6.7

The organization used tests for selection but believed they have other benefits: improving the quality of interviewing; a better understanding of the real personnel requirements for the job. Wilson (1975) concluded:

Our aim for the future is to improve our knowledge of the validity of the tests we are using and to improve interpretations which are more

meaningful to line managers . . . Having been doing concurrent validity
studies for some time, we are just coming up to the stage where tests have
been in use for long enough to carry out some predictive validity studies
(p.215).

Ingleton (1975) described the use of tests in an oil-marketing organization
in Great Britain. They used intelligence (Ravins Progressive Matrices), the
Thurston Interest Inventory and the 16PF. Among the initial difficulties
reported were preparing a report in a format helpful to the interviewing
panel, and gaining the confidence of bright but sceptical student applicants.
Although they met initial resistance from interviewers, things did improve.
They appeared to use the 16PF to determine, if offered, whether the applicant
accepted or declined the offer, which they would do statistically.

Randell (1975) was concerned with the selection of salespeople and notes
the number (well over 200) of references on salespeople selection. Using the
tests (16PF, Allport–Vernon–Linzey Study of Values, Thurstone Interest
Schedule) as well as various others including the EP1, SVIB and many
others, and biographical criteria, he looked at people in the gas, tyre and
oil industries. Although the tests were predictive, there was no general trait
of salespersonship across organizations and thus it was concluded:

> The search for the use of any general traits of 'salesmanship' would seem
> to be less useful to selling organizations than attempts at matching people
> to specific sales jobs. From this, the general implication emerges that
> organizations should be cautious about appointing salesmen just on the
> grounds of their previous sales experience (p.89).

Copeland (1975) reported on the selection of engineers using the Morrisly
Differential Test Battery – an ability/intelligence test that provides 12 separate
tests. Starting from a position of scepticism, the organization appeared to
have embraced testing as an extremely useful selection device, through
evidence of test validity.

Miller (1975a), on the other hand, was concerned with clerical selection
and used a large battery of ability, aptitude and personal value tests. Using
four groups in four locations (to check replicability and generalizability),
he found the ability tests (verbal, arithmetic and clerical) predicted training
grades. Beaton (1975) used a variety of tests in a retail business for a
number of reasons: improve selection; create an impression among potential
applicants; reduce turnover; and identify potential. He used intelligence and
mechanical reasoning tests as well as Cattell's 16PF, all of which proved to
have predictive validity.

Bentz (1985a, b) reported on a remarkable programme where executives
are given an extensive battery of personality and ability tests (called the
Sears Executive Battery). They were used mainly in selection but have
other obvious uses. Using sensitive, robust criteria, various attempts have

been made to validate the scale. For instance, the results from a validation of women executives engaged in buying was thus:

1. Strong predictive validity exists for the total group.
2. Validity patterns replicate across rating sources. This is particularly true for the promotability criterion.
3. Mental alertness is the best single predictor of all criteria.
4. The masculine/dominance scale is the most powerful predictor (of all criteria) among the personality measures.
5. Strong self-confidence generalizes across several variables as a predictor of effectiveness.
6. A group of personality variables indicative of emotional strength (optimism, emotional control and composure) relates to nearly all criteria. A kind of rugged emotional outlook is associated with effectiveness.
7. The more effective female buyer is strongly tied to objective reality, and her judgements are free from personal or emotional considerations.
8. A concern for the mechanics of how things run and an aversion to clerical pursuits reflect the interest patterns of the more effective buying executive.
9. Social competence and the aggressive assumption of responsibility and social leadership are associated with general effectiveness.
10. Current job performance, potentiality, and creative problem solving are all predicted at adequate levels of significance.
11. Effective application of ideas produced is more strongly predicted than production of creative ideas. 'Ingenuity' rather than 'pure creativity' makes good sense in terms of the nature of buying job requirements.
12. The psychological factors predicting effectiveness of female executives are not markedly different from those predicting effectiveness of other executives. It seems that 'an executive is an executive is an executive' rather than there being differential concepts of executive behaviour appropriate to gender identification (p.109).

Interestingly, a study of 179 manufacturing managers yielded the following findings:

1. Mental ability is a strong predictor of performance.
2. Self-confidence predicts 18 of the 23 criteria. The ability to initiate and act without need for external support is an extremely important predictor of executive performance in manufacturing.
3. A preference for selling and persuading others (persuasive interest) is associated with so many important criteria (15) that it must be requisite for executive effectiveness in manufacturing.
4. A strong concern for money, profit, and the economic value of the marketplace is a strong predictor (economic values).

5. Both importance of personal status and the natural assumption of the leading role when a member of a group are predictive of effective performance (political values and social ascendancy).
6. The criterion promotion potential is predicted by 14 psychological test variables.
7. Selling ideas to others in the face of resistance is a persuasive interest criterion predicted by a wide range (13) of mental ability, personality, and value variables.
8. Keeping track of efficiency, costs, and human performance is also predicted by 13 test variables (checking performance criterion).
9. Generating positive and productive attitudes in others (motivating criterion) is also predicted by a large number of psychological variables.

These results were summarized:

> Persuasive and socially assured, the person moves aggressively into a central role whenever a part of a social or business group (sociability, social ascendancy, persuasive interests). Confident to initiate and act without external support (self-confidence), the individual catches on rapidly (mental ability) and moves into action with energy and flexibility (general activity and serious versus carefree). With heightened personal concern for status, power, and money (political and economic values), the person will work hard to achieve positions that yield such rewards (p.109–12).

He also reports various longitudinal, follow-up studies which demonstrate both the stability of personality *and* the stability of personality–occupational behaviour relationships. He argues from his findings that the bias against paper-and-pencil personality tests is unjustified. The correlation he reports was frequently between 0.3 and 0.5, accounting for between a tenth and a quarter of the variance. But the results are consistent, replicated, robust and generalizable – surely a tribute to the measures used.

Yet despite evidence extending over 40 years showing evidence of the validity of some psychological tests there remain critics. In their review of the validity of personality measures in personnel selection, Guion and Gottier (1965) concluded that 'it is difficult, in the face of this summary to advocate with a clear conscience, the use of employment decision about people' (p.160). The low validity and utility of personality measures become particularly salient when compared to the validity and utility of other available selection methods, such as ability tests.

However, Hollenbeck and Whitener (1988) have argued that the dismal evidence currently available on personality traits as predictors can largely be traced to (a) theoretical inadequacies and (b) methodological problems associated with past research dealing with statistical power and contaminated measurement. They argue that personality traits which, as a whole, reflect individual differences in values, performances, needs or beliefs would seem to be more strongly related to one's motivation to perform than one's capacity (i.e. ability) to perform.

Essentially, their thesis is that personality in interaction with (i.e. moderating) ability impacts on work performance. They argue that although there are some studies that support this position, the vast number of personality–occupational behaviour validation studies have not assessed *ability by personality interaction*.

In conclusion, the purpose here was to demonstrate that previous reviews documenting the relatively low validity coefficients associated with personality measures have had an unnecessarily discouraging impact on selection research dealing with such variables. Theoretical and methodological inadequacies in this past research limit the ability to evaluate the potential of these variables. In order to resolve the theoretical problems in this area, a model was developed that placed emphasis on the moderating influences of ability and the mediating effects of motivation. A review of past research in light of this model suggests that personality measures have validity only when used interactively with ability tests, and only when there is some strong theoretical rationale to support a relationship between the personality variable in question and motivation. With respect to methodological issues, it was demonstrated that statistical power has not been sufficient in many tests of validation models. Moreover, it was also suggested that self-inventory and observational measurement methods have unjustifiably dominated this area. Measures of personality traits based on individual differences in perception and judgement, although clearly in a developmental stage, appears to be a promising approach to obtaining undistorted indices of such variables in applied contexts. Several examples of this type of measurement approach were provided where distinguishing individuals on the dimension of self-esteem was the objective. Future selection research that avoids the problems of the past may provide a more positive picture with respect to the utility of personality traits as screening devices. It would be unfortunate if the study of personality, so long a focus of attention for psychologists, was prematurely and permanently abandoned by personnel psychologists (p.89).

2.5 THE OCCUPATIONAL APPLICATION OF MAJOR TESTS

Perhaps the most useful way to review this highly scattered and varying literature is to examine research concerning a number of specific instruments. Only the most widely used and psychometrically assessed will be considered however. A cursory review of both the academic 'pure' and applied literature, as well as a poll of the test usage and familiarity in occupational settings, seems to suggest that a fairly limited number of tests have been used to predict occupational behaviour. These will be reviewed systematically.

The Myers–Briggs Type Indicator (MBTI)

The theoretical background to the measure of personality is derived from the theoretical work of Jung (1953). The test was devised by a mother and daughter team – Myers and Myers–Briggs – over 30 years ago and has been extensively and aggressively marketed ever since. According to McCrae and Costa (1988), the MBTI is unusual among personality assessment devices for three reasons: it is based on a classic theory; it purports to measure types rather than traits of continuous variables; and it is widely used to explain individuals' personality characteristics not only to professionals but also to the individuals themselves, and their co-workers, friends and families. But they also point out its limitations: the original Jungian concepts are distorted, even contradicted; there is no bi-model distribution of preference scores; studies using the MBTI have not always confirmed either the theory or the measure. Yet Devito (1985) has described the MBTI as 'probably the most widely used instrument for non-psychiatric populations in the area of clinical, counselling, and personality testing' (p.1030). The criticism of the typology theory is also cogently put by Hicks (1984). He points out that even the evidence in the manual provides less evidence for type than for continuous trait-like measurement which is against the spirit of the test. However, after careful evaluation, he argues that the MBTI merits serious consideration by psychologists.

In an extensive review of the instrument, Carlson (1985) pointed out that the MBTI has been used somewhat unsystematically in a very wide range of areas, but generally with favourable validity assessment. The limited reliability research shows satisfactory internal (alpha) and test–retest reliability, but is limited by student samples and short test–retest intervals. He reviewed criterion-related studies in treatment and research settings and noted that 'it is to the credit of MBTI that the instrument successfully predicted behaviours as far apart as personal problems to imagery and group conformity' (p.364). However, he does note that the introvert–extraversion dimension of the scale has shown most validational evidence, which is perhaps not surprising given that this dimension is perhaps the most well established in all personality testing.

Hirsh and Kummerow (1989) have looked at work style preferences of the four type dimensions:

- *Extraversion–introversion*. The extraversion (E) and introversion (I) preferences are applicable to the work that people choose, the work setting that maximizes their strengths, and the kinds of workers with whom they feel most congenial and productive. Extraverts copy a work setting that is actively oriented, has variety, and allows for frequent interactions with others. Introverts enjoy a work setting that is quiet and private, and that allows for concentration on the task:

'*I am more likely to work like an extravert and*:

Become impatient and bored when my work is slow and unchanging.

Seek a variety of action-oriented tasks.

Be focused equally on what is going on in the work site as well as with my work.

Respond quickly to requests and spring into action without much advanced thinking.

Enjoy phone calls as a welcome diversion.

Develop my ideas through discussion.

Use outside resources to complete my tasks.

Need frequent changes in pace and seek outside events.

I am more likely to work like an introvert and:

Become impatient and annoyed when my work is interrupted and rushed.

Seek quiet to concentrate.

Be focused more on the work itself than on what is going on in the work site.

Think through requests before responding, even to the point of delaying action.

Find phone calls intrusive, especially when concentrating.

Develop my ideas through reflection.

Use myself as my basic resource to complete my tasks.

Get caught up in my work and disregard outside events'.

(p.17–18)

They further note:

Extraverts frequently choose occupations that encourage activity and interaction with others on a regular and frequent basis. Introverts frequently choose occupations that encourage reflection and in-depth concentration on concepts and ideas.

While extraverts can and do enter all occupations, some are more appealing to them than others. According to available research, some occupations (in alphabetical order) seem to be especially attractive to extraverts: consultant, dental assistant, food service worker, home economist, insurance agent, marketeer, receptionist, restaurant manager, sales manager, sales clerk, and other occupations in which they can put their energy to active use. These occupations are not meant to be an exhaustive list but serve to illustrate some areas than an extravert might enjoy.

While introverts can and do enter all occupations, some are more appealing to them than others. According to available research, some occupations (in alphabetical order) seem to be especially attractive to introverts: chemist, computer programmer, electrical engineer, lawyer, legal secretary, librarian, maths teacher, mechanic, surveyor, technician, and other occupations in which their energy is focused internally on facts or ideas. These occupations are not meant to be an exhaustive list but serve to illustrate some areas that an introvert might enjoy (p.20).

- *Sensing–intuition*. The sensing (S) and intuition (N) preferences are applicable to the work that people choose, the work setting that maximizes their strengths, and the kinds of workers with whom they feel most congenial and productive. Sensors generally choose a work setting that produces practical, useful products or services for people or organizations. They are likely to be where they are able to use their sensing preference to work carefully with people, things and data. They tend to prefer work settings that allow them to learn a skill and practise it to the point of mastery. Intuitives are likely to choose a work setting that produces new products or services. They like to be where they are able to use their intuition preference to meet future needs or to find new possibilities for people, things and data. They tend to prefer work settings that allow them the opportunity to learn continually to do new things:

'I am more likely to work like a sensor and:

Use my previously acquired work experience.

Appreciate standard ways to solve problems and reach solutions.

Apply skills that are already developed, rather than take the time to learn new ones.

Distrust and ignore my inspirations.

Like things to be concrete and seldom make errors of fact.

Prefer work that has a practical aspect to it.

Want to understand how the details of my work make up a complete picture.

I am more likely to work like an intuitive and:

Do things differently than my previous work experience may dictate.

Use new and different ways to solve problems and reach solutions.

Enjoy learning new skills for the challenge and novelty involved.

Follow my inspirations regardless of the facts.

Like things to be generally stated and seldom worry about specific facts.

Prefer work that has an innovative aspect to it.

Want to see what is involved in the overall picture first and then fill in the details.

| Prefer to continue with what is tried and true and make adjustments for fine tuning. | Prefer change, often with major readjustments, to continuing on with what is'. |

(p.31–2).

Hirsh and Kummerow note:

Sensing types frequently choose occupations that require more hands-on and direct experience dealing accurately with problems. Usually the jobs sensors enjoy call for attending to and mastering detail. Intuitives frequently choose occupations that call for seeing relationships and patterns and dealing with them. Usually the jobs that intuitives enjoy call for attending to underlying meanings and anticipating future possibilities and needs.

While sensors can and do enter all occupations, some are more appealing to them than others. According to available research, some occupations (in alphabetical order) seem especially attractive to sensors: accountant, bank manager, cleaning service worker, dentist, farmer, food service worker, law enforcement officer, mid-level manager, secretary, steelworker, and other occupations that allow for specific experience. These occupations are not meant to be an exhaustive list but serve to illustrate some areas that a sensor might enjoy.

While intuitives can and do enter all occupations, some are more appealing than others. According to available research, some occupations (in alphabetical order) seem to be especially attractive to intuitives: artist, attorney, clergy, consultant, counsellor, entertainer, journalist, psychologist, social scientist, writer, and other occupations that allow for generalization. These occupations are not meant to be an exhaustive list but serve to illustrate some areas than an intuitive might enjoy (p.35–6).

- *Thinking–feeling.* The thinking (T) and feeling (F) preferences are applicable to the jobs that people choose, the work settings that maximize their strengths, and the kinds of workers with whom they feel most congenial and productive. Thinkers are likely to choose a work setting that is more impersonal and governed by logic. Feelers tend to prefer a work setting that is personal, focusing on relationships between people and meeting people's personal need:

'I am more likely to work like a thinker and:	I am more likely to work like a feeler and:
Orient myself toward the tasks.	Orient myself toward my relationships.
Like harmony, but can get along without it and still be effective at work.	Need harmony in order to work most effectively.

Use logic and analysis as a basis for my work.

Hurt people's feelings without being aware of it.

Decide impersonally and some-times overlook others' wishes so I can get my work done.

Manage and deal firmly with others.

Readily offer criticisms or sug-gestions for improvement.

Factor in principles and truths when making work-related decisions.

Include others' opinions in addition to my personal values as a basis for my work.

Pay attention to others' feelings and enjoy pleasing them even in unimportant things.

Allow others' likes and dislikes to influence my decisions, sometimes taking precedence over getting my work done.

Manage and relate sympathetically with others.

Avoid and dislike giving and receiving unpleasant feedback, even when well deserved.

Factor in underlying values and human needs when making work-related decisions'.

(p.46–7)

As regards career information, Hirsh and Kummerow note:

Thinking types frequently choose occupations that encourage the use of logical and impersonal analysis. Feeling types frequently choose occupations that have a values basis and involve people relating per-sonally.

   While thinkers can and do enter all occupations, some are more appealing to them than others. According to available research, some occupations (in alphabetical order) seem to be especially attractive to thinkers: attorney, auditor, bank officer, chemist, computer systems analyst, engineer, farmer, manager, police officer, systems researcher, and other occupations that allow them to be logical. These occupations are not meant to be an exhaustive list but serve to illustrate some areas that a thinker might enjoy.

   While feelers can and do enter all occupations, some are more appealing to them than others. According to available research, some occupations (in alphabetical order) seem to be especially attractive to feelers: child care worker, clerical supervisor, clergy, counsellor, dental hygienist, librarian, nurse, physical therapist, secretary, school teacher, and other occupations that reflect their values. These occupations are not meant to be an exhaustive list but serve to illustrate some areas that a feeler might enjoy (p.49).

- *Judgement–perception*. The judgement (J) and perception (P) preferences relate to the work that people choose, the settings that maximize their strengths, and the kinds of worker with whom they feel more congenial and productive. Judgers are likely to choose a work setting that is structured and organized, with plans in place. Judgers like settings in which decisions get made. Perceptives tend to prefer a work setting that is spontaneous, flexible and open to change. Perceptives like gathering information as a part of their work:

'*I am more likely to work like a judger and*:	*I am more likely to work like a perceptive and*:
Do my best when I can plan my work and work my plan.	Do my best when I can deal with needs as they arise.
Enjoy getting things settled and finished.	Enjoy keeping things open for last-minute changes.
Like checking items off my 'to do' list.	Ignore my 'to do' list even if I make one.
Overlook new things that need to be done in order to complete my current job.	Postpone my current tasks to meet momentary needs.
Narrow down the possibilities and be satisfied once I reach a decision.	Resist being tied down to a decision in order to gather more information.
Decide quickly and seek closure.	Put off decisions to seek options.
Seek structure in scheduling myself and others.	Resist structure and favour changing circumstances.
Prefer to regulate and control my work and that of others.	Prefer to free up my work and that of others'.

(p.61–2)

Finally, as regards careers information, Hirsh and Kummerow noted:

To perform well at work, individuals may need to use all of the eight preferences at the appropriate time and when required by the situation. Knowing this, people tend to select occupations that allow them to use the preferences that are most natural to them.

Judgers frequently choose occupations that have requirements for organization and closure. Perceptives frequently choose occupations in which they can define their own schedules, be flexible, and remain open to new information.

While judgers can and do enter all occupations, some are more appealing to them than others. According to available research, some occupations (in alphabetical order) seem to be more attractive to judgers: accountant, administrator, bank officer, dentist, elementary school teacher, guard, judge, manager, nurse, police supervisor, and other occupations that allow for closure. These occupations are not meant to be an exhaustive list but serve to illustrate some areas that a judger might enjoy.

While perceptives can and do enter all occupations, some are more appealing to them than others. According to available research, some occupations (in alphabetical order) seem to be more attractive to perceptives: artist, carpenter, counsellor, editor, entertainer, journalist, labourer, researcher, surveyor, waiter and waitress, and other occupations that allow for flexibility. These occupations are not meant to be an exhaustive list but serve to illustrate some areas that a perceptive might enjoy (p.64).

Relatively few of the empirical studies in this area have addressed the relationship between MBTI variables and occupational behaviour. Most of the better studies have addressed clinical or counselling dependent variables. Some studies have yielded impressive evidence. For instance, Carlson (1980) was able to conclude:

> Results of all three studies gave unambiguous support for hypotheses derived from Jungian type theory. Type differences in memorial and perceptual processes, previously identified in laboratory set-ups, also operate in the personal world, where individuals remember, construe, and imagine their significant moments and relationships (p.818).

In an early and much quoted study, Stricker and Ross (1964) looked at personality, ability and interest correlates of MBTI. Many of the findings, such as the relationship between the E–I scale and vocational interests, showed somewhat contradictory results. They concluded:

> The empirical support for the alternative interpretation does suggest that the indicator's scales are strongly subject to influences other than the typological variables . . . the E–I and J–P scales seem to reflect something quite different from their postulated dimensions, and the S–N and T–F scales at best seem to reflect restricted aspects of them (p.642).

Although there has been a vast amount of work on the MBTI, little has examined the relationship between types and occupational behaviour such as productivity or satisfaction. Yet this literature has increased rather than decreased over the past 15 years. Some of these studies have shown few predicted differences. For instance Slocum (1978) examined changes in cognitive style (MBTI scores) and the tactics that subjects would most likely use to bring about organizational and individual change. He found only limited evidence that different types use different amounts of information in the diagnosis of the client/organization problems, and may use different tactics to bring out organizational change. Not all studies have been empirical. Also, Blaylock and Winkofsky (1983) used MBTI concepts to explain the unrated problem-solving differences between scientists and managers. They point out that most scientists are STs or NTs, while many R&D managers are SFs and NFs and their given preferences for seeing the world lead to various conflicts.

But most of the studies in this area have been empirical. Rahim (1981) tested the hypothesis that there would be a congruence between MBTI type and occupational type (technical, intellectual and social) as measured by a job satisfaction index. The results did not confirm the person–job hypothesis but did show that extraverts were more satisfied than introverts, and that judging types were more satisfied than perceiving types irrespective of their occupation. Other results have also shown evidence of the main effects of personality on job satisfaction (Furnham and Zacherl, 1986). A good example is the work of Nutt (Henderson and Nutt, 1980; Nutt, 1986a,b,c) who has completed a number of very competent, simulated decision-making studies. Nutt (1986a) described how MBTI type was related to managers' decisions concerning leadership, team building, control and future orientation.

Henderson and Nutt (1980) conducted a study in which experienced decision makers from hospitals and private firms were asked to assess several capital-expansion projects (likelihood of adoption, perceived risk etc) after completing the MBTI. Cognitive style was a significant correlate: ST subjects scored the highest risk and were reluctant to adopt the projects, while SFs were risk tolerant and more likely to adopt the same projects.

> Decision style was influenced by setting. The NT executives in hospitality were more conservative than NT's in firms. The NT's in firms were more apt to adopt and score less risk in the same projects. We speculate that the experience of NT executives in hospitals may suggest that they cannot deal with demand and other environmental factors in a structured manner which may encourage them to take a conservative posture (p.384).

Nutt (1986b) related the MBTI scores of 137 top executives to the way in which they evaluated hypothetical capital-expansion scenarios with strategic importance. The MBTI score was once again found to be a higher significant factor in explaining the adoptability and perceived risk for strategic decision. Executives with SF profiles were found to be action oriented, STs' executive action was adverse, with NTs and NFs taking nearly identical and neutral positions. SFs were inclined to adopt the capital-expansion projects and found less risk in this decision than did other styles. INFPs tended to reflect on the reactions of people involved and to modify their decisions to cater for them. Interestingly, ENTJs were less risky and comprehensive in their analyses than INTJs.

Nutt (1988) used the MBTI to define various organizational decision-making styles – ST (analytical), NF (charismatic), SF (conservative) and NT (speculative) – and showed how items affected decision making. In a later study, Nutt (1989) showed that the organizational culture was more powerful than the person's individual style in determining decision making. In a more recent study, Nutt (1990) showed that top executive and middle management decision style was a key factor in explaining the likelihood of taking strategic action and the risk associated with this action. He concluded:

> The decisions of top executives were more *style* dependent than those of middle managers. The judicial (SF) top executives were action-averse, with the speculative and charismatic (NT and NF) top executives taking nearly identical and neutral positions. Using the extended definition of decision style and its categories, top executives with a sensate (S) style were found to be much like top executives with pure (narrowly defined) systematic or analytic style (ST), and top executives with a feeling (F) style similar to top executives with a pure judicial (SP) style. Top executives with a pure ST style were much more conservative than the traditional ST's, and the pure SF's far more action-orientated than the traditionally defined SF (p.192).

In a similar simulated study, Haley and Stumpf (1989) tested real managers in groups of twelve. The simulation revolved around a hypothetical commercial bank with 12 senior management posts across three hierarchical levels and two product areas. After selecting managerial roles, participants received information on the financial issues and then they ran the bank as they saw fit. Trained observers rated the information-gathering methods that the participants used, which were then related to their MBTI scores. The hypotheses, derived from the work of Tversky and Kahneman (1982), which all received support, revolved around the idea that managers' information input biases have subsequent output biases which may lead to operational biases. For instance, STs succumb to functional-fixedness and regularity-and-structure biases while NFs succumb to reasoning-by-analogy and illusory-correlation biases. They argued that this research indicated the choices that different personality types usually make under the various environmental conditions. Thus, managers' predominant styles may lead to good or poor strategies. This information could help managers sensitize themselves to sequential biases in decision making by identifying appropriate and erroneous tactics.

Researchers are aware of the criticism that simulated decisions, as in these studies, may not replicate the decisions that executives would face in real-world situations but argue that the strength of the findings overcomes this problem. Other empirical studies have, however, overcome these problems of ecological validity by looking at actual occupational behaviour. For instance, Rice and Lindecamp (1989) correlated MBTI types with gross personal income of small business managers to return on assets. Although extraverts tended to do better than introverts, and thinking types better than judging types, the authors concluded:

> The study found no convincing support for any link between Jungian personality types and performance of small businessmen, and this included failure to support the expectations of Myers (p.181–2).

Yet other studies have found significant and predictable relationships. For instance, Marcia, Aiuppa and Watson (1989) compared the MBTI, self-esteem and job satisfaction scores of 102 American managers with the organizations' 'normative' personality type. It was hypothesized that managers who had the norm personality type of their particular organization should show higher self-esteem, greater job satisfaction and a lower turnover rate. The results were confirmed for self-esteem but not for job satisfaction. They argue that those with high fit tend to be more rewarded by the organization, which tends to increase their self-esteem.

Many studies using students have demonstrated behavioural correlates of the MBTI which are clearly related to the world of work. For instance, Danziger, Larsen and Connors (1989) found a relationship between MBTI types and time-keeping and appointments for an experiment on problem solving. Also, Schurr, Ruble and Herriksen (1988) found that MBTI types were significantly related to self-reported academic problems, skills and scholastic aptitude. For instance, personality type scores could explain 21 per cent of the verbal score variance, and 8 per cent of the mathematics score variance.

More recently, Moore (1987) has noted that the use of personality tests in industry is wide, and Haley and Stumpf (1989) have pointed out, quite correctly, that the popularity of the MBTI in executive circles affords researchers tremendous opportunities for research. Moore (1987) noted that most companies use the MBTI to help managers better understand how they come across to others who may see things differently. Other applications include team building, improving customer service, smoothing out group differences, working on projects, adapting to change, analysing troubles, behaviour between employees, and between employees and their jobs, and facilitating competitive strategic thinking.

In a fairly large representative study of American managers, Campbell and Van Velsor (1985) found 46 per cent with ST preferences and 37 per cent with NT preferences, with few SF or NF types. Thus, according to Haley and Stumpf (1989):

> Organizations may adopt conservative recommendations or those based on patterned data more often than people-oriented or innovative recommendations. These biases may account in part for organizational

difficulties in adapting to environmental changes. Ideally, decision tasks should dictate cognitive styles managers use. Good managers should at least be able to apply and to understand conclusions drawn from different decision models and processes, or to understand when their specific skills should come into play and when they prove counter-productive. However, these ideal decision making approaches may not be possible ... Only about 17 per cent of American managers see things in personal and interpersonal dimensions: 83 per cent tend to see things in technical and structural dimensions (p.493).

Eysenckian Theory: Extraversion, Neuroticism and Psychoticism

Without doubt, the most sophisticated trait personality theory is that of H.J. Eysenck which has been likened to finding St Pancras railway station (e.g. elaborate, Victorian structure) in the jungle of personality theories. The theory, which has spawned the Maudsley Personality Inventory (MPI), the Eysenck Personality Inventory (EPI) and the Eysenck Personality Questionnaire (EPQ), has been latterly revised. These questionnaires have been subjected to extensive investigation and proved robust (Helmes, 1989). The theory, which has undergone various changes over a 30-year period, argues for the psychophysiological basis of personality, and locates three major factors which relate to social behaviour: extraversion, neuroticism and psychoticism. Although the theory has been applied to a wide range of activities including criminality, sex, smoking, health and learning, less work has been done on the Eysenckian dimension correlates of occupational behaviour. However, over the last 25 years, there is evidence not only of the application of Eysenck's theory but its predictive usefulness in the occupational sphere.

In an early study, Rim (1961) looked at personality determinants of job incentives. He found students scoring low on extraversion and neuroticism ranked 'opportunity to learn new skills' as more important than high scorers, while high neuroticism scorers ranked 'good salary' as more important than low scorers.

Bendig (1963) used the SVIB with the MPI and discovered that introverts preferred scientific and theoretical jobs such as journalism, architecture and the teaching of mathematics, whereas extraverts expressed more interest in occupations involving more social contact (e.g. selling life insurance and social work). Extraversion was consistently and negatively correlated with preferences to become an architect, dentist, mathematician, physicist, engineer or chemist, while neuroticism was negatively correlated with accountant, office manager, banker, sales manager and teacher. Overall, the results showed social extraversion was negatively correlated with SVIB scales in Strong's areas I (general professional), II (science and engineering) and IV (practical) for both sex groups. Stable extraversion (SE) was positively correlated with area V (social service) and negatively correlated with areas VIII (business) and III (production manager) for men, while SE was positively correlated with interests in area IX (sales) for women. SE was also negatively related to the author–journalist interest scale for both sexes. The 'emotionality' (EM) trait, as measured by the neuroticism scale, was negatively correlated with SVIB scales in areas III (production manager) and VIII (business) for both men and women, and with areas IV (practical) and V (social service) for women.

In a study more useful for its norms than theory, Eysenck (1967b) collected EPI data on 1504 businessmen. His results are shown in Table 2.8.

Table 2.8 Personality scores of businessmen in different areas of business

Area of business	N	Neuroticism		Extraversion		lie scale	
		Mean	SD	Mean	SD	Mean	SD
General management	165	7.04	4.03	11.13	3.58	2.80	2.12
Production	135	6.90	3.77	11.05	3.72	3.08	1.69
R&D	574	7.42	4.05	9.98	3.88	2.76	1.49
Finance	132	7.53	4.49	10.12	3.40	2.93	1.97
Sales	168	7.04	3.64	11.33	3.98	2.93	1.92
Personnel	88	7.11	4.04	11.34	4.36	2.95	1.72
Consultancy	218	7.32	3.93	10.09	3.93	2.91	1.66
More than one of above	24	7.70	5.16	11.91	3.26	2.66	1.49
Total	1504						
Standardized data							
Normal population	2000	9.06	4.78	12.07	4.37	–	–
Salesmen	37	8.38	4.72	13.63	3.76	–	–
Professional	23	7.95	5.11	11.40	4.91	–	–
Normal population	651	–	–	–	–	2.26	1.57

Source: Eysenck (1967b)

On the E scale, the business groups are relatively introverted, but significantly different between themselves, with finance, R&D and consultants being the most introverted, and those belonging to more than one group being the most extraverted. Eysenck noted:

> Successful businessmen are on the whole stable introverts; they are stable regardless of what type of work they do within business, but their degree of extraversion may be related to type of work. The data are probably reasonably reliable because relatively few respondents failed to answer, and because scores on the lie scale did not indicate any market tendency to 'fake good'. The results suggest that the E.P.I. may have some modest role to play in furthering research into the personality patterns of persons engaged in business and industry' (p.250).

The notion that introverted workers are better able than extraverted ones to handle routine work activities was investigated by Cooper and Payne (1967) in a study carried out in the packing department of a tobacco factory where the work was repetitive and light. Job adjustment, as assessed by two supervisors, was negatively related to extraversion, and those workers who left the job in the 12 months following testing were significantly more extraverted than those who remained. Neuroticism was also implicated, being related to poor job adjustment and to frequency of non-permitted absence. They note:

> Beginning with the withdrawal indices, we find that the only appreciable correlations are with length of service and non-permitted absences. The more extraverted workers in this study have shorter periods of service to their credit than the less extraverted (more introverted); this finding may be taken as evidence that the more extraverted individuals will withdraw permanently from work of a routine nature. Non-permitted absence offers further interesting support for the withdrawal assumption. The correlation between extraversion and surgery attendance, although in the expected direction, is probably too small to merit serious attention. Surprisingly, certified sickness absence is almost completely unrelated to extraversion; it would be tempting to account for this non-relationship on the basis of certified sickness requiring a visit to a doctor and subsequent submission of a medical certificate to the employer, all of which may not be considered worth the effort when there exists the alternative of taking one or two days' uncertified absence (i.e., non-permitted absence) with virtually no trouble at all. However, such an explanation is not in keeping with an unpublished finding of Taylor that extraversion scores for 194 male oil refinery workers correlated .22 with sickness absence (p.112).

The use of both conditioning and arousal theory is evident in Cooper and Payne's thinking:

> Because extraverts condition poorly and introverts readily, extraverts are less able to tolerate tasks of routine nature since inhibition accumulates and inhibits sustained task performance;
>   Because extraverts are under aroused they seek arousal and do not function as well as introverts with a minimal or moderate sensory variation input.

Savage and Stewart (1972) also found that 100 female card-punch operators in training showed negative correlations between extraversion and supervisor ratings of output per month, although there was no relationship between this personality variable and drop-outs from the programme.

In another relevant paper, Hill (1975) compared the behaviour of introverts and extraverts on a monotonous task. He found, as predicted, that extraverts tend to build more variety into their responses on a monotonous task compared to introverts. Wankowski (1973) investigated a random sample of students at Birmingham University. He found that extraverted students tended to choose practical or people-oriented courses, whereas introverted students preferred more theoretical subjects. Introverts had greater examination success than extraverts in the physical sciences. Low neuroticism scorers opted for practically biased courses, whereas high neuroticism scorers preferred people-oriented courses. In terms of examination success, low neuroticism was associated with success in the applied sciences. Wilson, Tunstall and Eysenck (1972) used various ability and personality tests (including the EPI) to predict three criteria among gas fitters: examination results, supervisor ratings, college attendance. Neuroticism was a much better predictor than extraversion and results showed high scores were negatively associated with both exam results and absenteeism.

Morgenstern, Hodgson and Law (1974) demonstrated that introverted subjects function less efficiently in the presence of distractions, while extraverts show actual improvement in the presence of distractions. They concluded:

> It would seem that the extraverted subjects do not merely prefer to be in the company of others, but that their work efficiency actually improves in the face of distractions, while the solitary preferences of the introverts are reflected in their reduced efficiency of work when distracted. Paying heed to such preferences, as measured by the Eysenck Personality Inventory, is therefore not only a method of increasing contentment at work by means of personnel selection, but should also result in improved efficiency of output (p.220).

Rim (1977) got several job applicants to complete the EPI and rated statements according to how well they described their ideal job. Among the male subjects, the neurotic extraverts had the most distinctive ratings, valuing social contact, economic and social position, patterning of time and power functions of work more than neurotic introverts, stable extraverts or stable introverts. There were only modest and uninterpretable effects of personality on the description of the ideal job among female subjects.

Since neurotic individuals in general, and neurotic introverts in particular, are especially susceptible to stress, it might be thought that such people would prefer jobs that involve minimal stress. However, Rim (1977) did not find any large differences in the ideal job as a function of either neuroticism or neurotic introversion, while Bendig (1963) reported only that high neuroticism was associated with a dislike of business-type occupations such as banking, office management and accountancy.

Organ (1975a) examined personality correlates of conditionability in organizations as operationalized by students getting bonus points for performance on random quizzes. Introverts did better than extraverts, who presumably got diverted from the routine discipline of the daily preparation for classes regardless of contingencies.

Extraverts are more likely than introverts to prefer occupations that involve social contact. There is therefore a danger that introverted workers may become over-aroused if their jobs involve considerable extra organizational contact and a relative absence of routine. Blunt (1978) argued that introverted managers would thus tend to choose positions involving relatively routine duties (finance, production or technical managers), whereas extraverted managers would be more likely to select jobs in sales, marketing or transport. The results were broadly as hypothesized, except that transport managers were less extraverted and production managers more extraverted than predicted.

The relationship between personality and occupational success has been frequently examined. Fairly impressive findings were obtained among trainee pilots by Jessup and Jessup (1971). They tested would-be pilots with the EPI early in their course and discovered that the subsequent failure rate varied considerably as a function of personality. Specifically, 60 per cent of the neurotic introverts failed, against 37 per cent of the neurotic extraverts, 32 per cent of the stable extraverts and only 14 per cent of the stable introverts. Thus, high levels of neuroticism had a much greater adverse effect on introverts than on extraverts. They note that they expect the introverted cadet to learn better both in the aircraft and lecture room than extraverts. Jessup and Jessup concluded:

> The comparative failure of the specifically neurotic introvert may be tentatively explained as follows. High arousal in the visceral system is associated with high N; high cortical arousal with low E. Given that there is an optimal level of arousal for learning to fly and that this is a particularly stressful experience, it seems likely that the neurotic introvert will be aroused beyond the optimum; the learning of the stable introvert on the other hand profits from cortical arousal with suffering from additional visceral arousal (p.120).

Similar findings were reported by Reinhardt (1970), who carried out a battery of personality tests on a sample of the United States Navy's best pilots. Their mean score on the neuroticism scale of the MPI was only 11, compared with a mean of 20 among American college students. Okaue, Nakamura and Niura (1977) divided the extraversion and neuroticism scores of military pilots into three categories (high, average and low) on each dimension. Of the sample of 75 pilots, 38 fell into the stable extravert category, with the highest frequency in any of the other eight categories being only 8. In more recent research with military pilots in the United Kingdom, Bartram and Dale (1982) found a tendency for successful pilots to be more stable and more extraverted than those who failed flying training. They had data on over 600 pilots from the Army Air Corps (AAC) and the Royal Air Force. The consistent finding that neuroticism is negatively related to flying success makes intuitive sense. Flying can obviously be stressful, with a single mistake proving fatal. In such circumstances, pilots who are especially susceptible to stress are likely to perform less well than those who are more stable.

This association prompts a number of questions: whether all aviators have this personality pattern; whether military pilots are pre-selected with respect to it; or whether military flying training regimes filter out those who do not have it. But they do note:

> Consideration of the nature of operational military flying and military training regimes has some bearing on the question of whether they effectively filter out men as a function of their personality. Flying training in the services is a strictly paced, stressful exercise. Students are enrolled in classes of about 15 members in which competition is encouraged. For various practical reasons, all members of the class are under pressure to learn at the same rate. In addition, there is some physical danger involved, so errors can result in death or serious injury. Viewed in this way, it is intuitively reasonable to expect the more stable candidates to have a higher success rate. Failure, however, is rarely attributed to neurosis. The most common attribution in the AAC is 'lack of flying ability'. Enquiries at a deeper level are rarely initiated when a man fails, since failure is relatively commonplace.

> To regard flying training as a straightforward learning situation is possibly a simplification. Flying instructors do not simply monitor progress, they attempt to predict future performance. A student who exhibits occasional lapses when flying dual sorties may well be considered a bad risk, since just one lapse when he is captain of an aircraft could result in disaster. Also, hesitation when faced with decisions in training might be seen as another serious limitation in a man being trained to fly in battle. We believe these predictions of future performance represent another way in which personality may influence success in flying training. To put it another way, training is used as a basis of further selection and men thought to be unsuitable as operational pilots are eliminated as 'training failures' (p.293).

Looking at more common jobs, Kirton and Mulligan (1973) found attitudes towards organizational change to be related to a combination of neuroticism and extraversion among 258 managers from eight companies with at least 1000 employees each. The four extraversion-by-neuroticism groupings were compared and the finding was that the two personality variables interacted, although there was no effect of either taken separately. Subjects scoring high on both neuroticism and extraversion, and subjects scoring low on both scales (neurotic extraverts and stable introverts) had more positive attitudes toward change in managerial practices in general, more positive attitudes toward specific, innovative appraisal schemes or promotional policies being introduced, and the lowest level of discontent with the institution and with superiors.

Yet Turnbull (1976) found that among more than 100 male college students involved in a summer of book sales, neither EPI extraversion scores alone nor in combination with other personality scales predicted sales success. Sales success was determined on the basis of total wholesale business and a sales index indicating amount of business per call made. In the global studies presented earlier, the sales vocations were only weakly related to extraversion. Turnbull noted a wide range of scores on the extraversion–introversion dimension among the individuals applying for the job and no personality differences between those who completed the summer of sales and those who dropped out. It was found, as predicted, that extraversion scores increased from the beginning of the summer to the end of the summer as a result of the sales experience, an increase that was equal for more successful and less successful salesmen.

Studies of personality correlates of mood have revealed interesting results. Christie and Venables (1973) asked 80 volunteers, whose jobs ranged from office clerks to heads of academic departments in the various schools, to complete a mood adjective checklist on Monday and Friday mornings and afternoons for four successive weeks. They combined the scales of concentration, activation and deactivation to form an efficiency index, for which there was a significant four-way interaction effect involving day of week, time of day, extraversion and neuroticism. The authors described a pattern of high arousal and low euphoria experienced by neurotic introverts on Monday morning to Monday absenteeism, and a pattern of high arousal and high euphoria experienced by stable extraverts on Friday afternoon to premature departures from work at that time. Bishop and Jean Renaud (1976) related end-of-day moods to amount of change in daily activities and personality. Choosing people at random in a community, representing a number of different vocations, they asked subjects to keep a diary in which entries were made each 15 minutes during both a work day and a leisure day. Mood ratings were taken from the last hour before bedtime. Again, there was a four-way interaction effect. Activity variation was not related to mood on work days but it was on leisure days. The fact that activity variation was related to pleasantness of mood for stable extraverts and neurotic introverts but related to unpleasantness of mood for neurotic extraverts and stable introverts indicates how increased variation and stimulation (and its opposite, monotony) has different value for different individuals.

Kim (1980) using undergraduates on a simulated work task found, as predicted, that introverts were less dissatisfied on a non-stimulating task than extraverts who were more satisfied on a stimulating task, although there was a difference in their actual performance. It was also found that introverts and extraverts differed in their perception of expectancy and motivating characteristics of objective tasks.

More recently, in a study of personality correlates of job preference and satisfaction, Sterns et al. (1983) found that extraverts preferred jobs with higher levels of cognitive task demands, pace of task demands, cognitive closure, extrinsic rewards and intrinsic rewards. Neuroticism, on the other hand, was negatively related to each of these preferences, except for extrinsic rewards. Extraverts were less satisfied with the clerical work itself, supervision and co-workers than introverts. It should be pointed out that subjects were non-managerial civil service clerical employees in a job that would suit stable introverts more than extraverts.

The Eysenckian trait dimensions have also been found to predict 'negative' occupational variables. There has been some interest in the relevance of personality to performance under rather monotonous conditions. It might be predicted that under-aroused extraverts would find it more difficult than introverts to maintain performance over time. Extraverts showed a greater deterioration than introverts in driving performance over a four-hour period (Fagerström and Lisper, 1977). However, their performance improved more than that of introverts when someone talked to them or the car radio was turned on.

Shaw and Sichel (1970) compared the personality characteristics of accident-prone and safe South African bus drivers. Most of the accident-prone drivers were neurotic extraverts, whereas the safe drivers were predominantly stable introverts. As might have been expected, it is the impulsiveness component of extraversion rather than the sociability component that is more closely related to poor driving and accident proneness (Loo, 1979) (see Chapter 8).

Eysenck and Eysenck (1985) have concluded:

> In sum, it appears that preferences for different kinds of occupation and occupational success are both determined to some extent by personality. The research to date mostly suffers from the disadvantage that job characteristics are discussed in an *ad hoc* fashion. A major dimension along which jobs can be ordered is the extent to which the behaviour of an individual doing that job is constrained by external factors. For example, a car worker on an assembly line has minimal control over his work activities, whereas a university lecturer has greater control. It seems likely that personality will be a more consequential determinant of job satisfaction and success when severe constraints exist. It may be coincidence that two of the occupations wherein personality has been found to be relevant (flying and driving) both involve considerable constraints. In other words, the fit of a worker to his job is especially important when the worker has little scope for tailoring the work environment to his needs (p.329).

However, it is possible to argue the precise opposite. That is, where there are few external demands, personality (and ability) factors may be primary causes of success and failure. Thus, it may be argued that personality factors are more relevant and crucial under these conditions.

Finally, what happens if an individual finds himself/herself in a job that is ill-suited to his personality? If he remains in that job, then the obvious answer is that his job performance will tend to be relatively poor. An alternative possibility that has rarely been considered is that his personality may alter as a result of being exposed to a particular job environment. Turnbull (1976) found that there was no tendency for success among male student salesmen to be related to extraversion. However, the experience of selling and making numerous contacts with strangers produced a highly significant increase in the average level of extraversion.

Cattell's 16PF

Perhaps the most famous of all personality tests applied to industrial, organization and occupation settings is R.B. Cattell's 16PF which was published initially over 40 years ago. For Cattell, the test has a number of advantages: it is unusually *comprehensive* in its coverage of personality dimensions; it is based on the *functional* measurement previously located in natural personality structures; the measurements are relatable to an *organized* and *integrated* body of practice and theoretical knowledge in clinical education and industrial psychology.

The test measures 16 dimensions of personality (and six to nine second-order factors) which are supposedly independent and identifiable; reliably and validly measureable. The psychometric properties of the scale are well documented as well as the problem of deception. The very fact that the test has been around so long; very shrewdly and aggressively marketed in a variety of countries; and that Cattell himself has been such an active researcher and zealous advocate of the test for so long, all have attracted incredible attention. For instance, if one consults the handbook printed 20 years ago (Cattell, Eber and Tatsuoka, 1970), one finds incredible evidence of the application of the test. This data is in fact divided into two sections. The first concerns available specification equations against criteria: here various weights are given (per dimension), derived from multiple regressions. Police officers to school counsellors are considered. For instance, consider the following:

Salesmen: Retail. Two studies, the larger by Industrial Psychology Inc., have related actual sales volume in comparable situations (retail bakery route salesmen, soft-drink salesmen) with the following average equation:

Salesmanship $= 0.44A - 0.11B + 0.11C - 0.22E + 0.11F - 0.11G + 0.22H - 0.33L - 0.11M + 0.11N + 0.11O + 0.44Q_3 + 0.22Q_3 - 0.22Q_4 + 1.87$ [Group mean = 5.56]

In this case, even the smaller weights have been retained because the sign was the same in the two studies. It will be clear from this, as from some other instances, that the popular stereotypes and impressions on which occupational selections are still often based can be erroneous. Thus, dominance, E+, is actually not effective in face-to-face selling, and the view of the successful salesman as an 'extravert' has to be modified. For although gains are shown through exviant deviations (the temperament source traits of A, F, and H), self-sufficiency, Q_2, is actually oppositely weighted to the extravert direction; i.e., the inviant endowment is required.

Salesmen: Wholesale. On wholesale (grain) salesmen, personality has similarly been correlated with *actual sales income*, resulting in the following equation:

Wholesale sales success = $0.21A + 0.10B + 0.10C + 0.10E + 0.21F + 0.10G - 0.10L - 0.31M + 0.21N - 0.31Q_2 + 0.21Q_3 - 0.21Q_4 + 3.80$ [Group mean = 5.09]

It will be noted that intelligence shifts to a positive effect here, autism (M) is more of a drawback than it was in the retail field, and so on, but otherwise there is a 'family similarity' between the two types of sales activity (p.166–7).

Secondly, equations are indirectly calculated as they are derived and cross-validated on samples. Occupations as varied as accountants to athletes; military cadets to musicians; and sales personnel to social workers are considered. For example, considering executives and industrial supervisors, Cattell *et al.* (1970) noted:

Perhaps the classing together of several types of executives has smoothed out some special characteristics that will later be found; but at present, except for high warmth, intelligence, and independence, the profile diverges little from that of 'the man in the street'. However, the characteristics are in the direction that psychological analysis would suggest, namely, a high tolerance of people in affectothymia (A+), toughness in factor H, shrewdness in N, some self-development in (Q_3+), and a marked willingness to try new ideas and new methods (Q_1).

At the second order the executives are not high in cortertia (QIII) as one might expect, and the chief characteristics are some independence and exvia.

The pattern for the supermarket personnel is one of interpersonal warmth (A+), as might be expected, but it is clearly not a sales pattern, nor even an exviant (extraverted) one. A glance at the second-order anxiety component (C–, O–, Q_4+, L+) shows an appreciably raised anxiety level, and one wonders about the degree to which the personal tensions and detailed cares of the manager's position have produced this, or the degree to which a position of this kind simply tolerates performance by quite anxious persons. The sober desurgency (F–) seems consistent with the need for doing a precise job and paying attention to detail. Mediocre general ability (B−) may indicate that shop tasks are numerous and harassing rather than intrinsically complex.

Above-average intelligence (B+), a practical, sober, and industrious attitude (M−, F−), and indications of a slightly raised general sensitivity (G+, O+, Q$_3$+) to superego demands, mark the industrial plant foreman as an effectively and appropriately functioning type in industrial organizations with the characteristics of management. It is interesting to compare the profile of these men appointed for efficiency in getting the work done, with those of elected leaders, with whom there are major resemblances but also some intriguing differences (p.201).

Some of these findings have received moderate corroboration by replicative studies. For instance, Cattell *et al.* (1970) reports on 139 cabin crew:

The most noteworthy features of the primaries are high ego strength, parmia (insusceptibility to sympathetic-system upset by stress), high self-sentiment (control), low pretension (tolerance of 'difficult' passengers!), low inadequacy–guilt proneness, and especially, low ergic tension. With this high general strength of character and self-control, there is, however, only average dominance. Such an unusual degree of deviation toward character and control (along with sociability), and away from neuroticism, suggests (along with rather small standard deviations) that the air line is doing an excellent job (p.189).

Twenty years later, using cabin crew from a British airline, Furnham (1991) showed the Spearman rank-order correlation between the two to be $r = 0.63$ which is significant at 0.01. Yet he did find the 16PF did not discriminate between good, average and poor employees. One hundred and thirty-six crew completed the Cattell 16PF at the beginning of their training as the personnel department wanted to determine the effectiveness of the test in predicting occupational success. Over the course of a six-month period, detailed daily reports were kept on their in-flight behaviour. These reports were later used to categorize the subjects into above average, average, below average, and to note those who left the airline. Pearson correlations and one-way analysis of variances (ANOVAs) across various groups (i.e. above vs below average; stayed vs left) failed to yield significant differences, although some clear trends were apparent.

Yet it is not only the relationship between personality and vocational/occupational variables that has interested Cattell and his colleagues. For instance, Cattell and Butcher (1968) looked at the relationship between personality and clinical and educational outcomes. In fact, the occupational correlates of personality seem to have excited Cattell least, although many followers have pursued this path.

There have been a very large number of studies looking at cross-cultural differences in personality as measured by the 16PF. These have important implications because there are notable and significant personality differences between different countries, and these may be reflected in the organizational structures that occur in that country. For instance, if country A tends to be more extraverted than B, one might expect organizations in country A to have more open-planned offices; to have a more explicit performance reward structure; to have many more social events than country B.

Studies have shown some clear patterns. For instance, Cattell and Warburton (1961) found, in comparable student groups, that the British were more conservative, less emotionally sensitive, with higher ego strength and self-sentiment, but lower super-ego development and self-sentiment than Americans. Similar subject studies have shown them to be consistent but relatively minor.

As regards an occupational application, Cattell has outlined two approaches to deciding a person's suitability for a specific occupation or a particular job. First is the effectiveness estimate approach in which goodness of performance is estimated by a quantitative value. Second is the adjustment approach, whereby a person is allocated to a specific group – for example, a group of 'successful' salesmen. This is usually done by computing a similarity coefficient relating that person's profile to the mean profile of that group.

The first approach assumes a linear relationship between the various factors and the criterion, and is usually expressed as a linear regression equation with weights attached to each factor. The second approach assumes a curvilinear relationship as there is an 'optimum' value for each factor, that 'optimum' value being the mean score of the successful group in that factor. Most of the research in this area, under Cattell's guidance, has adopted the first route.

A review of the occupational literature has shown that Cattell's 16PF has also worked well in a variety of practical situations. Bernardin (1977) studied absenteeism and turnover in a sample of 51 sales personnel; he found correlations between the 16PF conscientiousness and anxiety scales and absenteeism and turnover varying between 0.21 and 0.40. Karson and O'Dell (1970) studied 568 air traffic controllers and found a number of low but significant correlations with peer and supervisory ratings. Toole et al. (1972) used the 16PF to study the relationship between personality and job performance in minority and non-minority employees; they found zero-order correlations less than .30, but a multiple r of 0.41 between scale scores and performance ratings. There is also considerable concurrent validity of the 16PF. Jones, Sasek and Wakefield et al. (1976) found the 16PF correlates significantly and predictably with the Work Motivation Inventory, a measure of Maslow's needs.

Rather than look at correlates (predictors) of success, some researchers have looked specifically at personality predictors of failure. McLoughlin, Friedson and Murray (1983) compared 49 'terminated' male executives to an employed sample on the 16PF. Compared to those not sacked, the terminated group were less warm-hearted (A), more emotionally stable (C), more assertive (E), more conscientious (G), more imaginative (M), more unperturbed (O), more self-sufficient (Q$_3$) and more controlled (Q$_4$). Curiously, then, the sacked executives appeared on the whole healthier and happier than the employed executives, but neither scores were outside the average range. The authors noted that the personality characteristics of the sacked may have been less contributory or causal factors in their dismissal, yet they show the pattern of the driven, self-absorbed and successful executive. However, it is crucial to know *why* people were dismissed to make sense of this data. Similarly, Moore and Stewart (1989) found various 16PF correlates of employee honesty and integrity. Although the study did not show a consistent pattern of 16PF correlates of four quite different measures, the size and number of the correlations indicated effects well above chance level.

More recently, Fraboni and Saltstone (1990) used the 16PF to see if it could distinguish between first-generation entrepreneurs who had established their own businesses, and those second-generation entrepreneurs established by their parents. The results showed that compared to second-generation entrepreneurs, the first-generation entrepreneurs were *more* suspicious (L), assertive (E), imaginative (M), controlled (Q$_3$), and reserved (A), but *less* trusting, humble, practical, undisciplined and outgoing. First-generation entrepreneurs are more innovatively oriented while second-generation entrepreneurs are more administratively oriented.

Perhaps predictably, because of their similar approach and methods but relatively subtle differences, such as the fact that Eysenck stresses super-factors and orthogonal factor rotations, and Cattell stresses simple factors and oblique rotations; these two figures have occasionally taken swipes at each other. For instance, Eysenck (1985a) has claimed that Cattell's 16 factors are unstable:

> When results are thus completely unreplicable, it would seem that the theory based on the original analysis is unacceptable, and that such scales should not be used in theoretical or practical scientific work (p.9).

Cattell (1986) in reply quotes 41 published studies that replicated his system. He notes:

> Eysenck's resort to 3 factors is shown to be theoretically faulty and unable to equal the criterion predictions obtainable from the 16PF primaries (p.153).

And later:

> Eysenck's attack on the continuing lack of clear paradigms in current personality discussion is well merited, but he does not need to criticize one of the most scientifically established maps of human personality structures because it is not quite as simple as his own idea of things (p.158).

Yet both men, graduates of London University, have developed question-naires useful in the world of occupational testing.

2.6 MORE RECENT RESEARCH ON OTHER TESTS

Over the past 40 years, various personality tests have been developed which have been correlated with occupational performance. Hogan (1990) has reviewed some thesis research.

Guilford–Zimmerman Temperament Survey

The most recent version of the Guilford–Zimmerman Temperament Survey Manual (Guilford, Zimmerman and Guilford, 1976) reports 23 separate studies of managerial performance. Harrell and Harrell (1984) tested 336 MBA students who graduated between 1961 and 1964, and the class of 1966, to see if scores predicted earnings five, ten and 20 years after graduation. The correlations between compensation, sociability and ascendance averaged about 0.20 across all three follow-up periods and were the most stable coefficients in the study. Harrell and Harrell (1984) note that personality predicted success better than academic aptitude; they thought this was because 'business success is usually ... dependent upon relating effectively with people, rather than solving a scholastic puzzle' (p.29–30).

Sparks (1983) tested 2478 men in a large oil company and found consistent relationships between scale scores and indices of job success, job effectiveness and managerial potential. Bentz (1985b) describes 30 years of research designed to identify 'general executive competence' using a test battery selected by L.L. Thurston in the early 1940s. Bentz showed that sociability, energy and ascendance are modestly but steadily and significantly correlated with a surprising variety of criterion data (ratings, nominations, compensation level, promotability) across a large number of samples. Bentz concluded that:

> It has been demonstrated that personality measures are reliable over a considerable time span; tests taken years ago predict both job progress and current performance. From the perspective of this research it is appropri-ate to conclude that the pervasive academic bias against paper-and-pencil personality assessment is unjustified (p.143).

Californian Personality Inventory

The Californian Personality Inventory (CPI) has been used for a very long time in managerial settings. For instance, Goodstein and Schroder (1963) used the CPI to develop a reliable and valid 'good manager' scale. Gough (1984) later showed the subscale diagnostic of behavioural effectiveness, self-confidence, cognitive clarity and good orientation. Other measures of the whole scale have shown to be useful. Orpen (1983) found significant correlations between the CPI and ratings of managerial effectiveness. These accounted for about 10 per cent of the variance. Mills and Bohannon (1980) used the CPI in a study of 49 highway patrol officers; for six scales and two criterion ratings, they found nine significant correlations varying between 0.26 and 0.43. There is also an interesting CPI literature concerned with forecasting educational performance (Gough, 1968). Gough (1985) developed a work orientation scale for the CPI and it showed high scores to be dependable, moderate, optimistic, persevering and conservative. He hypothesized that individuals with strong managerial drive and high Wo scores should be circumspect, judicious and cautious; while those with strong drive but low Wo scores would be more venturesome, quick and risk taking. More recently, Gough published CPI scales designed to assess individual differences in devotion to the work ethic and in managerial effectiveness (Gough, 1989).

Rawls and Rawls (1968) used the EPPS and CPI to see if they could discriminate 30 more and 30 less successful executives based on salary, title and appraisal performance ratings. They also administered a biographical information form. In all, five of the 15 EPPS scales and ten of the 18 CPI scales showed significant differences. The successful executives made significantly higher scores on the dominance, heterosexuality and aggression scales of the EPPS, and on the dominance, capacity for status, sociability, social presence, self-acceptance, intellectual efficiency, psychological-mindedness and flexibility scales of the CPI. Less successful executives, on the other hand, scored significantly higher on the deference and order scales of the EPPS, and on the self-control and femininity scales of the CPI.

The biographical items showed that successful executives' fathers more often had a high-school education, while less successful executives' fathers more frequently had only a junior high-school education. Successful executives had more often belonged to the Boy Scouts. They were younger than less successful executives when they learned to swim, travelled alone on a trip over 100 miles, started to date, earned their own living in a regular job, and started to drink alcoholic beverages. As youngsters, successful executives were more frequently chosen as leaders in group activities and felt their general athletic ability to be above average. Successful executives belonged to more social organizations and had more close friends. In contrast to less successful executives, they felt prestige and 'coming up with something new' to be major motivations in their lives.

Successful executives read more books, newspapers and periodicals (better informed), felt more confident in most areas (self-reliant, self-confident), expressed their opinions freely (forward), expected to make more money and attain higher levels in the organisation (ambitious), were at ease in social situations (confident in social interaction), and felt that they had been more aggressive and successful in life (aggressive, dominant).

Continued occupational applications of the CPI certainly suggest that it has validity for predicting behaviour at work.

Gordon Personal Profile

Various studies are attested to the usefulness of this measure. Dodd, Wollowick and McNamara (1970) reported significant correlations between the Gordon ascendancy scale and a criterion measure of progress for 396 maintenance technical trainees over nine years, and 103 sales trainees over 11 years. Spitzer and McNamara (1964) divided a sample of 102 manufacturing managers into four groups. In three of the four groups, ascendancy correlated .28, .27 and .31 with peer ratings for managerial potential. Palmer (1974) corroborates these results with both versions of the Gordon Personal Profile in a different sample.

Personality Research Form

In a recent study, Tetl and Jackson (1990) correlated PRF scores with the in-basket exercise scores derived from 78 Canadian managers. Although many of the correlations were significant, a number were contrary to predictions (i.e. PRF autonomy and dominance correlated positively with participative tendency). In a recent study of accountants, Day and Silverman (1989) found, even with cognitive ability taken into consideration, three personality dimensions (orientation to work; degree of ascendancy; degree/quality of interpersonal orientation) significantly related to important aspects of job performance. They conclude:

> In summary, it appears that scores on specific, job-relevant personality scales are significantly related to important aspects of job performance in this sample of accountants. One of the three significant predictor scales (viz., interpersonal orientation) also provided a significant increase in validity for the global or overall measure of job performance. It has been argued that this would be expected due to collinearity among the different behavioural dimensions at the true score level. However, relying solely on the global measure would mask the significant relationships found between work orientation and ascendancy and some of the specific performance dimensions. In addition, examining the individual behavioural dimensions is interesting because it reveals that some of the highest correlations are found between those personality–performance links that are theoretically most similar, such as interpersonal orientation and ratings of cooperation. From the results of this study, it also can be concluded that particular, job-relevant aspects of personality are significantly related to ratings of job performance above what can be predicted by cognitive ability measures alone (p.34).

Kuder Occupational Interest Survey

Numerous attempts have been made to validate this measure. For instance, Lester and colleagues (Lester and Purgrave, 1980; Lester and Ferguson, 1989) found that it could not predict success/failure for police graduates or success 10 years later.

Occupational Personality Questionnaire

Various versions of this British-normed measure have been developed. It has been shown to be reliable (Budd and Paltiel, 1989), but there are doubts about the dimensional structure (Matthews *et al.*, 1990) and its predictive validity.

Locus of Control

The locus of control concept and scale (developed by Rotter, 1966) has been used extensively but not programmatically to look at occupational behaviour. But the scale has consistently proved a predictable and significant correlate of work related behaviour. For instance, Broedling (1975) used over 200 naval officers to test five hypotheses, all written in the expectancy–valence framework. The hypotheses were:

1. Internals are more likely to use rewards as being generally contingent upon job performance than externals.
2. Internals are more motivated to perform on the job than externals.
3. Internals are better performers on the job than externals.
4. Self-expectancy and instrumentality (inner locus of control) are positively correlated.
5. Those with higher pay grades are more internal to those occupying lower pay grades.

All these hypotheses received support but there was no discriminant validity for ratings by supervisors, peers and the subjects themselves on job effort and performance. However, the results do point to the fact that locus of control beliefs is closely related to occupational behaviour.

Ahmed (1985) showed, as predicted, that compared to non-entrepreneurs, Bangladeshi immigrant entrepreneurs in Great Britain scored higher on internal locus of control (and need for achievement and risk taking), although it is unclear on which criteria the two samples were matched.

Locus of control has also been shown to be related to a tendency to take part in office politics. Biberman (1985) found internal locus of control was correlated with job satisfaction and a tendency to engage in office politics (which of course may be a powerful moderator variable).

Ad Hoc and Multiple Inventory Studies

Many studies have failed to report interesting, significant or in any way theoretically important findings, mainly because of very poor choice of both independent and dependent variables. They have not been chosen for their psychometric or theoretical constructs and hence yield few interesting findings.

For instance, Ling and Putti (1987) related the six personality dimensions of the Bernreuter Personality Inventory to the 12 dimensions in the Leader Behaviour Description Questionnaire. Neuroticism and introversion correlated significantly negatively but poorly ($r = \pm 0.15$) and dominance and confidence positively with about half of the leadership style. Rather unfairly, the authors concluded that personality traits *per se* do not determine the leadership style adopted. It certainly was not warranted from their data and may be a natural consequence of their choice of independent and dependent variables.

There are, of course, numerous studies which have used multiple measures to attempt to identify occupation success. For instance, Burgess (1955) used six tests in a battery to attempt to isolate under- and over-achievers in engineering. He found the MMPI, the Bernreuter Personality Inventory, part of the Strong Vocational Interest Blank and Rosenzweig test 'when given and scored in the conventional manner, are not suitable instruments for differentiating groups of academic deviates' (p.98).

Dyer (1987) used the Strong–Campbell Interest Inventory, the CPI and biographical inventory to try to predict university success and first-year job performance. In all, the personality variables accounted for 3 to 5 per cent of the variance. The CPI scale – socialization – accounted for most of the variance for all CPI scales.

Rabinowitz, Hall and Goodale (1977) looked at various individual difference predictions of job involvement (based on a few items, self-report measures). Various personality measures were used, like growth need, locus of control, work ethic. The former and the latter in conjunction with length of service and job scope accounted for 25 per cent of the variance.

Cognitive Attitude and Learning Style Test

Various studies have shown that intelligence or cognitive tests predict occupational success. There is a significant literature on cognitive structure, style and complexity, all relating to the processing of information. Streufert and Nogami (1989) have recently reviewed this vast and scattered literature, and shown how cognitive style relates to organizational flexibility, leadership, performance, stress etc.

Also, a number of attitude questionnaires have been developed which appear to predict occupational behaviour. For instance, Johnson, Messé and Crano (1984) developed a simple 35-item work opinion questionnaire, measuring five factors (co-operation, self-confidence, maturity, security and fairness) that actually correlated with supervisors' ratings of actual work behaviour. Another such measure is the Management Effectiveness Profile System (Cooke, 1989).

Although various attempts have been made to develop a theory, taxonomy and measure of learning style, the theory and questionnaire that has attracted most attention is that of Kolb (1976, 1984). The model focuses on two orthogonal dimensions: active–reflective (i.e. from direct participation to detached observation), and abstract–concrete (i.e. from dealing with tangible objects to dealing with theoretical concepts). Kolb (1984) defines a four-stage cycle of learning: the acquisition of concrete experience (CE); reflective observation (RO) on that experience; followed by abstract conceptualization (AC) and then active. Each stage of the cycle requires different abilities, and because people are more skilled in some, rather than others, they tend to develop a particular style. According to the theory there are four types, as shown in Figure 2.4.

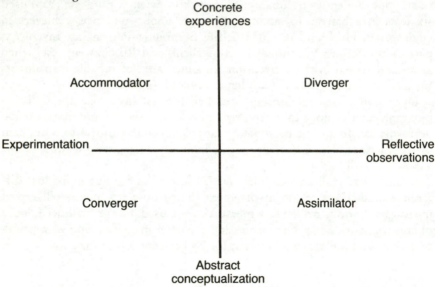

Figure 2.4 The four learning styles according to Kolb's theory
Source: Kolb (1984)

The identified strengths of divergers are described as their imaginative abilities and understanding of people, while their weaknesses are found in their inability to make decisions or being paralyzed by alternatives. Assimilators are said to be oriented toward building theoretical models and using inductive reasoning. A weakness of this style may occur with the lack of practical applications generated from theory. Convergers use deductive reasoning and prefer the application of ideas; convergers are also relatively unemotional and would rather work with things than people. Making decisions too quickly and solving the wrong problem have been identified as weaknesses of convergers. The accommodator is quick to get involved in new situations in a trial-and-error manner; risk taking is a strength of this style. Trivial improvements and being involved in seemingly meaningless activities are noted as weaknesses. These learning styles describe the four distinct cognitive modes of information processing.

The test has been subjected to psychometric scrutiny and improvement (Atkinson, 1988, 1989; Wilson, 1986), and alternative measures like the Honey and Mumford (1982) learning styles questionnaire (LSQ), which has also undergone psychometric investigation (Allison and Hayes, 1988). Certainly, the fit between preferred learning style and the way one is taught could improve management efficiency.

2.7 CONCLUSION

Personality tests have been used fairly extensively in management for over 50 years. Robertson and Makin (1986) contacted 304 major British companies in the mid-1980s of which 108 (34 per cent) replied. Whereas just under 10 per cent used personality tests fairly frequently, 65 per cent said they never did. They mainly used interviews and references, although a very small minority (under 5 per cent) used graphology, astrology, biodata or assessment centres. In America, the number is probably higher.

There remains considerable scepticism in applied circles as to the usefulness of personality tests. Stone (1988) refers familiar objections to the use of personality tests: they were designed to identify mental disorders; they are difficult to validate; there is a great deal of vagueness in the trait definitions; they are open to faking and response bias; respondents frequently lack self-awareness; they are not reliable on equal opportunity issues, and legislation prevents them being used anyway; there is a lot of research evidence to support them etc. He concludes:

'All in then, personality testing is not a very rewarding approach for selecting managers and probably shouldn't be used at all' (p. 54).

There has also been a significant increase in the development of specialist tests for use in personnel selection. For instance, Sackett, Burns and Callahan (1989) survey tests aimed specifically at measuring employee integrity (dishonesty, theft). These have been developed mainly by test publishers but seem to do the job well.

This chapter has attempted a fairly comprehensive review of the early, as well as more recent, literature on personality test correlates of occupational behaviour. This literature is widely scattered, of uneven quality and frequently a-theoretical, but there is sufficient evidence to suggest that there is a place for psychological (particularly personality) testing in the workplace.

Chapter 3

Personality and vocational choice

Nothing that is worth knowing can be taught.

Oscar Wilde

A little uncertainty is good for everyone.

H. Kissinger

A round man cannot be expected to fit in a square hole right away. He must have time to modify his shape.

Mark Twain

Choose a job you love, and you will never have to work a day in your life.

Confucius

Some people quit working as soon as they find a job.

Anonymous

3.1 INTRODUCTION

The fundamental purpose of vocational guidance and counselling is obvious and quite straightforward. It is to help people make appropriate vocational choices and adjustments; and to facilitate the efficient and cost-effective functioning of organizations by the appropriate exploitation of individual assets and abilities. To a large extent, the work on vocational guidance is identical to that of employee selection, except the former takes the perspective of, and is primarily concerned with the best interests of the employee, while the latter is mainly the concern of the employer. Because there are individual differences in ability, aptitude, needs, personality and interests, and job difference in the demands they make in personal attributes and skills, people will do better in jobs for which their abilities are suited than those not congruent with them.

Vocational (occasionally termed career) psychology focuses on people thinking about careers, preparing for the occupations of their choice and, where appropriate, changing jobs or even leaving the world of work.

Vocational guidance is one of the oldest areas of applied psychology. Super

(1953) has reviewed the history of what he calls the differential psychology applied to occupations and the developmental psychology of careers. He noted the impetus both world wars gave to the classifying of large numbers of drafted men and assigning them to appropriate military jobs. He noted particularly the theoretical work of Ghiselli in the 1950s and Holland in the 1960s.

The *Journal of Vocational Behaviour* publishes annually a very comprehensive critical review of current work in the field. For instance, Greenhaus and Parasuraman (1986) found quite distinct themes in the literature: person–environment fit, gender influence, cultural group differences, career planning and decision making, and job search and recruitment. Rarely, however, are personality factors mentioned explicitly. Much of the research in this field remains concerned with the assessment of interests, rather than the assessment of individual differences and their interests (Walsh and Osipow, 1986). More recent approaches include looking at a life-span approach to career development (Vondracek, Lerner and Schulenberg, 1986), but, again, traditional personality and individual difference variables are neglected.

Certainly, as regarding the interface of personality and vocational psychology, there appears to be little mutual interest in each other's areas of concern. Yet since the 1930s it has been suggested that there may be greater influences on occupational choice (Carter, 1932). Indeed, this demonstrable heredity component in occupational choice has been seen to operate through the media of personality variables (Vandenberg and Stafford, 1967).

Many organizations are becoming aware of the career development of employees. Over time it is quite common for people to be promoted in rank or level (concomitant changes in responsibilities and skills), or to move horizontally or laterally (with functional or technical changes). These lead to significant changes which the individual might or might not be able to cope with.

According to Shullman and Carder (1983), there are three critical phase processes that occur for each individual's career in an organization:

- *Entry*. This includes the process of recruitment, selection and socialization, the first two of which, at least, seem obsessed by individual differences.
- *Establishment and movement*. This involves such things as the way in which performance reviews and promotion policies affect career development.
- *Late careers*. This involves the issue of career plateauing, obsolescence and preparation for retirement.

While demographic variables are frequently considered in this literature, personality variables are not. There are, however, always exceptions.

Do people who make mid-career changes have a different personality structure from those who are vocationally stable? Wiener and Vaitenas (1977) gave the EPPS and the Gordon Personal Profile and Inventory to matched groups of mid-career changers, and the vocationally stable in management and sales occupations. Career changes were *lower* on dominance, ascendancy, responsibility, endurance and order. They argue that the career changers seemed less disciplined, and because they were less enterprising in what were essentially enterprising occupations this led them to leave. Certainly, these results fit nicely within the person–environment fit model.

Super (1953) set out ten propositions that define some of the major issues in the field, although not all would necessarily agree with his terminology:

1. People differ in their abilities, interests and personalities.
2. They are qualified, by virtue of these circumstances, each for a number of occupations.
3. Each of these occupations requires a characteristic pattern of abilities, interests and personality traits, with tolerance wide enough, however, to allow both some variety of occupations for each individual and some variety of individuals in each occupation.
4. Vocational preferences and competencies, and situations in which people live and work, and hence their self-concepts, change with time and experience (although self-concepts are generally fairly stable from late adolescence until later maturity), making choice and adjustment a continuous process.
5. This process may be summed up in a series of life stages, characterized as those of growth, exploration, establishment, maintenance, and decline, and these stages may in turn be subdivided into (a) fantasy, tentative and realistic phases of the exploratory stage, and (b) the trial and stable phases of the establishment stage.
6. The nature of the career pattern (that is, the occupational level attained and the sequence, frequency, and duration of trial and stable jobs) is determined by the individual's parental socio-economic level, mental ability, and personality characteristics, and by the opportunities to which he is exposed.
7. Development through the life stages can be guided partly by facilitating the process of maturation of abilities and interests and partly by aiding in reality testing and in the development of the self-concept.
8. The process of vocational development is essentially that of developing and implementing a self-concept; it is a compromise process in which the self-concept is a product of the interaction of inherited aptitudes, neural and endocrine make-up, opportunity to play various roles, and evaluation of the extent to which the results of role playing meet with the approval of superiors and fellows.
9. The process of compromise between individual and social factors, between self-concept and reality, is one of role playing, whether the role is played in fantasy, in the counselling interview, or in

real life activities such as school classes, clubs, part-time work, and
entry jobs.

10. Work satisfaction and life satisfaction depend upon the extent to
    which the individual finds adequate outlets for his abilities, interests,
    personality traits, and values; they depend upon his establishment in
    a type of work, a work situation, and a way of life in which he can
    play the kind of role which his growth and exploratory experiences
    have led him to consider congenial and appropriate (p.189–90).

Many have pointed out that Super's observations are no doubt true,
self-evident even, but do not make up a theory, or really provide new
insights into, or procedures for, vocational guidance.

3.2 THEORIES IN VOCATIONAL PSYCHOLOGY

There is no shortage of theory in vocational psychology, although there is
something of a dearth of well-designed, conducted and analysed studies to
test them. Indeed, there are so many theories in the area it is necessary to
group or classify them:

- *Developmental*. These are theories that focus on developmental stages,
  tasks or phases, typically as aspects of a life-long process. The individual
  has some measure of control and some freedom of choice. Environmental
  factors, however, play a part. Super, Ginzberg and Tiedeman are major
  representatives of this approach.
- *Needs*. Psychological needs are considered the paramount determinants.
  Roe, Holland and Hoppock are the principal spokesmen for this approach,
  although the importance of needs is acknowledged in the statements of all
  theorists.
- *Psychoanalytical*. Psychoanalytic vocational development theory deals
  with personality dynamics as interpreted by this psychological system.
  Bordin, Nachmann, Segal and Galinsky are perhaps best known for this
  approach.
- *Sociological*. Theorists in this group consider sociological factors to be
  major influences. Such factors include the home, school and community.
  Miller and Form, Hollingshead and Blau and others are well known for
  their theories in this area.
- *Decision making*. This is an emerging approach focusing on the way
  the individual utilizes information, self-knowledge and perceptions of
  rewards in making the successive choices involved in career development.
  All theories, however, focus on decisions and state with varying degrees
  of specificity how decisions are made. Some theorists, however, such as
  Gelatt, Hilton, and Hershenson and Roth consider decision making central
  to this approach.
- *Existential*. Comparatively little has been written from this point of view,

but there are some indications that it is an area of concern. Simon and Standley are the only theorists who use this approach exclusively, although much of existential psychology, as it relates to choice, becoming and fulfilling potentialities, inevitably touches upon career development.

Vocation psychology has been catholic and eclectic in its reliance on theories from other areas, especially cognitive and moral development, achievement motivation and decision-making skills. Yet it has developed various relatively new themes: the vocational behaviour of women, black and linguistic minorities, career development; worker adjustment problems (Fretz and Leong, 1982).

The importance of sex differences in occupational choice has received particular attention (Hollenbeck *et al.*, 1987). Recent issues have concerned sex differences in occupation perceptions and expectations (Bridges, 1988). Few studies have looked at sex and personality differences in occupational interests. Kirkcaldy (1985) is an exception. He found, perhaps quite predictably, that females displayed less interest in technical trades and scientific occupations, but more interest in design-oriented and social–educational occupations. Overall, females emerged as less likely to choose task-oriented jobs and more inclined to select creativity/expressive occupations, indicating a preference for more permissive, less structured occupations in environments allowing for artistic, emotional and introspective forms of expression.

There has also been a great deal of renewed interest in young people's occupational expectations (Crowley and Shapiro, 1982), although there is nothing new in this (Nelson, 1963). Studies have examined pre-school and elementary school children (Tremaine, Schau and Busch, 1982), secondary school children (Borgen and Young, 1982) as well as university students (Taylor, 1985).

Schemata's theory has been particularly useful in investigating stereotypes of occupations. Levy, Kaler and Schall (1988) asked 110 people to rate 14 occupations along various personality characteristics including introvert–extrovert, feminine–masculine and intelligent–non-intelligent. As a result of multi-dimensional scaling, two orthogonal factors emerged – achievements vs helping orientation and high–low educational level – and it seems possible to 'plot' people on each dimension.

Kline (1975) has questioned all theories in vocational psychology on the grounds, firstly, that the theories do not travel across culture and country and, secondly, that vocational (choice) theories should be part of more general theory:

> Thus the value of theories is suspect on the grounds that they are likely to be too specific and perhaps hindrances to the development of a more general theory of greater power which would predict far more developmental characteristics than just those of career choice (p.170).

He concluded his review thus:

Vocational guidance is seen as fitting men to jobs. It therefore involves man and job assessment. We have shown in the earlier sections of the book that psychometric tests are the best means of measuring abilities, personality and interest. Nevertheless none of these tests is perfectly reliable or valid so that mechanical interpretation of test scores and mathematical predictions of occupation success or satisfaction, in the individual case, is not possible. This means that interview techniques, although unsatisfactory, have to be used to amplify test scores and to obtain further information. It is admitted that job satisfaction and success involves more than merely being able to do the job or not. Nevertheless these other determinants of job satisfaction are seen as falling outside the purview of vocational guidance. Indeed, from the theories of occupational development we argue that there are two classes of occupational difficulty, one the province of vocational guidance, suitability to the job, and the other general occupational difficulties reflecting problems of mental health, the province of counselling or psychotherapy. From this we argue that vocational guidance officers need training in counselling but should restrict themselves to the first group of occupational difficulties, i.e. fitting men to jobs (p.225-6).

3.3 PERSON–JOB FIT

One of the oldest ideas in psychology is that productivity and satisfaction are directly related to the fit between the characteristics of individuals (ability, personality, temperament) and the demands of the job. A fit is where there is congruence between the norms and values of the organization and those of the person. This concept has both antecedents in selection and socializing processes, and consequences in job-related behaviour. Put more simply, the 'fit' idea is that the greater the match between the individual's needs and the environmental attributes, the greater will be the potential for the individual's satisfaction and believed performance.

Furnham (1987a) provided a simple illustration of this thesis using one famous individual difference (introversion–extraversion) and one dimension of work (whether people work in open- or closed-plan offices). Extraverts with high needs for arousal and stimulation perform well in an open-plan office with all the excitation of noise, movement and variety, but poorly in closely planned offices that may be relatively deprived of sensory stimulation. The opposite will, of course, be true of introverts whose high levels of cortical arousal mean that they will perform best under conditions of low arousal (that is, closed-plan offices) and vice versa (see Figure 3.1). Ignoring individual differences, then, may well obscure these differences. Organizations that attract extraverts (such as the media) may well increase productivity in open-plan offices, while those that attract introverts (such as universities) may have to provide places of limited external stimulation to ensure that work is done most efficiently or effectively. Of course, this is not to suggest that other features such as the task itself do not mediate between personality factors and office design, but rather that individual differences should not be ignored.

In a field experiment, Morse (1975) examined the effects of congruence between five personality dimensions and the degree of certainty (routineness and predictability) of clerical and hourly jobs on self-estimates of competence. He measured the following personality dimensions: tolerance for ambiguity, attitude toward authority, attitude toward individualism, cognitive complexity, and arousal-seeking tendency. New applicants who clustered on the high end of all or most of these dimensions were assigned to lower-certainty jobs, while those falling on the lower end were assigned to high-certainty jobs. The rest of the applicants were placed in jobs through the company's regular selection procedure. On the basis of ratings taken shortly after placement and eight months later, both congruence groups had significantly higher self-ratings of competence than the employees placed in the conventional manner. Furthermore, there were no differences in self-estimates of competence between the two job-congruent groups, even after eight months. It should be noted, however, that no measure of actual performance was taken, and it is not clear what construct, or set of constructs,

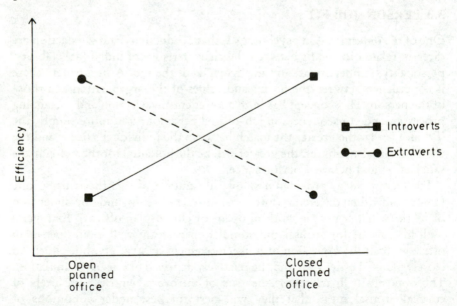

Figure 3.1 Hypothetical relationship between personality and efficiency in two types of office design

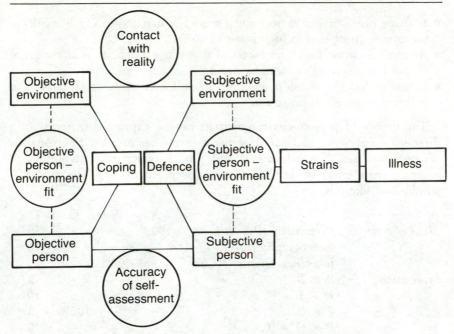

Figure 3.2 A model describing the effects of psychosocial stress in terms of fit between the person and the environment. Concepts within circles are discrepancies between the adjoining concepts. Solid lines indicate causal effects. Broken lines indicate contributions to interaction effects
Source: Furnham and Walsh (1991)

self-estimated competence actually refers to. All this seems to suggest the importance of 'fit'.

There is no doubt that personality factors are important in how people perform at work. But it is equally important to take into account environmental/organizational factors and the fit between person and environment. According to Caplan (1983), the theory of person–environment fit distinguishes between two types of fit: *needs* such as for achievement and values of the person, with the environmental *supplies* and *opportunities* to meet them, which in the employees' terms may be seen as the needs and supplies fit, or in the employer's terms as abilities and demands fit. The second type of fit distinguishes between objective and subjective person (P) and environment (E) characteristics – the correspondence between objective and subjective P is labelled *accuracy of self-assessment* (or self-awareness) while the correspondence between objective and subjective E is labelled *contact with reality* (or environmental awareness). This is illustrated in Figure 3.2.

Furthermore, the exact relationship between *fit* and its opposite, *strain*, is not clear. Caplan (1983) has mentioned three types of relationship:

- *U-shape curve*. Excesses (too much work) or deficits (too little work) in the environment lead to high levels of strain.
- *Asymptotic curve*. Either an excess of P (but not a deficit) or an excess of E (but not a deficit) can lead to strain.
- *Linear effect*. The absolute amount of one PE component (P relative to E) has a linear effect on strain.

The theory of person–environment fit can be expressed in terms of a three-way analysis of variance. Imagine that one has measured personality, demography (sex, age, education) and job characteristics attempting to ascertain their effect on job satisfaction (or productivity). The ANOVA would look like this:

		A	B	C	D
Main effects:	Personality (P)	100%	–	–	30
	Demography (D)	–	–	–	10
	Job characteristics (JC)	–	100%	–	20
Interaction:	P × D	–	–	–	5
	D × JC	–	–	–	10
	P × JC	–	–	100%	15
	P × D × JC	–	–	–	10
Error:		–	–	–	–

A, B, C and D refer to hypothetically different outcomes

One can calculate the amount of variance from main effects and interaction. Column A shows the hypothetical result showing that JS = f(P) or that job satisfaction is a function purely of personality. Alternatively, column B shows JS = f(JC) where job satisfaction is a function purely of the characteristic of the job. The person–job fit is shown in column C where JS = f(P × JC). Of course, it is probable that all the main effects and interactions account for some of the variance but the question concerns how much of the variance (see column D). This debate is of course very similar to the person–situation debate which concerned whether personality or situational factors determined social behaviour (Argyle, Furnham and Graham, 1981). In fact, O'Reilly (1977) adopted this approach when examining navy personnel. He found an interaction between *expressive* (or desiring achievement and self-actualization on the job) and *instrumental* (desiring job security and high financial reward) facts on job attitudes and performance. Caston and Branto (1985), on testing nurses, also found evidence of an interaction between intrinsic and extrinsic features.

Chatman (1989) has shown how one might develop (and test) specific hypotheses on the basis of the person–organization fit model. Here are nine propositions:

Proposition 1: When a person with discrepant values enters an organization characterized by strong values, the person's values are likely to change if that person is open to influence. Furthermore, this person is more likely to behave in accordance with specified norms of the organization.

Proposition 2: When a person with discrepant values enters an organization characterized by strong values, the person's values will not be expected to change if the person is not open to influence. This person would be likely to leave the organization.

Proposition 3: When a person with discrepant values enters an organization characterized by strong values and he/she scores high on self-efficacy or personal control, or when many new members enter at once who share the same values with one another, but not with the organization's values, norms will become more like the individual's over time.

Proposition 4: In organizations characterized by weak values (low crystallization and intensity), a person's values are likely to remain the same; that is, his/her values will not change as a function of organizational membership.

Proposition 5: Person–organization fit will be positively related to extra-role behaviour.

Proposition 6: Potential recruits who either initiate or are asked to spend more time with an organization and who are involved in a variety of organizational activities (e.g., interviews, phone calls, receptions) before being hired will have profiles of values similar to those of the firm upon entry.

Proposition 7: The behavioural outcome of high person–organization fit at entry will be that the person conforms to the pivotal norms of the organization. Further, changes in individual values will be negatively associated with high person–organization fit at entry.

Proposition 8: In organizations that have strong values, a greater variety and number of socialization processes, which include such activities as social and recreational events, formal training, and mentor programs, will be positively associated with person–organization fit and will bring about greater changes in individual values, resulting in a closer fit over time.

Proposition 9: At early stages in organization membership (0–1 year), selection experiences will explain more variance in person–organization fit than socialization experiences. However, as the recruit becomes 'less new' in the organization, the number and type of socialization experiences will explain more variance in person–organization fit than person variables will (p.337–8).

On attempting to measure PE fit, the two items (one measuring P and the other E) are usually commensurate. For instance, in a well-known vocational choice theory, Holland (1973) has suggested that one can characterize people by their resemblance to each of the six personality types: realistic, investigative, artistic, social, enterprising and conventional – which are a product of characteristic interaction among a variety of cultural and personal influences. As a result of developmental experiences, a person learns at first to prefer some activities rather than others; later, these activities become strong interests which lead to a particular group of competencies. Finally, when this has occurred, a person's interests and competencies create a particular disposition that leads him/her to perceive, think and act in ways which are more appropriate to some occupations than others. By comparing a person's attributes to those of each model type, one can determine which type he/she resembles most. The three types which the person most resembles are placed together in descending order to provide what is termed as the person's 'personality profile'.

There can be little doubt that there is a great deal of support, if fairly modest, for the PE fit theory. Studies have been done on people from widely different occupations (Harrison, 1978), in different countries (Tannenbaum & Kuleck, 1978) and on different age groups (Kahana, Liang and Felton, 1980). Furthermore, a large number of dependent variables – career change, labour turnover, performance – have been shown to be associated with PE fit (Kasl, 1973). For instance, Caplan *et al.* (1980) have shown that PE fit (but *not* P *or* E on its own) predicted depression in an occupationally stratified sample of 318 employees from 23 occupations. Similarly, Furnham and Schaeffer (1984) showed PE fit was positively associated with job satisfaction and negatively associated with mental health and vice versa. Henry (1989) found congruence was related to academic achievement in medical students. Using scores on Holland's inventory, students were classified congruent and incongruent and these were related predictable to overall and science grade-point average. As Caplan (1983) has concluded:

> In general, however, PE fit has explained only an additional 1 per cent to 5 per cent variance in strain. It has, consistently, doubled the amount of variance explained (p.42).

In an attempt to improve the predictive power of PE fit theory, Caplan (1983) has proposed an elaborated cognitive model with the concept of retrospective, non-retrospective and future, anticipated fit. He has also noted the importance of the buffering effects of social support on PE strain. These new developments seem particularly promising.

There is, then, a wealth of evidence to suggest that a positive fit between a person (their ability, needs, values etc) and his/her working environment (its demands, output) leads to satisfaction, good performance, and higher mental and physical health. However, as has been noted, one of the major problems of the PE fit literature has been the measurement of P and E. Although researchers have become more and more sophisticated in the identification and measurement of salient, work-related, individual differences, less developments have occurred on the description, measurement and established consequences of work situations. Researchers have used various psychological theories to test person–job congruence theories (Sims and Veres, 1987a,b).

This need for congruence between a person's interests, preferences and abilities, and the factors inherent in his/her environment forms the basis for a theory of vocational choice proposed by Holland (1973) and continually updated (Holland, 1985), which offers a measure of PE fit. Although a very popular and well researched theory, it does have its critics (Bates, Parker and McCoy, 1970; Schwartz, Andiappan and Nelson, 1986).

Recent work by Smart (1985) provided clear support for Holland's general premise that vocational type development is a function of a complex series of events resulting from family backgrounds, initial personal orientations, and occupational preferences and interactions with alternative environmental settings. The results showed that vocational type development is a function of a long series of life-history experiences that extend from individuals' family backgrounds through their experiences in further education, but that the magnitude, direction and method by which these influences are exerted differ dramatically among the three vocational types.

The environments in which people live and work can also be characterized according to their resemblance to six model environments corresponding to the six personality types stated earlier. Because the different types have differing interests, competencies and dispositions, they tend to surround themselves with people and situations congruent with their interests, capabilities and outlook on the world. People tend to search for environments that will let them exercise their skills and abilities and express their personality, i.e. social types look for social environments in which to work. It has, however, been suggested that some environments are more satisfying than others, irrespective of the personality of the person (Mount and Muchinsky, 1978), and that some jobs are simply more desirable than others (Furnham and Koritsas, 1990). Congruent environments provide job satisfaction for the subjects because they are among people with similar tastes and values to their own, and where they can perform tasks which they enjoy and are able to do so. Some environments, such as the social or investigative environment, contain people with whom a wide variety of individuals can get along. Mount and Muchinsky's (1978) results suggest that even if a person's aptitudes would be more congruent with a realistic or investigative environment, the person finds a social environment interesting enough to obtain satisfaction from it.

Smart (1985) pointed out that Holland's theory suggests that model/fit/congruent environments *reinforce* the characteristic predispositions and attitudes of their corresponding personality types. Using over 2000 graduates traced over the period 1971–80, evidence was found for the thesis.

For example, graduates educated in investigative environments have higher intellectual self-esteem scores, and those prepared in artistic environments have higher artistic self-esteem scores when pre- and post-university measures are controlled. And, predictably, it was possible to show that student satisfaction with the programme, the staff–student relations and peers, was a function of congruence (Smart, 1987).

In addition to the core idea of PE fit, some secondary concepts are proposed which can be used to determine more efficiently the goodness fit between P and E. Holland (1973) suggests that within a person or environment some pairs of 'types' are more closely related than others, and that the relationship within (which yields a measure of *consistency*) and between (which yields a measure of *congruency*) personality types or environments can be ordered according to a hexagonal model, in which distances within and between the personality profiles and job codes are inversely proportional to the theoretical relationships between them. These degrees of relatedness or *consistency* are assumed to affect job satisfaction and general well-being. The types are ordered in a particular manner (RIASEC) – realistic, investigative, artistic, social, enterprising and conventional. The letters are listed in rank order so that the type listed first is the type that the person most resembles. As a useful and approximate way of showing the degrees of relatedness among the six types, they are arranged at the vertices of a hexagon such that those which are closest are most similar. Thus, the investigative and artistic types are similar and hence closer together because both are concerned with intellectual pursuits, although in different ways – the investigative type is more methodological and data oriented while the artistic type is more spontaneous. By contrast, the investigative type, who is relatively asocial and analytical, differs most from the self-confident and persuasive enterprising type. Similarly, the spontaneous, disorderly and creative artistic type contrasts sharply with the self-controlled, conforming and unimaginative conventional type. By inference, intermediate proximities on the hexagon depict intermediate degrees of psychological similarity, although the correlated results do not totally support that particular shape.

A second concept is *differentiation*, which means that some people and environments are more clearly defined than others; for example, a person or environment may be dominated by a single type (well differentiated), or may resemble many types equally well (undifferentiated). The better the environment or person is differentiated, the more likely the person is to find a congruent job, and the more likely he/she will be to have high job satisfaction and good mental health as a result. Holland (1973) suggests that for inconsistent subjects, with little differentiation, an incongruent environment in which they work can become less stressful as they meet people involved in that environment and adopt their needs and values.

The third measure is *congruence* or compatibility, referring to a person and job type which are very similar, e.g. a realistic type in a realistic environment.

This measure is also derived from the hexagon model. Incongruence occurs when a type lives or works in an environment that provides opportunities and rewards foreign to a person's preferences and abilities, e.g. a realistic type in a social environment. Congruence is therefore the best measure of PE fit as defined by French *et al.* (1974). Strictly speaking, it is only congruence and not consistency or differentiation that measures person–environment fit. Consistency is a characteristic of either a person's profile or an environment, but it says nothing about the relationship between the two; nor does differentiation, which is only a measure of the 'peakedness' of a profile. The hexagon model is used in Holland's theory to derive both consistency and congruence but not differentiation. This model is given pictorially in Figure 3.3 including the correlational results from Holland (1973) and both studies reported by Furnham (Furnham and Schaeffer, 1984; Furnham and Walsh, 1991).

Holland's (1973, 1985) theory has probably attracted more empirical attention than any other theory in the area (Wigington, 1983). Most empirical studies have looked at the relationships between the three measures of PE fit and a specific occupational-dependent measure that would be predicted from Holland's model (Raphael and Gorman, 1986). Thus, many studies have looked at the relationships between PE fit and job satisfaction

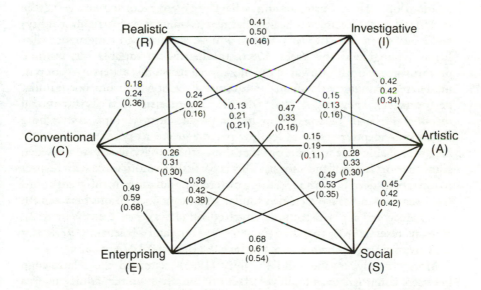

Figure 3.3 Correlations from the hexagonal model. The correlations in parentheses are from Holland's original work, the uppermost correlations are from Furnham and Schaeffer (1984) while the lower correlations are from Furnham and Walsh (1991)
Source: Furnham and Schaeffer (1984); Furnham and Walsh (1991)

(Mount and Muchinsky, 1978; Wiggins *et al.*, 1983; Furnham and Schaeffer, 1984; Smart, Elton and McLaughlin, 1986). However, a wide variety of other variables have been considered including mental health (Furnham & Schaeffer, 1984), Protestant work ethic beliefs (Furnham and Koritsas, 1990) and entrepreneurship (Venkatapathy, 1984). Finally, there have been a number of studies that have attempted to correlate other personality systems with Holland's (1973, 1985) six types (Perairo and Willerman, 1983; Costa, McCrae and Holland, 1984; Naylor, Care and Mount, 1986).

Perairo and Willerman (1983) compared Holland's typology and the 16PF and found, as expected, social and enterprising occupations (requiring sociability, enthusiasm, adventurousness) were associated with more extraversion than investigative and realistic occupations, which were more temperamentally independent. Costa *et al.* (1984) used the neuroticism, extraversion, openness model of personality and found openness to experience closely associated with investigative and artistic preference, and social and enterprising interests with extraversion. They argue that Holland's typology appears to lack 'neuroticism', one of the major dimensions identified in most personality research.

Whereas PE fit in this research is seen as the independent variable, the dependent variable has varied considerably. Most, but not all, of the studies in this area have yielded modest but significant (and predictable) relationships. Thus, Furnham and Schaeffer (1984) recorded $r = -0.24$ ($p < 0.01$; $N = 82$) for mental health (defined as minor psychiatric morbidity) and $r = 0.37$ ($p < 0.001$; $N = 82$) for job satisfaction and congruence. For Ferris, Youngblood and Yates (1985), the dependent variable was training performance and withdrawal of organizational newcomers. Person–group fit moderated training performance–withdrawal relationships but not training performance. They argue that whereas absenteeism is a dysfunctional response for high person–group fit, employee turnover appears to be a functional, adaptive response for low person–group fit types.

It is probably true to point out that these studies have nearly all provided some support for Holland's thesis. This is particularly noticeable with respect to job satisfaction. For instance, using different populations in different countries, various studies have yielded similar significant correlations between PE congruence and job satisfaction; Gottfredson (1978), $r = 0.28$ ($N = 112$); Wiggins *et al.* (1983), $r = 0.57$ ($N = 247$); Dore and Meacham (1973), $r = 0.38$ ($N = 54$); Furnham and Schaeffer (1984), $r = 0.37$ ($N = 82$).

More recently, Swaney and Prediger (1985) examined the relationship between congruence and job satisfaction for 1688 young adults over a six-year period. They found a modest but significant relationship that was higher in certain samples. Smart *et al.* (1986) confirmed the positive relationship between congruence and satisfaction, but found gender-specific differences with congruence being related to extrinsic job satisfaction in males and overall job satisfaction in females. Heesacker, Elliott and Howe (1988) used two job satisfaction measures in examining the relationship between congruence and satisfaction, and productivity in rural factory workers. One satisfaction measure showed a significant correlation with congruence ($p <$ 0.03), and weakly predicted the other ($p < 0.09$). Overall, 'social' subjects were most satisfied followed by conventional and realistic types and then the lower three types. In accordance with the theory, social, conventional and realistic types were more productive (and satisfied) than the other types, but the types were not related to either absenteeism or insurance claims. But overall the results did not support the thesis that congruence is related to increased satisfaction and productivity.

Elton and Smart (1988) also provided modest support for Holland's theory by demonstrating, in a large sample of nearly 2000 young people, that those at the highest level of congruence tended to be less dissatisfied than those at the lowest level of congruence. The theory has been applied to many groups in many countries including Indian entrepreneurs (Venkatapathy, 1984) and American college-educated working black men and women (Walsh, Bingham and Sheffey, 1986). The theory has also been applied to leisure activities (Taylor *et al.*, 1979).

In two studies, Furnham and Walsh (1991) looked at the association between fit and absenteeism. Contrary to the predictions made, those more congruent (and consistent) with their environments had significantly more occasions of absence, and almost a significant number of days off, than those who were incongruent. Although these coefficients reduced to $r = 0.11$ and $r = 0.25$ respectively when sex, grade and job frustration are partialled out, there was still no evidence to support the hypothesis. The second hypothesis anticipated a negative correlation between congruency and frustration. The coefficient of $r = -0.49$ indicated that greater congruency is related to lower frustration rates. On the basis of the first two predictions, it was further hypothesized that absenteeism would be positively correlated with frustration. Values of $r = -0.15$ and $r = -0.12$ ($p > 0.05$) indicate the absence of any significant relationship between these variables. Congruent subjects were thus less frustrated and more often absent than less congruent subjects, but absence rates were not linked to frustration. It may have been that subjects were less frustrated because they were taking more days off, as opposed to the more intuitive hypothesis that job frustration leads to absenteeism, but the third finding, frustration not being related to absenteeism, precludes such a suggestion. The perhaps counter-intuitive conclusion offered by Furnham and Walsh (1991) was that job frustration does not lead to absenteeism, and that congruency implies less frustration but more occasions of absenteeism.

A second study looking at the relationship between fit and stress also proved equivocal. The results provide some support for the hypothesis that there would be significant negative correlates between PE fit and stress. It was predicted that all three of the Holland (1973) measures

– particularly congruence – would be. However, neither the congruence nor the differentiation measure was significantly associated with stress as predicted. Three possible factors could have accounted for these results. Firstly, various methodological problems may have accounted for these non-significant findings like the psychometric properties of the stress measure, the size and stratification of the sample etc. Although these objections may be raised, it should be pointed out that other studies using similar measures and samples yielded predictably significant findings. Secondly, it may be that a set of other important mediating variables, such as workload, time pressures, unemployment statistics etc, actually moderate the relationship between the PE congruency and stress such that the extant relationship disappears. This might well be true, but it is not clear why it should be more true of dependent variables such as stress compared say to satisfaction, nor is it clear why consistency did show a significant correlation if moderator or intervening variables were changing the relationship.

Apart from methodological issues, Furnham and Walsh (1991) provided two possible explanations relevant to much of the work in this case. Firstly, the concept of congruence appears too vague. Indeed, Joyce (1982) has already subdivided it into three areas for research purposes – namely effect congruence, general congruence and functional congruence. He found that different variables, e.g. performance and satisfaction, were explained by different models. Among the most recent research in the area is that by Payne (1988), who also divided up congruence. Indeed, the same objection may be profitably applied to both consistency and differentiation. In other words, Holland's (1985) conception of congruence may be too vague or in fact multi-dimensional rather than undimensional as presently conceived. Furthermore, although cross-sectional studies such as those reported here may serve as validity tests for the theory, only longitudinal studies can determine whether PE fit or misfit is a cause or effect of other psychological or demographic measures.

Secondly, it may be too much to expect that PE fit variables alone can account for much of the variance in understanding behaviour at work. Absenteeism, frustration, satisfaction and stress are caused by numerous sociological, organizational and psychological factors, only one of which is PE fit. Certainly, partial correlation (particularly on sex, grade and class) significantly changed the size of the correlation, although others were no doubt important. But just as it may be unwise or indeed naïve to expect PE fit variables alone to predict specific work behaviours, it is equally unwise to neglect them in any analysis of the problem.

There have been a number of serious but not damning criticisms of Holland's work. For instance, Schwartz et al. (1986) have argued that it is achievement orientation (and not person–job congruence) that is responsible for the positive association between academic achievement and congruence. Thus, in an occupation that is characterized by low achieving types, those who are congruent (those with a low-achieving typing) have lower annual incomes than do those who are incongruent.

Nevertheless, Holland's work stands out above nearly all other theories in vocational psychology, which probably accounts for the reason why it has attracted so much attention. From the perspective of the personality theorist, it seems a pity that Holland's *six types* have not been 'married to' the 'big five' emerging from recent meta-reviews in personality psychology. However, it is possible that one may begin to classify occupations and vocations in terms of the big five, just as Holland has done in terms of his six types, so that both people and jobs are described in the same terminology. When this has been done, and only then, can the potentially very interesting concept of fit be fully investigated.

Not all congruence studies have used Holland's typology. For instance, Morse and Caldwell (1979) measured six personality variables: tolerance for ambiguity; attitude to authority; attitude to individualism; need for achievement; need for affiliation, and machiavellianism. They also measured six job environmental factors labelled: structure, standards, responsibility, warmth, support and identity. They then derived a matrix of hypotheses reduced to two basic suppositions:

- Individual satisfaction in task group performance will be positively related to the total amount of congruence between personality and environmental characteristics.
- More of the variance in individual satisfaction in task group performance can be accounted for by the congruence or fit of personality and environment than either alone or added without the concept of fit.

Both of the hypotheses received support and the authors note that rather than there being an ideal organizational climate, the 'ideal' or 'optimum' climate probably differs from individual to individual. Clearly, the concept of 'fit' remains a useful theoretical heuristic in understanding individual differences in vocational choice and satisfaction.

3.4 EXPECTANCY THEORY AND OCCUPATIONAL CHOICE

Vroom's (1964) application of expectancy–value theory to vocational psychology presupposed the generally accepted, underlying principle of maximization of expected value of various outcomes. Expectancy–value theory assumes that the strength of a tendency to act in a certain way depends on the strength of an *expectancy* that the act will be followed by a given consequence (or outcome) and on the *value* or attractiveness of that consequence (or outcome) specifically to the actor. Typically, the two components are seen as combining in a multiplicative manner. This basic formulation has been central, and has proved useful, to many of the major theories of learning, decision making, attitude formulation and motivation.

Occupational preference is viewed as a function of attraction (occupational valence, V_j) to an occupation such that:

$$V_j = \sum_{i=1}^{n} (V_i I_{ij}),$$

where V_j is the value of occupation j, V_i is the value of outcome i, I_{ij} is the cognived instrumentality of occupation j for the attainment of outcome i and n is the number of outcomes. Occupations that are most instrumental for important rewards and outcomes will naturally have the most positive occupational valence and will be preferred over other occupations.

The second model predicts force toward, or *choice of*, occupations. The force on a person to choose an occupation is seen as a function of the valence of an occupation and that person's expectation that this occupation is attainable. Specifically:

$$F_j = E_j V_j$$

where F_j is the force to choose occupation j, E_j is the strength of the expectancy that the choice of occupation j will result in attainment and V_j is the valence of occupation j. Essentially, the model states that an individual will choose the occupation with the greater F_j or force level.

Within the past 20 years there have been several articles reviewing the empirical research relating to the success of expectancy–value theory at predicting occupational preferences and choices (Wanous, Keon and Latack, 1983; Brooks and Betz, 1990). These reviews have analysed the empirical results from differing perspectives, and the conclusions within and between reviews are predictably equivocal.

Wanous *et al.* (1983) reviewed 16 studies and found a within-person correlation between a valence × instrumentality index and an overall measure of occupational attractiveness to be 0.72. This means that the average 'hit rate' is 63.4 per cent. More recently, Brooks and Betz (1990) found the expectancy × valence interaction accounted for between 12 per cent and 41 per cent of the tendency of introductory psychology students to choose an occupation.

A particular concern of reviewers of this literature has been the nature of the analysis used by researchers in the field, and its adequacy in light of the various definitions of motivation. Vroom (1964) proposed that the expectancy – value model be studied in the form of a *within-subjects* framework. Many initial tests of the model used a *between-subjects* analysis which is thought to contribute to the equivocal results often reported (Zedeck, 1977).

A second inconsistency within the expectancy–value theory literature is with respect to the form of the expectancy model and the relationship of the scores that it yields to effort and behavioural criteria. It remains unclear at this point whether the components of the model should be combined additively, multiplicatively, or whether they should be combined at all.

A recent development in the expectancy–value theory field has been the attempt to apply a decision-modelling approach to examinations of the theory. Behavioural decision theory has been used to study human decision-making procedures.

Researchers in decision-modelling frequently model decision making via the general linear model:

$$Y_j = \sum_{i=1}^{n} (B_i X_{ij}), \quad j = 1 \ldots m,$$

where Y_j is the decision, B_i is the beta-weight or value attributed to outcome i (these beta-weights are typically derived from regressing Y_j on X_{ij}), X_{ij} is the likelihood that outcome i will be present in choice j, n is the number of outcomes considered and m is the number of occupations considered.

Conceptual imitations between the linear model used in decision modelling and the valence model used by expectancy–value suggest that the decision-modelling approach be used in expectancy–value theory studies. A comparison between expectancy–value theory and decision modelling illustrate the reason for this suggestion. In expectancy–value theory, a V_j value is computed for each potential act or choice of acts available to the subject. It can be seen that the Y_j, B_i and X_{ij} of the decision-modelling formulae correspond to the V_j, V_i and I_{ij} of the valence equation.

There is a general difference in the manner in which these variables are measured. In expectancy–value theory, the subject must provide evaluative responses of V_i and I_{ij}; that is, the assumption is made that he/she has sufficient information to start the instrumentality and *value* associated with each particular outcome. Since there are many different ways used to measure V_i and I_{ij}, there is confusion as to reliability and comparability. The decision-modelling approach, however, focuses on an individual's response; either a specific behaviour or a behavioural intention. The V_i of the model is incorporated in the Y_j formulation but is inferred from the computed beta-weights. An important distinction here, then, is between the initial objectives of the two models. Expectancy–value theory may be seen as an attempt to predict choice behaviour from information provided *purely by the subject*. Decision modelling was not, at least originally, intended to predict either behavioural intent or behaviour itself, but rather attempted to infer a *person's policy or strategy* for using various kinds of information to arrive at some sort of judgement. Prediction is accomplished by applying the inferred policy to new information on the assumption that the individual will continue to use that policy for subsequent judgements. Thus, Zedeck (1977) argued that a decision-modelling approach could act both as an extension of, and improvement upon, the expectancy–valence theory approach to motivation and choice behaviour.

The paradox of both expectancy–valence and decision-modelling approaches is that while both take into consideration individual differences, they do not take into consideration systematic individual differences. Thus, neither expectancy nor valence is seen to be related to stable, predictable individual differences. This is not impossible to do, however. There are many measures like locus of control, the Protestant work ethic and need for achievement which are clearly related to expectations of success or failure. Similarly, there are various measures of valence that allow people to be categorized along various dimensions. As there are strong theoretical underpinnings of both, it seems a logical step to develop an individual difference model of expectancy–valence theory.

3.5 PERSONALITY PROFILES OF 'SUCCESS' IN VARIOUS OCCUPATIONS

Is it worthwhile using one of the many standard (but well validated) personality questions (16PF; Myers–Briggs, EPQ) in vocational guidance? The answer must be yes if the test reliably discriminates between occupational groups on theoretically acceptable grounds. Hence, one can build up an *occupational profile* which shows the mean score (and standard deviation/or range) for the particular occupational group. The more a person's score resembles those of a given group profile, the more he/she is for membership of that occupational group. However, the profiles must be based on an adequately sampled group which has been selected against some robust and sensitive measure of occupational success. The profiles are the mean score for each different occupational group, on each factor/dimension, and the degree of fitness must be based on the pattern similarity. This may be on a correlation or other statistical coefficient (multiple point–biserial regression equation) or some mile-based system.

Some test developers have been more interested than others in making their tests useful for vocational guidance. Both Cattell *et al.* (1970) and Eysenck and Eysenck (1975) have published occupational profiles, although not all are based on sufficiently large samples. One of the personality traits most frequently used in this area is extraversion.

There have been various other 'theoretical systems' that have variables closely akin to extraversion, such as sensation-seeking or stimulus screening. The arousal level hypothesis – the idea that performance has an inverted U-relationship to arousal – suggested that performance is optimal when arousal is intermediate, but hindered when extremely high or low. The thesis has been tested successfully in various work settings. For instance, Russell and Mehrabian (1975) showed arousal-seeking tendencies interacted with the desire to work in various settings.

Various attempts have been made to ascertain the profile of various professional groups. While the concept is straightforward – namely to describe the profile of successful people – the following factors are not clear:

- How success is measured – whether the criterion or criteria are robust.
- Who the comparison group is – those that fail, those that are average.
- What measure of personality to choose – what the criteria of the test are.
- How the profile is validated – once this is 'discovered' how is it validated.

Nevertheless, despite all of these problems, many studies exist for different occupational groups. Stevens, Hemstreet and Gardner (1989) used the CPI, 16PF and EPPS to discriminate those coastguard cadets who resigned from those that graduated. Their results are given in Table 3.1.

Table 3.1 Mean scores of scales that differentiate female cadets who resign from those who graduate

Scale	Resigned	Graduated	t	p
CP Capacity for status	40.21	49.86	−2.13	0.02
CP Sense of well-being	41.75	45.22	−1.60	0.10
CP Good impression	43.06	46.19	−1.69	0.05
CP Achievement via conformance	40.64	48.14	−3.26	0.005
CP Intellectual efficiency	48.51	51.14	−1.62	0.05
CP Flexibility	52.12	48.10	2.27	0.02
PF Warm-hearted	9.67	8.28	2.05	0.02
PF Abstract	7.14	8.42	−1.69	0.05
PF Emotionally stable	9.83	12.28	−2.02	0.02
PF Assertive	8.50	11.17	−2.04	0.02
PF Enthusiastic	10.61	12.30	−1.46	0.10
PF Self-sufficient	6.58	8.42	−1.76	0.05
PF Self-controlled	9.14	11.14	−2.41	0.01
PF Driven	9.06	11.42	−1.97	0.025
EP Achievement	52.67	55.88	−2.10	0.025
EP Exhibition	51.19	48.75	1.73	0.10
EP Dominance	51.08	53.77	−1.52	0.10
EP Heterosexuality	49.92	46.00	1.65	0.05
EP Aggression	49.97	46.50	1.90	0.05

CP: California Personality Inventory, PF: Cattell 16 Personality Inventory, EP: Edwards Personal Preference Scale, *t*: test, *p*: probability
Source: Stevens *et al.* (1989)

Elton and Rose (1973) compared the personalities of university students with, as opposed to those without, work experience. Those with more experience were more sociable, emotionally sensitive, tolerant of ambiguity, ambitious and aggressive, and possessed wide-ranging academic interests. Although they realized that their research is, at best, preliminary, they believe it could highlight the concept of 'work personality': a hypothetical construct which attempts to link motivation, ability and previous experience.

Various personality tests have been used to test specific occupational groups: to see if they have distinct profiles; to see if they can predict occupational success; to see if they can discriminate between success and failure on the job. Two rather different examples are considered here: police officers and medical students.

Police Officers

Burbeck and Furnham (1985) examined the fairly extensive literature on psychological testing among police officers. As well as looking at tests of values (the Rokeach Value Survey) and conservatism/authoritarianism (Californian F; Wilson–Patterson), they looked at the EPI, the 16PF and the MBTI.

Eysenck's Personality Inventory

A good deal of research on the difference between police officers and the general population relies on normative data for its comparisons. Potter and Cook's work (1977, reported in Colman and Gorman, 1982) described in a study by Clucas (Colman and Gorman, 1982) found 219 police officers in a northern British police force to be relatively extraverted, tough-minded and conservative compared to normative data tested on Eysenck's Social and Political Attitude Inventory, Eysenck's Personality Inventory and some other tests. Gudjonsson and Adlam (1983), working with eight British police forces, administered Eysenck's Personality Questionnaire (which measures extraversion, neuroticism, psychoticism and lying) and Eysenck's I5 (which measures impulsiveness, venturesomeness and empathy) to 84 recruits, 84 probationary constables with about 18 months' experience, 73 experienced constables with a mean length of service of 19.9 years, and 112 officers of the rank of inspector or above with a mean length of service of 19.5 years. The recruits were highly extraverted, impulsive and venturesome when their scores were compared to normative data. Their empathy scores did not differ from the normative scores, but the empathy scores for the other three groups were significantly lower than the norm. The experienced constables and senior officers were significantly less impulsive and venturesome than the norm and the recruits. The probationers, experienced constables and senior officers did not differ from the norm for extraversion. Unfortunately (unlike the EPQ data), the normative data for Eysenck's I5 is not scaled for age, so the changing results could be an artifact of age, rather than the result of socialization, as one would expect to find decreasing impulsiveness and venturesomeness with increasing age. However, the reducing extraversion and empathy scores seem likely to be caused by socialization, as they occur by 18 months' service.

Burbeck and Furnham (1984) found that 319 applicants to the Metropolitan police displayed much higher levels of extravert stability on Eysenck's Personality Inventory than the norm. These results were obtained before the candidates were selected and included those who were turned down, which would be evidence for the predispositional model. However, because the test was administered at the time of the selection interview, the authors had reason to believe that there was extensive 'faking good' on the part of the applicants.

Cattell's 16PF

Gibson (1982) used Cattell's 16PF to test 98 constables with 18 months' service in northern England. He found that constables had a distinct profile on the 16 factors and were generally more intelligent, more emotionally stable, more enthusiastic, adventurous, dependent on groups and relaxed than the general population. Few other studies appear to have used this measure.

Myers–Briggs Type Indicator

Research by Males (1983) on a sample of 171 British officers of chief superintendent, superintendent and chief inspector ranks showed that they were predominantly ISTJ (38.5 per cent) and ESTJ (29 per cent) types. Such types may have difficulty with sensitive handling of other people and lack innovative skills. Males points out that where a high proportion of people in an organization see the world in the same way, a strong organizational subculture is likely to develop, and with these particular personality types which he has found, it will be resistant to change.

There are a variety of problems with the research just discussed which make its direct application to selection procedures difficult. First, the results are often equivocal, and it is not clear why different samples, instruments and nationalities could all account for these different findings. Often, there are methodological weaknesses with the controls not being properly matched, or comparisons are made with normative data which are not directly comparable, usually because of age differences.

Second, it does not follow that serving police officers display certain characteristics and that those characteristics are in existence at the time of selection. Much of the research quoted is concerned with answering the question: Is there a personality type which makes people particularly likely to join the police force (predispositional model), or are people who join the police force much the same as everybody else but develop a certain personality type over a period of time as a result of the job that they do (socialization model)? There are also the possibilities that, although a wide range of personality types seek to become police officers, only a certain type is selected, or that, although quite a range of personality types join the force, selective wastage caused by the nature of the job results in the departure of non-conforming types. These issues have been discussed at considerable length in the comprehensive reviews of the literature by Balch (1972) and Lefkowitz (1975). Lefkowitz concluded that 'the data substantiate, with some qualifications, the existence of a non-pathological "model police personality"' (p.3) determined by a combination of predispositional and socialization factors. Balch concluded that 'there is simply not enough good evidence to support or refute any side of the controversy' (p.119). If it is the case that a police personality develops as a result of socialization, this is of no use for selection purposes, for the characteristics will not be salient at the time of selection. Because the evidence, one way or the other, is inconclusive, attempting to select recruits who display 'a police personality' may simply not be feasible.

Finally, even if there is such a thing as 'a police personality', and that is by no means proven as shown by the differing results of the research and the varied arguments presented by Balch (1972) and Lefkowitz (1975), it does not follow that it is desirable in candidates to the force. For instance, it has been suggested that police officers tend to be authoritarian (Colman and Gorman, 1982). It by no means follows that police forces should attempt to select such candidates. Research comparing good with bad police officers is likely to indicate which are desirable characteristic traits to be looked for in recruit selection.

Other Tests

Spielberger (1979) concluded from his assessment of police selection techniques that value, attitude and interest profiles of police officers differ from those of the general population but do not seem to predict success in the job. Interest and personality measures are not correlated to academy grades but are correlated with instructor and peer evaluation of general suitability for police work, and with supervisor ratings of probationers.

In a study by Blum (1964), 87 police officer recruits were given the MMPI, Rorschach Test, SVIB, Machover Draw a Picture Blank and an 'F' Scale, and the Otis Intelligence Test Performance on ten variables was measured seven years later using data from personnel folders. The magnitude of the relationship between any one psychological characteristic and any one work measure was low and never accounted for more than 22 per cent of the observed variation. The highest correlation described the relationship between evidence of misconduct and tests indicative of personality disorder, which is what one might have predicted.

Lester (1983) also points out that 'there is not much evidence that psychological testing has any use in predicting performance as a police officer' (p.53), and quotes research by Cohen and Chaiken who found that using the best predictors they could find for promotion they could only account for 10 per cent of the variation.

Levy (1967) also came to the conclusion that psychological tests seemed to have little predictive value. She decided to study the personnel file of 4500 law enforcement officers in 14 police jurisdictions to see whether she 'could find any known and recorded preappointment factors which would significantly discriminate between those who left their positions because of occupational inadequacies and those who were considered adequate or successful' (p.265). Officers who had been dismissed or whose resignations had been requested were classified as failures. Officers who had left for other reasons were called 'non-failures', and serving officers were described as 'current'. A total of 140 variables appeared in at least 50 per cent of the records and were included in the analysis.

Levy found that the failures show a pattern of greater mobility and uncontrolled impulsivity than the others. They tended to be better educated, younger at the time of appointment, to have had a greater number of marriages, more job mobility, and more convictions for traffic violations. She also concluded that 'those who leave police employment with a clean record may be affected by the stresses inherent in their new occupations'.

It should now be obvious that comparing the performance of successful and unsuccessful officers has not revealed any clearcut differences that would be of use in the selection procedure. One problem seems to be that law enforcement in different types of police force, different geographic areas and different countries are not directly comparable, and it is not necessarily to be expected that one common denominator will be found.

Second, different researchers have used differing, and not necessarily equivalent, criteria of success and failure. The following are all considered failures: candidates who are rejected (Saxe and Reiser, 1976); recruits who fail their training (Balch, 1977); officers who leave the force (Levy, 1967; Saxe and Reiser, 1976); officers who are required to resign (Levy, 1967); and serving officers who are rated unsatisfactory (Blum, 1964). Spielberger (1979) points out that the measures of performance which are often used to identify unsatisfactory officers are not always reliable. Absenteeism, sickness, complaints, requirements to resign, commendations and numbers of arrests are nearly always too low in frequency to be of a great deal of use. They may also vary between busy urban and rural areas. Promotion is not a good measure either because a good officer will not necessarily be promoted or seek promotion.

Clearly, what is needed is a multi-dimensional, reliable and robust set of criterion measures on which police officers could be judged by superiors, peers and junior officers. Discriminant analysis can then be used to determine which factors discriminate between successful and unsuccessful police officers.

Medical Students

There is a fairly considerable literature on medical students' beliefs about, knowledge of, and choices in medicine. There are also a number of studies comparing attitudes, beliefs, and knowledge before and after specialist courses or clerkships in the various specialist areas of medicine. Many reports exist of medical students' choices of proposed future specialities as they rate to their personality. However, this literature is not without its critics.

As Fishman and Zimet (1967) point out, this interest emerges partly from the fact that despite being fairly homogeneous in background and socialization, students end up in highly dissimilar vocations:

> There is no other field where the congruence of a long-term educational experience is so great but where differences in the actual work performed are so striking. The psychiatrist and the surgeon, the public health officer and the laboratory researcher, and the pathologist and the paediatrician work in very different kinds of settings and very different kinds of skills and interests (p.524).

There is, however, no agreement on why medical students prefer or choose one speciality over another. Most of the work in this field has been instigated by researchers in one of the less prestigious or declining areas of medicine (i.e. psychiatry), but even there the reasons remain unclear.

All sorts of variables have been considered as they relate to career choice or beliefs about the various specialities. These include personality (especially anxiety, authoritarianism, dominance); demographic factors (religion, socio-economic class, size of home community); sex and marital status; and beliefs about various features of the speciality (efficacy, patients etc).

Some attempts (Furnham, 1986a,b) have been made to develop inventories specific to the medical profession (Savickas, 1984). But the usual approach has been to use standard questionnaires.

Bartnick et al. (1985) administered the CPI to four years of medical students at the beginning and end of their medical school training. Their hypothesis was that career choice could be predicted from the CPI data but it was not confirmed, possibly because they used the wrong test.

Zeldow et al. (1985) used a whole battery of psychological tests to try to predict adjustment in medical students. They were tested at the beginning of their course and eight months later. The independent variable was a measure of masculinity–femininity while the dependent variable was depression, neuroticism, locus of control, satisfaction etc. The results showed, quite dramatically, that femininity was associated with depression, pleasure capacity, extraversion, neuroticism, interpersonal satisfaction, concern for the opinions of others, and humane attitudes toward patient care. They believe that masculinity, femininity and androgynous scores may be very helpful in predicting medical student success, particularly the latter.

Clearly, attempts to find the 'profile' of specialist doctors has, at this stage, not met with much success.

3.6 PERSONALITY, ACADEMIC PERFORMANCE AND VOCATIONAL IMPLICATION

Various studies of personality and education have important but often neglected implications for vocational guidance. Scholarly extraverts seem superior to introverts in the pre-school and primary school ages, up until perhaps 12–15 years of age. At that point, a transition occurs, and beyond that level introverts are superior to extraverts. However, the correlation between extraversion and educational achievement is consistently positive before age 12 or 13, and consistently negative after age 15 or 16. Literature reviews by Entwistle (1972) and Anthony (1973) each support this conclusion. Entwistle found extraverts, particularly stable extraverts, to be superior to introverts up until age 13 in studies using Eysenck's scale, and until age 12 or 14 in studies using the Cattell scales. Research using both scales shows introverts to be superior beyond that age level. For instance, using university students, Entwistle *et al.* (1972) found extraversion and neuroticism correlated negatively with measures of grade attainment, study methods and self-ratings of industry. Bennett and Youngman (1973) have argued that extraversion and neuroticism relate clearly to adjustment and compliance, and then to educational attainment.

Anthony (1973) cites cross-sectional studies that indicate that extraversion increases in the general population until about age 14 and then begins to decline from that point throughout the life-span. On the other hand, development of ability follows a linear progression, increasing until the early 20s before levelling off. The superiority of the extraverted child arises from the fact that he/she is an early developer both in terms of personality and ability; as long as both lines are increasing in parallel fashion, say up to age 13, there is a positive relationship between extraversion and ability. At that point, however, extraversion reaches a peak and begins to decline, whereas ability continues to increase so that beyond the age of 13 or 14 the person who is more advanced in both personality and ability progressively becomes more able and less extraverted, thus the negative correlation between the extraversion and ability beyond age 14. This explanation, however speculative, highlights the important fact that we cannot simply assume that the same individuals who are introverted at age 9 and performing more poorly are the ones who are also more introverted at age 16 and performing better. Anthony suggests that those who are introverted at an earlier age and performing more poorly are the ones who are more extraverted at the age of 16 (because they reach their peak later) and continue to perform poorly. Thus, whereas one position holds that the level of extraversion and introversion remains the same and the academic performance changes, the other position assumes that the level of performance stays the same and the degree of extraversion–introversion changes.

In a study of the reading achievements of eight-year-olds, Elliott (1972) determined that the positive relationship between extraversion and reading achievement at this age level was not a function of either chronological age differences among the eight-year-olds or mental age (IQ) differences. With these two factors partialled out, the explanation of the superiority of extraverts over introverts lay within the interaction between personality and educational practices. Extraversion was related to reading achievement in three restricted samples: one based on similarity of chronological age between 8 years 6 months and 8 years 11 months; another based on similarity of mental age of IQ; and a third based on similarity of reading age. With each of the three held constant, extraversion could be related to the other two in each sample and thus clarify the relationship. The high positive relationship of extraversion to reading age remained even when chronological age and IQ were controlled for, but the reverse was not true. Therefore, the reading superiority of extraverts was not a function of either chronological age or IQ differences.

In another study of younger students, the correlation between extraversion and both intelligence and achievement was consistently positive but small. White, black and Mexican-American students in the fourth through the eighth grades (i.e. 10–14 years) in California were given a battery of tests, including the Junior Eysenck Personality Inventory, at the beginning of the school year and tested by the Stanford Achievement Test at the end of the school year (Jensen, 1973).

A detailed longitudinal study of 345 boys, covering the ages of 11–15, by Banks and Finlayson (1973) compared school examination performance in relation to Junior Eysenck Personality Inventory scores. In general, introverts performed better, especially in two schools where ability and aspiration levels were higher. And the relationship between introversion and performance increased with age, particularly for students with higher neuroticism scores. Results were clearer when extreme over- and under-achievers were considered. There were two clusters of variables in the study that were related to successful academic performances. One centred around achievement motivation, whereas introversion was an important element of the other. Included with introversion were (1) intellectual curiosity, (2) homework orientation, (3) parental warmth and support, combined with (4) dependence and conformity on the part of the boy, and (5) a slower development of interest in girls.

A study by Seddon (1975) used 741 chemistry students aged between 15 and 19 years at various educational levels. Employing multiple-regression analysis, he found that extraversion–introversion was not related to IQ but was related to achievement in chemistry. For the sample as a whole, there was a negative correlation of extraversion with chemistry achievement, an indication that for these students the transition had already occurred. There was also an interaction between extraversion and age that indicated that the negative correlation of extraversion with performance increased at each age level so that the prediction of the superiority of introverts over extraverts continued to increase with each year of experience. A few weeks after this data was collected, the same subjects were exposed to a nine-session, self-instructional chemistry programme (Seddon, 1977). According to pre- and post-treatment scores on a background chemistry test, there was an interaction, as in the earlier data, between extraversion and chronological age.

Goh and Moore (1978) found generally negative correlations between extraversion and grade-point average among 78 university students, 48 vocational technical institute students and 49 high-school students, in the United States. There were no differences between groups on EPQ extraversion scores, indicating that differential correlations were not the result of different levels of extraversion at the three educational levels. The negative correlation between extraversion and achievement was significant only at the university level and was much higher for a group of science students than for social studies students.

One study conducted with black Ugandans (Honess and Kline, 1974) and another with South Africans (Orpen, 1976) seemed to pinpoint the transition point at a slightly later age. With black rural Ugandans aged 14, 15 and 17, the only relationship between extraversion and achievement occurred in the younger girls, for whom there were positive correlations with three of the five academic subjects used. Orpen compared rural South African blacks and Afrikaans-speaking rural whites. The results were the same for both groups. In a group of 14-year-olds of both races, the correlation between extraversion and achievement was positive, whereas in a group of similar students of both races at the college level the relationship between extraversion and year-end academic achievement was negative.

In general, however, studies conducted in other cultures indicate that either the transition to introvert superiority occurs considerably later or that there is simply no relationship between extraversion–introversion and scholastic performance in those cultures. Paramesh (1976) found no relationship between extraversion or neuroticism and performance in seven different subject areas among 155 high-school boys in India, and Mehryar et al. (1973) found no relationship between college achievement and extraversion in Iran. They correlated an Iranian version of the Eysenck Personality Inventory as well as a psychoticism scale with college entrance exams. Only a small positive relationship of extraversion with IQ, and a relationship between extraversion and either maths or natural science scores, were found for either females or males.

Shadbolt (1978) carried out two experiments. In the first, 211 students were taught introductory genetics with the aid of programmed text. In the second, 145 students of the history of education served as subjects. Personality was measured by the Eysenck Personality Inventory. In both experiments, students were exposed to either a structured–deductive or an unstructured–inductive teaching approach. Based on post-test assessments, there was an interactive effect of extraversion and teaching strategy in Experiment 1, and an interaction between neuroticism and strategy in Experiment 2. In the first case, introverts performed better with a structured approach; in the second, neurotics performed better with a structured approach. Results showing the same trend are reported by Rowell and Renner (1975), who examined the performance of masters level education students in Australia in four different courses. Unexpected scores on the Eysenck Personality Inventory were unrelated to a preference for written essay work versus formal examinations, as well as performance. Extraverts outperformed introverts in only one course, educational sociology, and the authors surmised that this may have been the result of a lower degree of class structure in that course.

Recent studies have even shown that there is a clear and interpretable link between personality variables (introversion, neuroticism and psychoticism) and occupational interests among psychiatric patients.

Other attempts to relate personality differences to teaching variables have not met with similar success. Robertson (1978) was interested in attention deployment in grammar school students; attention deployment was defined as whether they chose to study only one or more than one topic simultaneously in a programmed study of probability theory. No relationship to Eysenck Personality Inventory scores was found. Power (1977) likewise could find no effect of extraversion and rate of interaction with teacher on several indices of achievement in eighth-grade science classes.

It seems that there is a consistent relationship of extraversion–introversion to academic performance. Younger extraverts seem to perform better than introverts. There are non-significant differences between the groups in the early teenage years, and in late high school (and university) introverts perform better than extraverts. It appears that these differences are *not* accounted for by differences in intelligence, and differences in neuroticism or anxiety do not interact with the extraversion–introversion variable in such a way as to explain the differences between groups. As Entwistle (1972) points out, there are a number of variables that may enter into this transition that have not yet been fully explored, not the least of which is the continuing selectivity that occurs in samples as the researcher moves from primary grades to university. The population covered by a random sample of third graders (nine-year-olds) is clearly not the same population as a random sample of university students who differ on many variables related to academic specialization and vocational goals. More longitudinal studies in which the same subjects are tested year after year for a period of six or eight years through the transition period would seem to be essential in clarifying the relationships involved.

The information relating to introverts' vocational choices seems clearer than that for extraverts. Because of aptitude differences, college/university achievement differences and/or vocational interests, introverts are more likely to end up in the task-oriented, technical professions than are extraverts. An introvert's orientation seems to be toward ideas, often abstract ideas, and structured, detailed work as opposed to the less well-ordered and perhaps more practical person-oriented occupations. One of the reasons why the picture is clearer for introverts than for extraverts may be that introverts are more consistent in stating their occupational interests, values and aspirations than are extraverts. Pillai (1975) investigated more than 400 high-school students in India who completed an occupational values questionnaire and an occupational aspirations questionnaire separately. Disparity between the two was related to both extraversion and neuroticism. The author explains that more introverted students both value and aspire to traditional, high-status, professional vocations. More extraverted students state more liberal, less socially conforming values, but their actual aspirations are governed more by immediate status and monetary considerations.

The global studies of the SVIB reviewed earlier indicate a moderate preference of introverts for the profession of artist. These findings are corroborated in a study by Gotz and Gotz (1973), who administered the Maudesley Personality Inventory to students at an art academy. Art teachers were asked to nominate the young adult students with whom they had worked for a minimum of two years for inclusion in either the gifted or the ungifted category. Fifty of each were utilized in the study and 15 of the 50 gifted students were designated highly gifted. The findings indicated that the gifted students were significantly more introverted and more neurotic than the ungifted students and standard norms. There was no difference between the ungifted students and standard normative data on introversion and neuroticism. Furthermore, the 15 highly gifted students were significantly more introverted and more neurotic than the remaining 35 gifted students. Therefore, the relationship of introversion to the degree of creativity among professional art students seems relatively clear.

Edwards (1977) set out to establish personal traits associated with schooling and occupational success. However, both the independent variable (group peer ratings on 16 personality dimensions) and dependent variable (supervisor rating of job performance) consisted of 'other' ratings. Individual traits which were highly correlated with wages, supervisor's ratings and school grades were 'consistent attender', 'practical', 'dependable', 'empathizes', 'identifies with job/school' and 'quitting'. To some extent, this sort of method may seem tautological as the dependent and independent variables are confounded.

The work on personality and academic performance/preference is highly salient to vocational psychology. It is a truism that people tend to be attracted to tasks and activities that they do well, that suit their temperament, arousal needs and skill. Studies in educational settings have consistently shown how introverts and extraverts differ in their ability to do different tasks. They are also attracted to different teaching and learning styles. Hence, it may be predicted that introverts and extraverts seek jobs that provide opportunities for them to do things both that they like and also that they are good at. Understanding the nature and type of academic/educational task preferred by different personality types is therefore highly salient to vocational psychology.

3.7 INTEREST LEVELS

Interest tests obviously measure the extent to which people are interested in particular activities in jobs. But interest need not correlate with ability, nor does it explain motivation. The term has little psychological meaning, is usually defined tautologically, and simply refers to the fact that people seek out and enjoy some activities more than others. Nevertheless, the major psychometric preoccupation of vocational psychologists has been in the development of interest scales of which one or two are very well known.

The Strong Vocational Interest Blank Test

The SVIB test consists of 400 items to each of which the person taking the test answers 'like', 'indifferent' or 'dislike'. The items are concerned with vocations, school subjects, amusements, activities and kinds of people. The test can be scored for more than 40 occupations for men and more than 20 occupations for women. A, B and C scores are given to each person taking the test for each occupation. The score for a particular occupation is determined by comparing a person's answers with the typical answers made by people actively and successfully engaged in that occupation. An A score means that a person's interests are very similar to those in that field; B, somewhat similar; and C, not at all similar.

Vocational interests are generally set *before* a person enters an occupation and change little thereafter. Strong tested 50 men when they were college freshmen and again 20 years later; the median correlation of scores was 0.72. He tested 228 students when they were seniors and again 22 years later. The median correlation was even higher: 0.75 (Strong, 1951). While some men change their interests after entering an occupation, the odds are against it. Furthermore, those who change are more likely to become *less* interested in the occupation, not more interested.

Scores on inventories do predict job success. Ghiselli and Barthol (1953) found 113 studies where scores had been related to success in different occupations: supervisors (52 studies), clerks (22), sales workers (20), skilled workers (8), service workers (6) and protective workers (5). For each of these job categories, there was a low but positive median correlation between scores and success. Although inventories have been used most often to predict supervisory success, the correlations were lowest for this group. Inventories were best in predicting sales success.

The method by which a car salesman scale was created illustrates the long process of developing a valid inventory. Kennedy (1958) first collected nearly 300 multiple-choice items covering personality, interest and attitudes that he thought might be related to success as a salesman. He then sent the questionnaire to a representative sample of General Motors car dealers throughout the country, some of whom were selling a high-priced car. At his request, the dealers had several hundred of their salesmen complete the questionnaire. The dealers returned the completed questionnaires along with a record of the gross earnings of each salesman. The salesmen were divided into a successful and an unsuccessful group on the basis of their earnings. The answers of the two groups to each item were then compared. The 40 items that most sharply differentiated the successful from the unsuccessful were chosen for the final form of the scale. This final form was again sent to the dealers, who had over 700 more of their salesmen complete it. They again returned the completed inventories with records of the earnings of the salesmen. The result was that the scores of the salesmen were significantly related to their earnings (correlation: 31). The scale worked equally well for salesmen selling the low- and high-priced cars.

Kline (1975) has cast doubt on the usefulness of the SVIB for a number of reasons:

- It seems less applicable outside America.
- Jobs have changed and hence criteria need to be changed.
- The test performs no better than simply getting a person to tell you their vocational interests.
- People deceive themselves into thinking they have interests when they don't.

The Kuder Interest Tests

There are various Kuder tests, all of which are very similar to the Strong test. *The Kuder General Interest Survey* (Kuder, 1970), which is the revised form of the Kuder Preference Record-Vocational, and suitable for 13-year-olds upwards, measures ten interest areas: outdoor, mechanical, computational, scientific, persuasive, artistic, literary, musical, social service and clerical.

There is evidence that the test was valid – for instance, people who were more satisfied/content in their jobs tended to have higher relevant Kuder scores than those who were not. However, Kline (1975) is critical of the test and makes four basic objections:

1. There is no evidence that Kuder scores predict better than simple expressed interests or goals.
2. There is evidence that interest dimensions are not those purportedly measured by the Kuder.
3. Ipsative scores can be misleading and need other data for interpretation. They are also worthless for multi-variate statistical analyses – necessary for research into interests.
4. Finally we should stress again that with our concept of interest as merely inferred from voluntary activity it is not surprising that expressed goals and interests are as good predictors as criterion keyed inventories (p.139).

3.8 CONCLUSION

Hogan *et al.* (1985) noted that psychologists have been doing 'vocational assessments' in industry since just after the start of the century, while academics have been interested in the topic since the 1920s. Over the century the pendulum has swung, among different groups (practitioners, academics), from extreme enthusiasm to guarded scepticism about the usefulness of personality tests in industry. Hogan *et al.* (1985) have attempted to refute the traditional academic cynicism regarding the utility of personality assessment in occupational selection:

1. Classic, well-cited reviews of occupational validity of personality measures are, if considered carefully, much less damaging than typically believed.
2. Too many 'personality inventories' exist which are not equivalent in their theoretical origin, construction, their measurement goal; hence, the equivocal results which are relatively easily explained.
3. Too many of the personality measures used in occupational settings were devised to detect psychopathology; hence, their limited usefulness.

They note:

Key terms are seldom defined; the goals of measurement are often unspecified; the meaning of test scores is rarely examined; and validity issues are often ignored. In the midst of all this confusion, it is a testimonial to the robustness of the enterprise that significant empirical results are ever reported (p.24–5).

Unfortunately, as Hogan *et al.* (1985) observe, both applied psychologists and managers tend to think of personality in clinical terms, and hence choose clinical measures. However, they see the importance of organizations doing personality audits so that sensible decisions about training and selection can be made.

This chapter has not focused extensively either on the various theories in occasional psychology or the specific vocational guidance measures, because of problems associated with both. Two theoretical concepts were explored partly because of their proven success and fecundity for generating hypotheses: person–job fit and expectancy theory. One way of exploring the usefulness of personality variables is to examine their predictive and discriminating validity with specific groups. This chapter looked at the rather diverse groups of police officers and medical students. Finally, the relationship between personality and academic performance was explored, because it seems that this relationship is moderated through such things as teaching style. The idea that there is a link between personality and preference for learning style has clear implications for vocational guidance (Furnham, 1992).

Chapter 4

Personality and work motivation

Business is like a wheelbarrow. Nothing ever happens until you start pushing.

Anon

I was made to work; if you are equally industrious, you will be equally successful.

J.S. Bach

There is no substitute for talent. Industry and all the virtues are of no avail.

A. Huxley

The brain is a wonderful organ; it starts the moment you get up in the morning and does not stop until you get to the office.

Robert Frost

Luck is not something you can mention in the presence of self-made men.

E.B. White

The secret of success is constancy to purpose.

Benjamin Disraeli

The three great American vices seem to be efficiency, punctuality and the desire for achievement and success.

Lin Yutang

Nobody talks more of free enterprise and competition and of the best man winning than the man who inherited his father's store or farm.

C.W. Mills

4.1 INTRODUCTION

One of the most interesting but difficult questions with regard to personality at work is why people work: what motivates them to work as hard or as little

as they do? Despite the voluminous literature in this area there is a paucity
of studies which look at individual differences except on the most general
level. Hence, this chapter is partly tentative and speculative as it attempts to
understand individual differences in work motivation.

It is an important area, as the findings in Table 4.1 (Vroom, 1960)
illustrate.

Table 4.1 Relationships between a measure of non-verbal reasoning and
ratings of job performance as a function of the motivation of the worker

Correlations between non-verbal reasoning scores and supervisory ratings of:

Motivation	N	Overall perfor- mance	Summary appraisal	Overall results (Prod. cost qual.)	Overall results (Skill, methods, effort)
High motivation group	31	0.47**	0.56***	0.33**	0.21
Moderate motivation group	28	0.06	−0.04	−0.19	−0.05
Low motivation group	32	−0.07	−0.23*	−0.17	−0.31**

*$p < 0.05$
**$p < 0.01$
***$p < 0.001$
Source: Vroom (1960)

What the table illustrates is that ability relates to output only in highly
motivated employees. Indeed, high-ability workers show the very opposite
effect when not motivated. From the table, it seems that a primary, if not *the*
primary, determinant of work output (qualitative and quantitive) is personal
work motivation.

4.2 THE MOTIVATION TO WORK

There are various self-evident reasons why people work: work provides a
source of income; a source of activity and stimulation; a source of social
contacts; a means of structuring time; and a source of self-fulfilment
and self-actualization. Nearly everyone chooses to work because of the
explicit and implicit rewards that it brings. However, people experience
quite different amounts and types of motivation to work. The quantity,
quality, enthusiasm and productivity shown at work seems to be a function
of work motivation.

There are a number of economic and psychological theories of work
motivation. A number of points could be made about the (psychological)
theories in general:

- Firstly, few if any of the theories were developed to account specifically for *work* motivation. Nearly all are general motivation theories applied to the world of work and supposedly applicable to all individuals.
- Secondly, nearly all of the theories have received, at best, limited empirical support for their propositions. Indeed, there seems to be almost no relationship between a theory's popularity and its empirical support. Most it seems have at least heuristic value, and sometimes not even that.
- Thirdly, it is probably true to say that the theories are neither overlapping nor contradictory given the diversity of their epistemological origins, although they may be contradictory on certain issues.
- Fourthly, there has been almost no interest in individual difference correlates of work motivation within each theory.

The various theories will be reviewed here. Because they have almost totally neglected personality and individual differences, various speculative hypotheses will be presented after each of which could (after suitable reflection) be worked up into testable hypothesis. It is really very surprising that so little work has been done on individual difference correlates of motivation, given that individuals differ so noticeably in their behaviour at work.

4.3 NEED THEORIES

Need theories are based on the simple idea that work-related behaviours are directed to satisfying certain needs. Depending on the type and quality of that need, people will strive in, and out of, work to satisfy them.

Maslow's Theory

Without doubt the best-known theory is that of Maslow (1954). It often seems as if people who have only been given one lecture on psychology in their entire lives have had it dedicated to Maslow's theory.

Maslow supposed that people have five types of needs which are activated in a *hierarchical* manner, and then are aroused in a specific order such that a lower-order need must be satisfied before the next highest-order need is activated. Once a need is met, the next highest need in the hierarchy is triggered, and so forth.

Psychological needs

Psychological needs are the lowest order, most basic needs and refer to satisfying fundamental biological drives such as the need for food, air, water and shelter. To satisfy these positive needs, organizations must provide employees with a salary that allows them to afford adequate living conditions (e.g. food and shelter). Employees need sufficient rest breaks to allow them to meet their psychological needs. Organizations may provide exercise and physical fitness programmes for their employees, because providing such facilities may also be recognized as an attempt to help employees stay healthy by gratifying their physiological needs. It is only in rare or exceptional circumstances (war, natural disaster, disease, epidemic) that organizations would find their employees 'stuck' at this level. However, many organizations in Third World countries might find their employees struggling to satisfy these more primitive needs.

Safety needs

Safety needs are activated only after physiological needs are met. Safety needs refer to needs for a secure, predictable, habitable, non-threatening environment, free from threats of either physical or psychological harm. Organizations may provide employees with life and health insurance plans, opportunity for savings, and secure contracts that enable work to be performed without fear of harm. Similarly, jobs that provide life-long tenure and no lay-off agreements enhance psychological security. Individuals are of course threatened (or feel threatened) by a wide range of factors and it is not clear whether organizations should attempt to distinguish between real and imagined safety threats.

Social needs

Social needs are seen to be activated after both physiological and safety needs are met. Social needs refer to the need to be affiliative – to have friends, to be loved and accepted by other people. These friends, relations and work colleagues help to meet social needs, and organizations may encourage participation in social events such as office parties, sports competitions, or social events which provide an opportunity for meeting social needs. Many organizations spend vast sums of money on facilities for out-of-work activities for their staff. Social needs are especially likely to be aroused under conditions in which 'organizational uncertainty' exists, such as when there is the possibility of a merger or closure. Under such conditions, employees may be likely to seek their co-workers' company to gather information about what's going on, and how best to combine their efforts to deal with the problem.

   Taken together, these three needs – physiological needs, safety needs and social needs – are known as *deficiency needs*. Maslow believed that without having these needs met, an individual will fail to develop into a healthy person, both physically and psychologically. The next two higher-order needs are known as *growth needs*: gratification of these needs is said to help a person grow and develop to his/her fullest potential.

Esteem needs

Esteem needs refer to a person's need to develop self-respect and to gain the approval of others. The desire to achieve success, have personal prestige and be recognized by others, all fall into this category. Companies may have awards or banquets to recognize distinguished achievements. Printing articles in company newsletters describing an employee's success, assigning private parking spaces, and posting signs identifying the 'employee of the month' are all examples of things that can be done to satisfy esteem. The inflation of job titles could also be seen as an organizational attempt to boost employees' self-esteem. Cultural and subcultural factors determine which sort of reward actually contributes to self-esteem. These policies seem most popular in low-paid service industries or in sales forces where people have limited contact with peers. Most people in most organizations seem to have difficulty satisfying this level and, hence, never go beyond it.

Self-actualization needs

Self-actualization needs are aroused only after all the lower-order needs have been met. They refer to the need for self-fulfilment – the desire to become all that one is capable of being, developing one's potential and fully realizing one's abilities. By working at their maximum creative potential, employees who are self-actualized can be extremely valuable assets to their organizations. Individuals who have self-actualized supposedly work at their peak, and represent the most effective use of an organization's human resources.

The definition of self-actualization is by no means clear; hence, it becomes very difficult to operationalize, measure and test. Few jobs provide total, free and open scope for employees to achieve total self-fulfilment. Maslow conceived of the dynamic forces of behaviour as deprivation and gratification. Deprivation, or lack of satisfaction with respect to a particular need, leads to dominance of that need where the person's behaviour is entirely devoted to satisfying that need. Once satisfied, or gratified, however, the need recedes in importance and the next highest level of need is stimulated or activated. Thus, beginning with the lowest level, the entire process involves deprivation leading to dominance, gratification and activation of the next level.

The fact that the theory is all-embracing has attracted a great deal of attention. It has also been enthusiastically applied to the world of work. Predictably perhaps the research has been highly critical. Few have been able to find evidence of the five (or two) tier system (Mitchell and Mowdgill, 1976), and there is precious little evidence that the needs are activated in the same order. It is not certain how, when or why the gratification of one need stimulates or activates the next highest category. But it does seem that some of the ideas are useful: individuals clearly have different needs; needs do relate to work behaviours; organizations as a whole may be classified in terms of the need that they satisfy.

Possible Personality Hypotheses

- Individual differences are more noticeable in the higher-level needs (growth needs) than in the lower-level needs.
- Neurotics, those with external locus of control and those with conservative values have difficulty fulfilling self-esteem needs.
- Definitions of self-actualization needs are a function of personality itself.

Alderfer's ERG theory

This theory is much simpler in that Alderfer (1972) specifies that there are only *three* types of needs but that they are not necessarily activated in any specific order. Furthermore, any need may be activated at any time.

The three needs specified by the ERG theory are the needs for existence, relatedness and growth. Existence needs correspond to Maslow's physiological needs and safety needs; relatedness needs correspond to Maslow's social needs – the need for meaningful social relationships; growth needs correspond to the esteem needs and self-actualization needs in Maslow's theory – the need for developing one's potential.

The ERG theory is much less construing than Maslow's need hierarchy theory. Its advantage is that it fits better with research evidence suggesting that, although basic categories of need do exist, they are not exactly as specified by Maslow. Despite the fact that need theorists are not in complete agreement about the exact number of needs that exist and the relationships between them, they do agree that satisfying human needs is an important part of motivating behaviour on the job.

The theory has not attracted as much attention as Maslow's theory but seems a reasonable modification of it. However, like Maslow's theory, it is potentially rather difficult to test.

Possible Personality Hypotheses

- Extraverts have stronger relatedness needs than introverts.
- Neurotics are most obsessed by, and find it more difficult to, achieve growth needs than non-neurotics.
- Growth needs are less stable over time than the other needs.

Murray's Needs and Presses

Murray (1938) believed that motivation represents the central issue in personality theory and argued that people are motivated by the desire to satisfy tension-provoking drives (*needs*). He defined need as a force in the 'brain region' which energizes and organizes perceptions, thoughts and actions, thereby transforming an existing, unsatisfying situation in the direction of a particular goal. Murray expanded the list of biological ('viscerogenic') needs to include hunger, thirst, sex, oxygen deprivation, the elimination of bodily wastes, and the avoidance of painful external conditions (such as harm, heat and cold); he also posits the existence of mental ('psychogenic') needs, which are derived from the viscerogenic ones. Murray (1933) eventually settled on a list of 20 identifiable and presumable distinct needs (see Table 4.2).

Ascertaining an individual's needs is not an easy task. Some needs are inhibited or repressed because of their unacceptable nature, rather than overt and readily observable. A need may focus on one specific goal or it may be so diffuse as to permit satisfaction by many different objects in the environment; or an activity may provide its own pleasures, rather than being directed toward a particular goal. Furthermore, needs often operate in combination: one need may assist another, as when a person actively persuades a group to complete a challenging task (*n*Dominance subsidiary to *n*Achievement), argues passionately for freedom (*n*Dominance subsidiary to *n*Autonomy), or rules others through the use of force and punishment (*n*Aggression subsidiary to *n*Dominance). Alternatively, needs may 'fuse' into a more equally weighted composite. Thus, an individual may humbly serve a domineering master (*n*Defence fused with *n*Abasement), or become a prize-fighter (*n*Aggression fused with *n*Exhibition). Needs may also conflict with one another (e.g. *n*Affiliation with *n*Dominance).

Needs can be triggered by external as well as internal stimuli, so personality cannot be studied in isolation from environmental forces. 'At every moment, an organism is within an environment which largely determines its behaviour . . . (usually) in the guise of a *threat of harm or promise of benefit* . . . The *press* of an object is what it can *do to the subject* or *for the subject* – the power it has to affect the well-being of the subject in one way or the another' (Murray, 1938, p.39–41, 121). Thus, *press* refers to those aspects of the environment that facilitate or obstruct a person's efforts to reach or avoid a given goal.

Murray distinguished between an individual's interpretation of external events ('beta press') and actual reality as defined by objective inquiry ('alpha press'). In addition, a single need–press interaction is referred to as a *thema*. For example, if a person is rejected by someone else and responds in kind, the thema would consist of *p*Rejection (the environment event) causing a rejection (the need evoked). Alternatively, *p*Rejection might lead to (say) *n*Abasement or *n*Aggression; or the thema might be initiated by a need, as when an excessive *n*Affiliation causes inappropriate behaviour that provokes disdain and *p*Rejection; or other people may actually be favourably disposed toward oneself (*p*Affiliation, alpha press) but be misperceived as hostile and threatening (*p*Aggression, beta press) (Murray, 1938, p.123).

The number of people that have been strongly influenced by Murray's (1938) theory is some testament to its worth. Compared to Maslow's theory, Murray has many more needs (enabling one to be diagnostically much more specific) which are not hierarchically arranged. However, these needs are categorizing tools or labels because they do not help to understand when, why or how a need will be activated, expressed or satisfied. Descriptively and taxonomically, the system devised by Murray has immense appeal but its explanatory value is limited.

Murray was overly fond of neologisms, and his taxonomy has been criticized as making too many finicky distinctions, whereas other important details remain unclear (e.g. how psychogenic needs are derived from viscerogenic ones). Perhaps the major criticism of Murray's work is the failure to provide robust empirical evidence of the distinct nature of the 20 needs. Clearly, multi-variate statistics need to be employed in order to examine the structure of these needs which are likely to be interrelated.

Possible Personality Hypotheses

- Extraverts are likely to have greater affiliation, exhibition and play needs than introverts.
- Neuroticism is associated with abasement, defendance and harm avoidance needs.
- Needs for achievement and dominance are associated with particular forms of business success.
- Successful, caring professionals have high nurturance needs while successful academics rate high on need for understanding.

Table 4.2 Murray's original taxonomy of needs

Need	Description	Representative questionnaire item	Accompanying emotion(s)
*n*Abasement	To submit passively to external force; to accept blame, surrender, admit inferiority or error	My friends think I am too humble	Resignation, shame, guilt
*n*Achievement	To accomplish something difficult; to master, manipulate, surpass others	I set difficult goals for myself which I attempt to reach	Ambition, zest
*n*Affiliation	To draw near and enjoyably co-operate or reciprocate with liked others; to win their affection, loyalty	I become very attached to my friends	Affection, love, trust
*n*Aggression	To overcome opposition forcefully; to fight, revenge an injury, oppose or attack others	I treat a domineering person as rudely as he treats me	Anger, rage, jealousy, revenge
*n*Autonomy	To get free of confinement or restraint; to resist coercion, be independent	I go my own way regardless of the opinion of others	Anger due to restraint; independence
*n*Counteraction	To master or make up for a failure by restriving; to overcome weakness, repress fear	To me a difficulty is just a spur to greater effort	Shame after failure, determination to overcome
*n*Defendance	To defend oneself against assault, criticism, blame; to vindicate the ego	I can usually find plenty of reasons to explain my failures	Guilt, inferiority
*n*Deference	To admire and support a superior; to praise, be subordinate, conform	I often find myself imitating or agreeing with somebody I consider superior	Respect, admiration
*n*Dominance	To control one's human environment; to influence, persuade, command others	I usually influence others more than they influence me	Confidence

nExhibition	To make an impression, be seen and heard; to excite, amaze, fascinate, shock others	I am apt to show off in some way if I get a chance	Vanity, exuberance
nHarm avoidance	To avoid pain, physical injury, illness and death; to escape danger, take precautions	I am afraid of physical pain	Anxiety
nInfavoidance	To avoid humiliation; to quit or avoid embarrassing situations; refrain from acting due to the fear of failure	I often shrink from a situation because of my sensitiveness to criticism and ridicule	Inferiority, anxiety, shame
nNurturance	To give sympathy and gratify the needs of someone helpless; to console, support others	I am easily moved by the misfortunes of other people	Pity, compassion, tenderness
nOrder	To put things in order; to achieve neatness, organization, cleanliness	I organize my daily activities so that there is little confusion	Disgust at disorder
nPlay	To act fun without further purpose; to like to laugh, make jokes	I cultivate an easygoing, humorous attitude toward life	Jolliness
nRejection	To separate oneself from disliked others; to exclude, expel, snub others	I get annoyed when some fool takes up my time	Scorn, disgust, indifference
nSentience	To seek and enjoy sensuous impressions	I search for sensations which shall at once be new and delightful	Sensuousness
nSex	To form and further an erotic relationship; to have sexual intercourse	I spend a great deal of time thinking about sexual matters	Erotic excitement, lust, love
nSuccorance	To have one's needs gratified by someone sympathetic; to be nursed, supported, protected, consoled	I feel lonely and homesick when I am in a strange place	Helplessness, insecurity
nUnderstanding	To ask or answer general questions; an interest in theory, analysing events, logic, reason	I think that *reason* is the best guide in solving the problems of life	A liking for thinking

Source: Based on Murray (1958)

Jahoda's Latent Needs

Based on her work dating from the 1930s, Jahoda (1982) has developed a theory based on the idea that what produces psychological distress in the unemployed is the deprivation of the latent functions of work. These include:

- *Work structure time.* Work structures the day, the week and even longer periods. The loss of a time structure can be very disorientating. Feather and Bond (1983) compared the structure and purposeful activity among employed and unemployed university graduates. They found, as predicted, that the unemployed were less organized and less purposeful in their use of time, and reported more depressive symptoms than the employed.
- *Work provides regularly shared experiences.* Regular contact with non-nuclear family members provides an important source of social contact. There is a vast literature on social skill deficits which suggests that social isolation is related to disturbed mental states. There is now a growing interest in the social support hypothesis which suggests that social support from family and friends buffers the major causes of stress and increases coping ability, so reducing illness. If one's primary source of friends and contacts is work colleagues, then the benefits of social support are denied precisely when they are most needed. There are also a wealth of studies in organizational psychology which suggest that one of the most frequently cited sources of job satisfaction is contact with other people.
- *Work provides experience of creativity and mastery, and a sense of purpose.* Both the organization and the production of work imply the interdependence of human beings. Take away this daily experience and the sense of purpose, and the unemployed are left with a sense of uselessness. Work, even not particularly satisfying work, gives some sense of mastery or achievement. Creative activities stimulate people and provide a sense of satisfaction. A person's contribution to producing goods or providing services forges a link between the individual and the society of which he/she is a part. Work roles are not the only roles which offer the individual the opportunity of being useful and contributing to the community, but, without doubt, for the majority they are the most central roles. Consequently, people deprived of the opportunity to work often feel useless and report that they lack a sense of purpose.
- *Work is a source of personal status and identity.* A person's job is an important indicator of his/her personal status in society – hence, the often amusing debates over job titles such as sanitary engineer for street cleaner! Furthermore, it is not only to the employed person that the job gives certain status but also to his/her family. The employed person therefore is a link between two important social systems – family and home. An unemployed person has lost his employment status and hence identity. Not unnaturally there is a marked drop in self-esteem following unemployment.

• *Work is a source of activity.* All work involves some expenditure of physical or mental effort. Whereas too much activity may induce fatigue and stress, too little results in boredom and restlessness, particularly among extraverts. People seek to maximize the amount of activity that suits them by choosing particular jobs or tasks that fulfil their needs. The unemployed, however, are not provided with this possibility and have consistently to provide stimulation to keep themselves active.

Table 4.3 Possible matching characteristics for each environmental category

Category		Possible matching characteristics
1.	Opportunity for control (AD)	High growth-need strength (ES) High desire for personal control High need for independence (ES) Low authoritarianism (ES) Low neuroticism High relevant ability
2.	Opportunity for skill use (AD)	High growth-need strength (ES) High desire to use/extend skills (ES) Relevant skills which are unused Low neuroticism
3.(a)	Externally generated goals: Level of demands (AD)	High growth-need strength (ES) High desire for high workload (ES) Type-B behaviour High need for achievement Low neuroticism High relevant ability (ES)
3.(b)	Externally generated goals: Task identity (AD)	High growth-need strength (ES) High desire for task identity
4.	Variety (AD)	High growth-need strength (ES) High desire for variety (ES)
5.(a)	Environmental clarity: Feedback (AD)	High growth-need strength High desire for feedback
5.(b)	Environmental clarity: Role clarity (AD)	High need for clarity/intolerance of ambiguity (ES) External control beliefs (ES?) Low need for achievement (ES?)
6.	Availability of money (CE)	High desire for money
7.	Physical security (CE)	High desire for physical security
8.	Opportunity for interpersonal contact (AD)	High sociability Lack of contact in other environments High desire for social support
9.	Valued social position (CE)	High desire for social esteem

ES: empirical support is available for a significant person–situation interaction in respect of job satisfaction
AD: vitamins that at high levels cause decrement in mental health
CE: vitamins that at high levels do not cause decrement
Source: Warr (1987)

This 'deprivation theory' has had its critics. Fryer (1986) has offered three kinds of criticism:

1. *Pragmatic* – the theory is very difficult to test.
2. *Methodological* – one cannot be sure which or how the deprivations are caused by unemployment; people *not* deprived do not necessarily enjoy, appreciate or acknowledge this state.
3. *Empirical* – the theory does not take into account changes over time and undivided difference in reaction.

In a sense, Jahoda argues that people are *deprived* while Fryer argues that institutions *impose* things on people (like stigma). Furthermore, whereas the former underplays individual choice and personal control, the latter tends to underplay social identity and interdependence of people at work.

Jahoda's theory is essentially that work provides people with both explicit and implicit, obvious and latent, sources of satisfaction. Studies on unemployment have made apparent some of the less obvious needs that work fulfils. While Jahoda's theory is not easy to test in its entirety, it has stimulated both research and theorizing. For instance, Warr (1987) developed a vitamin theory that suggested that work provides nine specific beneficial 'opportunities'. These are tested in Table 4.3.

Table 4.3 shows that Warr has a clear concept of fit whereby certain personality types or those with specific need profiles would presumably seek out and respond to jobs that offered more of these characteristics. To some extent, these are tautological yet the concept is important: to the extent that certain jobs fulfil specific needs, it is likely that those with these needs will be satisfied in them. Presumably, this relationship is curvilinear rather than linear, so one may have the concept of the optimal fulfilment of needs.

Possible Personality Hypotheses

- Extraverts seek out jobs that provide regular social contact and stimulation.
- Instrumentalists (internal locus of control) respond best to jobs that provide the experience of mastery and sense of purpose.
- People with high neuroticism scores benefit from the status and identity that work can provide.
- More intelligent people seek out and benefit from jobs which require the exercise of considerable skill.

4.4 EQUITY THEORIES

Equity theory, borrowed by psychologists from economics, views motivation from the perspective of the social comparisons that people make among themselves. It proposes that employees are motivated to maintain fair, or 'equitable', relationships among themselves and to change those relationships that are unfair, or 'inequitable'. Equity theory is concerned with people's motivation to escape the negative feelings that result from being treated unfairly in their jobs once they have engaged in the process of *social comparison*.

Equity theory suggests that people make social comparisons between themselves and others with respect to two variables – *outcomes* (benefits, rewards) and *inputs* (effort, ability). Outcomes refer to the things that workers believe they and others get out of their jobs, including pay, fringe benefits or prestige. Inputs refer to the contributions that employees believe they and others make to their jobs, including the amount of time worked, the amount of effort expended, the number of units produced, or the qualifications brought to the job. Equity theory is concerned with outcomes and inputs as they are *perceived* by the people involved, *not* necessarily as they actually are, although that in itself is often very difficult to measure. Not surprisingly therefore, workers may disagree about what constitutes equity and inequity on the job. Equity is therefore a subjective, not objective, experience, which makes it more susceptible to being influenced by personality factors.

Equity theory states that people compare their outcomes and inputs to those of others in the form of a ratio. Specifically, they compare the ratio of their own outcomes/inputs to the ratio of other people's outcomes/inputs, which can result in any of three states: *overpayment*, *underpayment* or *equitable payment*.

- Overpayment inequity occurs when an individual's outcome/input ratio is *greater than* the corresponding ratio of another person with whom that individual compares himself/herself. People who are overpaid are supposed to feel *guilty*. There are relatively few people in this position.
- Underpayment inequity occurs when an individual's outcome/input ratio is *less than* the corresponding ratio of another person with whom that individual compares himself/herself. People who are underpaid are supposed to feel *angry*. Many people feel under-benefitted.
- Equitable payment occurs when an individual's outcome/input ratio is *equal to* the corresponding ratio of another person with whom that individual compares himself/herself. People who are equitably paid are supposed to feel *satisfied*.

According to equity theory, people are motivated to escape the negative emotional states of anger and guilt. Equity theory admits two major ways of resolving inequitable states. *Behavioural* reactions to equity represent things that people can do to change their existing inputs and outcomes, such as working more or less hard (to increase or decrease inputs), or stealing time and goods (to increase outputs). In addition to behavioural reactions to underpayment inequity, there are also some likely *psychological* reactions. Given that many people feel uncomfortable stealing from their employers (to increase outputs), or would be unwilling to restrict their productivity or to ask for a salary increase (to increase inputs), they may resort to resolving the inequity by changing the way that they think about their situation. Because equity theory deals with perceptions of fairness or unfairness, it is reasonable to expect that inequitable states may be redressed effectively by merely *thinking* about the circumstances differently. For example, an underpaid person may attempt to *rationalize* the fact that another's inputs are really higher than his/her own, thereby convincing himself/herself that the other's higher outcomes are justified.

There are a number of quite different reactions to inequity. People can respond to overpayment and underpayment (i.e. being under-benefitted) inequities in behavioural and/or psychological ways (i.e. being over-benefitted), which help change the perceived *inequities* into a state of perceived *equity*. Table 4.4 shows the four 'classic' reactions to inequity.

Table 4.4 Reactions to inequity

Type of inequity	Type of reaction	
	Behavioural	Psychological
Overpayment inequity (guilt): I < O	Increase your inputs (work harder), or lower your outcomes (work through a paid vacation, take no salary)	Convince yourself that your outcomes are deserved based on your inputs (rationalize that you work harder, better, smarter than equivalent others and so you deserve more pay)
Underpayment inequity (anger) I > O	Lower your inputs (reduce effort), or raise your outcomes (get pay increase, steal time by absenteeism)	Convince yourself that others' inputs are really higher than your own (rationalize that the comparison worker is really more qualified or a better worker and so deserves higher outcomes)

An analogous set of behavioural and psychological reactions can be identified for overpayment inequity. Specifically, a salaried employee who feels overpaid may raise his/her inputs by working harder, or for longer hours or more productively. Similarly, employees who lower their own outcomes by not taking advantage of company-provided fringe benefits may be seen as redressing an overpayment inequity. Overpaid persons (few though they are!) may readily convince themselves psychologically that they are really worth their higher outcomes by virtue of their superior inputs. People who receive substantial pay raises may not feel distressed about it at all because they rationalize that the increase is warranted on the basis of their superior inputs, and therefore does not constitute an inequity.

Research has generally supported the theory's claim that people will respond to overpayment and underpayment inequities in the ways just described. For instance, Pritchard, Dunnette and Jorgenson (1972) hired male clerical workers to work part-time over a two-week period and manipulated the equity or inequity of the payment that the employees received. *Overpaid* employees were told that their pay was higher than that of others doing the same work. *Underpaid* employees were told that their pay was lower than that of others doing the same work. *Equitably paid* employees were told that their pay was equal to that of others doing the same work. People who were overpaid were more productive than those who were equitably paid; and people who were underpaid were less productive than those who were equitably paid. Moreover, both overpaid and underpaid employees reported being more dissatisfied with their jobs than those who were equitably paid.

As one might expect, equity theory has its problems: how to deal with the concept of negative inputs; the point at which equity becomes inequity; the belief that people prefer and value equity over equality. Nevertheless, the theory has stimulated an enormous literature which partially addresses itself to the issue of motivation. In essence, then, the theory predicts that people are motivated to achieve subjectively perceived equity.

Possible Personality Hypotheses

- Instrumentalists would tend more to behavioural than psychological responses to inequity.
- Neurotics tend to experience more inequity than non-neurotics.
- Extraverts, because they are more often concerned with social comparison, are more aware of equity than introverts.
- People may refuse promotion if they believe that it promotes them out of an equity situation.

4.5 VALUE THEORIES

Researchers on the topic of social values have conceived of them as a system of beliefs concerned with such issues as competence and morality, which are derived in large part from societal demands. These value systems are organized summaries of experience that capture the focal abstracted qualities of past encounters; have a normativeness or oughtness quality about them; and which function as criteria or frameworks against which present experience can be tested. It is also argued that these act as general motives.

Various instruments have been devised to measure a person's value system but the one that has probably attracted the greatest following is that of Rokeach (1973), who distinguished 18 terminal and 18 instrumental values. A value is considered an enduring belief that a specific instrumental model of conduct and/or a terminal end state of existence is preferable. It is argued that once a value is internalized, it consciously or unconsciously becomes: a standard criterion for guiding action; for developing and maintaining attitudes toward relevant objects and situations; for justifying one's own and others' actions and attitudes; for morally judging self and others; and for comparing oneself with others.

Research by Feather (1985) and others has demonstrated that these value systems are systematically linked to culture of origin, religion, chosen university discipline, political persuasion, generations within a family, age, sex, personality and educational background. Feather has argued that social attitudes precede values which emerge as abstractions from personal experience of one's own and others' behaviour. These values become organized into coherent value systems in time which serve as frames of reference that guide beliefs and behaviour in many situations, such as work. He has argued that values, attitudes and attributions are linked into a cognitive–affective system. Thus, people's explanations of unemployment are 'linked to other beliefs, attitudes and values within a system in ways that give meaning and consistency to the events that occur' (p.805). Thus, it may be expected that there are coherent and predictable links between one's general value system and specific work-related beliefs.

Furnham (1987b) predicted that Protestant work ethic (PWE) beliefs as measured by two different scales would be associated with values such as security, cleanliness, obedience and politeness; and negatively associated with values such as equality, harmony, love, broadmindedness, imaginativeness and being intellectual. It was also predicted that work-involvement beliefs would be associated with values such as sense of accomplishment, security, social recognition, ambitiousness, responsibility and self-control; and negatively associated with values such as a comfortable life, pleasure, imaginativeness and loving. On the other hand, it was predicted that Marxist work-related beliefs would be positively associated with values such as equality, peace, inner harmony, love and forgiving; and negatively associated with a sense of accomplishment, salvation, ambition, obedience, politeness and responsibility. Similarly, the leisure ethic was expected to be associated with values such as a comfortable life, happiness, pleasure, imaginativeness and independence; and negatively associated with a sense of accomplishment, salvation, ambitiousness, capability, obedience and politeness. The actual results are set out in Table 4.5.

Thus, many of the hypotheses were confirmed, especially with respect to instrumental values. Work-related beliefs thus relate to a whole range of values which, in part, may explain why PWE beliefs are so predictive of such a wide range of behaviours (Furnham, 1990b). However, the work on social values has concentrated less on how these values are socialized and maintained in individuals and groups.

One of the most interesting studies on values has been that of Hofstede (1984) who, in a study of organizational values, isolated four dimensions that have been successfully applied to all cultures. The four dimensions are as follows:

- *Power distance*. The extent to which the less powerful numbers of institutions and organizations accept that power is distributed *unequally*:

Low	High
Less centralization	Greater centralization
Flatter organization pyramids	Tall organization pyramids
Fewer supervisory personnel	More supervisory personnel
Smaller wage differentials	Large wage differentials
Structure in which manual and clerical work are equally valued	Structure in which white-collar jobs are valued more than blue-collar jobs

- *Uncertainty avoidance*. The extent to which people feel threatened by ambiguous situations, and have created beliefs and institutions that try to avoid these:

Low	High
Less structuring of activities	More structuring of activities
Few written rules	More written rules
More generalists	More specialists
Variability	Standardization
Greater willingness to take risks	Less willingness to take risks
Less ritualistic behaviour	More ritualistic behaviour

- *Individualism/collectivism*. This reflects either a position in which people are supposed to look after themselves and their immediate family (individualism), or a situation in which people belong to in-groups or collectivities which are supposed to look after them in exchange for loyalty (collectivism):

Low	High
Organization as 'family'	Organization is more impersonal
Organization defends employee interests	Employees defend their own self-interests
Practices are based on loyalty, sense of duty and group participation	Practices encourage individual initiative

Table 4.5 Product–moment correlations relating the terminal and instrumental values to each of the seven work beliefs

Values	PWE	Work ethic	Organizational beliefs	Marxist beliefs	Humanistic beliefs	Leisure ethic	Work involvement
Terminal values							
Comfortable life	−0.02	0.09	−0.06	−0.04	−0.16**	−0.06	−0.09
Exciting life	0.06	0.23***	0.21***	−0.08	−0.12*	−0.04	−0.01
S.O.A.†	0.03	0.08	−0.10*	−0.11*	0.05	−0.02	0.13*
World at peace	−0.03	−0.12*	0.15*	0.25**	0.07	0.12*	0.05
World of beauty	−0.08	−0.07	−0.13*	−0.01	−0.03	−0.04	−0.05
Equality	−0.30***	−0.17*	0.16**	0.41***	0.07	0.19***	−0.06
Family security	0.06	−0.03	−0.04	−0.15*	0.11*	−0.13*	0.18**
Freedom	−0.02	0.03	−0.04	−0.04	0.04	−0.03	−0.00
Happiness	0.12*	−0.01	0.04	0.00	0.00	−0.07	0.02
Inner harmony	−0.10*	−0.15*	−0.05	0.10*	0.10*	−0.02	−0.05
Mature love	−0.12*	−0.08	−0.11*	0.12*	0.00	−0.06	0.00
National security	0.14*	0.00	0.04	−0.10	−0.03	−0.09	0.00
Pleasure	0.06	−0.17*	−0.03	0.05	−0.24***	0.13*	−0.14*
Salvation	0.17*	−0.06	0.22***	−0.01	−0.02	−0.13*	0.02
Self-respect	0.00	0.00	−0.10*	−0.09	0.00	−0.04	0.02
Social recognition	−0.05	−0.03	0.00	−0.07	−0.04	0.05	0.02
True friendship	0.02	−0.18***	0.03	−0.04	0.02	−0.08	0.12*
Wisdom	−0.02	−0.02	−0.06	−0.03	0.14**	0.05	0.00
Instrumental values							
Ambitious	0.09	0.25***	0.11*	−0.11*	0.00	−0.11*	0.11*
Broadminded	−0.15*	−0.18*	−0.05	0.09	0.09	0.06	0.03
Capable	−0.04	0.02	−0.15*	−0.15*	−0.01	−0.12*	0.04
Cheerful	0.00	−0.06	0.10*	0.04	−0.08	0.03	−0.01
Clean	0.19***	−0.14**	0.10*	0.00	−0.15**	0.00	−0.15**
Courageous	−0.10*	−0.06	−0.07	0.10*	0.04	0.06	−0.05

Forgiving	-0.10*	-0.25***	0.08	0.13*	-0.03	-0.04	-0.00
Helpful	0.04	0.06	-0.09	-0.02	-0.06	0.13*	-0.03
Honest	0.07	0.14**	0.13*	0.05	0.10*	0.03	0.11*
Imaginative	-0.15**	0.04	-0.22**	0.11*	-0.01	0.25***	0.15**
Independent	-0.06	0.19***	-0.16**	-0.08	0.01	0.02	-0.06
Intellectual	-0.14**	0.03	-0.18**	0.00	0.02	0.04	-0.05
Logical	-0.00	0.11*	-0.13	-0.06	-0.09	-0.03	-0.13*
Loving	-0.07	-0.15**	0.00	0.11*	0.13*	0.12*	0.02
Obedient	0.19***	0.02	0.20***	-0.07	-0.07	-0.18***	0.05
Polite	0.15**	0.07	0.10*	-0.16**	-0.09	-0.22***	0.14**
Responsible	0.13*	0.02	-0.02	-0.12*	0.05	-0.11*	0.13*
Self-controlled	0.04	0.10*	0.13*	-0.09	0.01	-0.03	-0.02

* $p < 0.05$
** $p < 0.01$
*** $p < 0.001$
(† S.O.A. = Sense of accomplishment
Source: Furnham (1987a)

- *Masculinity/femininity*. A situation in which the dominant values in society are success, money and things (masculinity). A situation in which the dominant values in society are caring for others and the quality of life (femininity):

Low	71 1High
Sex roles are minimized	Sex roles are clearly differentiated
Organizations do not interfere with people's private lives	Organizations may interfere to protect their interests
More women in qualified jobs	Fewer women in qualified jobs
Soft, yielding, intuitive skills are rewarded	Aggression, competition and justice are rewarded
Social rewards are valued	Work is valued as a central life interest

Despite the fact that these value dimensions have been applied mainly to organizations and cultures, there is no reason why they cannot be applied on the individual level. If this is done, it becomes possible to determine a measure of fit between the person, the organization in which they work, and the culture as a whole. Presumably, work motivation (quality and quantity) would be a measure of the 'fit' between the two (person and organization) added up over the four dimensions.

The problem with the current research on values is that there does not appear to be any agreement on what the definitive list of values is and how they are interrelated. Nevertheless, they do provide an interesting approach to the whole area of motivation.

Possible Personality Hypotheses

- Authoritarians will prefer to work in, and be motivated by, high power–distance organizations.
- Neurotics will be demotivated in low uncertainty avoidance situations.
- Instrumentalists, as opposed to fatalists, will prefer individualistic vs collectivistic organizations.
- People whose personal values coincide with those of the organization feel more satisfied, work harder and are less prone to leave.

4.6 REINFORCEMENT THEORIES

These theories, for there are many, specify how a history of past benefits, or reinforcements, modifies behaviour so that future benefits will be secured.

The direct application of behaviour modification principles to the work situation claims to provide procedures by which human performance can be shaped and altered. At the centre of behaviour modification is the concept of reinforcement contingency. The rate of performance will increase when valued outcomes (reinforcers) are made contingent on the performance. It makes no difference to the theory what the person needs, expects, values or wants. It is sufficient merely to establish the reinforcement contingency in order to effect a behavioural change. Clearly, individual differences dictate what are, and what are not, reinforcements. The argument is that people perform certain work-related acts that are subject to reinforcement (or punishment and extinction) contingencies. People work with a certain degree of effectiveness and when a particular behaviour results in a reward (there is a reinforcement contingency between, say, payment and work efficiency), performance improves. Learning theorists assert that all behaviour is shaped and sustained through the action of contingent reinforcement; work-related behaviours are simply special examples of this more universal phenomenon. Behaviour modification has not met with universal approval, either as a theory of work behaviour, or as an ethically acceptable approach to work management (behaviour modification may severely restrict a worker's freedom of choice).

A second type of reinforcement theory is the social learning theory. Whereas need theory attributes work solely to the person (internal motives), and behaviour modification theory explains work in terms of the action of the environment (contingent reinforcement), social learning theory emphasizes *both* the person and the environment. The individual (who has unique traits, cognitions, perceptions, attitudes, emotions) and the environment (which provides reinforcement) combine to affect performance. It is not sufficient to say merely that a person works because he/she is reinforced; one needs to take the person's cognitions, attitudes or emotions into account as well. For example, a person learns work performance through copying the behaviour of others as a consequence of the reinforcers they are perceived to obtain, not simply through a series of discrete trial-and-error experiences. Because cognitive processes appear to mediate behaviour, feelings, images and thoughts, all affect the way that people experience and perceive reinforcers and thus the way that they perform.

A number of managers have begun to use social learning theory in the workplace. Some of the strategies have been directed at changing the environmental stimuli which set the occasion for rewarded behaviour, while others have manipulated the consequences of behaviour in such things as performance appraisal schemes.

Reinforcement and learning theories are among the oldest in psychology. Advocates of operant conditioning emphasize that punishment (negative reinforcement) is not usually effective since it suppresses rather than eliminates undesirable responses. They also noted that the more quickly reinforcement is given after the response, the more effective it becomes. Finally, when complex responses are desired, *shaping* is sometimes useful. This involves positively reinforcing responses that are part of the more complex one until the desired response is obtained.

Jablonsky and De Vries (1972) have suggested the following guidelines for applying operant conditioning as a motivating technique:

1. Avoid using punishment as a primary means of obtaining desired performance.
2. Positively reinforce desired behaviour and ignore undesired behaviour if possible.
3. Minimize the time lag between response and reinforcement.
4. Apply positive reinforcement frequently on a variable ratio schedule.
5. Determine the response level of each individual and use shaping to obtain the final complex response.
6. Determine environmental factors that are considered positive and negative by the individual.
7. Specify desired behaviour in operational terms.

Clearly, points 5 and 6 require that the 'motivator' be cognizant of individual differences.

Possible Personality Hypotheses

• Extraverts will be more motivated by social reward, introverts by punishment.
• Instrumentalists will attempt to manipulate their environment and set up contingencies more than fatalists.

4.7 EXPECTANCY THEORIES

Expectancy theory asserts that people are motivated to work when they expect that they will be able to achieve and obtain the things that they want from their jobs. Expectancy theory characterizes people as rational, logical and cognitive beings who think about what they have to do to be rewarded and how much the reward means to them before they perform their jobs.

Expectancy theory specifies that motivation is the result of *three* different types of belief cognitions that people have. These are known as:

1. *Expectancy* – the belief that one's effort will result in performance.
2. *Instrumentality* – the belief that one's performance will be rewarded.
3. *Valence* – the perceived value of the rewards to the recipient.

An employee may believe that a great deal of effort will result in getting a lot accomplished, while others believe that there are other occasions where hard work will have little effect on how much gets done. For example, an employee operating a faulty piece of equipment may have a very low *expectancy* that his/her efforts will lead to high levels of performance, and hence probably would not continue to exert much effort.

It is also possible that even if an employee works hard and performs at a high level, motivation may falter if that performance is not suitably rewarded by the organization – that is, if the performance was not perceived as *instrumental* in bringing about the rewards. So, for example, a worker who is extremely productive may be poorly motivated to perform if he/she has already reached the top level of pay given by the company. If behaviour is not explicitly or implicitly rewarded, people are unlikely to repeat it.

Even if employees receive rewards based on their performance, they may be poorly motivated if those so-called 'rewards' have a low *valence* to them. Someone who doesn't care about the rewards offered by the organization would not be motivated to attempt to attain them. It thus behoves an organization to determine what rewards its employees value, because rewards of low valence will not affect motivation. To a large extent, personality factors determine valence – the value of rewards.

Expectancy theory posits that motivation is a multiplicative function of all three components. This means that higher levels of motivation will result when valence, instrumentality and expectancy are all high, than when they are all low. The multiplicative assumption of the theory therefore implies that if any one of the components is zero, then the overall level of motivation will be zero. Thus, even if an employee believes that his/her effort will result in performance, which will result in reward, motivation may be zero if the valence of the reward that he/she expects to receive is zero.

The specific way in which the components are formally related involves two equations. First, the valence of outcome *j* (the attractiveness of that particular outcome) is a function of the valence multiplied by the instrumentality summed over all of the alternative outcomes. In symbols, the equation is as follows:

$$V_j = f \sum_1^N V_k I_{jk}$$

where f is a constant, V_j is the valence of outcome j, I_{jk} is the perceived instrumentality for achieving j with outcome k, V_k is the valence of outcome k and N is the number of outcomes. Instrumentality, according to Vroom (1964), varies from -1 (the outcome k never leads to the attainment of outcome j) to $+1$ (outcome k is perceived as always leading to outcome j). The classic situation to which this equation has been applied is workers' satisfaction. Satisfaction with a job (outcome j) is related to how instrumental that job is at achieving certain other outcomes, such as salary (outcome k) and the valence of attractiveness of those outcomes (V_k).

The second equation involved in the theory deals with a person's motivation to perform. Vroom (1964) notes that the force acting on a person is the sum of products of the valences of the outcomes and the strength of the expectancies that the behaviour will result in the outcome. Specifically:

$$F_i = \sum_1^N E_{ij} V_j$$

where F_i is the motivational force to perform act j, E_{jk} is the expectancy that act j will be followed by outcome k, V_j is the valence of outcome j and N is the number of outcomes. This equation has been used to predict the choice of occupation, duration of work and effort. For example, it has been shown that the stronger the attractiveness of a certain outcome, and the more a person believes that his/her job is instrumental in achieving the outcome, the stronger the person will be motivated to perform the work behaviour.

Expectancy theory assumes that *motivation* is not equivalent to job performance, but is only one of several determinants of job performance. In particular, the theory assumes that *personality, skills* and *abilities* also contribute to a person's job performance. Some people are better suited to perform their jobs than others by virtue of the unique characteristics and special skills or abilities they bring to their jobs.

Expectancy theory also recognizes that job performance will be influenced by people's *role perceptions*: what they believe is expected of them. Poor performance results *not* necessarily from poor motivation, but from misunderstandings concerning the role that one is expected to play in the organization.

Expectancy theory also recognizes the role of *opportunities to perform* one's job. It is possible that even the best employees will perform at low levels if their opportunities are limited. Even the most highly motivated sales person will perform poorly if opportunities are restricted – if the available inventory is very low (as is sometimes the case among certain popular cars), or if the customers are unable to afford the product (as is sometimes the case among sales persons whose territories are heavily populated by unemployed persons).

It is important to recognize that expectancy theory quite realistically views motivation as just one of several determinants of job performance. Motivation, together with a person's skills, personality traits, abilities, role perceptions and opportunities, combine to influence job performance.

Expectancy theory has generated a great deal of research and has been successfully applied to understanding behaviour in many different organizational settings. However, although some specific aspects of the theory have been supported (particularly the impact of expectancy and instrumentality on motivation), others have not (such as the contribution of valence to motivation and multiplicative assumption). Despite this mixed support, expectancy theory has been a dominant approach to the field of organizational motivation due, in part, to the theory's important implications for organizational practice.

One important recommendation is to *clarify people's expectancies that their effort will lead to performance* (see Table 4.6). Motivation may be enhanced by training employees to do their jobs more efficiently, thereby achieving higher levels of performance for their efforts. It may also be possible to enhance effort–performance expectancies by following employees' own suggestions about ways of changing their jobs. To the extent that employees are aware of the problems in their jobs that interfere with their performance, attempting to alleviate these problems may help them to perform more efficiently. Where possible therefore a manager should *make the desired performance attainable*. It is important to make it clear to people what is expected of them *and* to make it possible for them to attain that level of performance.

Table 4.6 Suggestions from expectancy theory as to how to motivate

Recommendation	Corresponding practice
Clarify the expectation that working hard will improve job performance	Design jobs so as to make the desired performance more attainable
Clearly link valued rewards to the job performance needed to attain them	Institute *pay-for-performance plan*, paying for meritorious work
Administer rewards that have a high positive valence to workers	Use a *cafeteria-style benefit plan*, allowing workers to select the fringe benefits they most value

A second practical suggestion from expectancy theory is to *clearly link valued rewards and performance*. Managers should therefore attempt to enhance their subordinates' beliefs about instrumentality – that is, make it clear to them exactly what job behaviours will lead to what rewards. To the extent that it is possible for employees to be paid in ways directly linked to their performance, such as through piece-rate incentive systems, or sales commission plans equity options, expectancy theory specifies that it would be effective. Performance increases can result from carefully implemented merit systems (management–performance systems).

One most obvious practical suggestion from expectancy theory is to *administer rewards that have positive valiance to employees*. The reward must be valued by employees if it is to have potential as a motivator. It is a mistake to assume that all employees care about having the same rewards made available to them by their companies. Values are in part personality dependent. Some might recognize the incentive value of a pay rise, while others might prefer additional vacation days, improved insurance benefits, or day-care facilities for children, free health insurance, a motor car or an impressive job title. With this in mind, more and more companies are instituting cafeteria-style benefit plans – incentive systems through which the employees select their fringe benefits from a menu of available alternatives. The success of these plans suggests that making highly salient rewards available to employees may be an effective motivational technique.

Possible Personality Hypotheses

- Instrumentalists have higher expectancy and instrumental beliefs (by definition) than fatalists.
- Social contact and stimulation have higher valence for extraverts than introverts.
- Neurotics tend to be less certain about instrumentality in general than non-neurotics.

4.8 CURRENT MOTIVATION-ENHANCING TECHNIQUES

Management science is notoriously faddish; hence, theories and associated techniques move in and out of favour. For a short while, they enjoy unparalleled popularity and are adopted by certain organizations. Disillusionment inevitably follows unrealistic, indeed naïve, expectations and the techniques are dropped and replaced by others. One reason (of many) why the techniques do not work might be because the role of individual differences is ignored. Consider the following recent techniques.

Goal Setting

It is supposed that if an organization (or a departmental/section head) sets *difficult but attainable* goals, within the capacity of employees, workers will strive harder to achieve them. It is suggested that if the workers are *involved* in the goal-setting process, it will encourage ownership of the set standards. Further psychological, even formal, *contracts* are encouraged so that agreed goals are able to be referred to. A final crucial component refers to the frequency, quality and veridicality of the feedback received by employees on how their performance is matching up to the planned goal. No doubt the quality, quantity and difficulty of attaining the goal will be influenced by individual preferences and perceptions.

Job Enlargement and Enrichment

The idea behind this technique is to expand the *content* of a job (by increasing task number and variety) while also encouraging employees to perform at a higher *level*. Thus, simultaneously it is possible to increase job responsibility and control as well as task variety and level. This approach stresses various specific principles: combine jobs to enable workers to perform an entire job; form natural work units to allow workers to be identified in their work; establish client relationships to allow service/product providers to meet recipients/clients; load jobs vertically to allow greater responsibility and control at work; and open feedback channels to give workers knowledge of their results.

4.9 WORK-RELATED LOCUS OF CONTROL

The locus of control concept has been effectively and enthusiastically applied to occupational behaviour. It is one area in which an individual difference variable has been extensively and systematically examined with relation to work motivation. This is not surprising given that locus of control is similar to numerous expectancy theories in occupational psychology. A number of studies in the 1970s illustrated this point: Lawler (1971) found that among managers, internals are more likely to feel performance leads to outcome while externals are less likely to have performance-to-outcome expectancy; while Broedling (1975) found a predicted significant relationship between locus of control and the well-known expectancy model constructs of valence, valence X instrumentality, and superior's ratings of effort and performance. Similarly, Szilagiji and Sims (1975) found internals perceive stronger performance-to-reward *and* effort-to-performance expectancies than externals across various occupational levels. Earlier studies are reviewed in the next section.

Some studies have been longitudinal in their approach. Andrisani and Nestel (1976) related locus of control to a whole range of occupational variables in 2972 respondents studied cross-sectionally and longitudinally. Regressional analysis showed that locus of control beliefs are significantly related to occupational attainment, hourly earnings, job satisfaction, annual earnings and perceived financial progress. The longitudinal analysis showed changes in occupational attainment, annual earnings and dropping out of the labour force were related to locus of control beliefs. The authors note:

> These findings ... suggest that internal–external expectancies both affect one's behaviour toward the environment and are affected by one's environment ... It suggests that opportunities for success and success itself are effective means for raising initiative to succeed, and that the somewhat more external outlook of those at the lower end of the socio-economic spectrum may reflect unfulfilled expectancies of success, rather than – or as well as – a lack of initiative (p.162–3).

In another longitudinal study, Frantz (1980) also used an abbreviated Rotter locus of control scale to study the work-related behaviour of 976 young men. Internal control was associated with race (being white), years of formal schooling, weeks worked and hourly wages. He too believes that locus of control and work experience are reciprocal such that labour market success affects locus of control beliefs which in turn affect work-related behaviour. Becker and Krzytofiak (1982) examined the effect of labour market discrimination (over a two-year period) of a large sample of 2857 on subsequent locus of control beliefs. They found, for instance, that perceptions of employment discrimination influenced the level of externality among blacks, over and above their racial status. The results provide powerful evidence for the fact that work experiences (labour market discrimination) can powerfully affect locus of control. Vecchio (1981) also used a large population of 1131 full-time male American workers to demonstrate that belief in external control was significantly related to overall job satisfaction; black workers believed more in external determinants of success, and locus of control did not moderate the relationship between job quality and satisfaction. These results must be treated with caution, however, as both locus of control and job satisfaction were measured by single-item, self-report measures.

Richards (1983) used four locus of control questions (all external) in a longitudinal study of over 8000 young subjects. He failed to find evidence for the hypothesis that internal control furthers differential goal attainment or vice versa. One obvious explanation for this finding lies in the psychometrically poor measures used to operationalize both independent and dependent variables.

Hammer and Vardi (1981) tested a number of hypotheses regarding the effect of locus of control on work-related behaviour. They believed that in organizational settings which facilitate career self-management, internals more than externals will: exert more effort towards attaining the jobs they want; use more specific strategies to attain preferred jobs; initiate more job moves; experience more upward mobility; perceive mobility as contingent upon personal factors such as skills and competence, experience and performance rather than seniority or sponsorship. Most of the hypotheses were confirmed and the authors were sensitive to the reciprocal causation:

> There is a feedback loop from career experience to locus of control, where favourable experiences increase tendencies toward internal control, which in turn increases the employee's initiative in self-development with future favourable outcomes. Unfavourable experiences increase the tendencies toward external control which reduces a person's willingness to take an active part in career management . . . One might consider the role which locus of control plays in career self-management as similar to the role of need achievement in successful job performance. If the need is present but is allowed to lay dormant by an unstimulating, non challenging environment, it will benefit neither the employee nor the organization (p.28).

Apart from large-scale survey studies, there have been a number of smaller-scale studies with a variety of subjects. For instance, Brownell (1982) used business school students and middle managers in a laboratory simulation. He found that internally oriented subjects performed best in conditions on high participation, while externally oriented subjects performed best in conditions of low participation. He argued that his results are consistent with the hypothesis that performance is the result of the interaction between locus of control and source of control in a particular situation. Payne (1987) reported on a study where locus of control correlated significantly with four out of five 'objective' success measures of R&D professionals.

Miller, Kets de Vries and Toulouse (1982), on the other hand, used top executives and actual business behaviour to show that locus of control is directly related to strategy making. Locus of control was powerfully correlated with many strategic variables, but shown to be mediated by the organizational structure and the business environment. In attempting to interpret their findings, the authors note:

> Though these congruencies appear to be very significant, some doubt remains as to the causal network that induces them. Some might argue that the locus of control of the chief executive influences his strategy making behaviour, and that this in turn has an impact on structure and environment. For example, internals may perceive 'constraints' in the environment as loose and malleable; they turn competitors' challenges into opportunities for innovation. Externals may see their environments as having many rigid boundaries that cannot be violated. The result in the first case is an innovative, proactive, risk embracing strategy, and, in consequence, a more sensitized differentiated structure capable of operating in a more dynamic and heterogeneous environment. The result in the second case is a conservative strategy and a more monolithic and closed structure that is confined to operating in a stable, undifferentiated environment. The data here are most consistent with these conjectures.
>
> But a different causal network might be at work. There might be a selection or a developmental activity performed by structure and environment that influences chief executive locus of control. Perhaps externals are selected by and thrive in untechnocratized, monolithic structures facing stable environments, and internals are chosen by and rise to the top of more open and differentiated structures in more dynamic and heterogeneous environments. This may even be a 'training' influence whereby stable environments push personality in an external direction and dynamic ones do the opposite. These hypotheses are cast into doubt but are by no means entirely ruled out by the findings presented here. Further longitudinal research might be very useful in helping to establish the most important one (p.251).

The idea that locus of control is a moderator variable has been noted by many subsequent authors. For instance, studying nurses, Blau (1987) found locus of control moderated the relationship between withdrawal cognitions (thinking of quitting, intention to search) and job turnover. Internals showed significantly stronger negative relationships than externals between these satisfaction facets and withdrawal cognitions and turnover. Similarly, Storms and Spector (1987) examined frustration in 160 community mental health workers and found that externals are more likely to respond to frustration with counter-productive behaviour (sabotage, aggression, then withdrawal) than persons with an internal locus of control.

Various reviewers have tried to summarize the role of locus of control in organizations: Spector (1982) argued that because internals tend to believe that they can control the work setting through their behaviour, they should attempt to exert more control than would externals, *provided that* control is perceived to lead to desired outcomes and rewards. He noted:

> The internal would probably attempt control in the following areas: work flow, task accomplishment, operating procedures, work assignments, relationships without supervisors and subordinates, working conditions, goal setting, work scheduling, and organizational policy . . . Internals should be easier to motivate. Thus, one should find internals more responsive than externals if the appropriate performance-reward contingencies can be presented (p.485–6).

He examined the literature on seven relevant areas which showed the following:

- *Motivation* – internals are more likely to believe that their efforts will result in good performance, and that they exhibit stronger belief in their own competence.
- *Job performance* – internals perform better because of their greater effort, seeking of more information in complex task situations, and exhibition of greater personal career effectiveness.
- *Job satisfaction* – internals should be more satisfied than externals (generally as well as in the job) partly because of their success.
- *Leadership* – internals prefer participative approaches from their supervisors, rely more on personal persuasion with their subordinates, and seem more task oriented and less socially oriented.
- *Job perception* – internals perceive more personal control over their environment, report more feedback on the job and perceive less role strain.
- *Turnover* – highly job satisfied internals exhibit the same rate of turnover (presumably low) as externals, but for highly dissatisfying jobs, internals would exhibit more turnover than externals.

Although Spector is acutely aware of the methodological shortcoming of research in this area (measurement tools, direction of causality, intervening variables), he believes locus of control measures can be used both for selection and better management. His final cautionary note is well taken:

> One further note is that internals seem to behave in ways that validate much theory in organizational psychology. That is, internals respond to reinforcement contingencies (incentive systems) on the job, they seem to prefer participative supervision, they demonstrate initiative, and they tend to take personal action on the job. Externals on the other hand, seem unresponsive to incentives (they want them but will not necessarily work hard for them) and prefer directive supervision. Thus, much organizational theory might well be limited to internals (p.495).

In a very extensive review O'Brien (1984) tabulated and criticized the by-now extensive literature on the relationship between locus of control beliefs and work (as well as unemployment, retirement and leisure). He starts examining internal–external determinants of occupational choice and career planning. He drew three conclusions on the basis of this:

1. Internals are more likely than externals to choose jobs that have higher skill requirements and provide greater personal autonomy. However, this appears to apply to choices of ideal occupations. When internals and externals are asked about their actual or realistic choices, they display few differences. Actual choices are probably constrained by situational factors, such as social pressures and accessibility of various jobs. It is possible that actual job choices are determined jointly by locus of control and situational factors, but further research is needed for this to be demonstrated.

2. Internals sometimes report more effort than do externals in career planning. It appears that the extent of the difference between internals and externals is determined by the degree to which their organizational environment encourages and provides opportunities for career development. Evidence suggests that internals are more likely to report greater career planning than externals if they are in organizations where career advancement is possible and the criteria for advancement are related to personal motivation and skill. Further research is needed before this hypothesis can be considered to have been supported.

3. Nearly all research studies use self-reports as measures of occupational choice and planning. Hence the results may not extend to objective choices and objectively measured planning behaviour. Another qualification that needs to be made is that results from various studies may differ because of the use of different locus of control scales. The score of different scales is not necessarily unsound, but interpretations are difficult when no information is provided about the degree of correspondence between revised scales and one or more commonly used locus of control scales (p.14–15).

Results seem to indicate that internals perform better than externals on the job and obtain jobs with higher skill utilization and occupational status. According to O'Brien, three possible explanations could be put forward to account for this:

- Internals show great job mobility as a function of their career planning and choice.
- Internals get better jobs because of greater effort, work motivation and therefore promotion.
- Internals get promoted because they choose task behaviours that approximate more closely the behaviours required for optimal job performance.

In attempting to provide an answer to the above, O'Brien tabulated various salient studies but found equivocal results. However, he lists four possible explanations for the different results from various studies:

1. *Situation factors.* In some studies, the performance of internals and externals could have been affected systematically by differences in their situations. In addition, the failure of some studies to measure situational factors precluded estimation of locus of control–situational interactions.
2. *Valence differences.* Many studies did not establish that the value or attractiveness of performance outcomes was equivalent for internals and externals.
3. *Ability.* Some studies found that significant differences between internals and externals disappeared when ability was controlled for. Hence studies that failed to measure ability might be interpreted as showing different ability distributions among internals and externals.
4. *Use of performance ratings.* Although ratings are more often associated significantly with objective performances when both types of performance measures are used, the degree of correspondence is often low.

Despite these difficulties of interpretation, some generalizations are possible. Locus of control accounts for a small percentage of the variance in performance measures (the direct effect is generally less than 10 per cent). When interaction between locus of control and structure is estimated, the percentage of variance accounted for is increased. Internals tend to be rated by supervisors as higher on performance than externals. However, the results do not allow one to infer actual performance differences, as the ratings could be due to an interaction between the public presentation of internals and externals with raters' stereotypes of the better-performing employee. The results could also be attributable to systematic differences in the abilities of internals and externals and in the job structures in which they are found (p.28–9).

O'Brien is critical of studies that interpret findings that individuals with external locus of control report higher stress levels. He believes that locus of control might play a part in distorting responses to stress questions and that most studies fail to measure objective stress factors, the objective degree of structure in jobs, or the behaviour of internals and externals *subsequent* to the onset of stressors.

Locus of control is an important *moderator* variable that together with biographical and job facet variables determine work-related behaviour. It is also a reciprocal variable in that it determines *and* is determined by work-related behaviour. Unfortunately, many extant studies prevent clear interpretations.

More recently, Spector (1986) did a meta-analysis of locus of control studies. He found that high levels of perceived (internal) control were associated with high levels of job satisfaction (overall and individual facets), commitment, involvement, performance and motivation; as well as lower levels of physical symptoms, emotional distress, role stress, absenteeism, intent to leave and actual turnover. Correlates seemed to range from 0.2 to 0.5, suggesting that between 5 per cent and 25 per cent of the variance in occupational behaviour can be accounted for by the locus of control variable. There is no doubt therefore that the locus of control variable accounts for an important and significant amount of individual difference variance with regard to work motivation and productivity.

Sphere-specific Scales

Just as in the other areas, specifically health, researchers attempted to improve the predictive power of locus of control measures by making them specific to a particular domain of behaviours. It was felt that there was sufficient incremental validity to be obtained by having locus of control questions made highly specific to work.

Jones and Wuebker (1985) noted, as research had shown, that the safety conscious were more internal in their beliefs, and that they might profitably develop a *safety locus of control scale* designed to predict employees' accidents and injuries. They ended up with a 17-item scale (ten external, seven internal) which looked at industrial and general accidents. Using undergraduate subjects, they found good split-half reliability and discriminatory validity in that total scores correlated with actual (self-report) history of accidents and injuries. In addition to the impressive, concurrent criterion-related validity, they report on a number of technical reports which provide additional evidence of validity. If, indeed, locus of control is stable and predicts safety-related behaviour, this might constitute partial evidence for the illusive accident-prone personality.

Furnham (1986a), on the other hand, developed an *economic locus of control scale* to measure economic and work-related beliefs. The 40-item scale which revealed a four-factor structure (internal, chance, external, powerful others) had satisfactory reliability and concurrent validity. The demographic correlates of the locus of control beliefs were particularly interesting for a number of reasons. First, it was the chance economic locus of control beliefs that most clearly differentiated between the various demographic groups (age, sex, education and vote). Predictably, in terms of previous research on all aspects of locus of control, females more than males, older rather than younger people, and politically left-wing more than right-wing people tended to rate the power of chance as determinants of both wealth and poverty more highly. Educational level, however, showed a curvilinear pattern; the relatively poorly educated and the very well educated had lower chance economic locus of control beliefs than the intermediary group probably because of the economic position of people with moderate levels of education. The fact that some people (i.e. older, working class, and females) believe that both wealth and poverty are uncontrollable (unobtainable in the former case, and unavoidable in the latter) may explain aspects of the (somewhat irrational) behaviour on the part of certain groups. For instance, working class gambling (on bingo, fruit machines and football pools) may be seen as an attempt by certain groups of people to become wealthier in the only way that they know how. Similarly, it may explain the low incidence of saving or any form of financial planning on the part of poorer people, which may partly explain why they remain in poverty.

Van Daalen, van Niekerk and Pottas (1987) have provided validation of the economic locus of control scale for Black Africans. Similarly, in an Australian study, Heaven (1990) showed, as predicted, that internals on the economic locus of control scale supported tough-minded options for reducing unemployment, while those who felt that their own economic well-being was due to chance factors or powerful others supported tender-minded options (like increased government spending). He argues that economic locus of control beliefs are related to a wide range of socio-political and organizational attitudes.

In order to improve the size of the correlations between locus of control and work-related variables, Spector (1988) developed a 16-item *work locus of control scale* validated on six business administration and industrial psychology students (totalling 1151). The test showed acceptable levels of internal reliability and acceptable concurrent validity, although as yet there was little evidence of predictive or construct validity.

More recently, Trice, Haire and Elliott (1989) developed an 18-item scale useful for students in career-development situations. From their psychometric assessments of the *career locus of control scale*, they believe it to be 'related to the construct of locus of control, reliable, uninfluenced by the social-desirability response set, and a valid index of job-search behaviour among college seniors and major selection and career service use among college juniors' (p.555).

4.10 ATTRIBUTIONAL STYLE, LOCUS OF CONTROL AND WORK MOTIVATION

Attributional style is a personality characteristic that was first introduced by Abramson, Seligman and Teasdale (1978) and further elaborated by others (Peterson *et al.*, 1982). According to the reformulated, learned helplessness model of depression (Abramson *et al.*, 1978), individuals vulnerable to depression differ from the non-vulnerable in the causal judgements they habitually make for the good and bad events in their lives. Abramson *et al.* speculated that a 'depressive attributional style' is characterized by the tendency to view aversive events as caused by *internal* factors (in contrast to external factors, such as the environment or the actions of others); by factors that are *stable* (rather than unstable or temporary); and by factors that exert *global* influence across many domains in one's life (rather than specific or narrow influence in only a few situations).

Seligman and his colleagues developed the Attributional Style Questionnaire (ASQ) which presents subjects with 12 different hypothetical situations, half of which are interpersonal/affiliative in nature, while the other half are achievement related – to allow for the possibility that attributional style for affiliative events is different from attributional style for achievement events, as well as to build cross-situational generality. Within each class of situations, there are three positive outcomes and three negative outcomes. Subjects are required to imagine themselves in the situations described, write down one major cause of the outcome and then rate the cause on separate seven-point scales for the three attributional dimensions of internality, stability and globality, as well as the degree of importance of the situation. The ASQ has been mainly employed in studies of depression, although the causal relationship between attributions and depression is still unclear.

Despite the documented importance of attributions in achievement motivation (Weiner, 1980), little attention has been paid to the role of attributional style in occupational settings. One exception is the work of Seligman and Schulman (1986). Utilizing a sample of 94 experienced life insurance sales agents who as a result of their job repeatedly encounter failure, rejection and indifference from prospective clients, Seligman and Schulman tested whether explanatory style predicts work productivity and quitting. They found, as predicted, that individuals who habitually explained failure by internal, stable and global causes initiated fewer sales attempts, were less persistent, produced less, and quit more frequently than those with a more optimistic explanatory style. The results showed that agents who had an optimistic explanatory style on the ASQ sold 37 per cent more insurance in their first two years of service than those with a pessimistic style. Agents in the top decile sold 88 per cent more insurance than those in the bottom decile. In a prospective one-year study of 103 newly hired agents, individuals who had an optimistic explanatory style when hired remained in their job twice as long and sold more insurance than agents with a pessimistic explanatory style.

The theoretical significance of these findings is that they support the reformulation's claim that a bad explanatory style predisposes to poor performance, and poor performance is then triggered by failure in those individuals with the predisposing style. The interaction of the two components increases the likelihood of helplessness deficits, here operationalized by quitting and poor productivity. These results suggest that a depressogenic explanatory style predicts performance deficits in a work setting, beyond the clinical syndrome of depression, wherein it has most often been tested.

Furnham, Sadka and Brewin (1992) described a new measure of attributional style, the *Occupational Attributional Style Questionnaire* (OASQ), which was designed to assess how a person makes causal attribution for specifically occupational outcomes. Despite the development of numerous alternative measures of attributional style, such as Russell's (1982) Causal Dimension Scale and Feather's (1985) Balanced Attributional Style Questionnaire, the OASQ is exceptional in that it describes hypothetical events which are specifically related to the work setting. Studies have shown that predictability is improved with specific sphere-related questions (Furnham and Procter, 1989). In addition, the OASQ is multi-dimensional, measuring nine dimensions of beliefs.

The OASQ was closely modelled on both the ASQ in terms of its basic format, instruction and response scales, and the measure of perceived control over diabetes developed by Bradley *et al.* (1984) which incorporates various attributional dimensions not found in the ASQ (e.g. controllability and foreseeability).

The measure consists of nine items that present brief descriptions of hypothetical situations which are commonly experienced by, or particularly relevant to, employed individuals. Five of the hypothetical events describe positive outcomes and five describe negative outcomes. The hypothetical events are presented in Table 4.7, along with the rating scale.

For each hypothetical event, respondents were asked to imagine vividly themselves in the situation, and to write down the single most likely cause of the event. They then rated this cause on nine separate seven-point scales concerned with internality, stability, externality, chance, personal control, colleague control, foreseeability and importance respectively. The scale showed impressive internal reliability and a clearly interpretable factor structure.

The attributional correlates of salary were most consistent and explicable: high salaries were positively correlated with internal, personal control and importance judgements but negatively correlated with external, chance and *superior* control attributions. Dimensions of the scale correlated strongly with job satisfaction and motivation. The pattern of correlations is strongest for the positive rather than the negative events. Eight of the nine attributions for positive events correlated with job satisfaction in the predicted direction. That is, job satisfaction was associated with internal, personal control, and foreseeable attributions but negatively associated with *unstable, specific*, external, chance, and *superior* control attributions. Very much the same pattern emerged for intrinsic job motivation, although it is probably worth pointing out that the correlations were somewhat higher.

About a third of the attributional dimensions for negative events correlated with job satisfaction and intrinsic motivation. The pattern of correlations for the combined scores also showed an interesting pattern. While only one (foreseeability) correlated with job satisfaction, seven correlations

Table 4.7 First-order and partial correlations (in parentheses) between attributional style, job satisfaction and job motivation, controlling for age, sex, education, occupational status and salary

	Job satisfaction		Job motivation	
Positive events				
Internality	0.24**	(0.22*)	0.29***	(0.21**)
Stability	−0.20*	(−0.20*)	−0.44***	(−0.43***)
Globality	−0.21*	(−0.20*)	−0.31***	(−0.29**)
Externality	−0.28**	(−0.19*)	−0.14	(−0.08)
Chance	−0.28**	(−0.22*)	−0.25**	(−0.20*)
Personal control	−0.29**	(0.25**)	0.26**	(0.20*)
Colleague control	−0.30***	(−0.26**)	−0.16	(−0.18*)
Foreseeability	0.30***	(0.25**)	0.30***	(0.17)
Importance	−0.08	(−0.07)	−0.40***	(−0.37***)
Negative events				
Internality	−0.20*	(−0.22*)	0.04	(0.02)
Stability	0.00	(0.12)	−0.19*	(−0.13)
Globality	0.27**	(0.31**)	0.00	(0.01)
Externality	0.15	(0.25**)	0.01	(0.04)
Chance	0.01	(0.11)	−0.21*	(−0.20*)
Personal control	−0.12	(−0.13)	0.03	(−0.02)
Colleague control	0.12	(0.20*)	0.08	(0.14)
Foreseeability	0.20*	(0.10)	0.18*	(0.04)
Importance	0.04	(0.05)	−0.31***	(−0.33***)
Combined events				
Internability	−0.01	(−0.01)	0.21*	(0.19*)
Stability	−0.07	(−0.03)	−0.37***	(−0.33***)
Globality	0.06	(0.08)	−0.27**	(−0.23*)
Externality	−0.06	(0.04)	−0.27**	(−0.33***)
Chance	−0.14	(−0.07)	−0.24**	(−0.15)
Personal control	0.13	(0.07)	0.22*	(0.14)
Colleague control	−0.10	(−0.01)	−0.07	(0.04)
Foreseeability	0.37***	(0.28**)	0.35***	(0.20*)
Importance	−0.02	(−0.03)	−0.33***	(−0.32***)

*$p < 0.05$
**$p < 0.01$
***$p < 0.001$

(five partial correlations) were significant for intrinsic job motivation. The direction of the correlations was similar to that for positive events (see Table 4.8).

Attributions for positive events particularly (and to a lesser extent with positive and negative combined) were correlated with social class, salary, job satisfaction and intrinsic motivation. These attributions were what Seligman and Schulman (1986) called the optimistic vs pessimistic explanatory style for bad events. They found that an optimistic attributional style for both good and bad events predicted survival and productivity in the job of sales

Table 4.8 The hypothetical events used in the OASQ

Positive outcomes
Imagine that you apply for promotion and get it.
Imagine that you solve a major problem that has occurred at work.
Imagine that you very successfully lead a group project with a positive
   outcome.
Imagine that you are voted as the most popular boss in your section.
Imagine that you are given a special performance reward at work.

Negative outcomes
Imagine that you are turned down at a job interview.
Imagine that your boss always acts aggressively toward you.
Imagine that you can't get all the work done others expect of you.
Imagine that you give an important talk in front of your colleagues and they
   react negatively.
Imagine that you are given a poor annual report by a superior.

Source: Furnham, Sadka and Brewin (1992)

agents just as the same style predicted salary, satisfaction and motivation in
this study.

Contrary to the predictions of learned helplessness theory, attributions
for positive events were uniquely linked to job attitudes and salary. Similar
findings have been reported by Brewin and Shapiro (1984), who found
that responsibility for positive outcomes, but not negative outcomes, was
linked to academic achievement. In contrast, it is attributions for negative
outcomes rather than positive outcomes that are most strongly associated
with depression. Further research is necessary to explain these discrepancies.
However, to find an individual difference variable with such widespread
predictive power is relatively rare in psychology (Furnham, 1990b).

Of course, correlational results do not show direction of causality or
rule out the probable likelihood of bi-directionality. Just as an optimistic
attributional style may lead to success and satisfaction, so success may
enhance, maintain or change attributional style. The literature in this field
suggests a mutual, reciprocal causative model is probably operating.

Clearly, these findings have implications for both selection and training.
If, as has been shown, attributional style is a correlate of satisfaction and
motivation, it can be selected for in job applicants. Attribution training
techniques have been successfully used to enhance academic attainment,
and could be adapted to meet the needs of employers.

4.11 CONCLUSION

It is surprising that despite the number of theories concerning work motivation, there is so little research on individual difference in this area. There
could be many reasons for this: for instance, there is not a large amount of

empirical research in this area anyway; secondly, many theorists do not focus on individual difference but rather 'universal' principles; thirdly, personality researchers have not been impressed with the theories in the area.

However, it is neither difficult to derive individual difference types nor hypotheses for each of the theories considered. Both from a personality psychology and an organizational psychology point of view, it seems as if a set of reasonable studies could be done to test hypotheses with clearly very important implications.

One area of research that does seem both highly relevant and very promising is the research using the locus of control concept. The fact that this expectancy–valence type concept correlates so powerfully and frequently with so many occupational variables implies its importance in the area. Extensions of the idea to attributional style as a whole seem most promising. Clearly, the development of sphere-specific measures applicable to occupational behaviour would seem to be a natural outcome of this very promising line of research.

Chapter 5

Personality and productivity

My two new assistants are incompetent dullards, so they should do very well in British Industry.

Michael Green

Well, we can't stand around here doing nothing, people will think we're workers.

Spike Milligan

Few people who do business well do nothing else.

Lord Chesterfield

Too much work and too much energy kill a man just as effectively as too much assorted vice or too much drink.

Rudyard Kipling

Work was like cats were supposed to be; if you disliked and feared it and tried to keep out of its way, it knew at once and sought you out.

Kingsley Amis

Visionary people are visionary partly because of the very great many things they don't see.

Berkeley Rice

Behind every successful man there stands an amazed woman.

Anon

To be successful you have to be lucky, or a little mad or very talented, or to find yourself in a rapid-growth field.

Edward de Bono

All you need in this life is ignorance and confidence, and then success is sure.

Mark Twain

5.1 INTRODUCTION

It is self-evident that some people work harder than others. Working hard probably correlates with productivity, but as the Americans say it is better to work 'smarter' rather than harder to be productive. Assuming that it is possible to provide a robust, sensitive and reliable measure of productivity, can it be shown that some personalities are more productive in certain jobs? Unfortunately, the measurement of work productivity is highly problematic. In some jobs, productivity is fairly easy to measure; for instance, it is simple to measure the number of pots a potter throws in a day or words a journalist writes. Where people work on their own (as opposed to on a conveyor belt), producing specific and finished goods, it is fairly easy to count their productivity. However, where (more usually) people work in teams where they are interdependent, it becomes much more difficult to determine productivity of individuals. In some jobs, determining productivity is almost impossible. How does one determine the productivity of, say, a night watchman, a clergyman or meteorologist?

There are various types of measures that might be used to determine productivity:

- *Quantity* – how much is produced. This may be calculated in a variety of ways referring to wholes or parts. Most easily, this can be calculated in terms of money, such as revenue generated, mark-up items etc.
- *Quality* – the perfection of the goods/services produced. This is much more difficult to calculate reliably and may be highly sensitive to personal tastes and preferences.
- *Accidents/rejects* – the amount of rejected or unacceptable products. This is a more negative way of calculating productivity.

Eleven of these possible performance measures are set out in Table 5.1. Alas, each performance measure is associated with different biases and limitations and hence they may not be strictly comparable. Also, of course, they may not be available to the researcher, who may have to use what is available. Therefore the issue of personality correlates of productivity is fraught with experimental problems, mainly because of problems in the measurement of productivity.

5.2 PSYCHOLOGY OF THE ENTREPRENEUR

The quest for the ultimate, comprehensive and veridical description of the mechanism and process by which someone becomes an entrepreneur is a bit like the quest for the holy grail: extensive, full of myths and ultimately unsuccessful. A major problem for the psychologist is that the entrepreneur is not a psychological concept, being caught up in ideological cant and

Table 5.1 Different performance measures and different evaluation situations in industrial settings

Performance measure	Training performance	Actual job performance
Rate of work	Time to learn	Amount per unit time
Quality of work	Ratings	Ratings
Accidents and breakage	Accident rate	Accident rate
Money earned	Earnings	Earnings
Job knowledge	Ratings or test	Ratings or test
Job tenure	Time to learn	Length of time
Absenteeism	Number of days	Number of days
Rate of advancement	Improvement during training	Salary history–promotion history
Supervisory judgements	Ratings	Ratings
Peer judgements	Ratings	Ratings
Self-judgement	Ratings	Ratings

obfuscating jargon. Indeed, the concept has had a varied history and the term remains etymologically uncertain and multi-faceted. Tripathi (1985) uses an excellent metaphor to explain problems with the concept of the entrepreneur: it is like a hat that has lost its shape because of overuse by people who pull it into their preferred fashion. Indeed, Sexton (1987) laments all research in this area. He writes:

> The lack of definition of the sample, when combined with invalidated test instruments, small sample sizes, unsophisticated or simplistic mathematical analyses, limited comparable studies, and a paucity of longitudinal studies are characteristic of this . . . area (p.26).

Chell and Haworth (1988) prefer the definition of Meredith, Nelson and Neck (1982) who suggest the following:

> Entrepreneurs are people who have the ability to see and evaluate business opportunities; to gather the necessary resources, to take advantage of them; and to initiate appropriate action to ensure success (p.3).

For Carland *et al.* (1984):

> An entrepreneur is an individual who establishes and manages a business for the principal purpose of profit and growth. The entrepreneur is characterized principally by innovative behaviour and will employ strategic management practices in the business (p.258).

In a thorough and thoughtful review on the mixed literature on entrepreneurship, Low and MacMillan (1988) came to six conclusions:

1. Purpose. There is a need for future research programs to include a clear statement of purpose. Furthermore, we appeal to researchers to link

the specific purpose of their study to the more fundamental purpose we have proposed: to explain and facilitate the role of new enterprise in furthering economic progress. It is hoped that by linking to this overall purpose, a wide variety of research activities can be brought into a broad but unifying arena.

2. Theoretical perspective. In the past, much of the entrepreneurship literature has implicitly assumed a strategic adaptation perspective. The insights resulting from recent work using the population ecology perspective has challenged some of these assumptions and demonstrated the benefits of theory driven research. We suggest that future research should examine and clearly state theoretical assumptions and that additional theoretical perspective should be explored.

3. Focus. Recently, there has been a trend toward more contextual and process oriented research. This is an important advancement and moves the field closer to a position of being able to explain rather than merely document the entrepreneurial phenomenon. Future research should continue this trend.

4. Level of analysis. There has been a welcome initiation of studies that examined more than one of the individual, group, organization, industry, and society levels of analysis. Such multi-level studies provide a much richer understanding of the entrepreneurial phenomenon and should therefore be encouraged in future research programs.

5. Time frame. It appears that greater insights can be obtained from studies which employ wide time frames than from studies employing cross-sectional 'snapshots'. A push towards longer time frame studies is desirable, particularly since it is becoming clear that different strategic issues become important as firm and industry evolve.

6. Methodology. There has been disappointingly slow progress in research that addresses issues of causality, perhaps reflecting the elusiveness of the entrepreneurial phenomenon. Recent years have seen only limited examples of research designs that develop a priori hypotheses. Consequently formal modelling and experimental research have lacked a foundation for development. On the positive side, the incidence of studies that are both cross-sectional and longitudinal are on the rise (p.157).

In a similar critical review, Wortman (1987) has lamented the theoretical and methodological shortcomings of entrepreneurial behaviour. In so doing, he develops 25 research questions that in his opinion have not been answered. They include:

• What happens to entrepreneurs over time? How much do they change and why?
• What external and/or internal factors have had an impact on the effectiveness of an entrepreneur?

• Are there distinct competencies for individual entrepreneurs?

Hébert and Link (1982) classify economic writers on entrepreneurship initially as falling into 12 ideological categories:

1. The entrepreneur is the person who assumes the risk associated with uncertainty.
2. The entrepreneur is a supplier of financial capital.
3. The entrepreneur is an innovator.
4. The entrepreneur is a decision maker.
5. The entrepreneur is an industrial leader.
6. The entrepreneur is a manager or superintendent.
7. The entrepreneur is an organizer or co-ordinator of economic resources.
8. The entrepreneur is a proprietor of an enterprise.
9. The entrepreneur is an employer of factors of production.
10. The entrepreneur is a contractor.
11. The entrepreneur is an arbitrageur.
12. The entrepreneur is the person who allocates resources to alternative uses.

In a further effort to characterize the 12 categories listed, Hébert and Link have distinguished between static and dynamic theories of entrepreneurship. In a static world, neither change nor uncertainty is present, and the entrepreneur becomes a passive element, because his/her actions are repetitions of past procedures and techniques that have already been learned and implemented. On the other hand, 'dynamic theories' of entrepreneurship are based on a process view of competition. If a dynamic point of view is relevant, it becomes possible to reduce the 12 different views on entrepreneurship to a four-type taxonomy of economic theories of entrepreneurship. These are:

• *'Pure' uncertainty*. The entrepreneur is someone with foresight and is willing to take risks (with land, labour and capital); is well organized and is highly sensitive to response demand; and is a catalyst in a progressive and dynamic economy.
• *'Pure' innovation*. The entrepreneur is a creative manager and organizer whose role it is to innovate and initiate to promote and produce new processes or products.
• *Uncertainty and ability/innovation*. The entrepreneur has to rely on his/her knowledge and ability to take risks and innovate; he/she is able to bear the anxiety and stress of business. Cole (1946) best describes the position:

Entrepreneurship may be defined as the purposeful activity (including an integrated sequence of decisions) of an individual or group of associated individuals, undertaken to initiate, maintain, or aggrandize a profit-oriented business unit for the production or distribution of economic goods and services with pecuniary or other advantage the goal or measure of success in interaction with (or without the conditions established by) the internal situation of the unit itself or with the economic, political and social circumstances (institutions and practices) of a period which allows an appreciable measure of freedom of decision (p.88).

• *Perception and adjustment.* This approach minimizes the stress on risk but emphasizes the successful co-ordination of labour and capital to restore the economy to equilibrium.

According to Baran (1957), the entrepreneur is not the major figure responsible for economic development, but he/she is similar to the capitalist, a figure that has benefitted substantially from modern capitalism, and both radically and ideologically trained. He gives the following reasons. Much of the literature on entrepreneurship glorifies the 'genius' of the entrepreneur in the capitalistic system, and it does not explain how this 'genius' turned to the accumulation of capital. Secondly, many authors also imply that less developed countries are lacking in entrepreneurship because of a lack of the appropriate character traits, i.e. risk taking, imagination and frugality, which are presumably considered to be the strengths of Anglo-Saxon peoples. Thirdly, the problem in less developed countries is not a lack of the supply of entrepreneurship, but rather of the composition of entrepreneurship between the various sectors of the economy.

Others have attempted to provide a theory/explanation of the entrepreneur from the non-psychological perspective, such as Leibenstein (1966) and Druker (1985). Although Leibenstein originally developed his x-efficiency theory for other purposes, he has more recently applied it to analyse the role of the entrepreneur (Leibenstein, 1979). X-efficiency therefore arises because the resources are either used in the wrong way or not used at all. Entrepreneurship is, then, regarded by Leibenstein as a creative response to x-efficiency. Other people's lack of effort, and therefore the consequent inefficiency of the organizations that employ them, creates the opportunities for the entrepreneurial spirit, which has two major roles for the entrepreneur: 'input completion' – this involves making available the inputs which improve the efficiency of existing production methods or to help with the introduction of new ones; 'gap-filling' – this involves filling gaps in the production process and overcoming obstacles to production. It closely resembles the arbitrage function as introduced by Kirzner (1973).

Druker (1985), on the other hand, sees entrepreneurship in terms of management practice. Innovation and entrepreneurship can no longer be the domain of the gifted few with special personality characteristics. Instead, Druker identifies the practices and discipline of innovation and entrepreneurship and explains why these practices should be a necessary part of the repertoire of the behaviour of an individual and an organization. He defines systematic innovation as the 'purposeful and organized search for changes and the systematic analysis of the opportunities such change might offer for economic or social innovation' (p.35). Druker regards only businesses that introduce an innovation as entrepreneurial.

Clearly, not all innovative businesspeople are entrepreneurial, so while innovations may be necessary, it is far from sufficient in the definition of entrepreneurial behaviour! Also, organizations can be described in entire entrepreneurial terms just as much as in traditional terms. Peterson (1980) has argued that entrepreneurship is a process, not a person, and has to do with demand and opportunity, and not supply, and hence can be applied not only to individuals but whole organizations. Davidsson (1989) has attempted to trace the development of entrepreneurship which begins to answer some of these questions.

While anthropologists and sociologists have attempted explanations of entrepreneurship (Hagen, 1962; Whyte, 1963), few psychologists have attempted this. A clear exception is McClelland (1962, 1987). More recently, social psychologists have attempted a theoretical interpretation or perspective on entrepreneurship behaviour. Carsrud and Johnson (1989) stressed the social context of entrepreneurial behaviour, the power and usefulness of social networks, and the importance of impression management in the whole procedure. On the other hand, Scherer, Adams and Wiebe (1989) provide a social learning perspective which stresses the importance of early role models and reinforcement patterns on the maintenance and acquisition of entrepreneurial behaviours (see Figure 5.1). Their 'model' is thus:

> First, the individual observes the parent entrepreneur. The observer makes cognitive evaluations about the parent's reinforcements and the value of those reinforcements to the observer. These evaluations are influenced by observer attribute and the gender of the model and the observer (as a result of the socialization process). In addition, the observer's sense of identification or perceived similarity to the parent model will affect the observational learning. An observer who identifies with or perceives similarities between self and the model will conclude that similar outcomes might result for him/her in an entrepreneurial career. If, on the other hand, the child observing the parent identifies him/herself as essentially different from the parent model, the observer will not expect the same outcomes for the behaviours the parent is seen enacting. The child who does not identify with the parent is therefore less likely to choose an entrepreneurial path to achieve the observed outcomes even when those outcomes are evaluated as desirable. The net effect of the observational learning is different levels of entrepreneurial behaviours in the observers. Note that the conceptual model treats the individual's personality as a whole *set* of integrated elements rather than as isolated characteristics (p.22).

It should, however, not be thought that all studies of entrepreneurs see them in heroic terms. In an unusual paper, Kets de Vries (1985) points out some of the weaknesses that he found in entrepreneurs. These are a distrust and suspicion of others and yet a strong desire for applause.

For reasons that are not immediately apparent, there has been something of a renaissance in the interest in the process of entrepreneurship (Chell, 1985; Timmons, Smollen and Dingee, 1985). Chell and Haworth (1987) classify approaches to the study of the entrepreneurial personality into three categories: the trait approach, the behavioural approach and the contingency approach.

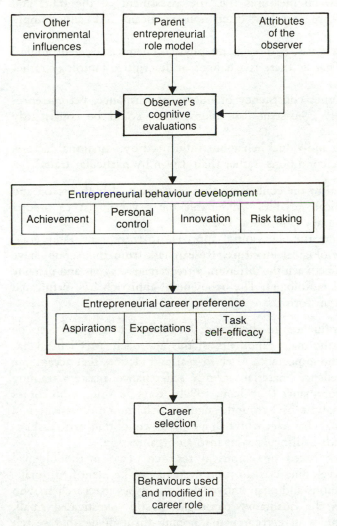

Figure 5.1 A model of entrepreneurship
Source: Scherer *et al.* (1989)

The majority of research on entrepreneurship has been aimed at discovering the trait(s) that could be used to describe entrepreneurs (Brockhaus, 1982a). According to Chell and Haworth (1987), this approach yielded only equivocal results. Different schools of thought have proposed different explanations of entrepreneurial behaviour. Some of these differences might be ascribed to different definitions or conceptualizations of the term entrepreneur – but also the research has been very weak. Major problems include the following:

• Correlations between measures (i.e. the assessment of the trait) and actual behaviour are very low, often non-significant and cannot imply causation.
• Exactly what are traits, if there is no physico-chemical or neurological basis to traits? That is, there is a danger of descriptive tautology rather than explanation.
• Trait theory assumes consistency of human performance, yet entrepreneurs seem rarely consistent. Of course, they could be consistently inconsistent.
• To what extent is individual behaviour influenced by situational factors, such as economic conditions, rather than driven by particular traits?

These arguments led to the contention that assessment of both person and situational/economical variables will enable the psychologist to predict behaviour with accuracy (Furnham, 1981).

On the other hand, the behavioural approach to entrepreneurship emanated from the sociological literature. Researchers from this school have tried to distinguish between the different entrepreneurial types and provide descriptively useful tautologies. The behavioural approach has manifested itself in three different forms:

• Developmental influences in childhood. McClelland (1965) and Kets de Vries (1977) are the main exponents of this approach. McClelland has always stressed the importance of child-rearing practices that accentuate standards of excellence, material warmth, self-reliance, mastery training and low father dominance (Furnham, 1990b). Kets de Vries, who comes from a psychoanalytic background, suggests that the entrepreneur is a deviant or marginal character who had a difficult childhood, who dislikes authority and finds it difficult to fit into an organization.
• Typological work based on empirical research. Two methodological approaches to developing classification systems can be identified: qualitative design methods and quantitative survey analyses. Researchers who have worked on the qualitative paradigm mostly investigated small, non-random samples of entrepreneurs hoping through depth research to understand their dynamics. The quantitative studies are exemplified by the Dunkelberg and Cooper (1982) factor analytic classification of 1805

entrepreneurs into three typologies, viz. growth/change oriented, independence oriented and craftsman oriented. The latter approach attempts to describe broad types.

● Developmental stages approach. This approach focuses on the different stages of development of the business that the entrepreneur grows. Gibb and Ritchie's (1981) social development model provides such an example of this approach. It postulates that learning experience and stage in the life-cycle have a significant influence on the business start-up process.

The third approach to the study of entrepreneurship assumes that the behaviour of an entrepreneur is a function of various specifiable contextual (i.e. socio-economic) variables. Exponents of this approach are Miller (1983), and Miller and Friesen (1982). Miller distinguishes between three types of firms. Single firms are small firms which operate in hostile and competitive environments; the owner/manager dominates the decision-making processes in these firms. Planning firms are much more highly differentiated in terms of organizational structure and internal decision processes, while organic firms are much more oriented toward their environment and attempt to develop the best plan from among different courses of action in order to meet and exploit external challenges. Each firm, of necessity, requires a different type of entrepreneur. The economic reality thus drives the individual behaviour.

Chell and Haworth (1987) acknowledge the contribution of Timmons, Smollen and Dingee (1977, 1985) in presenting 'one of the most comprehensive approaches to understanding entrepreneurship to date' (p.21). The Timmons model is presented in Figure 5.2. It comprises a set of *personality traits*, *cognitive elements*, and also emphasizes the ability to capitalize on opportunities (as opposed to mobilization of resources). The successful entrepreneur is also supposed to possess various skills, such as team building and getting things done through other people. Chell and Haworth are, however, critical of the Timmons model because it assumes that a successful entrepreneur is an ideal type – and should possess *all* the characteristics stipulated by Timmons *et al*. They further argue that the model is too complex and prescriptive and also needs empirical testing. Indeed, it is rather unclear how the model could be tested.

Chell (1985) has proposed a useful reconceptualization of the entrepreneurial process (see Figure 5.3). According to Chell, the entrepreneurial personality comprises five social learning person variables, i.e. abilities, skills, constructs, expectancies, values and strategies/plans. These variables can be considered as general features of people, which in combination with particular socio-economic and business situations will result in particular actions. They influence the entrepreneur's orientation and role behaviour in respect of his/her business. The entrepreneur therefore has to deal with a multitude of different situations which are shaped by different environmental conditions. The entrepreneur, in bringing his/her own set

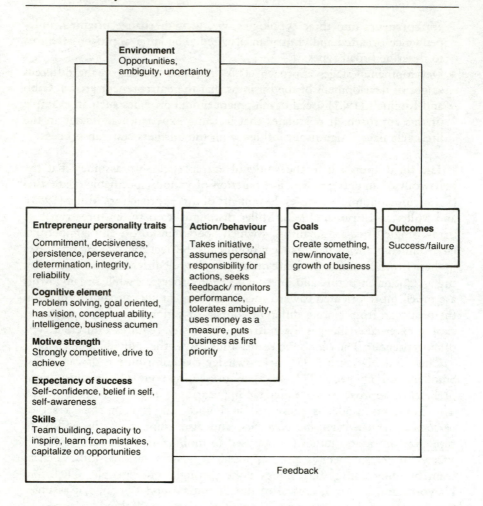

Figure 5.2 The process of entrepreneurship
Source: Chell and Haworth (1987)

of values and behaviours to bear in each situation, may or may not have the appropriate repertoire of behaviours to cope with, and deal with, the different situations that he/she is faced with.

Entrepreneurs often have to play a variety of roles, such as chief executive, production manager, salesperson or general handyman. In the acting out of appropriate roles, the entrepreneur can engage in various activities. Two main functions are associated with these activities according to Harré (1979): a *practical* function, to manage the situation and to fulfil the needs of the individual, and an *expressive* function, to convey impressions to others.

The expressive function contributes to the central function of human social activity, namely to develop style and reputation. Actions are often executed with particular judges and audiences in mind. For instance, the entrepreneur would probably try to convey a message of friendliness, reliability and trustworthiness to his/her customers aimed at maintaining longevity of the relationship, and therefore also the success of the business.

Chell (1985) reconceptualizes entrepreneurship into an interactionist model that encapsulates appropriate person variables and takes account of the variability in behaviour due to differences in people and situations. This model is typical of the interactionist approach of the early 1980s. One problem with the Chell model, and also duly pointed out by Chell and Haworth (1987), is that it contains no motivational elements. It is not clear what energizes the entrepreneur in the first place. Chell and Haworth further suggest that the Chell model needs to be tested empirically.

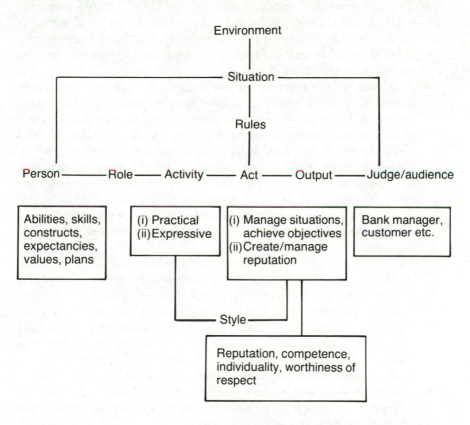

Figure 5.3 Person/situation influences of entrepreneurship
Source: Chell and Haworth (1987)

There have been innumerable attempts, often of very poor research quality, to distinguish (isolate) the characteristics of entrepreneurs. Using standardized, validated and popular, mainly vocational guidance questionnaires, Hornaday and Aboud (1971) found entrepreneurs, compared to the general population, higher on achievement, independence and leadership but low on support. However, they did point out that what would merit further work would be to determine whether these four scales could differentiate between the successful and unsuccessful entrepreneur.

More recently, Ray and Trupin (1989) compared how American, Canadian, French and Japanese entrepreneurs perceived success. Most believed it took three to five years to achieve success. Table 5.2 shows the factors rank ordered by the different national entrepreneurs. It also shows the factors thought to relate to success. The authors interpret these findings thus:

- The biotechnology entrepreneurs in the United States combined business and scientific skills and believe that such a combination is the key to their success. In a new industry, like biotechnology, this belief is probably well founded. This combination, however, may be applicable only to biotechnology.
- The Japanese entrepreneurs did not seem to attribute their success to hard work and persistence as did the samples from each of the other countries. However, it would be erroneous to assume that Japanese entrepreneurs do not work hard or appreciate the value of hard work. Rather, it may be that hard work and persistence are taken as a given in Japan, whereas in the West, it may be more characteristic of entrepreneurs than employees. Much the same point might be made by the relatively low percentage of Japanese who indicated that people/communication skills and teamwork were important to their success. These skills and behaviours may be taken for granted in Japan.
- The Japanese entrepreneurs, however, did acknowledge that creativity was important to their success. The high percentage for the Japanese sample may, again, reflect that creativity is not perceived by Japanese entrepreneurs to be highly valued in large companies. Previous research indicated that creativity was the single most important value in motivating individuals to become high technology entrepreneurs in Japan. Understandably, these entrepreneurs would be prone to view the central motivation as also being an attribute related to their success.
- Leadership skills were relatively unimportant to the US biotechnology entrepreneurs, which may reflect the nature of their technology and product and their scientific background.
- Whereas there are national variations, it appears that the entrepreneurs in these four national samples might view technical competence as more important than an MBA and people/communication skills and

Table 5.2 Perception of entrepreneurial success

(a) Cross-national comparison of how entrepreneurs judge success

Factor	US	Japan	France	Canada
I became rich	11	10	11	11
I became financially independent	4	7	6	7
I gained control of my own destiny	1	4	2	1
I commercialized a product that became well accepted by customers	2	1	1	2
I was able to develop a project that was truly my own	5	2	3	9
I created an organization that really reflects my values	3	3	4	4
My company reached a comfortable size in terms of sales volume	8	8	8	6
My company reached a comfortable size in terms of profits	7	6	5	3
My company reached a comfortable size in terms of employees	9	9	9	8
I enjoy a certain degree of power	10	5	7	10
I have not gone bankrupt	6	11	10	5

(b) Skills and training that contributed to success (percentage of sample indicating)

Factor	US	Japan	France	Canada
Work ethic and persistence	0.42	0.10	0.42	0.34
Combine business and science or engineering	0.38	0.04	0.06	0.06
Experiential learning	0.38	0.14	0.23	0.26
Technical competence	0.25	0.16	0.35	0.19
People/communication skills	0.25	0.10	0.18	0.38
Scientific method	0.15	0.04	0.06	0.15
Honesty and trustworthiness	0.17	0	0.02	0.04
Creativity	0.13	0.24	0.19	0.02
Leadership skills	0.04	0.16	0.13	0.08
Personal attributes (optimism, pragmatism, patience)	0.15	0.05	0.05	0.08
Courage	0	0.06	0.10	0
Teamwork orientation	0	0.02	0.13	0.02
General education/generalist orientation	0.17	0.14	0.05	0.04
MBA	0.13	0.02	0.02	0.11
MBA skills	0.10	0.04	0.11	0.11
Knowledge, intelligence, competence	0	0.02	0.08	0
Number of respondents	48	49	62	53

Source: Ray and Turpin (1989)

the scientific method as more important than the functional skills associated with most MBA programs. This may have interesting implications for entrepreneurship education (p.125).

Timmons *et al.* (1977) presented 13 general characteristics which, according to research findings at that stage, could be regarded as *important* for entrepreneurial success. These characteristics are:

1. Drive and energy.
2. Self-confidence.
3. Long-term involvement.
4. Money is regarded as a measure of success.
5. Persistence in problem solving.
6. Ability to set, and to commit themselves to, clear goals.
7. Moderate risk taking.
8. The ability to use failure as a positive learning experience.
9. Concern for feedback of performance.
10. Taking initiative and seeking personal responsibility.
11. Actively use resources, such as expertise of others, to accomplish goals.
12. Competing against self-imposed standards.
13. Tolerance of ambiguity and uncertainty.

Timmons *et al.* have, however, updated their attitudes toward entrepreneurial characteristics considerably in the latest edition of their book (1985). The trouble with these lists is legion: are they rank ordered?; how do the various characteristics relate to one another? (that is, what is their structure); is each necessary and sufficient to be an entrepreneur?; how does one measure both the independent and dependent variable? Burch (1986) came up with a not dissimilar and equally unsubstantiated list. Nine 'salient characteristics' seem to be: desire to achieve, hard work, nurturing quality, acceptance of responsibility, reward orientation, optimism, orientation to excellence, organization and profit orientation. He offers a way of self-diagnosis (see Figure 5.4):

> In this schema, the *laborer* is the least entrepreneurial and the *inventrepreneur* is the most entrepreneurial. In fact, the inventrepreneur is the epitome of entrepreneurial activity. This special entrepreneur has the ability both to invent a new product or service and to bring it successfully to the marketplace. The *bureaucrat*, *leader*, (bank loan officer), *professional*, and *manager* tend to be non-entrepreneurial. *Copycat entrepreneurs* simply imitate someone else's product or service and business. They have fairly strong entrepreneurial tendencies except in innovation. *Opportunist entrepreneurs* have fairly strong overall tendencies toward entrepreneurial activity, especially the tendency toward spotting and exploiting opportunities. *Venture capitalists* are not entrepreneurs as such, but are primary

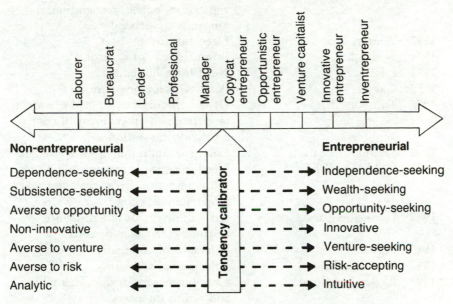

Figure 5.4 Tendencies toward non-entrepreneurial or entrepreneurial activity
Source: Burch (1986)

sources of equity financing for business ventures, especially for start-ups and early-stage expansion. They have a strong wealth-seeking tendency. Both the *innovative entrepreneur* and the *inventrepreneur* have very strong overall tendencies toward an entrepreneurial activity (p.15).

Historically, one can trace thinking about the characteristics of particular entrepreneurs. The following list is not exhaustive but illustrative:

Date	Authors	Characteristics
1848	Mill	Risk bearing
1917	Weber	Source of formal authority
1934	Schumpter	Innovation: initiative
1954	Sutton	Desire for responsibility
1959	Hartman	Source of formal authority
1961	McClelland	Risk taking; need for achievement
1963	Davids	Ambition; desire for independence, responsibility, self-confidence
1964	Pickle	Drive/mental; human relations; communication ability; technical knowledge
1971	Palmer	Risk measurement
1971	Hornaday and Aboud	Need for achievement, autonomy,

		aggression, power, recognition; innovative/independence
1973	Winter	Need for power
1974	Borland	Internal locus of control
1974	Liles	Need for achievement
1977	Gasse	Personal value orientation
1978	Timmons	Drive/self-confidence; goal oriented; moderate risk taker; locus of control; creativity/innovation
1980	Sexton	Energetic/ambitions; positive setbacks
1981	Welsh and White	Need to control; responsibility seeker; self-confidence/drive; challenge taker; moderate risk taker
1982	Dunkelberg and Cooper	Growth oriented; independence oriented; craftsman oriented
1982	Scheré	Tolerance of ambiguity
1987	Begley and Boyd	Tolerance of ambiguity
1987	Begley and Boyd	Curvilinear relationship: risk taking and return on assets

Other studies have asked entrepreneurs their theories on the origin of entrepreneurship. Birley and Watson (1988) asked 100 British owner–managers to rank the top five characteristics which they value for executive/entrepreneurial success in their company. The results are given in Table 5.3.

Table 5.3 Characteristics valued by entrepreneurs

Characteristic	No. of mentions	Mean rank	Standard deviation
Aggressiveness	9	3.3	1.3
Ambition	18	2.9	1.5
Appearance	3	4.7	0.6
Concern for people	12	2.9	1.2
Concern for results	23	2.3	1.5
Conformity	1	0.5	0.0
Creativity	12	3.1	0.9
Desire for responsibility	10	3.1	1.5
Integrity	20	2.4	1.6
Intelligence	10	2.5	1.5
Lateral thinking	11	3.5	1.3
Loyalty	8	3.7	1.1
Self-discipline	9	3.8	1.3
Sense of humour	8	3.7	0.9
Social adaptability	3	3.7	0.6

Source: Birley and Watson (1988)

Those factors which are not particularly rated by the group include aggressive, appearance, conformity, desire for responsibility, intelligence, loyalty, self-discipline, sense of humour, social adaptability. However, the factor which was mentioned the most, and was generally rated the highest, was a commercial attitude in the employees which focused on 'concern for results'. This was combined with the second most important factor of 'integrity', and the third of 'ambition'. The other two factors which were mentioned frequently, but did not achieve high rankings, were 'lateral thinking' and 'creativity'. 'Concern for people' was ranked highly in the limited number of cases it was mentioned.

Some researchers have attempted to highlight and integrate different features into a model. Olson and Bosserman (1984) hypothesize that individuals will exhibit entrepreneurial behaviour when they possess a combination of three attributes: role orientation, abilities and motivation. They argue that individuals will only exhibit the proper role behaviour when they know and understand what they are expected to accomplish. Aspirant entrepreneurs should therefore realize that entrepreneurship is not a single act, but rather a process involving many activities. To have this particular role orientation implies learned attitudes or specific beliefs about activities and situations. These include focusing on opportunities instead of on problems and recognizing that innovation is accomplished by a process involving many activities.

As far as abilities are concerned, they suggest that an entrepreneur must be able to think intuitively as well as rationally (being both S and N in Jungian terms). Intuitive thinking applies to the initial step of the process where new ideas are produced as a function of the imagination, not the senses. The entrepreneur must become aware of the environment, view it in different ways and find new connections between previously unrelated subjects. Solutions should be found intuitively by divergent thinking patterns.

The rational mode of thinking involves thinking that is rational, logical, sequential and analytical. It should be used to understand the current environment rather than to create something new. This mode of thinking becomes more important when the entrepreneur must determine success potential, analyse ideas, projects and plans, and communicate them, and do planning and implementation. Another important ability is to be able to discriminate between situations and to know which mode of thinking to use for each situation. Olson and Bosserman are, however, agnostic on the topic of motivation.

McClelland (1987) reports research done by McBer and Co. (1986) and lists nine 'competencies' that were found to be more characteristic of successful than average entrepreneurs in India, Malawi and Ecuador. Interestingly, he also noted competencies that *did not* distinguish successful from unsuccessful entrepreneurs, as follows:

1. Self-confidence. Expresses confidence in his/her own ability to complete a task or meet a challenge.
2. Persistence. Takes repeated or different actions to overcome an obstacle.
3. Persuasion. Convinces someone to buy a product or service, or provide financing; asserts own competence, reliability, or other personal or company qualities.
4. Use of influence strategies. Acts to develop business contacts; uses influential people as agents to accomplish own objectives.
5. Expertise. Had experience in the same area of business; had skill in financing, accounting, production and selling before starting business.
6. Information seeking. Does personal research on how to provide a product or service; consults experts for business or technical advice.

The positively discriminating competencies were categorized into three groups; namely 'proactive', 'achievement orientation' and 'commitment to others':

Proactivity
1. Initiative. Does things before being asked or forced to by events.
2. Assertiveness. Confronts problems with others directly; tells others what they have to do.

Achievement orientation
3. Sees and acts on opportunities. Seizes unusual opportunities to start a new business, obtaining financing, land, work space or assistance.
4. Efficiency orientation. Looks for or finds ways to do things faster or at less cost.
5. Concern for high-quality work. States a desire to produce or sell a top or better quality product or service.
6. Systematic planning. Breaks down a large task into subtasks, or subgoals; anticipates obstacles; evaluates alternatives.
7. Monitoring. Develops or uses procedures to ensure that work is completed or that work meets standards of quality.

Commitment to others
8. Commitment to work contract. Makes a personal sacrifice or expends extraordinary effort to complete a job; pitches in with workers or works in their place to get job done.
9. Recognizing the importance of business relationships. Acts to build rapport or friendly relationships. Sees interpersonal relationships as a fundamental business resource; places long-term goodwill over short-term gain.

Note that using the term competency as opposed to trait does not overcome some of the serious problems in this area; indeed, it may even make them worse (see Chapter 1). Consider the foregoing list:

- Is there empirical evidence for the clustering of the nine competencies into the three groups?
- How much of each of these competencies is necessary or acceptable?
- Is there a linear, curvilinear or some other relationship between these competencies and entrepreneurship?
- Can the competencies compensate for one another?

More recent studies have suggested that business planning, as manifest in the writing of business plans, is an important factor in predicting successful entrepreneurs (Frank, Liaschka and Roessel, 1989). Miner, Smith and Bracker (1989) found entrepreneurs differed from non-entrepreneurs on five related measures of motivation:

- Self-achievement. The desire to achieve through one's own efforts and to be able to attribute success clearly to personal causation.
- Risk taking. The desire to take moderate risks that can be handled through one's own efforts.
- Feedback of results. The desire for some clear index of the level of performance.
- Personal innovation. The desire to introduce novel, innovative or creative solutions.
- Planning for the future. The desire to think about the future and anticipate future possibilities.

The interest in the entrepreneur can be seen from a special issue of the *Journal of Creative Behaviour* in 1987 (No. 3, Vol. 22) and a large conference in Massachusetts in 1986. The former collection is highly varied and contains personal testimonies of successful entrepreneurs (Amos, 1987), and reviews (Soloman and Winslow, 1987) which found entrepreneurs confident, optimistic, independent, self-reliant and not risky, reckless or willing to be judged by others. Lipper (1987) outlined a number of important factors associated with successful entrepreneurs. These include the following:

- Measuring successes and understanding that winning a lot is the result of many small wins.
- Understanding that failures are common and inevitable.
- Having a long-term view of both success and failure but persevering.

Some of the papers are not unnaturally interested in the relationship between creativity and entrepreneurship. Whiting (1987) attempted to do this by listing separately characteristics associated with creative individuals and entrepreneurs. He found a large overlap suggesting a close association but admits that no real answers will emerge until the problems of definition are overcome. Weaver (1987) provided some evidence that corporate entrepreneurs (intrapreneurs) are also creative and innovative in making their organization responsive. Coyne (1987) and Fernald (1987) also argue that creativity and entrepreneurial behaviour are closely linked but it seems that this area is long on anecdote and personal history, and very short on theory or data.

The 1986 conference papers were, on the other hand, much heavier on data. Many papers were reported on attempts to describe the characteristics associated with successful entrepreneurs. Hornaday and Knutzen (1986) compared Norwegian and American entrepreneurs in terms of their social values and found them highly similar. In a comprehensive study, Begley and Boyd (1986) compared five personality variables thought to be indicative of entrepreneurship (need for achievement, locus of control, risk taking, tolerance of ambiguity, type A) and various 'bottom-line' measures like return on assets, liquidity, revenue and company age. Entrepreneurs had a higher need for achievement, internal locus of control and tolerance for ambiguity. However, there was little statistical relationship between psychological attributes and various measures of financial performance. They do note that it is possible that different characteristics are associated with starting-up vs maintaining an entrepreneurial business.

Bailey (1986) concentrated on the learning styles of successful entrepreneurs. Using the learning style questionnaire and a discriminate analysis, he found the learning modes of *low* performing entrepreneurs were the number of years of education, social questioning style, a perception of the influence of reading on learning, a perception of the influence of industry associations on learning, an active experimental learning style, a use of thinking back to past solutions for assistance in problem solving, a use of industry associations in problem solving, and a use of intuition (gut feeling) in problem solving.

Sexton and Bowman (1986) compared female entrepreneurs, managers, entrepreneurship students and business students on nine measures derived from the Jackson Personality Research Form. Comparing entrepreneurial students (and actual entrepreneurs) to business students (and managers) a very clear pattern was observed: the former scored higher on energy level, risk taking, social adroitness and autonomy change, and lower on conformity, interpersonal affect, harm avoidance and succorance. They note:

> A number of questions still remain for future research efforts. The impact of variables such as age, socio-economic level, and education upon the psychological traits must still be determined along with a determination of the actual impact of the psychological pre-disposition upon the new venture initiation decision (p.50).

5.3 BACKGROUND, BIOGRAPHICAL AND PSYCHOLOGICAL FACTORS ASSOCIATED WITH ENTREPRENEURIAL BEHAVIOUR

A number of researchers have attempted to determine the influence of various biographical factors on entrepreneurs. Brockhaus (1982b) mentions three classic demographic variables, i.e. age, education and residency.

Age

The years between 25 and 40 are usually regarded as the time when the entrepreneur is most likely to make the decision to go into and indeed succeed in business. This is because the potential entrepreneur has obtained sufficient experience, competence and self-confidence (but not capital), but has not yet incurred the family and financial obligations, or has not yet reached a position of prestige and responsibility in an organization.

According to Susbauer (1969), not too much emphasis is placed on this age interval. He found that the ages of high-technology entrepreneurs approximated that of the general population between 25 and 60. Individuals younger than 25 were still too much involved with education and military commitments while those over 60 lacked the physical energy for entrepreneurship. More recently, Begley and Boyd (1987a) in a study of 175 founders and 140 non-founders of small businesses used a discriminate analysis to show that age discriminated significantly between founders and non-founders. Age also correlated significantly with two criteria of business success over both groups; with debt/equity ratio (this means that older subjects had a more favourable debt/equity ratio than younger ones); with growth rate (this means that younger subjects had a faster growth rate of their businesses than older ones).

The concept of a critical age is obviously important, as well as a profiled life stage approach, but as yet neither is forthcoming.

Education

Views on the relationship between entrepreneurship and education are varied and conflicting. A number of studies reported entrepreneurs to have relatively low levels of education (Collins, Moore and Unwalla, 1964; Hameed, 1974). Lim (1977) showed that the majority of entrepreneurs had a low educational level and that most of them were not college graduates. The level of education of entrepreneurs was found to be significantly less than that of managers. This might be due to the fact that the entrepreneurs were not involved in high-level satisfying work to the same extent as the latter educated group and therefore subsequently started their own businesses (Brockhaus, 1982a). It could, of course, also mean that educational experiences socialized people out of entrepreneurial values and behaviour. Papanek (1971) and Babu (1978) concluded that education does not play a significant role in the making of an entrepreneur or in contributing to his/her success. On the other hand, investigations by Mancuso (1973) and others, and the Small Industry Extension Institute (SIET) concluded that entrepreneurs have high educational qualifications.

More recently, Deivasenapathy (1986) found among the 98 Indian entrepreneurs in his study that:

. . . though there is no significant difference, the entrepreneurs of healthy units were found to have a higher level of education when compared to those with sick units. Certainly, education helps the entrepreneur to understand technological changes and introduce new innovations and management principles (p.55).

Begley and Boyd (1987a), in their discriminant analysis study of 175 founders and 140 non-founders (managers) of small businesses, found that higher education was one factor that discriminated significantly between founders and non-founders. There was, however, no significant correlation between education and a number of business success criteria over both groups. Clearly, the literature on age determinants of entrepreneurial behaviour is equivocal, no doubt because the relationship is moderated by other variables.

Residency

Brockhaus (1982) seems to suggest that entrepreneurs tend to have resided in the areas of their businesses for long periods. He ascribes this to the fact that the higher educated managerial types were more mobile for the national job market, whereas the entrepreneurs had to remain closer to home and subsequently went into business. The question of the urban vs rural upbringing of entrepreneurs, an important issue, appears not to have been researched.

Family Support

Family (social) support affords the entrepreneur greater access to capital as well as support in decision making through a network of family connections. Deivasenapathy (1986) cites numerous studies that support this point of view. His own study among 98 Indian entrepreneurs also clearly showed that entrepreneurs of 'health units' received assistance from family members, whereas the unsuccessful ones did not receive it. Help from family members was mostly in the form of financial and moral support, and advice. The social support literature, however, would suggest various distinctions should be made such as the quality, quantity, timing and reciprocity of support.

Job Experience

After taking into consideration various research studies, Brockhaus (1982) concludes that:

. . . research strongly suggests that dissatisfaction with previous work experience is closely related to the entrepreneurial decision. Moreover, the person who is unemployed is more likely to decide to start a business than if he were employed (p.53).

In other words, entrepreneurs are pushed not pulled.

Deivasenapathy (1986) cites various Indian research studies, concluding that previous job experience has an important impact on the career of the entrepreneur. Because of experience in similar jobs, entrepreneurs have the necessary exposure to perform better as entrepreneurs when compared to others who had a different type of experience, or no experience at all. His own research also clearly showed that the number of entrepreneurs with previous experience in 'healthy units' is significantly larger than that of 'sick units'.

5.4 PERSONALITY TRAITS AND ENTREPRENEURSHIP

A review of the leading studies of entrepreneurial characteristics reveals that the following five attributes recur with regularity: the achievement motive (nAch), locus of control, risk-taking propensity, tolerance of ambiguity and, more recently, A-type behaviour (Van Daalen, 1989).

Need for Achievement

McClelland's name is perhaps synonymous with the concept of achievement motivation (McClelland et al., 1953; McClelland, 1962, 1965). His extensive research revealed a clear profile of the characteristics of high achievers. The need for achievement (or nAch) can be described as a desire to perform in terms of a standard of excellence, to be successful in competitive situations or, as Atkinson (1968) defines nAch,

> '. . . a capacity for taking pride in accomplishment when success at one or another activity is achieved' (p.181).

McClelland and Winter (1969) consider the following forms of behaviour as descriptive of those individuals who display a particular need to achieve:

- They take moderate risks and prefer to use their skill, not to rely on chance.
- They prefer to engage in energetic and/or novel instrumental activity.
- They prefer to assume personal responsibility for the outcome of their performance.
- They have a strong desire for immediate feedback of results of their performance.

These characteristics are, then, also regarded as important for success in entrepreneurial behaviour. Numerous research studies have supported the hypothesis that people with a high achievement motive behave like successful, rational business entrepreneurs; that is, they set moderate risks, become active, they assume personal responsibility, they desire feedback, and have a long time perspective.

Wainer and Rubin (1969) looked at the motivation of technical entrepreneurs as it related to company performance. They found, as predicted, that the relationships between the entrepreneurs' need for achievement, need for power, and need for affiliation were related to the performance of the small companies they founded and operated.

Achievement motivation can, however, also be fostered in adults by means of training courses. These courses have various goals, such as the following:

- To teach the participants how to think, talk and act like people with high achievement (to model the entrepreneur).
- To stimulate participants to set higher, but carefully planned and realistic, work goals for themselves over the following two years (cognitively to appraise differently).
- To provide the participants with knowledge about themselves (to provide self-insight).
- To create a group spirit from learning about each other's hopes and fears, successes and failures, and from going through an emotional experience together.

For a thorough review of the literature on the measurement of achievement motivation, Fineman (1979b) discussed the crystallization of the achievement motive construct in the literature. The 'formalization' of the construct, however, emanated from the work and theory of Murray (1938). From his work, a taxonomy of personality needs emerged, which he defined as: 'hypothetical constructs reflecting physiological "forces" which direct behaviour' (p.1).

The link between achievement motivation and entrepreneurship has been extensively studied by McClelland (1962, 1965). McClelland (1962) reports relationships between the need to achieve (nAch) and entrepreneurial behaviour in young men. In the USA, Poland and Italy, he found that school-leaving young men with high nAch scores have a preference for business occupations. In another study, this time a longitudinal study, McClelland (1965) confirmed his earlier findings. Eighty-three per cent of men in entrepreneurial positions had demonstrated high nAch 14 years earlier, while only 21 per cent of those in non-entrepreneurial positions had demonstrated nAch. This finding was later confirmed by Palmer (1971).

In a third study, McClelland and Winter (1969) reported that 48 per cent of Indian businessmen who had participated in a programme to increase the levels of nAch were more active in their entrepreneurial efforts. It is this study which helps disentangle the direction of causality.

Using Gordon's study of personal values, Komives (1972) measured the nAch values of 20 high-technology entrepreneurs who were considered to be successful. He found them high on achievement and decisiveness categories. However, in another study, Hull, Bosley and Udell (1980) reported that *n*Ach was a weak predictor of an individual's tendency to start a business. Achievement training had been given to executives, businessmen and entrepreneurs in the United States, Mexico and India, and, although there were some inconsistencies in the findings, it was generally found that those who had been on the achievement training course had more money, were promoted faster, expanded their business faster, and exhibited a higher rate of business activities than control groups, or groups trained otherwise (McClelland, 1965; Durand, 1972).

Cromie and Johns (1983), on the other hand, found that entrepreneurs did not score significantly higher on achievement motivation, nor on achievement values, than a group of managers. In a more recent study, however, Cromie (1987) found that a group of male and female entrepreneurs scored significantly higher on *n*Ach than a group of naval officers, and also significantly higher than a group of 200 university students. He found no evidence whatsoever of sex differences.

Ahmed (1985) gave tests of locus of control, risk-taking propensity and *n*Ach to 71 Indian entrepreneurs and 62 Indian non-entrepreneurs in England. He found significant differences between the two groups on all three scales. He concluded that these variables were positively related to each other and entrepreneurship and that it confirms earlier findings.

In another modest study done on Indian entrepreneurs, Venkatapathy (1983, 1985) found first- and second-generation entrepreneurs differed on a number of criteria. Specifically, first-generation entrepreneurs were significantly less impulsive, insecure, shy, gloomy and sensitive but more artistic and moody. They were also older, more highly educated, had healthy childhood experiences, had more friends, and showed more social involvement and awareness. In another study in a Third World country, Van Daalen, van Niekerk and Pottas (1989) found no relationship between need for achievement and entrepreneurial behaviour.

King (1985) reported that achievement motivation, internal locus of control and risk-taking propensity, among other independent variables, have a statistically discriminating effect on successful entrepreneurship. Other independent variables, such as sex, cognitive style, energy level and self-determination, did not meet the minimum criteria of significance for entering into the discriminant model. According to King, this was in contrast to earlier studies showing sex, cognitive style and both energy level and determination to discriminate between more, and less, successful entrepreneurs. However, King did not use psychometric trait questionnaires to measure these personality variables. He used a Behaviour Check Questionnaire, a 35-item questionnaire that supposedly measures achievement motivation, locus of control, risk-taking propensity, problem-solving behaviour and manipulating behaviour over seven items each. The questionable nature of this research suggests that results should be treated as speculative.

In a recent study, Begley and Boyd (1978b) distinguished between founders and non-founders of businesses; the former to be called entrepreneurs. They report that founders (N = 92) scored significantly higher on need for achievement, risk-taking propensity and tolerance of ambiguity. Among the non-founders, high nAch correlated positively with a high liquidity ratio. McClelland's (1987) most recent work reports on 45 average and superior entrepreneurs in Malawi who were assessed and compared on nine different 'competencies'. Five of these competencies are categorized under the heading 'achievement orientation'. A first study compared scores of these two groups on paper-and-pencil tests measuring these competencies. No significant differences between the two groups could be found. However, in a follow-up study the same competencies were measured by means of interviews and here the superior entrepreneurs scored significantly higher than the average ones on nAch. These rather equivocal findings make interpretation difficult.

A critical examination of the measurement of achievement motivation leaves a number of unanswered questions. The first of these relates to the predictive effectiveness of the Thematic Apperception Test (TAT) used in many of the studies, as judged by its low reliability and validity coefficients. Biesheuvel (1984), for instance, writes:

> . . . there is no compelling evidence, either statistical or logical, that behavioural clusters of the postulated kind exist. This applies even to the entrepreneurial pattern which constitutes the core of the nAchievement concept as seen by McClelland. Empirical support for the relationships between TAT achievement measures and entrepreneurial interest is slight and often contradictory (p.57).

Biesheuvel further warns that statistical significance should not be taken for behavioural significance. The variances accounted for in correlations studies 'are so small as to be virtually of no consequence' (p.238).

Heckhausen, Schmalt and Scneider (1985) have also been severely critical of the mechanistic approach to behaviour in McClelland's work and move toward more cognitive conceptualizations of human behaviour. Mancuso and Mascolo (1987) found the assumptions on which McClelland (1987) built his conceptualizations difficult to accept. McClelland's definition of a motive – '. . . a learned, affectively charged anticipatory goal state aroused by various cues' (p.132) – is severely questioned by these two reviewers. McClelland (1987) further states that motives activate the organism to learn 'the instrumental responses necessary to bring about the goal state' (p.132). These seemingly contradictory statements prompted Mancuso and Mascolo (1987) to ask: 'What activated the organism to learn the "learned affectively charged anticipatory goal states which are aroused by various cues"?' (p.324). Similarly, McClelland's discussion of the achievement motive as based on a 'variety incentive', and later in his book the definition of nAch as 'doing something better for its own sake', do not fit together conceptually. Heckhausen *et al.*'s contribution (1985), on the other hand, sets out to build mathematical formulae for predicting behaviours.

Locus of Control

The locus of control concept developed directly as a result of Rotter's social learning theory. This theory is based on the following four assumptions:

1. Prediction of human behaviour rests on an understanding of the interaction of people with their meaningful environments (Rotter, 1982, p.5).
2. Human personality is learned. Personality is not determined at any age of development but can be changed as long as people are capable of learning (Rotter, 1982, p.5).
3. Human personality has a basic unity. This means that experiences and the environment interact with one another to form a unified whole. The person cannot be separated from the environment and the environment has no meaning other than that given to it by the person (Rotter, 1982, p.8).
4. Motivation is goal directed. Rotter rejected the drive-reduction theories of, for instance, Freud, as an explanation of human behaviour. People are not motivated to seek pleasure or to reduce drives. Rather, they are motivated by their expectancies that their behaviours are moving them closer to their goals.

Rotter's main concern, however, was to predict human behaviour, and to make accurate predictions. However, the following four variables and their interaction must be analysed:

- *Behaviour potential*. This refers to the possibility that a particular response will occur at a given time and place.
- *Expectancy*. This is defined as the probability held by the individual that a particular reinforcement will occur as a function of a specific situation or situations. Expectancies can be general or specific. Generalized expectancies are learned through previous experience with a particular response (or similar responses) and are based on the belief that positive reinforcement will follow certain behaviours. Specific expectancies are bound to particular situations.
- *Reinforcement value*. This is defined as the degree of preference for any reinforcement to occur if the possibilities of their occurring are equal.
- *The psychological situation*. This is defined as a complex set of interacting cues acting upon an individual for any specific time period. No person behaves in a vacuum; rather, people respond to cues within this perceived environment. These cues from the environment will trigger certain expectancies, which in turn will lead to certain behaviours.

At the basis of Rotter's social learning theory is the supposition that reinforcement does not automatically extinguish behaviour, but rather that individuals have the ability to perceive the connection between their own behaviour and the occurrence of the reinforcer. Rotter's (1966) internal–external control scale is therefore an attempt to measure the degree to which individuals perceive the causal relationship between their own behaviours and the consequences in the environment (reinforcers). The central hypothesis of Rotter's research with the I–E scale is that people who believe that they can control their own fate will behave differently in a variety of situations from those who believe that their future is controlled by luck, chance or powerful others. Numerous research findings have used the by-now famous Rotter scale. Most studies seem to have shown a significant association between internality and achievement entrepreneurship.

Durand and Shea (1974) investigated 22 male and seven female entrepreneurs over a period of 18 months. Rotter's IE locus of control scale and a TAT were administered. Entrepreneurs with high nAch and internal locus of control were significantly more active than those with low nAch and low internality. Brockhaus (1977) administered the Rotter IE scale to a sample of 20 business school graduate students. Those who had strong intentions to become entrepreneurs were more internal than those who had no such intentions.

Borland (1975) used Levenson's measure of internal–external locus of control and eight items of Lynn's nAch questionnaire on a group of 302 students. Students scoring high on nAch and high on the internal scale were also higher on the expectancy to start a business than those who scored lower on the internal scale and lower on nAch. No difference in expectancy of starting a company was detected among those with high or moderate 'powerful others' and 'chance' scale scores.

The notion that locus of control may influence performance through its effect on intervening variables such as stress and decision behaviour was investigated by Anderson (1976) in a longitudinal study. Ninety entrepreneurs were investigated over a period of two-and-half years and internals were found to perceive less stress and employ more task-centred behaviours than externals. Anderson ascribed this to the possibility that the internals saw a stronger relationship between their task behaviour and goal accomplishment.

Using Rotter's IE scale, Brockhaus (1977) studied samples of entrepreneurs, moved managers and promoted managers. He found that entrepreneurs and promoted managers were more internal than the moved managers. Brockhaus (1977) compared the Rotter IE scores of entrepreneurs and managers. They found no significant differences between the scores of these two groups. They did, however, find that the scores on both groups were more internal than all of the scores reported by Rotter (1966), except those for peace corps trainees. Scanlan (1979) investigated the personality characteristics of two different categories of entrepreneurs, classified according to the relationship between the type of person and the type of firm. Thirty-three craft entrepreneurs and 31 opportunistic entrepreneurs were tested on Levenson's measure of locus of control. Both groups scored higher on the internal scale than the general mean.

In India, Pandey and Tewary (1979) studied entrepreneurs in a North Indian town and found that internality was associated with nAch. They further reasoned that the psychological characteristics of internals made them more suitable to be successful entrepreneurs. Venkatapathy (1983) compared a sample of 60 industrial entrepreneurs with 43 non-entrepreneurs. He found that entrepreneurs differed significantly from the non-entrepreneurs on all of the scales of the IE inventory.

Twenty franchise entrepreneurs and 31 independent entrepreneurs were studied by Mescon and Montanari (1982) using Rotter's IE scale. Both groups scored significantly higher than the national sample on internal locus of control. Independent entrepreneurs also scored higher than the franchise entrepreneurs, but not at a statistically significant level. A sample of 41 senior managers, 42 'established' entrepreneurs and 23 aspiring entrepreneurs was studied by Cromie and Johns (1983) using different types of psychological test. The established entrepreneurs were found to be significantly higher than the senior managers on internal locus of control. Furthermore, the aspiring entrepreneurs were again significantly higher than the established entrepreneurs on internality.

More recently, Cromie (1987) found that 35 men and 34 women entrepreneurs scored remarkably similar on Rotter's IE scale and on Lynn's achievement motivation scale, suggesting 'that these two groups are derived from the same population – entrepreneurs' (p.258). This sample also scored significantly higher on the locus of control scale (more internal) than a group of 41 managers, but not significantly less than a group of 42 entrepreneurs studied by Cromie and Johns (1983).

Begley and Boyd (1987b), however, reported that there was no significant difference between locus of control scores of founders ($N = 147$) and non-founders ($N = 92$) of small businesses. Both groups, however, manifested an internal locus of control. (Begley and Boyd prefer to reserve the title 'entrepreneur' only for founders of small businesses.)

Using Furnham's (1986a) economic locus of control scale, a multi-dimensional sphere-specific measure, Van Daalen and van Niekerk (1989b) found a clear relationship between internality and Third World entrepreneurship.

The recent work by Hunter, Schmidt and Judiesch (1990) has demonstrated how much more productive some workers are than less productive colleagues. Evidence showed that the percentage of mean (measurable) output increases as a function of the complexity level of the job – 19 per cent, 32 per cent to 48 per cent for low, medium to high complexity non-sale jobs, the difference being even higher for sales jobs. They also argue that general mental/cognitive ability is a simple but effective predictor of output, and that this can be measured.

In a recent review, Ginsberg and Buchholz (1989) attempted to categorize entrepreneurs, as shown in Figure 5.5. They believe this system will help sort out some of the conceptual confusion which currently exists. Clearly, there remains a serious problem in defining, describing and categorizing the dependent variable. However, until the problem is solved, it is impossible to progress in this field.

5.5 CONCLUSION

This chapter has concentrated on the psychology of the entrepreneur. Recent studies tend to be more theoretical and methodologically competent. For instance, Miner *et al.* (1989) compared 118 entrepreneurs and 41 manager scientists on a sentence completion scale, which has been developed to measure task motivation. According to the theory upon which the measure is based, entrepreneurial task motivation has a number of facets: self-achievement, risk taking, desire for feedback of results, evidence of personal innovation, concern with planning for the future. This study provided some validation of the theory and measure as they both discriminated between entrepreneurs and scientists, and also showed strong correlations with company growth in employees and sales.

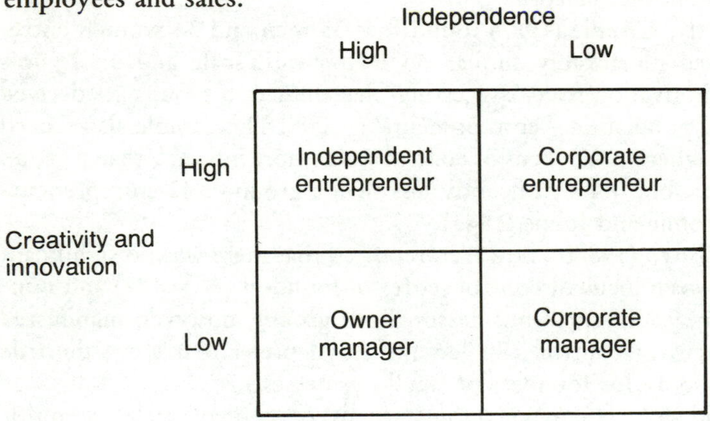

	Independence	
	High	Low
High	Independent entrepreneur	Corporate entrepreneur
Low	Owner manager	Corporate manager

Creativity and innovation

Figure 5.5 Decision autonomy and financial risk
Source: Ginsberg and Buchholz (1989)

Chapter 6

Personality and work satisfaction

One of the symptoms of an approaching nervous breakdown is the belief that one's work is terribly important.

Bertrand Russell

Business is a combination of war and sport.

A. Maureis

Men of genius do not excel in any profession because they labour in it, but they labour in it because they excel.

W. Haslitt

It seems a pity that psychology should have destroyed all our knowledge of human nature.

G.K. Chesterton

6.1 INTRODUCTION

Are some personality types more likely to be job satisfied than others regardless of the job? What sort of people are most satisfied in what sorts of jobs? Are job-satisfied individuals more productive than less satisfied individuals? Is job satisfaction a consequence, rather than a cause of, productivity at work? There are a number of important questions one may wish to ask of the literature on job satisfaction. Although there is a plethora of studies and available measures of job satisfaction, there is surprisingly little data on the role of individual differences in job satisfaction. Various demographic factors have been researched, such as age, sex and occupational status, but there are very few studies that for good theoretical or methodological reasons have included personality measures.

It seems completely self-evident that there should be major individual differences in job satisfaction. It is obvious that different people in the same job experience different sources and amounts of satisfaction, while two people doing quite different jobs experience comparable levels of satisfaction.

The most important question, however, is whether personality (and other individual differences) is a *main factor* or whether it works in *interaction* with the job to produce job satisfaction. Thus, we have the following possible equation:

$$JS = f(P * J * PJF * E)$$

where JS is job satisfaction, P is personality, J is job characteristics, PJF is person–job fit and E is error. There are two possible main effects: personality and job.

- If it can be shown that some personality types are more satisfied (or dissatisfied) irrespective of the nature of the job they are doing, presumably the main effect of personality accounts for a good deal of the variance.
- If it can be shown that some jobs cause their incumbents to be more satisfied (or dissatisfied) irrespective of the personality (skills, abilities etc) of the incumbents, the main effect of job probably accounts for a good deal of the variance.
- If it can be shown that a particular fit (or misfit) between a person (personality) and the job (demands) causes particular sources of satisfaction or dissatisfaction, the interaction between person and job is presumably the major source of the variance.

Alas, this equation is made somewhat more complicated by the fact that job satisfaction is itself multi-dimensional. Depending on the particular theorist that one reads or measures or adopts, there may be as many as ten different but inevitably related dimensions of job satisfaction like satisfaction with working conditions, co-workers and reward structure. Hence, one might find after extensive empirical evidence the following sort of hypothetical equations:

JS (working conditions)	=	4.86P + 1.35J + 2.41PJF + 2.14
JS (co-workers)	=	10.21P + 0.86J + 1.11PJF + 6.81
JS (reward structure)	=	3.11P + 9.87J + 2.23PJF + 1.33

The attraction of these sorts of equation is great; however, they can never be as simple as this. Both personality and jobs are multi-dimensional and the multiplication of the two means that there could be extremely awkward equations that are simply not cost effective to calculate. Nevertheless, the idea is a good one, although there will no doubt be considerable debate as to whether the P or J factor accounts for most of the variance!

6.2 THEORIES OF THE CAUSES OF JOB SATISFACTION

Despite the variety of variables suggested as having major, minor or moderating effects on job satisfaction, it is possible to divide these factors into three distinct groups:

- Organizational policies and procedures. These concern such things as the reward system (the perceived equity of pay and promotions), supervision and decision-making practices, perceived quality of supervision. Inevitably, each and all of these can effect job satisfaction.
- Specific aspects of the job such as overall workload, skill variety, autonomy, feedback, the physical nature of the work environment. These must have an important effect.
- Personal characteristics such as self-esteem, ability to tolerate stress, general life satisfaction probably determine job satisfaction.

Surveys consistently indicate that 80–90 per cent of people are relatively happy at work. However, it is clear that while job satisfaction is generally high, this is not true of all work settings and jobs; nor is it true of all socio-economic and ethnic groups. Given that sociological and organizational factors obviously contribute to job satisfaction, the question must remain as to the personality factors associated with those who claim either to be highly or not at all job satisfied. Consider, for example, the work by Locke (1984) which looks at how to increase job satisfaction (see Table 6.1). He identified eight factors of work and appropriate strategies but rarely considered the important moderating role of personality factors. Hence, with few exceptions, the proposed solutions are organizational rather than individual difference focused.

There are several theories of job satisfaction, most of which take relatively little cognizance of personality and individual differences. These will be briefly considered and the individual difference implications considered.

6.3 HERZBERG'S TWO-FACTOR THEORY

Herzberg *et al.* (1957) reviewed the early satisfaction research literature and found no relationships between job satisfaction and work performance. They concluded that there *were* systematic relationships between workers' attitudes and their behaviour, but that these relationships had gone unnoticed because researchers had confused job satisfaction and job *dissatisfaction*. According to them, job satisfaction depends on a certain set of conditions, whereas job dissatisfaction is the result of an entirely different set of conditions. Thus, although it is possible to think of satisfaction and dissatisfaction as the two extremes on a single continuum, they are determined by different factors. Hence, it may be more helpful to think of two factors.

Herzberg, Mausner and Snyderman (1959) tested the relationship between

Table 6.1 Major job values and ways to implement them

Job aspect	Job value	Wider value or need	Ways to implement
Work	Personal interest	Pleasure	Recruiting, selection, placement, job enrichment, goal setting, participation in decision making
	Importance		
	Chance to use skills	Growth	
	Responsibility		
	Autonomy		
	Variety		
	Achievement, progress	Self-esteem	
	Feedback		
	Clarity		
	Harmony		
	Participation		
	Pressure		
	Fatigue avoidance	Physical well-being	Design of workplace
	Fairness	Justice, need satisfaction	Job analysis; wage surveys; objective work measurement or performance ratings; high pay and benefits; incentive plans
Pay and benefits			
Promotions	Job security	Justice, visibility, growth	Manpower planning
Recognition	Fairness	Justice, visibility	Promotions on merit
	Recognition		Praise and credit for work and effort
Working conditions	Resources	Helps to get work done	Provide resources
	Hours	Helps get off-the-job values	Flexitime, four-day week
	Shift work(-)	Interferes with home life, health	Compensation (through pay, time off)
	Safe physical conditions	Health, well-being	Remove hazards, safety programmes

Co-workers/ subordinates	Privacy	Facilitates concentration; privacy	Closed office design
	Similarity	Friendship	Recruiting, selection, placement
Management/ supervision	Competence, co-operation	Helps get work done	Same as above, plus training
	Respect	Self-esteem	Being honest with employees; concerned with their wants
	Trust		Consistent honesty
	Two-way communication		Listening to employees
	Provide above values	See above	Participation, influence
Unions	Pay	See above	Higher pay, benefits

Source: Locke (1984)

satisfaction and performance, and formalized a theory based on their results. According to the theory, people have two major types of needs. The first of these was called *hygiene needs*, which are influenced by the physical and psychological conditions in which people work. The second set of needs were called *motivator needs*, and these were described as being very similar to the higher-order needs in Maslow's (1954) need hierarchy theory.

Herzberg *el al.* (1959) claimed that these two types of needs were satisfied by different types of outcomes or rewards. Hygiene needs were said to be satisfied by the level of certain conditions called *hygiene factors*, or *dissatisfiers*. The factors that they found to be related to hygiene needs are: supervision, interpersonal relations, physical working conditions, salary, company policies and administrative practices, benefits, job security. These factors are all concerned with the *context* or *environment* in which the job has to be done. When these factors are unfavourable, then job dissatisfaction is the result. Conversely, when hygiene factors are positive, such as when workers perceive that their pay is fair and that their working decisions are good, then barriers to job satisfaction are removed. The fulfilment of hygiene needs, however, cannot by itself result in job satisfaction, but only in the *reduction* or elimination of *dissatisfaction*. Herzberg *et al.* compared hygiene factors to modern water- and air-pollution controls: whereas such controls do not cure any diseases, they serve to *prevent* the outbreak of disease. In the same way, he and his colleagues believed that hygiene factors did not cause satisfaction but that they could prevent dissatisfaction.

Unlike hygiene needs, motivator needs are fulfilled by what Herzberg *el al.* called *motivator factors*, or *satisfiers*. They identified the following motivator factors: achievement, recognition, work itself, responsibility, advancement. Whereas *hygiene* factors are related to the *context* of work, *motivator* factors are concerned with the *nature* of the work itself and the consequences of work. According to the theory, the factors that lead to job satisfaction are those that satisfy an individual's need for self-actualization (self-fulfilment) in one's work, and it is only from the performance of the task that the individual can get the rewards that will reinforce his/her aspirations. Compared to hygiene factors, which result in a 'neutral (neither satisfied nor dissatisfied) state' when present, positive motivator factors result in job satisfaction. When recognition, responsibility and other motivators are absent from a job, however, the result will not be dissatisfaction, as with the absence of hygiene factors, but rather the same neutral state associated with the *presence* of hygiene factors.

Attractive although the theory is, there is little empirical support for it. This is no doubt due to the fact that various methodological errors were introduced into the early theory-testing work. These included the real possibility that all of the results were the result of classic attribution errors such that failure is attributed externally (to hygiene factors), and success internally (to motivation factors). Secondly, the theory-testing work was nearly all done on white-collar workers – accountants and engineers – who are hardly representative of the working population. Essentially, five objections are frequently made:

1. Selective bias and defensive behaviour. Responses to critical incident questions may 'selectively recall' situational factors and project failures to external factors.
2. Method dependency. When there are variations in methodology, different results are obtained. This suggests that results are dependent on how information is gathered.
3. Assumptions about the nature and measurement of satisfaction. There appears to be substantial evidence questioning the dual-factor argument that hygiene factors lead only to dissatisfaction when absent and motivators are only capable of providing satisfaction.
4. Individual variations. Evidence leads to questions of how well the theory applies to all people in different sexual, socio-economic, age etc categories.
5. Organizational differences. Effects of the two-factor theory vary with the climate of the organization within which it is implemented.

Despite serious doubts about the validity of the theory, researchers were very eager to implement one key implication of the theory, namely job enrichment.

The idea that repetitive and boring jobs cause employees to produce below potential and feel dissatisfied was suggested by human-resource researchers in the 1930s, who suggested such things as *rotating* workers among a variety of jobs and *enlarging* individual tasks to enable workers to identify more closely with a total product, thereby increasing their pride in craftsmanship. Herzberg and his colleagues recommend *job enrichment* (and by implication job satisfaction), defined as an attempt by management to design tasks in such a way as to build in the opportunity for personal achievement, recognition, challenge and individual growth. It provides the worker with more responsibility and autonomy in carrying out a complete task and with timely feedback on his/her performance. In summary, job enrichment consists of several steps:

1. Removing controls from a job while retaining accountability.
2. Increasing the accountability of the individual for his/her own work.
3. Giving each person a complete and natural module of work.
4. Granting job freedom for a person's own work.
5. Making timely reports on performance available to the worker instead of to the supervisor.
6. Introducing new tasks not previously performed.
7. Assigning specific tasks so the employee can develop expertise in performing them.

Various problems have also been noted in implementing the two-factor theory. Some are characteristic of all change efforts, while some are unique to alterations in motivational programmes:

1. *Education*. Many managers simply do not understand or approve of job enrichment.
2. *Ideology*. Division of labour or specialization and control are a part of the way that jobs have traditionally been performed.
3. *Organization*. Job enrichment is a long-term investment, whereas organizational controls demand immediate returns. Since job enrichment often requires that jobs be redesigned, vested interests cause resentment when a task is taken from one organization unit and placed in another.
4. *Management*. Managers frequently fear loss of control over operations knowing that knowledge is power.
5. *Technology*. Technology dictates the design of many jobs and leaves little flexibility for redesigning them.
6. *Employees*. Some employees do not wish to perform enriched jobs. Indeed, they are threatened by these steps.
7. *Implementation*. Implementors often become overly enthusiastic and unrealistic in what can or should be done.
8. *Diagnosis*. Job enrichment has become almost a fad, and many attempts have not been preceded by adequate diagnosis of the problems.
9. *Uniqueness of setting*. Some say a particular organization is unique and such a programme would not work in a specific setting.
10. *Nothing new*. This is the contention that job enrichment is 'nothing new' for a particular firm: all the jobs are meaningful.

Reif and Luthans (1972), who made the following observations, suggest that the two-factor theory be used selectively as a motivational technique:

1. Some workers are alienated by the middle class values inherent in job enrichment rather than by the job itself. Contentment on the job is not necessarily related to satisfaction since many people are perfectly capable of finding satisfaction outside the work environment.
2. Some people do not view improved job design and meaningful work as an adequate compensation for the alteration of existing patterns of social interaction which sometimes result.
3. Enrichment may have negative effects because some workers feel inadequate and fear failure.

Two major implications for the study of individual determinants of job satisfaction stem from the work of Herzberg and the celebrated two-factor theory. The first is that while certain personality traits are positively associated with job satisfaction, they have no impact on dissatisfaction. That is, different traits can, and do (in appropriate conditions), determine dissatisfaction but not satisfaction. Thus, for instance, extraversion might relate to satisfaction and neuroticism to dissatisfaction. The idea that different trait dimensions operate on satisfaction and dissatisfaction differently is a testable thesis derived directly from Herzberg. The second implication of this work refers to the personality characteristics of people who either shun or yearn for job enrichment. Various hypotheses could be entertained and hence tested: people with internal locus of control favour enrichment (and respond to it) better than those with external locus of control; extraverts seek out job enrichment more than introverts; ability is positively correlated with attitudes to job enrichment etc.

Some have argued that most industrial and organizational psychology has been designed by and tested on middle class, white-collar workers and hence shows a bias in that regard. That may well be true. It could also be true that because of volunteer effects, subjects in job satisfaction studies have been predominantly from some personality groups (i.e. extraverts) that may well have biased results.

6.4 NEED THEORIES

Perhaps the earliest application of the comparison approach to understanding job satisfaction involved the concept of needs. Need theories were developed primarily to explain motivation, and state that people have certain physiological and psychological requirements or needs that may be fulfilled through the work that they do. Workers continually compare the current status of their needs to the level of need fulfilment that they desire from their jobs. When needs are unfulfilled, an unpleasant state of tension results and hence workers are not likely to experience job satisfaction. Fulfilment of needs removes the tension, thereby allowing people to feel satisfied. In this sense, this is a strictly individual difference theory of job satisfaction.

Maslow's (1954) need hierarchy theory positions human needs in a hierarchy of importance or prepotence, with lower-level needs, such as physiological needs and safety needs, dominating behaviour until they are fulfilled, at which time higher-level needs, such as needs for esteem and belongingness, are activated. This gratification/activation principle has an interesting implication for job satisfaction. Because the fulfilment of any one level of needs activates the next level, a worker will always have an active need, making long-term job satisfaction seem unlikely, even impossible. The theory does not state that the satisfaction of one need but the lack of attainment of another is any more or less frustrating for higher or lower needs.

Murray's (1938) manifest needs theory assumes that different people may be motivated by, or satisfied with, different conditions, depending on their current need level in the hierarchy. However, *all* of the needs are potentially of equal importance to *all* people under the appropriate circumstances. Murray's manifest needs theory, on the other hand, allows for relatively permanent differences between people in the overall importance of different needs. Consequently, those workers who are high in need for achievement are likely to be more satisfied when they are solving problems and successfully accomplishing their job tasks. In contrast, those workers who are high in need for affiliation will probably be most satisfied by maintaining social relationships with their co-workers. Using Murray's relatively complicated system, then, one could, after completing a sensitive and robust job analysis, predict whose needs would be satisfied and whose frustrated. Similarly, one could predict the sorts of jobs that would make people with different need patterns highly satisfied.

Research has identified a number of problems with the need approach to studying job satisfaction. The most troublesome of these problems is the inability of psychologists to define adequately the concept of needs, or to identify a full set of needs that is adequate to explain behaviour over a variety of situations. Based on the research evidence so far, it appears that although the manifest needs approach may have some value in explaining and predicting managerial behaviour, including satisfaction, more general satisfaction theories will have to rely on other processes. In principle though, by focusing on some fundamental work-related needs – need for achievement, affiliation, dominance, variety – one could devise testable hypotheses about the specific source of satisfaction and dissatisfaction among workers.

6.5 LOCKE'S VALUE THEORY

A comparative theory of job satisfaction is the value theory developed by Locke (1976), who classified actions following positive and negative emotions (see Table 6.2). Rather than focusing on needs, Locke argued that job satisfaction may be more closely related to whether or not work provides people with what they *want, desire* or *value*. Workers examine what their jobs provide in terms of, for example, pay, working conditions and promotion opportunities, and then compare those perceptions to what they value or find important in a job. To the extent that the two match, job satisfaction results.

There is a difference between Locke's theory and that of need theories such as Maslow's, partly because the latter are not specific and do not consider the need for money. It would be unlikely that money could be identified as a *need* for these workers, in the way that either Maslow or Murray define needs. It is easy, however, to believe that most workers would *value* more money than they are currently receiving.

An implication of Locke's theory is that while knowing the importance or value that a worker attaches to a particular outcome does not *by itself* predict how satisfied the worker will be, importance should predict the *range* of potential worker attitudes. Some workers attach a high value to the level of their pay: to them, money is one of, if not *the*, major outcomes

Table 6.2 Classification of action alternatives following positive and negative emotions

Positive appraisals (emotions)
1. Approach object; retain object; protect object; repeat act.
2. If satiated or if anticipate future boredom (or failure): switch activities; set new goal; choose new task; pursue new endeavour.

Negative appraisals (emotions)
1. Take no action; gather more information.
2. Avoid object; leave situation; think about leaving situation; make plans to leave; spend less time in situation.
3. Change or attack object.
   a. Physical attack; destroy, damage, injure, punish object or person (threaten attack).
   b. Persuasion; complain; argue; convince agent to modify actions; bargain; criticize; harass; strike.
   c. Change own actions or performance (if they are the disvalued object).
4. Change or blunt reaction to object.
   a. Modify content or hierarchy of own values (self-persuasion; counselling; therapy).
   b. Modify estimate of relationship between situation or object and one's values.
   c. Use ego-defence mechanisms: psychological withdrawal; drugs; repression; fantasy; displacement etc, to distort perception or appraisal of situation.
5. Tolerate situation (focus on valued aspects of situation).
6. Repeat previous action (rigidity, compulsion, fear of change).

Source: Locke (1976)

associated with working. Consequently, variations in pay will be strongly related to their satisfaction. Other workers, once they are making enough money to satisfy their basic needs, are not so concerned with how much they make. Variations in the pay of these workers will not have much effect, either positive or negative, on satisfaction. Thus, value theory states that the more important a job-related factor is to a worker, the greater its potential effect on his/her satisfaction.

Whereas there is some evidence consistent with Locke's value theory (Locke, 1969; Mobley and Locke, 1970), there has been limited empirical research on this approach. Nevertheless, the concept of values is an important addition to the satisfaction literature and can be easily interpreted in terms of other studies such as that of Rokeach (1973). Need theories imply that the satisfaction of all workers depends on the fulfilment of a small number of basic needs. This in turn implies that satisfaction can be achieved through a limited number of strategies designed to address whichever of these needs are unfulfilled for a particular worker. Worker values, on the other hand, introduce another dimension. Even though outcomes such as pay, fringe benefits and working conditions are the same for two workers, and even though these outcomes may provide equivalent levels of need fulfilment, the workers' satisfaction will differ to the extent that their values differ. This approach seems to be more consistent with the ways in which people actually react to their jobs. People choose and change their jobs on the basis of these principles or values. Landy (1985) pointed out that value theory is theoretically consistent with more general models of emotion, which state that emotional responses, such as attitudes, are triggered by a general state of physiological *and* psychological arousal. Landy noted that valued outcomes are more likely to lead to arousal, and thereby have implications for satisfaction, than non-valued outcomes.

Individuals differ in their values, although patterns are apparent. Furthermore, personality is clearly related to value (Furnham, 1984a). Furnham (1984) gave the Eysenck Personality Questionnaire (EPQ) and the Rokeach Value Survey to over 70 subjects. The findings showed a clear relationship between personality and values. The major differences were between the unstable introverts and the other three groups. For instance, the unstable introverts rated *freedom* and *self-respect* more highly than the other four groups. On the other hand, neurotics rated *inner harmony* more highly and a *comfortable life* less highly than non-neurotics. Furthermore, in accordance with the hypothesis, both stable and unstable extraverts rated an *exciting life* more highly than stable and unstable introverts. A correlational analysis showed that by far the highest correlation was between stable extraverts and introverts, while the other correlations varied from 0.45 (unstable introverts and stable extraverts) and 0.65 (unstable extraverts and stable introverts). This suggests that the neurotic factor is a more important predictor of values than the extraversion factor.

A discriminant analysis was also done in order to distinguish the most important factors between the three groups. Eight variables clearly distinguished between the groups, the most important of which were a *sense of accomplishment*, *freedom* and *self-respect*, and to a lesser extent a *world at peace*, an *exciting life, inner harmony* and *true friendship*. A canonical correlation of 0.63 was achieved which indicated that the discriminant function based on values was fairly strongly related to group membership.

6.6 LAWLER'S FACET SATISFACTION MODEL

Another comparison theory of satisfaction is Lawler's facet satisfaction model (1973). This theory is an elaboration on portions of the Porter–Lawler motivation model which is a combination of some of the basic ideas from several prominent theories. The facet satisfaction model derives its name from the fact that it is intended to describe the processes by which satisfaction with any individual job component, or *facet*, is determined. The comparison specified in Lawler's theory is between perceptions of what a worker believes he/she *should* receive, in terms of job outcomes such as pay, recognition and promotions, and perceptions of the outcomes that are *actually* received. Perceptions of what *should* be received depend on perceptions of the inputs the worker brings to the job, such as skill, education and experience, as well as perceptions of job characteristics, such as responsibility and difficulty, and perceptions of the inputs and outcomes of others. Perceptions of *actual* outcomes depend, of course, on the outcomes themselves, as well as perceptions of the outcomes of referent others, or people holding similar jobs with whom workers compare themselves. The facet model is highly cognitive in nature and reflects the view that people respond to their *perceptions* of reality more directly than to reality itself.

As with Adams' (1965) equity theory, the facet model states that the only desirable or satisfying condition is one in which the input–output comparison process indicates equality, when perceptions of what should be received balance perceptions of what is actually received. If the worker feels that he/she is receiving *less* than is due, dissatisfaction with the job results. If the worker perceives that he/she is receiving *more* than is deserved, uncomfortable feelings of inequity, and possibly guilt, ensue. The notion of feeling overpaid or over-compensated is the most controversial aspect of the equity theory of motivation, and it remains a problem of Lawler's (1973) satisfaction theory. One way to reduce the supposed guilt which results from overpayment is to work harder, so increasing input.

Research on Lawler's model has been limited and somewhat inconclusive. Wanous and Lawler (1972) examined satisfaction with 23 different job facets using several measures of satisfaction. One of the measures, as specified by the facet satisfaction model, was the difference between the current level of the facet and the level that the worker believed *should* be associated with the job. They found that overall job satisfaction ratings could be predicted from this different score, as suggested by the theory. The same data, however, was later re-analysed by Wall and Payne (1973), who found that perceptions of the level of outcomes received predicted overall satisfaction best, with those workers who perceived greater outcomes being more satisfied. Furthermore, what the workers thought they *should* receive did not improve the prediction of satisfaction. Wall and Payne therefore argued that the type of difference score suggested by Lawler's model is inherently flawed because the measure of equity was wrong.

Another problem is that the facet model assumes that people use rational cognitive processes, carefully weighing their own, as well as others', inputs and outcomes, and basing their attitudes on the logical comparative conclusions derived from those comparisons. There are good reasons to suggest that many people are *not* this rational. Furthermore, it is not at all clear, even if people do compare inputs and outcomes, that this comparison is as simple as Lawler's model suggests. Weiner (1980) showed that job satisfaction can be predicted more accurately if the difference between what you actually receive and what you think you should receive is computed as a percentage of what you actually receive (satisfaction = [actual − desired]/actual), rather than as a simple difference (satisfaction = actual − desired).

This model, like the previous one, allows for, but does not stress, the role of personality and individual differences. Clearly, personality factors may determine the perceptions of both inputs and outputs, and hence determine the perception and subsequent experience of equity and inequity. Thus, instead of having a direct association between personality and satisfaction, two intervening variables are posited: the perception of inputs and outputs and also the subjective experience of equity or inequity. Again, it is not difficult to see how personality factors could be introduced into the model and sensible theories tested.

6.7 SOCIAL LEARNING THEORY

Social learning approaches to job satisfaction and attitudes are similar to Lawler's facet model, in that attitudes are seen to be determined in part by an examination of the behaviour of other workers. Instead of comparing inputs and outcomes, however, social learning theory claims that workers use other people as sources of information for selecting appropriate attitudes and behaviours. Workers' attitudes, at least in part, are copied, reflected or modelled from the attitudes of other co-workers. Specifically, by observing co-workers, workers infer their attitudes toward the organization, the job as a whole and specific job facets. People perceive certain co-workers, usually those with similar jobs and interests, or those who are believed to be successful or powerful, as being appropriate *models*, and base their own attitudes on what they believe theirs to be. Thus, the theory maintains that a worker's job satisfaction is not determined internally but externally.

A number of studies conducted by Weiss examined the social learning of work attitudes of which job satisfaction could be seen as one. Weiss and Shaw (1979) studied the effects of models' evaluative comments on the task satisfaction of subjects who watched an instructional videotape, on which could be seen the hands of a 'trainee' who was assembling a simple electric circuit, while the voice of the 'trainer' explained the steps involved in the task. The subjects could also hear, in the background, the voice of the trainee and another person. In some conditions, the trainee made positive comments about the task, while in others he made negative comments. Weiss and Shaw found that subjects who overheard the positive comments had more favourable attitudes after performing the task than those who overheard the negative comments. Precisely how long these positive attitudes lasted is not known, nor is the causes of various individual differences observed.

Weiss (1978) also found that the modelling of work values was influenced by supervisors' behaviour; there was great similarity between the values of workers and supervisors when the supervisors demonstrated consideration toward their subordinates. He also discovered that workers who were low in self-esteem, or who had relatively negative perceptions of their own abilities and worthiness, modelled the values of successful and competent supervisors more strongly than high self-esteem subordinates. Weiss suggested that high self-esteem people may have greater confidence in their own judgements and therefore feel less of a need to rely on cues provided by others.

Social learning appears to be a means by which people develop attitudes, not only in work settings, but also in other social situations. However, not everyone is equally likely to model the behaviour of others, nor is everyone equally likely to serve as a model. Consequently, social learning is apt to be a better explanation for job satisfaction and other attitudes in certain situations and for certain people than for others. Essentially, social learning theory traditionally sees individual differences as error variance. However, there is no reason to deny that there are individual differences in the extent to which people are likely to be influenced by the ideas, beliefs and behaviours of those around them. Personality differences are not incompatible with social factors operating.

6.8 SATISFACTION AND ATTRIBUTION PROCESS

Landy (1985) suggested an approach to job satisfaction that is based on a general theory of emotions developed by Schachter and Singer (1962), who noted that certain events or environmental conditions cause a state of general physiological arousal. The qualitative, physiological nature of this arousal is the same for any such event; differences from one situation to the next involve only the intensity or level of arousal. To understand individual differences in emotions, we need to understand how the individual interprets the feelings of arousal.

According to Schachter and Singer, specific emotions depend on the attributions, or perceived causes, for physiological arousal, people examine the situation or context in which it has occurred, and infer emotions from the cues that are present. The person who has just received a large pay increase is therefore likely to attribute his/her arousal to more money, and is likely to be satisfied with the job (or at least with the pay). For the person who is forced to miss his/her child's birthday party, arousal is more likely to be attributed to the 'unreasonable' travel demands of the job, and dissatisfaction is the likely result.

Not only can the same physical arousal result in different emotions, but arousal caused by the *same event* can have different emotional consequences depending on the attributions we make. This is, in essence, an individual difference theory of satisfaction.

This approach to job satisfaction assumes that environmental, psychological and physiological conditions have some sort of direct effect on satisfaction. It suggests that the effects of such conditions depend, to a great extent, on individuals' perceptions of the causes of those conditions, which in turn may be determined by a number of factors that are unlikely to be the same for everyone. The question remains, however, what individual difference factors are the best predictions of attribution.

Recent researchers have stressed that the social/cognitive construction view of job satisfaction deals with the *effects* of emotions on other types of behaviour. O'Reilly and Caldwell (1979) demonstrated that work attitudes can indeed be related to other perceptions about jobs, such as the variety of tasks that make up a job, and the skills required to perform the job. This research is consistent with the notion that emotional responses may help to determine employees' reactions to their jobs, and with Landy's (1985) suggestions that general theories of emotion may be useful for understanding job attitudes.

6.9 PERSONALITY AND THE THEORIES OF JOB SATISFACTION

Clearly, none of the various fairly well established, but not always empirically supported, theories of job satisfaction admit the possibility of individual differences or focus on them. These theories focus on such things as needs fulfilment, value fit, perceptions of equity, modelling behaviour and attribution style. Each proposes an intermediate, usually comparison, process between the individual difference variable and the subjective experience of satisfaction. Few, if any, consider the possibility that trait measures directly related to job satisfaction either as a main effect or in interaction with job-specific factors. It is, then, quite possible that one might measure personality empirically through a psychometrically validated questionnaire, and following a comprehensive job analysis make a clear prediction as to the nature of a job holder's satisfaction. Thus, it is possible to predict that extraverted salespeople would be more satisfied (and productive) than introverted salespeople, while introverted accountants would be more satisfied than extraverted accountants.

Recently, Locke and Latham (1990) have offered a 'coherent data-based theory' of the relationship between work motivation and job satisfaction by focusing on the high performance cycle. It begins with organizational members being faced with high challenge or difficult goals. If high challenge is accompanied by high expectancy of success or self-efficacy, high performance results, given that there is: commitment to the goals, feedback, adequate ability and low situational constraints. High performance is achieved through four mechanisms: direction of attention and action, effort, persistence, and the development of task strategies and plans. High performance, if rewarding, leads to job satisfaction, which in turn facilitates commitment to the organization and its goals. They note:

Our model, moreover, reveals why scores of previous studies have failed to find a consistent or meaningful association between job satisfaction and productivity. *The effects of satisfaction on subsequent performance are indirect and contingent rather than direct.* Only if satisfaction leads to commitment to the organization and to its goals, and only if those goals are challenging and accompanied by a high self-efficacy will subsequent high performance result. Furthermore, commitment is dependent on the anticipation of future rewards; such anticipation is based on past rewards and on one's judgement of how the situation will change . . .

The usefulness of the high performance cycle, we believe, goes beyond the confines of work organizations. The basic ideas are also applicable, for example, to the process of self-management that has been shown to be effective in clinical as well as work-settings. Self-management procedures involve setting a goal for what one wants to accomplish, measuring progress toward the goal, developing strategies to attain it, and reward oneself for success. Satisfaction and self-efficacy increase as one succeeds in attaining proximal goals and this in turn increases commitment to the program (p.345).

This potentially useful model, then, stresses the importance of self-efficacy which is a well-known individual difference variable.

6.10 IS JOB SATISFACTION GENETICALLY DETERMINED?

Writers in the 1970s have lamented the paucity of research on personality/dispositional correlates (determinants) of job attitudes, especially job satisfaction. Three important papers have recently addressed this issue. Staw and Ross (1985) sought to investigate both traits and organizational factors as determinants of job satisfaction among middle-aged men. Specifically, they examined the temporal stability of a single, global job satisfaction response as a function of pay change, occupational status change and previous global satisfaction measured some five years before. They found that neither changes in pay nor changes in job status accounted for nearly as much variance as prior job attitudes, namely satisfaction. Hence, they question the value of various programmes to change worker attitudes and hence behaviours. Many reviewers have taken Staw and Ross's findings to mean that worker attitudes are to a major degree a function of stable personality traits (more than organizational status). Others have criticized this conclusion. Gerhart (1987) has criticized this conclusion on various grounds:

• Older people, such as those in this cohort, are in any event less likely to experience significant changes in the work situation.
• The test–retest correlation between pay and occupational status was 0.84, which shows more the stability of organizational factors than dispositional ones.
• The reliability of the occupational measures was poor.

Gerhart thus set about to replicate this study to overcome some of the problems: increasing the sample variance (in terms of time and age) and providing a measure of job design. Over 800 people were measured twice over a three-year period. In accordance with the findings of Staw and Ross (1985), previous job satisfaction was the best predictor of current job satisfaction, yet in this study pay status and job complexity added explanatory power to an equation predicting job satisfaction. The author believes that the contradictory results are due to methodological problems. He notes:

> Finally, until more compelling evidence for the impact of stable traits on job satisfaction is found, personnel selection based on traits may be premature. It is important to remember that even conceptually stable traits such as intellectual flexibility have been found to change in response to situational factors like job complexity. To the extent that traits lack stability, their predictive validity is diminished. The longstanding conclusion that personality traits have suspect predictive validity may still apply (p.372).

Arvey *et al.* (1989) invested 34 monozygotic twins reared apart to look at genetic and environmental components in job satisfaction. They were quite clearly provoked by the article by Staw and Ross (1985) who noted:

> Job attitudes may reflect a biologically based trait that predisposes individuals to see positive or negative content in their lives . . . Differences in individual temperament . . . ranging from clinical depression to a very positive disposition, could influence the information individuals input, recall and interpret within various social situations, including work (p.471).

There is, they argue quite correctly, no reason to believe that genetic factors do not affect job satisfaction, and thus examined 34 monozygotic twins (reared apart) just over 40 years old on average. They completed a multi-dimension questionnaire on job satisfaction and the results showed a significant hereditability of intrinsic and general, but not extrinsic and overall, satisfaction. They also demonstrated clear evidence that there is a genetic component in terms of the job that is sought and held by individuals. However, the fact that the sample held similar jobs cannot account for the hereditability co-efficient being significant.

The authors note, however, that the genetic factor accounted for about 30 per cent of the variance, which is not overwhelming, but does not necessarily imply that all of the remaining variance is due to the environment. The authors argue that intellectual capacity (shown to have a strong hereditary component) probably accounts for the similarity between the jobs chosen by the twins. They argue that these results have two major implications. Firstly, that workers bring dispositions to jobs that are more difficult to modify than heretofore acknowledged. Thus, job enrichment and other satisfaction-increasing programmes might miss the mean levels of satisfaction for workers, but the rank order is preserved. Secondly, that future satisfaction may be predicted from current satisfaction, i.e. it can be used as a criterion for prediction.

These results will remain, like the whole issue, extremely contentious, not so much because of the methods used but the socio-political implications of these results for selection and, more importantly, organizational and structural attempts to improve job satisfaction (and hence perhaps satisfaction).

6.11 NEUROTICISM AND SATISFACTION

A number of studies have suggested that neurotics are less productive and satisfied than non-neurotics. In a natural experiment, Organ (1975b) observed neurotic and non-neurotic business students as they took structured or 'ambiguous' exams under high or low pressure. Predictably, the neurotics reported much more emotional stress in the ambiguous exam than non-neurotics.

Furnham and Zacherl (1986) examined the relationship between personality and job satisfaction as measured by a multi-dimensional scale. The results are shown in Table 6.3. Both the psychoticism and neuroticism scales correlated *negatively* with all of the subscale scores while both extraversion and the lie scale correlated *positively* with all of the subscale scores. People with high psychoticism scores (tough-minded) tended to be significantly less satisfied with their supervisors, the nature of the work and their co-workers than people with low psychoticism scores (tender-minded).

Table 6.3 Correlations between the four personality measures and the eight job satisfaction factors (N = 88)

Job satisfaction factors	Personality scale			
	Psychoticism	Extraversion	Neuroticism	Lie
1. Supervision	−0.17*	0.01	−0.12	0.15
2. Nature of the work	−0.21*	−0.11	−0.14	0.32***
3. Amount of work	−0.01	0.10	−0.33***	0.28**
4. Working conditions	−0.05	0.10	−0.08	0.10
5. Co-workers	−0.19*	0.05	−0.31***	0.21*
6. Pay	0.01	0.20*	−0.29**	0.36***
7. Future with the organization	−0.07	0.04	−0.01	0.01
8. Overall job satisfaction	−0.03	0.18*	−0.06	0.10

*$P < 0.05$
**$P < 0.01$
***$P < 0.001$
Source: Furnham and Zacherl (1986)

People with high neuroticism scores (unstable neurotics) tended to be fairly highly significantly less satisfied with the amount of work that they were required to do, their co-workers and their pay. But it was the lie scale – a measure of social desirability – which in fact yielded the most and the biggest correlations.

The fact that neuroticism correlates consistently negatively with the job satisfaction factors suggests that neurotics are in general less job satisfied than non-neurotics. This may be because they are less productive or that rather their poor satisfaction might lead to poorer productivity. Whichever way the direction of causality, it seems to be that neurotics make less satisfied employees than non-neurotics.

More recently, Levin and Stokes (1989) looked at the trait of 'negative affectivity' which for them is a mix of anxiety, irritability, neuroticism and self-depreciation. They argue:

> High-NA individuals have ongoing feelings of distress and nervousness. They tend to dwell on their mistakes, disappointments, and shortcomings and to focus more on the negative aspects of the world in general. In contrast, low-NA individuals appear to be more satisfied, self-secure, and calm and to focus less on, and be more resilient in response to life's daily frustrations and irritations (p.753).

In both a laboratory and a 'natural' experiment, they found that negative affectivity (neuroticism) was related to lower job satisfaction. They argue that non-neurotics may be denying or repressing various frustrations, disappointments and problems, or that the cognitive processes of neurotics lead them to perceive the world more negatively. Whichever the case, organizations would seem wise to screen out extreme neurotics and those with negative affectivity.

Perone, De Waard and Baron (1979) found similar correlations when examining satisfaction with real and simulated jobs. They found neuroticism and sensation-seeking were negatively correlated with satisfaction, indicating that dissatisfaction is symptomatic of general emotional maladjustment.

Thus, it seems that neuroticism is a highly undesirable trait in the workplace. Yet there is fairly consistent evidence that neuroticism is correlated with academic success. McKenzie (1989) has reviewed two explanations for this:

- Neuroticism only correlates positively with success in highly selected groups – particularly those selected for intelligence.
- Neuroticism only correlates positively with achievement in people that have appropriate coping strategies and super-ego strength.

There is in fact evidence for both, suggesting that if neuroticism is 'moderated' by intelligence and appropriate coping skills, it will not seriously inhibit achievement.

6.12 SENSITIVITY TO REWARDS AND PUNISHMENTS, AND JOB SATISFACTION

The motivational differences between extraverts who are motivated to seek rewards and introverts who are motivated to avoid punishment have been examined by Gray (1973) who, in rotating Eysenck's two factors along a 45° axis, has presented one of the most coherent challenges to that theory.

Gray's theory asserts that extraverts will respond more readily to reward while introverts react primarily to punishment. Although extraverts will react positively to an achieved reward and introverts will react positively to an applied punishment, both extraverts and introverts perceive reward and punishment in terms of possible current or future realizations. The extravert is motivated to gain a *promised* reward; the introvert is motivated to avoid a *threatened* punishment. Also, the over-application of the principle tends to lessen the intended effects, dampening the motivational qualities of reward and punishment: because the extravert is motivated by opportunity to gain reward, too much rewarding reinforcement tends to create a sating effect on the extravert's desire to achieve. Also, since the introvert is motivated by a need to avoid punishment, too many threats or actual enforcement of the negative reinforcement places the introvert in the position of being unable to avoid punishment, and so he/she becomes immobilized and the motivational effect of punishment is decreased of course. The motivationing effects of reward and punishment are not mutually exclusive: an extravert does not wish to be punished and will react to negative reinforcement, and all introverts want to be rewarded and are motivated by positive reinforcement.

The two crucial factors in this theory are:

(1) The tendency of the extravert or introvert to perform more satisfactorily in the face of either reward or punishment.
(2) The degree of extraversion or introversion in a given personality. The more extraverted, the greater sensitivity a person has towards promises of reward, while a person closer to the introversion end would display greater sensitivity toward threats of punishment.

The practical application of Gray's theory to occupational settings is appealingly obvious and we can now more effectively apply to the car-rot/stick principle in socializing human behavioural responses. It becomes apparent that it would be a waste of time to try to motivate an extravert with threats of dire punishment (such as sacking, no pay rise), and it would prove equally unsuccessful to attempt to entice an introvert with promise of pay and benefits. To exact the highest level of performance from individuals, motivators must encourage the extravert with potential rewards and prompt the introvert with judicial use of punitive threats. Thus, extraverted organizations, like those involved in selling, could best motivate and satisfy their staff by providing regular but varied rewards. Equally, a primarily introverted organization, as in many bureaucracies, can best shape or motivate staff by the threat of sanctions.

Gray's theory concerning sensitivity to signals of reward and punishment attempts to explain individual differences in extraversion and introversion but also deals with neuroticism. Just as extraversion and introversion can be viewed on a continuum scale, so, too, can individuals be evaluated on a continuum of stability and neuroticism.

The degree of neuroticism heightens an individual's sensitivity to reward or punishment. The introvert, sensitive to punishment, who displays high neuroticism becomes more sensitive to *both* reward and punishment with the greatest increase in sensitivity being toward punishment. That is, the neurotic introvert becomes more concerned with reward but is even more anxious about punishment than the low neuroticism introvert. As neuroticism increases, the extravert (sensitive to reward) becomes more sensitive to *both* reward and punishment, with higher increases in reward sensitivity. Although extraverts and introverts increase in sensitivity to reward and punishment as neuroticism increases, each has the highest increase of sensitivity to that trait commonly attributed to extraversion or introversion.

Thus, an extraverted neurotic, being highly sensitive to reward, is less socializable in terms of legal, organizational norms and more likely to become maladaptive or difficult. Given moderated levels of extraversion, high N (neurotic) individuals are usually more responsive to control techniques than low N (stable) individuals. Whether reward or punishment is the controlling factor, the over-socialized individual will respond readily and may tend to become over-controlled, while under-socialized individuals may show little or no response to control measures. Consequently, the low N (stable) individual may necessitate the use of rigid control and severe disciplinary measures (Wakefield, 1979).

Empirical support for this thesis has come from various sources. Gupta (1976) used a linguistic task to show that extraverts condition more readily to reinforcement and introverts to punishments. Gupta used two experimenters. Although all subjects were male, one experimenter was male and the other was female. When the word 'good' was vocalized by the female, the young male extraverts showed a more significant response differential than when the word was spoken by the male experimenter. Gupta concluded that, apparently, the encouraging word from the female was sufficiently rewarding while it appeared probable that the more explicit reward was required from the male. 'The strength of conditioning is to a certain extent determined by individual's subjective attitude towards the person who administers the reinforcement' (Gupta, 1976, p.50).

Similarly, Wakefield and colleagues tried to apply Gray's theory to educational settings. They argued that achievement in the elementary classroom can be improved by applying differential modes of reinforcement to extraverts and introverts. Extraverts should be rewarded with extensive praise and consistently encouraged by reminders of potential rewards commensurate with competent performance. Introverts, on the other hand, should be judicially exposed to threats of punishment and made continually aware of the negative sanctions resulting from unsatisfactory performance.

Thus, McCord and Wakefield (1981) hypothesized that: (1) introverts have better arithmetic achievements than extraverts when exposed to higher levels of teacher-presented punishment in the classroom, and (2) a reversal would occur in which extraverts would achieve arithmetic advantages in classroom situations where teacher-presented reward was prevalent. They related the reward to punishment ratio to teachers, the personality of children and the arithmetic performance of elementary school pupils. They found that extraverts do meet expectations of higher achievement than introverts in classrooms where there is a predominance of teacher-presented reward, but when the gap between reward and punishment predomination narrows, introverts have a greater achievement advantage.

More recent studies have also confirmed Gray's work. Boddy, Carver and Rowley (1986) gave introverts and extraverts two tasks to do: a computer game involving initiation of cursor movements on a VDU to find a hidden target, and a task involving recoding of decimal numbers and letters, and doing calculations. As predicted, extraverts performed better under positive than negative reinforcement, while introverts performed better under negative than positive reinforcement. In a study looking at reactions to punishment, Patterson, Kosson and Newman (1987) found extraverts fail to pause following punished errors, but that longer pausing following punishment predicted better learning from punishment for both introverts and extraverts. They note:

> In the presence of reward incentive, extraverts are more prone to facilitate their approach behaviour than to elicit interruption and reflectivity. Without adequate reflection, extraverts fail to associate punishment with the incorrect response and are therefore less likely to inhibit that response on subsequent occasions. In contrast to stable extraverts, whose disinhibited reaction to punishment appears to depend on the presence of cues for reward, the reaction of neurotic extraverts appears to be less situationally determined. To the extent that this disinhibited reaction to punishment interferes with learning and subsequent inhibition, we might expect that stable extraverts' insensitivity to punishment will be more situation specific than neurotic extraverts (p.570).

A number of attempts have been made to devise measures of Gray's theory. For instance, Torrubia and Tobena (1984) devised a 'susceptibility to punishment' scale which showed predictable and satisfactory correlations with Eysenck's measure. Wilson, Barrett and Gray (1989) were less successful, however. They devised a five-dimension measure – approach, active avoidance, passive avoidance, extinction and fight/flight – which, although they showed satisfactory internal consistency, did not correlate with the Eysenckian dimensions as hypothesized.

Given the nature of this theory, what are the implications for organizational behaviour? They are indeed manifold and could be considered relatively profound:

- The organizational incentives (i.e. performance related to pay, promotion possibilities) and prohibitions (i.e. potential sacking, fining) work differently for different people in the organizations.
- Extravert organizations (that is, those that are dominated by extraverts) can motivate and shape staff by having small (but incremental and worthwhile) incentives that act as reinforcements. The more regular, consistent and public these are, the better. 'Salesperson-of-the-month' and annual awards for efficiency, tact, customer relations etc are likely to be more successful with extraverts.
- Introverted organizations (that is, those that are dominated by introverts, and highly sensitive to potential sanctions and punishments) could be used to shape, or at least prevent, various kinds of behaviours. Thus, threats of imminent job loss, compulsory retirement, working on half-time are likely to make introverts work harder than extraverts.
- Organizations dominated by extraverts would do well to maintain a 'culture' where people give each other open, honest and regular, positive feedback for work well done, while introverted cultures would have ways to remind people regularly that stepping out of line or under-performing will be punished.
- The obvious major implication of this work is that management systems devised to regulate the behaviour of employees should be sensitive to major individual differences. The carrot and the stick should both be available, but they will not have equal effect on all employees.

6.13 CONCLUSION

This chapter attempted to review the extant literature on personality determinants or correlates of job satisfaction. A large number of individual difference factors have been shown to relate to job satisfaction either directly or in interaction with other variables. These include genetic factors; traits such as extraversion and neuroticism; needs either hierarchically conceived or listed; values; perceptions of equity and attributional style. These theories are not mutually exclusive, being compatible. However, they do tend to focus on different individual difference factors and it could be argued that some are the result of others. Thus, it could be argued that values and needs are the result of genetically inherited traits.

Chapter 7

Ability, biography and sex differences at work

A diamond is a piece of coal that stuck to the job.

Anon

Knowledge is the only instrument of production that is not subject to diminishing returns.

J.M. Clark

It is a great ability to be able to conceal one's ability.

F. La Rochefoucauld

You don't have to be intellectually bright to be a competent leader.

Sir Edmund Hillary

A woman who strives to be like a man lacks ambition.

Anon

The great corporations of this country were not founded by ordinary people. They were founded by people with extraordinary energy, intelligence, ambition, aggressiveness. All these factors go into the primordial capitalist urge.

D.M. Moynihan

Everyone complains of his memory, and no one complains of his judgement.

Duc de la Rochefoucauld

The true leader is always led.

C.G. Jung

7.1 INTRODUCTION

What is the best predictor of work satisfaction or productivity: *demographic* factors such as sex, age and class; *biographical* factors uniquely associated with each individual, such as whether they grew up in the town or country, or whether their parents separated or not; *ability* factors like general intelligence factors; or *personality*?

This chapter concentrates on those non-personality factors which have, in the past, been shown to be predictive of job success.

7.2 ABILITY AND OCCUPATIONAL SUCCESS

It seems patently obvious to most people that nearly all jobs require a certain amount of specific ability to do them. Accountants require numerical skills and abilities, journalists the ability to write, and politicians the ability to persuade. Recent research has attempted to ask *why* ability tests should predict job performance. Quite simply, more able people seem to be better workers primarily because they learn more quickly what the job is about. Less able workers no doubt learn how to do the job productively, but take longer to achieve this. However, two fundamentally important questions need to be considered in examining the relationship between ability and occupational success.

What Is the Relationship Between Ability and Success?

A number of quite different relationships are possible:

1. *Positively linear*. If the relationship is linear, this implies quite simply that the more the ability the greater the success. Certainly, many practical professionals hold to this very simple, although somewhat improbable, relationship occurring.
2. *Plateauing*. This relationship suggests that once a plateau has been reached, no further increase in the ability has any effect on the organizational successfulness of the worker. Clearly, if this relationship is the correct one, the crucial issue becomes where the plateau begins.
3. *Exponential*. This relationship suggests that beyond certain levels of ability, the increase in occupational success is phenomenal. Thus, for instance, very able people achieve substantially and significantly more success than moderately able people.
4. *Curvilinear*. The relationship between success and ability is curvilinear, which implies that there is an optimal amount of ability to achieve occupational success – too much or too little can have equal, non-ideal effects.
5. *Negatively linear*. It is possible that ability may be perfectly negatively correlated with success such that the more ability one has, the less successful one is occupationally. This indeed may be the case in intellectually less demanding jobs.
6. *Asymptotic*. This is a negative plateau relationship which indicates that low amounts of ability are linked with occupational success, but that after a certain point the relationship ends and no further amount of ability is linked to occupational success.

7. *No relationship*. Here there is no relationship at all between ability and occupational success, the latter presumably being determined by other factors, be they organizational or personal.
8. *Ability specific*. If this relationship occurs, it implies that only one particular level of ability is associated with occupational success.
9. *Bi-modality*. If the relationship is bi-modal, it suggests that two levels of ability – one moderate-to-low, the other moderate-to-high – are the optimal ones for job success. Put another way, there are two population groups successful for different reasons.

There are doubtless other possible relationships. There is a vast literature on the correlates of abilities, but very little specifically on the occupational correlates of abilities. Perhaps given previous studies in the whole area, the most probable relationship is plateauing (2), or curvilinear (4). However, for both, the crucial question remains: At what ability range does the performance reach its maximum?

Which Precise Abilities Are Predictive of Occupational Success?

This apparently simple but important question opens up many other extremely important questions, such as: How are various abilities related to one another? When do abilities stabilize? Is creativity an ability? How reliable are ability tests? There is no shortage of ability tests in psychology. For instance, there are numerous types of the following tests:

1. *Mental ability*. These 'intelligence' tests vary enormously in length and complexity, and in what they supposedly measure: general knowledge, verbal vs non-verbal (i.e. numeric) ability, mental alertness, adaptability etc.
2. *Mechanical aptitudes*. Again, there is a vast range of tests, some devised well over 50 years ago, that measure such things as dexterity, spatial relations ability, mechanical knowledge and reasoning, comprehending instructions.
3. *Sensory ability*. These are tests that measure physical attributes such as visual activity, colour vision and sensitivity to hearing.
4. *Motor ability*. These tests measure fine and gross motor co-ordination.

There have been numerous attempts to distinguish between abilities (believed to be inherited) and aptitudes (the capacity to learn and develop abilities). A major issue has been whether aptitudes or abilities are unitary or multi-dimensional. The most frequently cited abilities include the following:

- Reasoning (verbal, numerical, abstract ability).
- Spatio–visual ability (practical intelligence, non-verbal ability, creative ability).
- Perceptual speed and accuracy (clerical ability).
- Manual ability (mechanical, manual, musical, athletic ability).

Many of these 'abilities' are a mixture of ability, interest and values, but mechanical ability (or aptitude) is a complex mix of other aptitudes and characteristics because it consists of spatial visualization, reasoning and experience. However, despite its complexity, it can be treated as a unit and measured reliably. Other complex aptitudes that can be measured in psychometric tests are musical aptitude, manual aptitude and artistic aptitude.

There exist a large number of assessment batteries for special programmes. For instance, the General Aptitude Test Battery (GATB) was developed by the United States employment counsellors in the state employment service offices. Factor analysis suggested 12 tests should be given under the final battery, which gives a total of nine factor scores, as follows:

- *General learning ability* (G). Found by adding the scores on three tests. Also used to measure other factors (vocabulary, arithmetic reasoning, three-dimensional space).
- *Verbal aptitude* (V). Measured by a vocabulary test requiring the test taker to indicate which two words in each set have either the same or opposite meaning.
- *Numerical aptitude* (N). Includes both computation and arithmetic reasoning tests.
- *Spatial aptitude* (S). Measured by three-dimensional space test, involving the ability to comprehend two-dimensional representation of three-dimensional objects and to visualize effects of movement in three dimensions.
- *Form perception* (P). Measured by two tests requiring the test taker to match identical drawings of tools in one test and of geometric forms in the other.
- *Clerical perception* (Q). Similar to P, but requiring the matching of names rather than pictures or forms.
- *Motor co-ordination* (K). Measured by a simple paper-and-pencil test requiring the test taker to make specified pencil marks in a series of squares.
- *Finger dexterity* (F). Two tests requiring the assembling and disassembling respectively of rivets and washers.
- *Manual dexterity* (M). Two tests requiring the test taker to transfer and reverse pegs in a board.

The nine factor scores on the GATB can be converted into standard scores with a mean of 100 and a SD of 20. These standard score norms were derived from a sample of 4000 cases representative of the working population of the United States in terms of age, sex, educational, occupational and geographical distribution. By testing many groups of employees, applicants and trainees in different kinds of jobs, decent norms were subsequently established, showing the critical aptitudes and minimum standard scores required for each occupation.

Another major application of multiple-aptitude batteries is to be found in the armed services. Such batteries were first developed and employed for classification purposes, following preliminary screening with more general instruments. All branches of the armed services in many developed countries, particularly those with conscripts, eventually prepared multi-factor batteries for assigning personnel to military occupational specialities.

The Americans use the Armed Services Vocational Aptitude Battery (ASVAB), a composite selection and classification battery developed jointly for use in all the armed services. Current forms of the ASVB include the following ten subtests:

• Arithmetic reasoning
• Numerical operations
• Paragraph comprehension
• Word knowledge
• Coding speed
• General science
• Mathematics knowledge
• Electronics information
• Mechanical comprehension
• Automotive and shop information

Each service selects and combines subtest scores from this battery to form aptitude composites that fit its particular personnel classification needs. For example, there are aptitude composites for military occupational specialities within the clerical/administrative, electronics repair, and surveillance/communication areas.

Four ASVAB subtests (arithmetic reasoning, numerical operations, paragraph comprehension, word knowledge) constitute the current Armed Forces Questionnaire Test (AFQT), which serves as the common qualifying composite across all services. These AFQT scores were calibrated against an earlier common selection battery designated by the same name. The original fixed reference population employed in this calibration consisted of approximately 11,700 officers and enlisted men tested in 1944. In 1980, a new reference population was established through a project conducted by the Department of Defense and representatives of each of the military services. This project involved the administration of one current form of the ASVAB to a national sample of nearly 12,000 men and women between the ages of 18 and 23. Including both civilian and military personnel, the sample was representative of the national youth population in age distribution, sex ratio, ethnic composition, urban–rural residence and major geographic regions.

One of the forms of the ASVAB is regularly released to high schools for testing and counselling students. Normative data for high-school populations is provided for this form as are reliability and validity data, which meets fairly high psychometric standards. Kuder–Richardson reliabilities cluster in the 0.80s for individual subtests and in the 0.90s for aptitude composites. Validities for the prediction of appropriate criteria for both high-school students and military personnel are substantial. For example, in groups of 256 to 1880 students, correlations between appropriate ASVAB composites and final grades in business or technical courses ranged from 0.64 to 0.69. In a study of nearly 65,000 army-enlisted personnel, predictive validities of ASVAB aptitude composites against both training and on-the-job criterion measures ranged from 0.44 to 0.58, with an average validity of about 0.48. For obvious reasons, the military has always been keen on assessing abilities. Perhaps it is surprising that so few business organizations have done likewise.

7.3 INTELLIGENCE, HEREDITY, AND VOCATIONAL CHOICE AND SUCCESS

Do more intelligent people choose different jobs from less intelligent people? Does intelligence predict occupational success? Without doubt, the most impressive research in this field was the work of Ghiselli (1965), who searched the literature for 45 years to look for intelligence test correlates of vocational success, aware of all of the errors involved in meta-analysis of this sort.

In over 10,000 studies, intelligence has an average correlation for all jobs of 0.42 with training success and 0.23 for professional success. Mechanical principles and perceptual speed are also both good measures. The value of intelligence tests in vocational guidance should be clearly stated: the highest coefficient in all studies (not averages) for any job and any test were both with intelligence tests – applied to trades and crafts – 0.77 for training and 0.66 for proficiency.

Table 7.1 shows some data collected by Ghiselli (1955) on the efficiency of testing for various types of industrial tests. Ghiselli examined a large number of validation studies and classified them in terms of the type of test being used and the type of criterion involved. All validities within a particular category were then averaged to give the figures shown in Table 7.1. Only three of the values exceed 0.40 in size, and two variables are *not* tests but personal history items. While the process of averaging used by Ghiselli definitely confounds some very substantial validities, it should be sufficiently clear that testing is not a complete solution to the selection problem.

Such correlations are too low for clear individual prediction purposes. The relationship is nevertheless useful, for even such slight help in predicting success is better than if no tests were given, as was made clear in the earlier selection of the selection ratio. Clearly, many other factors, in addition to an individual's ability, help to determine performance. Powerful personal motivation for continuing on a job can compensate for an employee's limited ability. On the other hand, for many reasons, a person may be a failure on a job even though he/she has the ability to be successful. Success or failure depends on many other things besides ability. Most industrial testing programmes limit the functions to be measured to certain specific abilities and do not consider the other contributing factors. Furthermore, the claim cannot be made that even ability is perfectly measured.

However, the issue of ability, more particularly intelligence (the g factor), predicting job performance remains highly debated. Hunter (1986) argued that it is general intelligence (general cognitive ability), not specific abilities, that predicts job performance. Prediger (1989) reviewed 34 studies showing the performance criteria predicted by g have little relationship to performance criteria based on measures of job knowledge and work task proficiency. Indeed, he reports several studies which show work-relevant differences in the ability patterns. His work is most interesting because he identified 14

Table 7.1 Average validity coefficients for various types of test

	Type of criterion	
Type of test	Training	Job proficiency
Intellectual abilities		
Intelligence	38[c]	19[c]
Immediate memory	29[c]	19[c]
Substitution	26[c]	21[c]
Arithmetic	41[c]	21[c]
Spatial abilities		
Spatial relations	31[c]	14[c]
Location	24[c]	15[c]
Perception of details		
Number comparison	26[c]	21[c]
Name comparison	25[c]	21[c]
Cancellation	29[c]	20[c]
Pursuit	19[c]	17[c]
Perceptual speed	39[c]	27[c]
Mechanical comprehension		
Mechanical principles	34[c]	26[c]
Motor abilities		
Tracing	16[c]	16[c]
Tapping	12[c]	14[c]
Dotting	14[c]	15[c]
Finger dexterity	22[c]	19[c]
Hand dexterity	38[a]	14[c]
Arm dexterity	30[b]	17[c]
Personality traits		
Personality	16	21[c]
Interest	14[a]	27[c]
Personal data	44[c]	41[c]

Less than 100 cases, no letter symbol
[a] 100 to 499 cases
[b] 500 to 999 cases
[c] 1000 or more cases
Source: Based on E.E. Ghiselli (1955)

cognitive and non-cognitive abilities (see Table 7.2), which he shows are related to six job clusters (see Table 7.3).

Table 7.2 Definitions of specialized abilities and related DOL abilities

Cognitive
1. *Reading*: Reading and understanding factual material (for example, in a textbook or manual).
    a. *Verbal*: Understanding the meaning of words and using them effectively; comprehending language, understanding relationships between words, and understanding meanings of whole paragraphs.[a](A)[b]
2. *Numerical*: Doing arithmetic accurately and quickly; applying arithmetic (e.g. in formulas and word problems).
    b. *Numerical*: Doing arithmetic operations quickly and accurately.[a](A)
3. *Language usage*: Recognizing correct and incorrect uses of the English language (grammar, punctuation etc). Related DOL ability not found.
4. *Spatial*: Looking at a drawing of an object (for example, a house, a coat, a tool) and picturing in your mind how it would look if you were seeing it from different sides.
    c. *Spatial*: Thinking visually of geometric forms and comprehending the two-dimensional representation of three-dimensional objects.[a](A)
    d. *Form perception*: Perceiving pertinent detail and differences in objects or in pictorial or graphic material.(A)
5. *Clerical*: Quickly and accurately doing tasks such as looking up information in catalogues or tables, recording address or expenses, sorting things.
    e. *Clerical perceptions*: Seeing pertinent detail in verbal or tabular material; proofreading words and numbers, and avoiding perceptual errors in arithmetic computation. Speed of perception is measured.[a](A)
6. *Mechanical*: Understanding everyday mechanical laws (e.g. warm air rises) and how simple mechanical things work (e.g. a lever or pulley).
    f. Working with *processes and machines*.[a](I)
7. *Scientific*: Understanding scientific principles; doing science course work.
    g. Doing *scientific and technical tasks*.[a](I)
    h. Using *measurable* or verifiable *criteria* to make generalizations, evaluations or decisions. (T)
8. *Creative/literary*: Expressing ideas or feelings through writing; and—
9. *Creative/artistic*: Drawing, painting, playing a musical instrument, acting, dancing.
    i. Interpreting *feelings, ideas or facts*.[a](T)
    j. Doing *abstract and creative tasks*.[a](I)

Non-cognitive
10. *Manual dexterity*: Making or repairing things easily and quickly with one's hands.
    k. *Manual dexterity*: Moving hands easily and skilfully; working with hands in placing and turning motions.[a](A)
    l. *Finger dexterity*: Moving fingers and manipulating small objects with fingers, rapidly or accurately. (A)
    m. *Motor co-ordination*: Co-ordinating eyes and hands or fingers rapidly and accurately in making precise movements with speed. (A)
11. *Meeting people* (*Social*): Talking with people; getting along with others; making a good impression.
    n. *Working with people* beyond giving and receiving instructions.[a](T)

12. *Helping others*: Caring for or teaching others; helping people with problems.
    o. Working for the *good of others*.[a](I)
13. *Sales*: Influencing people to buy a product or take a course of action.
    p. *Influencing* opinions or *judgements* about ideas or things.[a](T)
14. *Leadership/management*: Leading/managing people to work co-operatively toward a common goal.
    q. *Directing*, controlling or *planning* an activity.[a](T)
15. *Organization*: Keeping track of details; doing things in a systematic way.
    r. Doing *routine*, concrete, *organized* tasks.[a](I)
    s. Following *set procedures*, sequence or *pace* in doing the same work, continuously. (T)

Specialized abilities (numbered) and DOL abilities (lettered)
Definitions of US Department of Labor (DOL) abilities paraphrase those in the *Handbook for Analysing Jobs* (DOL, 1972). Key words are in italics
[a] This DOL ability served as a proxy for the specialized ability with which it appears
[b] The symbols A, T and I identify abilities categorized by the DOL as aptitudes, temperaments and interests respectively
Source: Prediger (1989)

Table 7.3 Four highest specialized abilities for each job cluster as determined from proxies

Ability	Job cluster					
	Business contact	Business operations	Technical	Science	Arts	Social service
Cognitive						
1. Reading				4X	3	X
2. Numerical	4X	4X	X	2X		
3. Language usage[a]						
4. Spatial				4X	3	4X
5. Clerical		2X				
6. Mechanical		3	1X			
7. Scientific				1X		
8. Creative/literary					1X	
9. Creative/artistic					1X	
Non-cognitive						
10. Manual dexterity			2X			
11. Meeting people	2					2X
12. Helping others						1X
13. Sales	1X					4
14. Leadership/ management	3X					3
15. Organization		1X	3			

Rank order of the four abilities with the highest mean scores is shown for each job cluster. An 'X' indicates assignment of a specialized ability to a job cluster
[a]Data not available. Language usage was assigned to all but the technical job cluster
Source: Prediger (1989)

Prediger argues, as others have, that specialized abilities, taken together, predict occupational success. The argument here is on the nature of the predictive abilities, not whether abilities predict performance. In fact, it is precisely because ability test scores are used by employers that political, legal and social policy questions have been asked. Indeed, the problem of racial group differences in ability test scores used for employment selection continues to raise thorny issues (Schmidt, 1988).

Essentially, there remain three major questions in this area:

- Which ability scores (i.e. general intelligence vs specific abilities) predict which types of job performance/occupational success?
- Given the size of the ability–performance correlations, can or should people use these scores to select, train or relocate people in a skill-based organization?
- What other personal (motivational, personality trait) and organizational factors serve to 'wash out' or suppress (or possibly enhance) the relationship between specific/general ability and job performance?

The extant literature is not conclusive. Certainly, there is evidence that abilities of both a general and specific nature do correlate with various measures of job performance. But the size of the correlations is not high and can be easily affected by structural factors and organizational procedures.

Cook (1988) has taken a historical perspective on researchers' attitudes to the validity of cognitive ability tests. Despite early enthusiasm in the 1960s, the 1970s saw a period of disillusionment where abilities (and intelligence) were thought of as necessary but not sufficient to predict occupational productivity. This occurred partly because of a general distrust of the idea (and measurement) of individual differences, but also the apparent failure to predict anything useful. Meta-analyses and reviews revealed substantial variation in the relationship between general and specific tests of ability and productivity. Moderate variables, situational specificity and measurement issues (sampling error, criterion reliability, restricted ranges, test reliability) were used to explain this.

More recent analysis has tended to explain the poor relationship between ability tests and job performance as being due to poor research methods. Cook argues that carefully designed and executed research has shown that ability tests predict productivity in various clerical jobs, army trades, technical and apprenticeship occupations, computer programmers etc. This has led Cook to make eight bold conclusions based on his reading of the experiment and review literature:

1. Cognitive ability tests are not a waste of time – the estimated true mean validity is generally much higher than 0.30.
2. Ability tests are transportable without having to do a local validity study.

3. There are no 'moderator' variables worth looking for, otherwise they would have been incorporated in a new theory.
4. Job analyses are not absolutely essential because ability predicted productivity within a wide range of jobs.
5. Ability selection tests can be used 'off the shelf' without a local validity study if carefully chosen by a panel of experts.
6. Tests work for minorities and there is, in general, no evidence of differential validity.
7. Ability tests are useful at all occupational levels, even for the least complex jobs.
8. Differential batteries of tests are useful but some are simple general tests of intelligence.

Not everyone would agree with Cook on all of these points. But there is no doubt that careful reviews and meta-analyses have indicated that ability differences are correlated with job performance. Certainly it would be disappointing if they were not!

7.4 BIODATA OR BIOGRAPHICAL PREDICTORS OF OCCUPATIONAL SUCCESS

It seems self-evident to the lay person that from a personal point of view, the past predicts the future. That is, the most useful predictor of a person's behaviour at work is his/her personal history – his/her biographical facts.

Over 60 years ago, Goldsmith (1922) devised an ingenious new solution to an old problem: selecting people who could endure selling life insurance. He took 50 good, 50 poor and 50 middling salesmen from a larger sample of 502 and analysed their *application forms*. Age, marital status, education, (current) occupation, previous experience (of selling insurance), belonging to clubs, whether candidate was applying for full- or part-time selling, whether the candidate himself had life insurance, and whether (not what) candidates replied to the question 'What amount of insurance are you confident of placing each month?', all collectively distinguished good from average and average from bad. He scored the various variables. (See top of the following page).

Goldsmith turned the conventional application form into what was called a *Weighted Application Blank* (WAB). The WAB works on the principle that the best predictor of future behaviour is the past behaviour, and the easiest way of measuring past behaviour is what the applicant writes on his/her application form. The principle is familiar to anyone with motor insurance, and is the basis of the *actuarial profession*. Goldsmith concluded:

Age		*Marital Status*		*Service*	
18–20	−2	Married	+1	Full time	+2
21–22	−1	Single	−1	Full time	−2
23–24	0				
25–27	+1	*Occupation*		*Insurance*	
28–29	+2	Social	+1	Carried	+1
30–40	+3	Unsocial	−1	Not carried	−1
41–50	+1				
51–60	0				
Over 60	−1				

Education		*Experience*	
8 years	+1	Previous life insurance experience	+1
10 years	+2		
12 years	+3	*Confidence*	
16 years	+2	Replies to question: 'What amount of insurance	
		are you confident of placing each	
		month?'	+1
		Does not reply	−1

> The study of these 502 blanks has, therefore, indicated that for a life insurance company, the score on the personal history blank bears a positive relationship to the applicant's future success, and that on this blank a lower critical score may be set, below which it would not be worth while to licence an applicant (p.155).

By the end of the 1930s, the WAB technique was well developed; ready-made tables had been drawn up from WAB construction. Furthermore, various studies continued to be done in this area.

Mosel (1952) found 12 personal data items that distinguished between high and low department store sales selling figures. These factors included age, education, height, weight, marital status and dwelling. The American Green Giant Co. found in the 1950s that its seasonal pea and corn canners often inexplicably left within a few days of starting work, causing the company great inconvenience and expense. Dunnette and Maetzold (1955) devised a WAB to reduce turnover:

> The typically stable Green Giant production worker lives locally, has a telephone, is married and has no children, is not a veteran (not an ex-serviceman), is either young (under 25) or old (over 55), weighs more than 150 pounds but less than 175, has obtained more than ten years education, has worked for Green Giant, will be available for work until the end of summer, and prefers field work to inside work.

The WAB was only used for male applicants; female employees didn't present a turnover problem. It proved successful for many years, so validating the use of WABs in selection.

This profile retained its predictive validity over three successive years, and for three other Green Giant canning factories, but it didn't work for non-seasonal cannery workers. Scott and Johnson (1967) found *permanent* workers' turnover predicted by regression equation:

Tenure = 0.30 (age) + 8.82 (sex) − 0.69 (miles from plant) + 5.29 (type of residence) + 2.66 (children) + 1.08 (years on last job) − 1.99

where female = 1, male = 0, live with parents, or in a room (bedsit) = 0, and live in own home = 1. Permanent cannery workers who stay the course had family and domestic responsibilities (and tend to be women), whereas the profile for seasonal workers identifies young college students or semi-retired people, both wanting a short-term job. Buel (1964) showed that the WAB had both concurrent and predictive validity with regard to voluntary female clerical turnover. Similarly, Scott and Johnson (1967) found that the WAB was useful for selecting unskilled employees. They found that females who lived close to the plant and those with family responsibility (married, older, several dependents) were more likely to become long-term employees.

Table 7.4 Significance of the differences between mean personal-history factor scores for the upper-rated and lower-rated salesmen on the paired-comparison performance indices

Personal-history factor	Upper-rated salesmen (N = 72)		Lower-rated salesmen (N = 52)		t
	M	SD	M	SD	
School achievement	1.96	1.52	2.19	1.65	0.82
Higher educational achievement	4.59	1.68	4.69	1.91	0.30
Drive	4.13	2.04	4.15	1.90	0.00
Leadership and group participation	2.90	1.66	2.44	1.78	1.48
Financial responsibility	5.54	1.43	4.11	1.79	4.92***
Early family responsibility	8.63	1.98	7.31	2.63	3.17**
Parental family adjustment	6.47	2.25	6.79	2.06	0.80
Stability	6.01	1.68	5.08	2.56	2.46*
School activities	3.32	1.88	3.08	1.76	0.73
Professional successful parents	3.79	1.46	3.60	1.55	0.73
Educational–vocational consistency	1.42	0.95	1.25	0.99	0.95
Vocational decisiveness	2.22	1.35	2.14	1.12	0.39
Vocational satisfaction	5.69	1.81	5.67	1.72	0.00
Selling experience	6.25	1.39	5.92	1.44	1.27
General health	3.42	1.15	3.27	1.11	0.71

* $p < 0.05$
** $p < 0.01$
***$p < 0.001$
Source: Baehr and Williams (1968)

Walther (1961) set about trying to see if he could find predictors of success and failure at foreign service clerical jobs. Employees filled out a 68-item

Table 7.5 Multiple-regression analysis

Accepted personal-history factor	Partial r	Simple r	Beta-weight
Criterion: paired-comparison performance rating (multiple $R = 0.42$)			
5. Financial responsibility	0.33	0.33	0.34
4. Leadership and group participation	0.14	0.14	0.14
13. Vocational satisfaction	0.14	0.06	0.14
7. Parental family adjustment	−0.12	−0.08	−0.11
6. Early family responsibility	0.12	0.18	0.11
1. School achievement	−0.10	−0.05	−0.10
Criterion: mean sales volume rank (multiple $R = 0.50$)			
5. Financial responsibility	0.31	0.43	0.33
8. Stability	0.21	0.39	0.22
15. General health	−0.12	−0.05	−0.10
2. Higher educational achievement	0.12	0.12	0.10
1. School achievement	−0.10	−0.08	−0.09
Criterion: maximum sales volume rank (multiple $R = 0.36$)			
5. Financial responsibility	0.20	0.31	0.22
8. Stability	0.12	0.27	0.13
7. Parental family adjustment	−0.11	−0.11	−0.10
6. Early family responsibility	0.10	0.17	0.10
Criterion: route difficulty (multiple $R = 0.27$)			
3. Drive	0.19	0.16	0.19
11. Educational-vocational consistency	0.17	0.12	0.17
6. Early family responsibility	−0.12	−0.09	−0.11
15. General health	−0.11	−0.11	−0.11
Criterion: tenure as a salesman (multiple $R = 0.30$)			
13. Vocational satisfaction	−0.20	−0.18	−0.20
6. Early family responsibility	−0.19	−0.18	−0.18
12. Vocational decisiveness	0.16	0.12	0.16

Source: Baehr and Williams (1968)

biodata-type questionnaire and were later categorized as above and below average. The questionnaire items seemed to fall into various clusters, most of which showed significant differences. The results seemed to indicate that above-average employees preferred to work closely with supervisors, were sensitive to his/her wishes; disliked routine and liked variety; wanted to do things well and can work within set tolerance or standard; were sociable and enjoyed working with people; had a tendency to placate, avoid, divert or ignore aggressive behaviour; preferred activities involving the influencing of others through social relationships. Interestingly, the measure seemed as good at predicting success as failure. That is, differences on the various dimensions – please authority, social isolation, social leadership – seemed to discriminate closely between success and failure.

In a more robust and comprehensive study, Baehr and Williams (1968) examined 210 salesmen and 16 district managers on 15 personal background dimensions including parental success and adjustment, general health and financial responsibility. The criteria were multi-faceted and inter-correlated, and consisted of such things as performance ratings, sales rank etc. Upper- and lower-rated salesmen differed on three criteria (see Table 7.4). Each of the 15 criteria were regressed on to the five dependent variables (criteria). These are shown in Table 7.5. Financial responsibility (ability to invest and save) and early family responsibility (early marriages, family interests) seemed powerful predictors.

WAB construction is entirely mindlessly empirical in the eyes of its critics: The procedure is raw empiricism in the extreme, the 'score' is the most heterogeneous value imaginable, representing a highly complex and usually unravelled network of information. It doesn't matter why an item differentiates successful estate agents from unsuccessful – only that it does. WABs have been used successfully to test the following:

- Job turnover.
- Oil company executive success.
- Military promotability and much more.

The classic WAB is supposedly invisible and unfakeable. It's invisible because the applicant expects to complete an application 'blank', and it's unfakeable because most of the items *could* be verified independently, if the employer could afford the time and the expense (some can: it's called 'positive vetting'). The classical WAB has tended to be supplanted since the 1960s by 'biodata', or biographical inventories, or life history data. Biodata uses a questionnaire format with multiple-choice answers.

Biodata has been used successfully to predict success as sales/research engineers, oil industry research scientists, pharmaceutical industry researchers, bus drivers, 'custodial officers' and police officers. Biodata is used for: professional, clerical, sales, skilled labour and unskilled labour. It has been shown to work similarly successfully in different countries. Biodata has been used most frequently for selecting sales staff, least often for managerial occupations. But it has been used to predict many occupational behaviours with many different groups. Smith *et al.* (1961) found research competence and creativity could be predicted from biodata.

For instance, Cascio (1976) used biographical data from both minority and majority group members to predict job turnover. Nevo (1976) used biographical data to predict success for both men and women in the Israeli army. Using only 13 biographical variables and military values as the criteria, they found various significant correlates: father's educational and occupational level, mother's age, intensity of athletic activities, sound attitudes in high school. Keinan *et al.* (1981) exercised biodata to predict successfully motion sickness in seamen. They found that a combination of biographical data and optokinetic tests explained 40 per cent of the performance variance. More recently, biodata was shown to be effective in predicting accidents (Hansen, 1989).

Most modern researchers use a mixture of classic WAB and biodata. They're also generally much more reticent about item content, so it's often unclear how much of each they include. The success of the classic WAB depends on the general public never suspecting that application forms have any but the usual bureaucratic purpose. Essentially, biodata permits the respondent to describe himself in terms of demographic, experimental, or attitudinal variables presumed or demonstrated to be related to personality structure, personal adjustment or success in social, educational or occupational pursuits.

A distinction can be made between 'hard' items and 'soft' items. The former represent historical and verifiable information about an individual, whereas the latter are of a more abstract nature and cover value judgements, aspirations, motivations, attitudes and expectations. While soft biodata may be open to distortion and could lead individuals to 'fictionalize' their past lives, it may be useful to tap into success-related constructs not readily measured by hard items (such as 'assertiveness' in the first of the foregoing examples). Some studies use both hard and soft data. For instance, Metcalfe (1987) used only five biographical factors – sex, age, education, marital and family status – as well as 'soft' data.

The definition of biodata seems to imply that biodata is obtained from autobiographical accounts. However, it can be obtained from other than self-report forms. Employers' references, for example, can provide a good source of work history-related items, and educational biodata can often be obtained from school or university reports. There is no reason why biodata cannot be obtained from a suitably structured interview, so long as candidates' responses can be recorded without too much interpretation by the interviewer.

Various attempts have been made to develop standardized biographical questionnaires. For instance, Owens (1976), and Owens and Schoenfeldt (1979) developed a biographical questionnaire that appeared to have a stable factor structure (Eberhardt and Muchinsky, 1982). The 13 factors that emerged are interesting for their own sake:

1. *Warmth of parental relationship* (e.g. warm relationship with parents; affection, praise and attention given by parents).
2. *Academic achievement* (e.g. competitive in academic situations, parents satisfied with grades, high academic standing).

3. *Social extraversion* (e.g. directed group activities, held leadership positions, effective in social situations, dated more frequently).
4. *Athletic interest* (e.g. frequent participation in athletic events, excellent performance in athletic activities).
5. *Intellectualism* (e.g. regularly read literary, business, or scientific magazines; watched educational and cultural TV shows).
6. *Aggressiveness/independence* (e.g. enjoyed discussion courses, tried to get others to see their point of view, regarded as radical, said what they felt).
7. *Socio-economic status* (e.g. high parental educational level, above average family income, high parental occupational level).
8. *Parental control versus freedom* (e.g. parents more strict, critical and punitive; parents allowed less freedom and tended to nag or push for better achievement).
9. *Social desirability* (e.g. wished to become more socially acceptable, 'took things out' on friends and parents, suffered 'attacks of conscience').
10. *Scientific interest* (e.g. enjoyed science and lab courses and found them quite easy, worked with scientific apparatus outside class).
11. *Positive academic attitude* (e.g. liked school and teachers, enjoyed courses more while doing more homework, teachers aroused interests).
12. *Religious activity* (e.g. active in church, religious or charitable organizations; went to church more often, had stronger religious beliefs, attended summer camp).
13. *Sibling friction* (e.g. felt more friction and competition toward siblings, argued or fought with siblings, more younger brothers and sisters).

Modified versions of this scale have been used successfully to predict success in real estate agencies (Mitchell and Klimoski, 1982). More unusual perhaps, Neiner and Owens (1982) showed two biographical questionnaires correlated highly and positively seven years apart. More recently, Lautenschlager and Shaffer (1987) showed that Owen's questionnaire revealed components that were stable over time (for men and women) and across geographic locations.

What is the difference between biodata and personality tests? There are essentially three differences:

1. Biodata questions allow a definite answer, whereas personality questions often don't. Most biodata questions could be answered by someone who knows the respondent well.
2. Personality inventory questions are carefully phrased, to elicit a rapid, unthinking reply, whereas biodata items often sound quite clumsy in their desire to specify precisely the information they want. For example, with regard to personal appearance, as compared with the appearance of my friends, I think that:

   (a) Most of my friends have a better appearance.

(b) I am equal to most of them in appearance.

(c) I am better than most of them in appearance.

(d) I don't feel strongly one way or the other.

In a personality inventory this would read more like: 'I am fairly happy about the way I look – TRUE or FALSE'.

3. Personality inventories have fixed keys, whereas biodata items are rekeyed for each selection task. Personality questions lose their validity faster than biographical questions.

Reilly and Chao (1982) reviewed various alternatives to ability tests for predicting a variety of criteria and found that the mean validities for biodata ranged from 0.32 against job tenure to 0.46 against productivity. All validities listed are from cross-validation studies since, as will be discussed, development sample validities will tend to capitalize on chance. Validities for clerical or sales occupations were also higher than those for military or non-specific, non-managerial occupations. Their overall conclusion was that '. . . of the alternative reviewed, only biodata and peer evaluation have evidence of validity equal of that of tests' (p.289).

Schmidt, Mack and Hunter (1984) review research published between 1964 and 1982. The weighted average of 99 validity coefficients was $r = 0.24$, definitely poorer than assessment centres, work samples and peer ratings, but definitely better than personality inventories. Biodata was used to predict the following:

Performance ratings	$r = 0.32$
Turnover	$r = 0.21$
Achievement/grades	$r = 0.23$
Status change	$r = 0.33$
Wages	$r = 0.53$
Productivity	$r = 0.20$

The high correlation with wages, based on seven samples and 1544 subjects, is unexplained.

Hunter and Hunter (1984) review biodata research, using validity generalization analysis to arrive at a single estimate of biodata validity, based on pooled samples of 4000–10,000, for four criteria:

Supervisor ratings	$r = 0.37$
Promotion	$r = 0.26$
Training success	$r = 0.30$
Tenure	$r = 0.26$

Generalizable validity implies certain biographical pointers have fairly general predictive validity. Early WAB research occasionally gave some very contradictory results. Owning one's own home is generally a 'good sign', but *it* wasn't for shop saleswomen, where the most efficient lived in boarding houses. Are there any biographical pointers that have fairly general predictive validity?

- *Experience* has very moderate predictive validity for supervisor ratings, but zero validity for training grades (Hunter and Hunter, 1984). Arvey *et al.* (1989) review a dozen studies and conclude that there's little evidence that experience predicts productivity. General experience, in supervising people, or selling, has no predictive validity. Research on air traffic controllers finds experience was only used when it's directly and specifically relevant; having used a radio or flown an aircraft doesn't predict efficiency as an air traffic controller, but experience of instrument flying does.
- *Seniority*. How long the person has been working in an organization is often used to decide who gets promoted: 'Buggins's Turn'. Unions, in Britain and America, often insist it should be the sole criterion. Seniority almost always plays a big part in deciding who is 'released' when the work force has to be reduced: 'last in, first out'. There's no reason to expect seniority to be related to efficiency, and not much research on the link; Gordon and Fitzgibbons (1982) found seniority quite unrelated to efficiency in female sewing-machine operators. Many would argue that the relationship between seniority and work productivity is in fact curvilinear (inverse U).
- *Age*. Hunter and Hunter (1984) reviewed over 500 validity coefficients and found age alone has zero validity as a predictor, whether the criterion is supervisor rating or training grade. Age does predict turnover: younger employees are more likely to leave. Age can distort WAB/biodata scoring: older men tend to have dependants, higher living expenses and belong to more organizations than younger men, so a WAB using age-related items for subjects with diverse ages could give misleading results.

More recently, Childs and Klimoski (1986) showed similar biodata criteria could be used to predict career success over a wide range of occupations. Over 500 people were traced over two years and measured on three areas of success. A 72-item biographical questionnaire was factored into five factors (see Table 7.6). These factors were regressed on to the success criteria and were found to account for almost 25 per cent of the variance. Social orientation and interpersonal confidence seemed very important and predictive factors. They note:

> The present data indicate that some of the predictors (causes?) of success vary more with the specific criterion component of interest than others. For example, looking at the significance of the regression weights for the factors, the two 'social' factors, social orientation

and interpersonal confidence, account for significant unique variance in all three criteria. These factors might be viewed as 'overall success' antecedents; that is, an outgoing and self-confident personality pre-ordains success in both job and non-job related situations. The educational achievement factor, however, is a significant unique predictor of job and career, but not personal success. Success in one's educational history, it seems, may especially aid the attainment of success in one's job and career, regardless of whether that job is personally satisfying. Work ethic orientation is a significant predictor of career success but, surprisingly, not of job success. Perhaps this factor is more related to the attainment of career stability, progression, or goal orientation, while being less uniquely important to success in one specific job. It therefore may contribute more to a history of job success, that is, career success. Finally, the economic stability factor is only significantly uniquely associated with career success. This is understandable in that financial independence occurs usually after a sequence of repeated job successes, but not necessarily in one job (especially at the early stages of one's career). Or, looked at in another way, early financial independence may help one survive the earlier, more unstable years of one's career, contributing to the attainment of career success (p.7).

Table 7.6 Biodata factors uncovered in the study

Factor	Description
Social orientation	Receives many social phone calls, enjoys meeting new people, 'cheers up' others, frequently went to parties as a teenager, enjoys social gatherings and talking to people he/she does not know, good conversational skills, enjoys introducing people to others, often has social gathering with others.
Economic stability	Owns home, most likely married, high net worth, tends to be older, spouse has high monthly income, high earnings, has several credit cards.
Work ethic orientation	Worked while in school, worked many hours, male, earned commissions on sales, expects high earnings five years from now, successful in sales work, worked long days regularly.
Educational achievement	History of educational success, extracurricular participation, felt school was successful and stimulating, completed college courses in several areas with a high grade-point average.
Interpersonal confidence	Comfortable introducing self to others, rarely depressed, enjoys meeting new people, self-confident, enjoys talking to others.

Source: Childs and Klimoski (1986)

Rothstein *et al.* (1990) looked at the cross validation of biodata using 11,000 first-line supervisors in 790 organizations. The results showed that, contrary to popular belief, biodata validities are intrinsically specific to particular organizations:

> In summary, this research has shown that the validity of a well-developed autobiographical questionnaire instrument generalizes across a major job family: first-line supervision. All biodata items were based on a review of information about the job. Each item was based on a rationale or hypothesis as to its applicability to the candidate population; no item was keyed unless the relationship could be explained in psychological terms and the item showed validity across different organizations. All developmental samples were large, and the stability of all relationships was determined through later replications in multiple organizations. The findings of this study indicate that the validity of this instrument is temporally stable as well as generalizable. The findings also provide evidence against the hypothesis that the validity of biodata stems from measurement of knowledge and skills acquired on the job. Finally, the results of this study constitute additional evidence against the general hypothesis of situational specificity of validities; the findings disconfirm that hypothesis in an important noncognitive domain. This is significant because it has been hypothesized that situational specificity can be expected to be greater in noncognitive than in cognitive domains (p.183).

Other attempts to use biodata in selection have been Russell (1990), and Szymanski and Churchill (1990).

Recent biodata studies have also proven successful. McDaniel (1989) noted that various organizations required (USA) government-issued security clearance, but that the application of background investigation information in personnel screening differs in various ways from biodata:

- Biodata screens applicants from a diverse set of occupations, while screening is used for people in a position of trust.
- Biodata is usually restricted to pencil-and-paper methodology, while screening uses interviews, references and other methods.
- Biodata is usually concerned with identifying occupational capability, while screening is concerned mainly with behavioural reliability, integrity and personal adjustment.

McDaniel (1989) sought to identify constructs measured in background screening investigations; to examine the inter-correlations among measures of the constructs; and to determine the value of the measures in predicting behavioural reliability in the workplace. Over 700 military applicants were screened and the data was found to form seven robust dimensions: school supervision, drug use, quitting school, employment experience, grades and school club participation, arrests and socio-economic status. Most importantly, five out of seven of these dimensions showed criterion-related (unsuitability discharge) validity. This suggests a focus on the negative (as well as the positive) end of the background continuum will add to the predictive validity of tests.

Russell *et al.* (1990) asked over 900 naval academy recruits to write retrospective life-history essays concentrating on individual accomplishments, group accomplishments, disappointing situations and stressful situations. From these, a five-factor score was obtained which measured five biographical features: life problems and difficulties, aspects of task performance, work ethic/self discipline, assistance from others, and extraordinary goals or effort. These factors, particularly work ethic/self-discipline, were clearly related to the five robust-like, academic-quality point ratio, military performance rating etc. The authors are at pains to stress the relative ease and cost effectiveness of gathering (and coding) the biodata from simple autobiographical essays.

More recently, Smernou and Lautenschlager (1991) gave nearly 2000 students a 389 autobiographical data form and the Maudsley Personality Inventory, which measures neuroticism and extraversion. They then did a cluster analysis on the autobiographical inventory and related the clusters to two personality variables. The clusters associated with neuroticism contained information about perceived parental expectations and evaluations, mode of disciplinary control, parental functions, adjustment modes, psychological needs and social maturity. Physical health, academic performance and attitudes, work and leisure time interests were also identified. With regard to extraversion, various clusters resulted, dealing with parental training, standards and socialization practices, intimate behaviours, socio-economic indicators and relations with important others. Behavioural antecedents of extraversion were found to be reliance on people, extensive participation in diverse activities, leadership tendencies, self-reliance, inquisitiveness and interests in many subjects. Feelings of self-satisfaction and good health were present in the lives of many extraverts.

The fact that biological clusters/factors are related to personality dimensions should cause no surprise. The question remains, apart from psychometric questions of reliability, which is the most efficient, effective, sensitive and non-feedback means of gathering data about people to be used to predict occupational success and failure.

7.5 SCIENTIFIC PRODUCTIVITY, EDUCATIONAL ACHIEVEMENT AND OCCUPATIONAL SUCCESS

Various studies have attempted the personality profile of eminent scientific researchers. Using the 16PF (see Chapter 2), Cattell and Drevdahl (1955) found that outstanding professional, academic scientists as a whole differ from the following:

- The general population, at beyond the 1 per cent level, in the personality factors called (B), ego strength or stability (C), dominance (E), desurgency (F−), lack of group super-ego standards (G_0), adventurousness (H), sensitive emotionality (24I), lack of paranoid trends (L−), lack of free-floating anxiety (O−), and compulsive super-ego (or will control) (Q_3). Except for administrators, they are at the same significantly higher level in radicalism (Q_1) and self-sufficiency (Q_2). Administrators alone differed the 1 per cent level showing lower somatic anxiety (Q_4−).
- The university undergraduate population, approximately age corrected, by being decidedly more schizothyme (A−) and self-sufficient (Q_2), more intelligent (B), desurgency (F−), withdrawn schizothyme (H−), radical (Q_1) and, probably, more paranoid (L) and of higher somatic anxiety (Q_4).
- Researchers, relative to teachers or administrators, were more schizothyme (A−), self-sufficient (Q_2), emotionally unstable (C−), bohemian, unconcerned (M) and radical (Q_1). They are also significantly, but less uniformly, male dominant (E), paranoid (L), withdrawn schizothyme (H−) and lower on compulsive super-ego (will control) (Q_3). In the latter, and in radicalism, they differ more from administrators than from teachers. There were some interesting differences indicated among the sciences, researchers in biology being, among biologists, less dominant and more desurgent.

Recently, Rushton and colleagues in Canada have done studies on personality correlates of university teachers' productivity. For instance, Rushton, Murray and Paunonen (1983) in two comprehensive studies found different variables discriminated the creative researcher and the effective teacher. The creative researcher was ambitious, enduring, seeking definiteness, dominant, a leader, aggressive, independent, non-meek and non-supportive; while the effective teacher is best described as liberal, sociable, a leader, extraverted, non-anxious, objective, supporting, non-authoritarian, non-defensive, intelligent and aesthetically sensitive. Erdle, Murray and Rushton (1985), however, showed that 50 per cent of the relationship between personality and teaching effectiveness was mediated by classroom behaviour. They argued that teacher personality traits lead to specific classroom behaviours which in turn determine student evaluation. Later, Rushton, Murray and Erdle (1987) found extraversion correlated $r = 0.51$ with teaching effectiveness and $r = 0.33$ (on average) with single teaching behaviours.

In three studies, Katz (1984) found a particular personality profile associated with eminent scientists. These research studies yielded consistent findings, namely that the thinking/research style of scientists tended to fall into four quite different types:

- *Group I.* This group are reflective, serious, intellectually driven, ambitious, adaptable, and have a tendency to be conceited, cynical and arrogant.

- *Group II*. This group is flexible, spontaneous, unconventional and impelled toward change.
- *Group III*. This group is placid, obliging, tactful, routinized, conventional, thorough and steady, and of *relatively* lower intelligence.
- *Group IV*. This group is rebellious, cynical, careless, arrogant, moody, dissatisfied, aloof, withdrawn, self-critical, complaining, apprehensive, pessimistic, non-trusting and restless.

The results showed that the first type was characterized by fluidity in responding to figural, divergent thinking tasks but difficult in finding a single correct answer; the second type by high verbal originality and figural elaboration; the third type by an ability to isolate meaning from a distracting background and a preference for complexity; while the fourth pattern was characterized by an aesthetic preference for research problems which lend themselves to elegant and formal solutions.

Gratton (1987) argued that research scientists differ from research managers on a number of quite specific characteristics. Research scientists tend to have the following characteristics:

- Be innovative, preferring to do things differently.
- Be unstructured, tolerating ambiguous situations and low need for clarity.
- Be self-reliant and independent (have internal locus of control).
- Have high self-esteem and confidence in themselves and their work.
- Be less sociable and interested in dealing with people.

On the other hand, research managers tend to be characterized by the following:

- Interested in people and the social aspects of their work.
- Interested in action rather than thought, and concrete vs abstract problems.
- Interested in enterprising and commercial work.
- Strongly achievement oriented.

Studies such as these indicate clear behavioural correlates of various specialist occupations. However, like biodata studies, they tend not to be theoretically driven, nor do they provide data generalizable across jobs.

7.6 SEX AT WORK

With the rise of feminism and the dramatic increase of women at work in the industrialized West, there has come more and more research on gender and sexuality issues in the working place. Some of this work has been of a socio-political nature (Hearn and Parkin, 1987), but much more work has gone into applying classic psychological theories to both investigating and explaining sex differences. For instance, various studies have looked at sex differences in expectation and attributions which may account for differences in achievement (Erkut, 1983; Fiorentine, 1988). Most studies have found that males have higher expectations for success than females, but this is probably job and task specific. Hence, studies have shown that on female-related tasks, females may have equal or higher expectancies than males.

Linked to the idea that job success may be a function of lower expectancies is a considerable literature on achievement motivation differences between men and women. As a result, some have attempted unsuccessfully to raise achievement motivation in young women (Erwee, 1986). However, as Farmer (1985) has noted, inevitable background demographic factors (age, race, schooling), environmental factors (such as parental and teacher support) as well as various other personal factors (self-esteem, competitive co-operativeness) all combine to affect the various dimensions of achievement motivation in different ways.

There is sizeable, but scattered, literature on sex differences. Consider the following three examples:

- *Sex differences in occupational interests*. This refers to the extensive literature on sex stereotyping when it comes to occupational choice. There is an extensive literature on this topic (Block, 1980).
- *Sex differences in preferred rewards*. Studies in this area have tended to concentrate on preferred rewards. For instance, early studies suggested that men preferred security, advancement and benefits most highly while women seemed to prefer type of work, co-workers and supervision. Recent research shows, however, that these differences are less apparent (Wheeler, 1981).
- *Sex differences in occupational values*. Is it true that females are attracted to different jobs on the basis of their values? Certainly, recent research, especially among young people, would suggest that this is true (Bridges, 1989).

Despite the fact that the topic has been researched for over 50 years, the results are equivocal (Herzberg *et al.*, 1957; Quinn, Staines and McCullough, 1974). For instance, Benge (1944), Stockford and Kunze (1950), and Chase (1951) all found evidence for women being more satisfied than men in the same job, while Cole (1940), Hulin and Smith (1964), and Shapiro and Stern (1975) found the reverse. More recently, Brief and colleagues (Brief and Aldag, 1976; Brief and Oliver, 1976; Brief, Rose and Aldag, 1977) have found no evidence of any sex differences, but rather a remarkable similarity in the response patterns of both sexes. Most of the earlier research hypothesized that women should, on average, be less satisfied than men, since they were usually in lower socio-economic group occupations with less variety, lower rates of pay, few promotional opportunities etc. Others have suggested that certain job-related factors (i.e. intrinsic vs extrinsic) are rated differently by males and females. For instance, Herzberg *et al.* (1957) reported that males find intrinsic factors (job variety, challenge, responsibility, participation) more important than females, although as Saleh and Lalljee (1969) pointed out and demonstrated, once age, education and organizational level were controlled, these differences would disappear. However, others (Marhardt, 1972; Bartol, 1976) found that males evaluate long-term career prospects as more important than females, who in turn evaluate a pleasant work environment and fellow employees as more important than males. Schuler (1975) confirmed his hypotheses, set out thus:

'Females will evaluate the following job outcomes as being more important than males, pleasant employees and working conditions, when age,
education, and organizational level are controlled . . .

Males will evaluate the following job outcomes as being more important
than females, competitive, aggressive and dominant outcomes such as
promotion, supervising others, working on important problems and
influencing and directing the work of others, and the opportunity to
earn money income' (p.367).

It was argued that these sex differences were the result of occupational role stereotyping. More recently, Sauser and York (1978) found females were more satisfied than males with pay, which they believe was a consequence of different expectations. But they note:

'If the tendency for females to be more satisfied than males with respect
to pay is indeed a function of sex differences in pay expectations, then
as the Women's Liberation Movement continues to gain momentum and
women's expectations towards pay increase, the sex–pay satisfaction
relationship found in this study should be diminished' (p.545).

Indeed, more recent studies have looked at sex differences in such things as knowledge of, and skill demands in, traditional male and female occupations (England, Chassic and McCormack, 1982; Yanico and Mihlbauer, 1983). Similarly, others have looked at sex differences in the perception of rewards desired and available in an occupation. Recent work by Wheeler (1981) has shown very few sex differences in these perceptions when the choice of occupation is held constant.

There may be a number of reasons for the equivocal findings in this area which are mainly methodological and historical. The methodological problems are manifold and relate firstly to the measures of job satisfaction. Most measures (self-reports, interview) have been designed for, and validated on, male workers in traditionally male jobs and may be inappropriate for females (Hulin and Smith, 1964). Studies are also difficult to compare because they have used different measures of job satisfaction that may be tapping different factors. Nearly every theory of job satisfaction and motivation makes a distinction between different aspects or factors in the job which either lead to satisfaction or no satisfaction, yet many of the measures provide one or a very limited range of factors. What is clearly needed is a robust, multi-factorial measure of job satisfaction, appropriate to both men and women.

Two other methodological problems are important – range of occupations studied and confounding factors. As Brief *et al.* (1977) have noted, many studies have used restricted samples that have been drawn from specific organizations with a very limited array of occupations represented. Thus, it may be that men may be happier in one type of job and women in another depending on what specific sources of satisfaction the job offered. As Furnham and Schaeffer (1984) have noted, people tend to seek out jobs that allow them to exercise their skills and abilities, express their personality and fulfil their needs. However, perhaps the most crucial criticism is the notion that any observed differences in job satisfaction are not due to the influence of sex *per se*, but rather to the effects of several variables which co-vary with sex. Thus, as Sauser and York (1978) demonstrated, significant, observed sex differences in job satisfaction 'washed out' when the effects of age, education, tenure in the organization and present position were held constant through analysis of co-variance. Also, for instance, Forgionne and Peeters (1982) found on-the-job training, education, number of dependants etc. all mediated between sex and job satisfaction.

A second major problem in trying to evaluate work in this area concerns the fact that these studies have been done at different times over a 50-year period in which there have been enormous social and occupational changes, especially in sex–role stereotyping. Not only do more women work than ever before, but more have assumed higher managerial jobs. Social attitudes and expectations regarding women (and presumably men) at work have been changing, albeit slowly (England *et al.*, 1982). Similarly, fixed, rigid, sex–roles have also been changing and there has been a great deal of interest in masculinity, femininity and androgyny (Bem, 1974). Research by Spence and Helmreich (1978) found (for a student sample) that whereas about one-third of males are masculine sex typed, and a third of women feminine sex typed, a quarter to a third of both sexes are androgynous and the remainder undifferentiated. Furthermore, innumerable studies in this area have shown that sex–role stereotyping relates to a whole range of social behaviours. It may be possible that the sex–role, rather than biological sex differences, relate to job satisfaction, either directly or in interaction. Thus, equivocal findings may be explained by the fact that it is sex–role and not sex differences that relate to job satisfaction, and that in some samples there were many masculine males and feminine females, whereas in other studies feminine males and masculine females or androgynous people predominated.

Furnham and Goddard (1986) in two studies noted that, in the present study, females were found to be significantly more satisfied than males with their working conditions. This is consistent with results obtained by Bartol (1976), who examined the importance of certain aspects for males and females. The preliminary analysis of the results showed that the males tended to occupy higher-level jobs than females. It also emerged that, although not significantly different, the group of subjects (male and female) occupying the highest level jobs were curiously the least satisfied with their working conditions. Given these two pieces of information, it follows that males – occupying better jobs – should be the least satisfied with their working conditions. Presumably, if the males and females in this sample were matched for job level, then even the difference in satisfaction with working conditions would disappear.

7.7 CONCLUSION

This chapter first considered ability correlates of job success. Despite the seemingly self-evident truth that the more able one is, both in a general and a specific sense, the more productive one is at work, the literature remains far from clear. Certainly, there does seem some well replicated evidence that overall ability (i.e. general intelligence) is positively and significantly correlated with job performance criteria, but these correlations range from about $r = 0.15$ to $r = 0.30$. Thus, only about 10 per cent of the variance appears to be accounted for by ability, although this may increase as the reliability and direct specificity of both the instrument and the criterion increases. Nevertheless, it seems that a half to three-quarters of work performance may be accounted for by factors other than ability.

A second, rapidly growing area of research and interest is that of biodata. Here the hypothesis is that the biographical life-history experiences of individuals teach, or at least shape, individuals and that these experiences are related to work performance. Studies using application form information, as well as autobiographical questions, do indeed suggest their predictive usefulness. But the method is both a-theoretical and job specific such that no attempt is made to find factors that generalize over many jobs or work-related performance criteria. Studies examining personality correlates of very specific jobs, like research scientist, have proved moderately useful.

Finally, there is increasing evidence of significant sex differences at work. Although the studies remain equivocal, and the literature highly scattered and of uneven quality, there seems sufficient evidence to suggest that there may be important sex differences in how people perceive their work and, hence, behaviour in the workplace. Gender, then, may be increasingly important, along with personality, in understanding behaviour at work.

Chapter 8

Personality and work-related problems
Absenteeism, accidents, illness and stress

So much of what we call management consists in making it difficult for people to work.

Peter Drucker

Unless a man has been taught what to do with success after getting it, the achievement of it must veritably leave him prey to boredom.

Bertrand Russell

Three characteristics of top executives are: slow speech, impressive appearance, and a complete lack of humour.

J.O. Connor

A well-adjusted executive is one whose intake of pep pills over-balances his consumption of tranquillizers just enough to leave him sufficient energy for the weekly visit to the psychiatrist.

A.R. Motley

We always think every other man's job is easier than our own. And the better he does it, the easier it looks.

E. Phillpots

8.1 INTRODUCTION

Are some personalities more likely to go absent than others? Is there an accident-prone personality? Are some personalities drawn to groups that advocate and carry out Luddite behaviour? Can it be shown that strikers have different personalities from those who don't go on strike? Nearly everyone experiences stress at work but are some personalities more prone than others?

This chapter is concerned with the 'down-side' of organizational behaviour, namely work-related problems. Chapters 3, 4 and 5 have demonstrated that there is a modest but important relationship between personality and occupational performance regarding motivation, choice, productivity and satisfaction. The major question of this chapter concerns whether there is an equally important relationship between personality and absenteeism, accidents and illness. Although other causes, like employee turnover, have been examined (Farkas and Tetrick, 1989), these rarely take personality characteristics into account.

8.2 ABSENTEEISM

Absence refers to the non-attendance of employees for scheduled work when they are expected to attend. The different ways in which absence is calculated has made inter-company comparison difficult and international comparison impossible. The issue is also something of a taboo in organizations for different, but related, reasons. First, it may be that organizations are just too embarrassed to address this issue internally – let alone discuss it publicly in management journals. Thus, for a company to admit that it has an absence problem is perhaps to admit to being perceived as being a bad employer. Second, managers may treat absenteeism as an act of God that has to be endured, rather than as an organizational problem that is capable of being solved. Even if they believe that something can be done about it, there is surprisingly little up-to-date information on absence causes and controls available in a form that can be directly used by management.

As well as definitional issues, there is a serious issue of people's *ability* to attend. Family responsibilities, transportation problems, illness and accidents all have a role to play. But what is perhaps noticeable about the plethora of studies in this area is the neglect of individual differences. Although there are fairly complicated and sophisticated models of absenteeism, few consider individual differences or subjectively perceived reasons for lack of attendance (Hendrix and Spencer, 1989). Studies appear to have focused on issues such as organizational commitment rather than personality factors (Farrell and Petersen, 1984) or demographic characteristics like age and length of service (Nicholson, Brown and Chadwick-Jones, 1977).

Measuring and Defining Absence

One of the persisting difficulties in assessing the influences on employee absenteeism has been one of clarity of definition. There are a myriad of definitions for absenteeism (Landy and Farr, 1983):

- Scheduled versus unscheduled absence.
- Authorized versus unauthorized absence.

- Certified versus uncertified absence.
- Avoidable versus unavoidable absence.
- Justified versus unjustified absence.
- Contractual versus non-contractual absence.
- Sickness versus non-sickness absence.
- Disability versus non-disability absence.
- Medical versus personal absence.
- Injury versus non-injury absence.
- Chronic illness versus acute illness absence.
- Long-term versus short-term absence.
- Repeater versus non-repeater absence.
- Voluntary versus involuntary absence.
- Intentional versus unintentional absence.
- Explained versus unexplained absence.
- Excused versus unexcused absence.
- Official versus unofficial absence.
- Compensable versus non-compensable absence.
- Insured versus non-insured absence.
- Occupational versus non-occupational absence.
- Legal versus illegal absence.
- Reasonable versus unreasonable absence.
- Illness versus self-induced illness absence.
- Certified illness versus casual illness absence.
- Monday/Friday absence versus midweek absence.
- Reported versus unreported absence.
- Employee-centred versus management-centred absence.

Gaudet (1963) reported the use of at least 41 different measures in research that he had reviewed (Chadwick-Jones *et al.*, 1977). Even if these definitions were conceptually comparable, they have shown widely differing empirical stability as measured by test–retest reliability coefficients. One of the main problems in deriving a satisfactory measure of absenteeism is that the correlations between different absenteeism measures can be quite low. Landy and Farr (1983) found the following sources of unreliability in absence data:

Individual
- General health and resistance to illness
- Work-induced fatigue
- Non-work-induced fatigue
- Current hobbies, leisure activities
- Shift

Environmental
- Ambient flu, virus etc
- Fluctuations in atmospheric conditions

Suborganizational
● Accuracy of supervisor in recording incident and reason
Administrative
● Accuracy of personnel office in transcribing supervisory attendance reports
● Administrative categories used for attribution of absence
● Level of aggregation of absence data (day, week, month, quarter, individual, work group, shift, plant, etc)
● Index of absence used (i.e. number of total days per unit time, number of periods, ratio of total days to periods)

Huse and Taylor (1962) found that only two such measures – absence frequency (the total number of times absent) and attitudinal absences (the frequency of one-day absences) – could be measured with sufficient reliability to warrant their use as criteria.

Nicholson *et al.* (1977) used three distinct measures of absence:

1. The time lost index (TLI), representing the total number of working days lost in a year.
2. The frequency index (FI), representing the total number of absence spells in a year, regardless of duration.
3. The attitudinal index (AI), representing the total number of one- or two-day duration absence spells in a year.

All three measures included all absences with the exception of holidays, rest days, strikes, lay-offs and days 'released' for training. These were seen as discrete variables, even though they were designed to measure the same single phenomenon of absence.

There are two basic features of absence behaviour – the frequency of the absence spells per person and the (average) duration of these spells. These can be calculated for short spells (e.g. one-day spells or spells up to a maximum of 14 days) and for longer spells (e.g. up to six weeks, six months or one year). Most other measures are in fact derivations of one of these two basic aspects (e.g. the frequency of spells of one day, two days, longer than two days etc), or are resultants or products of both (e.g. the time, cost index, the total number of absence days per employee in a certain period). In addition, frequency appears to be of less importance than duration in determining the total number of lost days, since the correlation between frequency and total days lost is between 0.30 and 0.40, whereas the correlation between average duration and total days lost is between 0.60 and 0.70.

Smulder (1980) found that the frequency of all absences (up to one year) per employee is roughly influenced by job tenure, the task, work group organization, delegation of responsibilities, leadership style, working conditions (noise, heat, heavy workload), shift work, sickness benefits and control measures, whereas average duration of all absences is influenced by age, physical working conditions, the degree of personal and medical guidance given by the personnel and medical departments of the organization, sickness benefits, and also the organization of the national health care structure (especially access time to medical specialists and hospitals). Thus, frequency and duration are only partly determined by the same variables.

A single continuous period of illness-absence may be called an episode, incident, occurrence or spell of illness. Illness-absence is recorded and reported in various ways. The length of duration of the individual spells of illness being recorded and used for reporting absence experience must be known. Commonly, these will be absences of one day or more, three days or less, seven days or less (less than one week), or eight days or more (longer than one week). Occasionally, absences of longer duration will be reported.

From illness-absence data, several basic or standard rates can be calculated. The frequency rate is the number of absences per employee in a given period of time. The disability rate is the number of days of absence per employee in the period. The severity rate is the number of days lost per absence. The amount of time lost from work, expressed as a percentage of the available work time, is called the ineffective rate. Another way of expressing absence is by reporting the proportion of the work force – the percentage of the employee group – absent at a given time, while the frequency with which employees are missing from their jobs, because it indicates the frequency of interruption of the work process, has a significance all of its own. The ineffective rate is probably the best single indicator of the total impact of work absence and is the one most widely used. Whenever absence is expressed as a percentage, one must be clear as to whether this is relative to absent people or to available work time lost.

Much attention has been devoted to the analysis of absenteeism as one member of a family of 'withdrawal behaviours', which also include lateness and turnover. Most researchers, operating under the employee-withdrawal model, have focused primarily on turnover, treating absenteeism with subsidiary interest (Burke and Wilcox 1972). Porter and Steers (1973) stated that staff turnover and absenteeism share common antecedents and hence can be treated with similar techniques. Absenteeism was seen as a category of behaviour and differs in three important respects from turnover:

1. The negative consequences associated with absenteeism for the employee are usually much less than those associated with turnover.
2. Absenteeism is more likely to be a spontaneous and relatively easy decision, while the act of resignation is typically more carefully considered over time.
3. Absenteeism often represents a substitute form of behaviour for turnover, particularly when alternative forms of employment are unavailable.

In addition, of the 22 studies cited by these reviewers that examined influences on both turnover and absenteeism, only six found significant relationships in the same direction between the factors under study and *both* turnover and absenteeism. In other words, sufficient reason exists to justify the study of employee absenteeism in its own right, instead of as an analogue of turnover.

Critics of absenteeism measures have observed that they are frequently loaded with error variance and are therefore contaminated because a person can be off the job for a variety of reasons. As soon as a company attempts to measure absences, reliability may be threatened because it is difficult for the record of absence to be certain of the true cause, and hence the correct classification (e.g. resignation versus malingering versus a true disability) of failure to attend. On the other hand, measuring absenteeism from the opposite side of the coin, in terms of the number of employees who come to work, is a relatively unambiguous event.

Hackett and Guion (1985) have further stressed the unsatisfactory understanding of the phenomenon provided by most theories of absence, and the inadequacy of traditional absence measures as indicators of the underlying nature and causes of the behaviour. These two problems have been exacerbated by the application of normal distributions that are based on statistics to absence and attendance distributions that are clearly skewed.

A recent alternative hypothesis about attendance has derived from a dynamic model. One assumption of the dynamic approach, which departs from the withdrawal theory, is that absence may occur not simply because of dissatisfaction with the work situation, but because non-work alternatives offer a more attractive way of spending time. Fichman (1989) did a study of absence and attendance in terms of a hypothesis derived from the dynamic model of attendance. Attendance data was treated as an event history: a series of spells of attendance and absence. The hypothesis proposed that the 'hazard rate' of absence increases with necessary duration of an attendance spell. To test this hypothesis, attendance records of 465 underground coal miners were assessed, generating 5509 attendance spells. A clerk was employed to record duty absenteeism, divided into three categories of absence reflecting degree of voluntariness:

1. Voluntary (V) absences. Absences categorized as discretionary or contract days, discretionary holidays, graduated vacation days and miscellaneous paid absences. All these absences were paid.
2. Semi-voluntary (VV) absences. Absences categorized as excused, unpaid and unexcused unpaid (AWOLS). All were unpaid.
3. Involuntary (IV) absences. Absences categorized as on-the-job injuries, illness, wildcat strikes and off-the-job injury. These absences were compensated in varying degrees. They were not voluntary.

Results strongly supported the hypothesis. The likelihood of going absent increased with increasing attendance duration. This research indicated that people switch from one activity to another with some regularity. This prediction held whether the switch was primarily an escape from work or an escape to a more attractive atmosphere. The results further revealed that absences are not random occurrences but are tied to duration of attendance. Furthermore, attendance cannot be conceived of as a habit, otherwise one might expect longer spells of attendance to be negatively rather than positively associated with absence.

Causes of Absenteeism

Any systematic approach to the problem of absenteeism has to acknowledge the myriad of discrete and interdependent factors which may underlie it. Reasons for non-attendance at work are often situation and organization specific, so much so that individual difference factors are 'washed out' by these more powerful factors.

Major reviews of existing research literature over the past 30 years have indicated that investigators of employee absenteeism have typically examined correlations between each of a set of variables and subsequent absenteeism (Muchinsky, 1977). Two basic assumptions permeate the work that has been done to date. First, much of the research literature has assumed that job dissatisfaction represents the primary cause of absenteeism, despite the fact that few findings point conclusively to this relationship actually playing a major part in the explanation of absence behaviour. Nicholson *et al.* (1977), in a review of 29 such studies, concluded that 'at best it seems that job satisfaction and absence from work are tenuously related' (p.734). Implicit in these modest findings is the probable existence of additional variables (both personal and organizational) that may serve to moderate or enhance the satisfaction–attendance (absence) relationship. In a later, more extensive literature review of 104 empirical studies, Steers and Rhodes (1978) included job satisfaction as one variable thought to influence motivation on the part of employees to go to work.

A second major problem in much of the work on absenteeism is the implicit assumption that employees are generally free to choose whether or not to go to work. Such, however, is often not the case. Important situational constraints have been found to influence whether or not employees, dissatisfied or not, will take time off work (Igen and Hodenbeck, 1977). Factors such as poor health, family responsibilities and transportation problems can all interfere with free choice in attendance at work. Absenteeism has also been observed to cluster around holiday periods.

There is a surprising paucity of conceptual frameworks for integrating the research findings of employee absenteeism. Yet, in understanding the reasons why it occurs, it is essential that the major sets of variables should be identified and fitted together in a systematic fashion. Steers and Rhodes

(1978) suggested that employee attendance at work is largely a function of two important variables: (a) an employee's motivation to attend and (b) an employee's ability to attend. The first, in turn, is perceived to be influenced by the employee's satisfaction with the work situation and various internal and external pressures; the second, by personal characteristics. It is worth therefore exploring the different sorts of personal and organizational variables that have been related to absenteeism.

There are, of course, both organizational and demographic correlates of absenteeism. Among the former are job scope (Hackman and Lawler, 1971); job level (Hrebiniak and Roteman, 1973); role stress (Miles and Perreault, 1976); work group size (Ingham, 1970); leadership style (Bragg and Andrews, 1973); co-worker relations (Garrison and Muchinsky, 1977); opportunity for advancement (Garrison and Muchinsky, 1977); and organization size (Ingham, 1970). Among the latter are employees, values and expectations (Cheloha and Farr, 1980); age (Porter and Steers, 1973); length of service (Lyons, 1972).

Pressures to Attend

There are other important factors which can be identified as affecting work attendance and these probably work in an additive fashion. Steers and Rhodes (1978) termed these variables as 'pressures to attend'. These pressures may be economic, social or personal in nature. Specifically, at least five major pressures can be identified: economic and market conditions (the state of the economy); the incentive/reward system (related to the actual posts), work group norms (specifically about absenteeism). Two individual difference variables are, however, salient. These are personal work ethic and organizational commitment (Furnham, 1990b).

A further influence on attendance motivation is the personal value system that individuals have. Research on the work ethic has shown considerable variation across employees in the extent to which they feel morally obligated to work. In particular, several investigations have noted a direct relationship between a strong work ethic and the propensity to come to work (Feldman, 1974).

Somewhat related to the notion of a personal work ethic is the concept of organizational commitment. Commitment represents an agreement on the part of the employees with the goals and objectives of an organization, and a willingness to work toward those goals. In short, if an employee firmly believes in what an organization is trying to achieve, he/she should be more motivated to attend and contribute toward those objectives. This motivation may exist even if the employee does not enjoy the actual tasks required by the job. Some evidence has emerged of a relationship between commitment and attendance (Steers, 1977).

Personality factors may be seen as either *independent* variables accounting for a small but important amount of the variable either as a main effect or in interaction, or as individual-level intervening (or moderating) variables.

Personality Factors and Absence

Although there is a surprising paucity of research in this field, a few studies have looked at individual difference factors. Bernardin (1977) looked at 16PF correlates of turnover and absenteeism in two samples to test a hypothesis that extreme scores on the traits of emotional instability, anxiety, achievement orientation, aggression, independence, self-confidence and sociability are related to absenteeism. Only two factors – G (conscientiousness) and Q_4 (anxiety) – were associated with absenteeism, but they were not at extremes. The author was able to conclude that personality variables account for a small but significant amount of variance in predicting absenteeism. Anxious individuals (those whose manifest trait is anxiety) and those not very conscientious (unsteady in purpose, casual, lacking in effort and social demands) were much more likely to go absent. In this sense, personality traits might be used to detect job hoppers.

Mowday and Spencer (1981) showed, perhaps as one could predict, achievement motivation linked to absenteeism. They demonstrated that low nAch people had higher absenteeism than high nAch people.

Keller (1983) found two personality factors – low self-esteem and external health locus of control – to be significant predictors of absenteeism along with various demographic factors like sex, marital status and job tenure. However, Arsenault and Dolan (1983) suggest that personality (i.e. locus of control and A-type behaviour) is not a 'main effect' variable in absenteeism research, but rather interacts with job content and context factors to predict absenteeism.

More recently, George (1989) considered the possible relationship between workers' moods and absenteeism. As predicted, she found that a positive mood at work significantly and negatively associated with absenteeism. Various variables were regressed on the absence figure but only two proved significant: positive mood and tenure. She also found the 'traits' of positive and negative affectivity had significant effects on the extent to which workers experience positive and negative moods. She notes:

> The results of this study also underscore the importance of considering personality influences at work. Such influences are receiving increasing attention in the literature. The results presented here suggest that personality may have particularly potent effects on mood at work. The current finding for absenteeism in consort with the extensive body of literature in social psychology suggest that moods and their dispositional antecedents may have profound effect on a wide variety of thought processes and behaviours at work (p.322).

Ferris, Bergin and Wayne (1988) found that sex and two 16PF-derived personality variables – independence and ability to control anxiety – correlated with absenteeism in teachers. Again, the personality variables (especially anxiety) interacted with job characteristics to determine absenteeism.

It seems, then, that the main effect of personality traits on absenteeism is relatively small, and less powerful than demographic variables. However, when in interaction with organizational factors, they can account for major proportions of the variance in predicting absenteeism behaviour.

8.3 ACCIDENTS

Accidents have many causes: personal and situational; foreseeable and random; major and minor. They are usually defined by their consequences or outcomes rather than by their antecedent behaviour. They occur in all settings (the road, the home, the workplace). Details of accidents that are required to understand the process include: class of work (task, equipment, shift); how the accident occurred (prevailing conditions, time, location); type of injury; and personal details of the victim (sex, age, length of service).

Hansen (1989) took a personality measure of general social maladjustment (socio-pathic attitudes) and distractibility (neurosis) as well as measures of cognitive ability, age and job experience in 362 chemical industry workers and showed how, in a causal path analysis, they independently predicted accidents. This confirmed previous earlier research which suggests that two personality types were most likely to have accidents (Shaw and Sichel, 1971): *socio-pathic extraverts* (self-centred, over-confident, aggressive, irresponsible, resentful, intolerant, impulsive, anti-social, antagonistic to authority) and *anxious-neurotics* (tension ridden, paunchy, unduly sensitive to criticism, indecisive, unable to concentrate, easily fatigued, depressed, emotionally labile, easily intimidated and with feelings of inadequacy).

Various models have been developed as frameworks for viewing the behavioural events that lead up to accidents. One such model, based in part on the one presented by Ramsey (1978), is shown in Figure 8.1. This shows hypothesized stages in the occurrence or avoidance of accidents. The first stages deal with the *perception* and *cognition* of the potential hazard. Failure to perceive and recognize the hazard typically leads to unsafe behaviour, although in some instances a person might happen to make a decision that leads to safe behaviour. At the *decision-making* stage, the individual can make a decision to try to avoid an accident, or, conversely, to take whatever risk is implied.

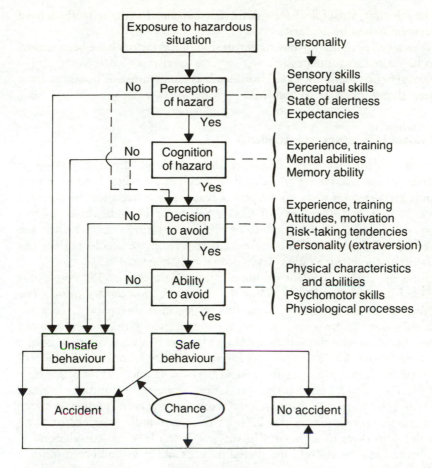

Figure 8.1 Sequential stage model in the development of an accident
Source: Ramsey (1976)

If the individual decides to take action to minimize the risk of an accident, the next stage depends on the person's *ability* to take action. The fulfilment of this sequence typically would result in the execution of some form of 'safe' behaviour. Failure to fulfil these stages typically would result in some form of 'unsafe' behaviour. Chance then plays a part. The term *chance* can be thought of as applying to events that we cannot predict. Such unpredictable circumstances (i.e. 'chance') certainly play their part in causing or avoiding accidents. Thus, even 'safe' behaviour might still not prevent an accident, and 'unsafe' behaviour might still avoid an accident. Situational factors that are important in accidents include the following:

- *The job itself.* Most jobs have risk factors associated with them which have been calibrated by actuaries.
- *Work schedule.* Time-of-day or chronobiological factors have been shown to be related to accident rate.
- *Atmospheric conditions.* Conditions such as temperature or humidity have been shown to relate to accidents.

Individual Differences and Accidents

It is self-evident that errors in perception, cognition, decision making or preferences for risk taking are related to accidents. Studies done over time in industrial settings seem to suggest a reasonable correlation of between $r = 0.30$ to $r = 0.60$ records of unsafe behaviour by individuals. In this sense, there appears to be evidence of *accident repetitiveness*, which is the systematic tendency for some individuals to have more accidents than can be attributed to chance (Whitlock, Clouse and Spencer, 1963).

Using the critical incident technique, the supervisors of 350 employees recorded the 'unsafe behaviours' of the employees for eight months. The number of unsafe behaviours served as an 'accident behaviour' score for each individual. These scores, in turn, were correlated with injuries recorded during the eight-month period, and for as long as five years after the study. The correlations, for 284 employees for whom injury records were available for periods of time, were for the first year $r = 0.35$ and for the fifth year $r = 0.56$. They also found that the correlation between the number of unsafe behaviours between the odd-numbered weeks and the even-numbered weeks for the eight-month period was 0.74. (The corresponding correlation for a sample of workers in a chemical plant was 0.93.) In turn, correlations of numbers of injuries for odd-numbered months and even-numbered months were also derived; these were computed separately for personnel for whom data was available for the different periods of time. The resulting correlations were 0.63 for one year of data, 0.58 for two years, 0.75 for three years, 0.66 for four years and 0.67 for five years. There is therefore substantial evidence, at least for certain work situations, that people tend to maintain their own rates of unsafe behaviour and accidents over time, regardless of whether the rates are high, average or low. This pattern is for individuals *within* individual work situations in which the accident liability is the same for all workers.

Various individual difference factors that may relate to accidents include the following.

1. *Perception of style.* One such variable that may be relevant is that of field dependency. In a laboratory experiment with subjects using a drive simulator, for example, Barrett and Thorton (1968) found that people who were field independent were able to decelerate more rapidly in an 'emergency' situation that those who were field dependent. In addition,

in an analysis of the accident records of vehicle drivers over a period of three years, Harano (1969) found that field-independent drivers had better accident records than field-dependent individuals.

From a review of relevant studies of perceptual style, Goodenough (1976) stated that evidence suggested that field-dependent drivers do not quickly recognize developing hazards, are slower in responding to embedded road signs, have difficulty in learning to control skidding vehicles, and fail to drive defensively in high-speed traffic. More data is necessary to nail down the relevance of perceptual style to vehicular driving, but the current cues suggest that this may be important in minimizing vehicular accidents.

2. *Perceptual motor styles*. Barbarik (1968) argued that drivers who make up for long 'initiation' time with fast movements (that is, have short movement times and thus stop their vehicles more abruptly after applying the brake) would be expected to have more rear-end accidents than drivers who – in the same time – initiate movements more rapidly but make less abrupt stopping movements. A ratio of these was found to be significantly related to rear-end accidents with a sample of 104 taxi drivers. Those with the most markedly different ratios were referred to as having 'desynchronizing' reaction patterns, whereas the others were referred to as 'normal.' Ten per cent of those who had a 'normal' reaction pattern had rear-end accidents while 38 per cent of the desynchronizing subjects showed rear-end accidents.

3. *Experience*. Job experience, measured by time on the job, has been related to accident rate. For instance, Butler and Jones (1979) looked at the deck and engineering divisions of 15 US destroyers and found a clearly linear pattern such that experienced personnel tended to have lower accident rates.

4. *Age*. Contradictory results appear. For some, there is a U-curve with the young (careless) and the old (with slower reaction) making more errors leading to accidents. Others have found an inverse *U* and suggest that very young and much older workers might have been placed in less hazardous jobs.

5. *Stress*. Not surprising, stress seems to both cause accidents and result from accidents. Stuart and Brown (1981) found that levels of self-reported stress correlate with accident (and disease) liability. Similarly, Allodi and Montgomery (1979) found that a positive history of medical, surgical and psychosomatic episodes differentiated a group of workers and a matched group of non-accident controls. Similarly, Melamed *et al.* (1989) found ergonomic stress levels clearly related to accidents.

6. *Life events*. Various studies have shown strong links between accidents and people's coping styles, mental health and work performance. Various causal mechanisms are likely. Personal problems associated with negative events may result in sleep loss, social isolation and increased alcohol/drug

consumption, all of which are related to accidents (Sheehy and Chapman, 1987).

7. *Risk perception*. Discrepancies between subjective estimates of risk and their actual objective counterparts leave people poorly prepared to detect and cope with potential hazards. The larger the underestimation, the greater the likelihood of risk and vice versa.

Accident Proneness

This concept originated when it was discovered that a small percentage of the population ('the accident prone') had a high percentage of accidents. The term 'accident proneness', taken to mean a psychological abstraction assumed to refer to the existence of an enduring or stable personality characteristic that predisposes an individual toward having accidents, became very popular in the 1920s and 1930s. Reviewers pointed out that individuals have a range of behaviours, much of which may be safe or unsafe, depending on environmental hazards. Obviously, it is not true that some individuals are more prone than others to all types of accidents, nor of course are *all* (or even most) accidents sustained by a small fixed group of people (Kay, 1981). But people drive as they live – that is, there are consistencies of behaviour (in response to particular stimuli) which suggest that they may be related to accidents. For instance, Quenalt (1968) observed bus driver habits and using behavioural measures like unusual manoeuvres, near misses, ratios of rear-mirror usage to manoeuvres, of being overtaken to overtaking etc; he found that definite classes of drivers could be identified. There are at least two objectives to the concept: statistical and conceptual.

Statistical

By chance alone, a certain small number of individuals would be involved in many accidents. The theory of accident proneness is based on identifying *individuals* who have certain characteristics. The theory would have validity if the *same* individuals *repeatedly* had large numbers of accidents. Some people do fall into this category, but we do not need a theory of accident proneness to identify them. For instance, alcoholics and drug addicts often have higher accident rates. Thus, alcoholism and drug addiction are valid predictors of accidents, and so we can reduce accidents by identifying and treating these conditions. However, on the basis of *group* data, it is fruitless to attempt to identify high-accident *individuals* without any other information. Despite rather convincing statistical evidence that accident proneness is not a necessary concept for explaining accidents, the notion has an appeal. Depending on how the concept is defined, it might be difficult to confirm or refute. The liability to accidents within the population can be described by a ponsson or negative binomial distribution, but the latter rests on the untenable assumption that exposure to accident situations and biases in accident reporting are equally distributed across the population.

Conceptual

The term is used ambiguously and inconsistently. Proneness can mean a number of things such as likelihood, whereas the term 'differential accident involvement' is far less loaded. For the personality theorist, the central question occurs: How stable is 'proneness'? How does it arise? Are accident-prone people more likely to have some accidents rather than others?

A more recent study by Dahlback (1991) has stressed two other individual difference factors implicated in accident proneness: those who repress the idea of unpleasant or conflicting outcome of action and those intolerant of ambiguity. In a study, he identified these two as independent factors but was unable to demonstrate that they had a clear relationship with accidents.

Personality and Accidents

There are a number of studies examining the relationship between personality (particularly extraversion and neuroticism) and accidents (particularly motor car accidents). Despite various methodological difficulties and differences, the results are fairly consistent. Venables (1956) found, as predicted, that driver consistency is related to neuroticism and extraversion in some groups. Presumably, erratic and inconsistent behaviour is closely associated with accidents.

Fine (1963) argued the following:

> Since extraverts are assumed to be less socialized than introverts, it is reasonable to assume that they should be less bound by prescribed rules of society regarding motor vehicle operation. Therefore, it was hypothesized that they would incur more traffic accidents and violations than introverts (p.95–6).

The study done on 937 college students showed, as predicted, that extraverts had more accidents and traffic violations than introverts.

Similarly, Craske (1968), who investigated 70 men and 30 women being treated after accidents in a minor trauma clinic, found a highly significant correlation between extraversion and accidents among the men, but not the women. Moreover, the positive correlation between accidents and extraversion was not significantly altered by examining severe and minor accidents seriously. A closer examination of the actual test items related to accidents showed that the few extraversion questions significantly related to accident repetition tended to be related to impulsiveness rather than sociability, while the three neuroticism questions were all concerned with guilt or depression. More recently, Schenk and Rausche (1979) found neuroticism closely associated with driving accidents.

Using Cattell's 16PF, Brand (1973) looked at the personality of drunken, dangerous and uninsured drivers, and a control group. Six factors differentiated offenders from controls. Compared to controls, offenders scored lower on B (intelligence), I (sensitivity), O (insecurity) and Q_3 (self-control) but higher on E (dominance) and L (suspiciousness). In short, offenders were less intelligent and more aggressive. There were also some interesting differences between the offender groups. For instance, compared to dangerous drivers, drunken drivers were more conscientious and insecure. Compared to controls, dangerous drivers are more assertive and uninsured drivers suspicious and lacking in control.

Perry (1986) argued that if *type A* behaviour (correlated positively with both extraversion and neuroticism) is associated with aggression, time urgency and impatience, type As more than type Bs would be more often involved in motor vehicle accidents. As predicted, type A students reported being involved in more accidents and receiving more tickets for driving violations than type Bs. Evans, Palsane and Carrere (1987) found that type A bus drivers, in comparison with B types, have more accidents, absenteeism, official reprimands and personal reports of occupational stress. Data from India also suggest that type As brake, pass and blow their hooters more frequently than B types.

Montag and Comrey (1987), on the other hand, were interested in *locus of control* correlates of fatal driving accidents. They devised two scales: driver internality (drivers are responsible for accidents) and driver externality (accidents are due to chance, situational or other people variables). These two scales were administered to 200 Israelis applying for a driver's licence and 200 individuals from the same population who had been involved in a fatal motor accident. Predictably, the accident group had lower driver internality and higher driver externality scores, which concurs with previous studies that show internality is linked with cautious behaviour, more attentiveness and an aptitude to avoid aversive situations.

Arnett (1990) focused on sensation-seeking and drunken driving among adolescents, looking at nearly 180 males of 17 and 18 years. He found that drunk driving was related to the total score on sensation-seeking as well as three out of four subscales (thrill and sensation-seeking, disinhibition, boredom susceptibility).

In a more comprehensive, multi-variate study, Hansen (1989) looked at biodata, personality and cognitive correlates of accidents in a causal model. Looking at 362 chemical industry workers, it was hypothesized that traits of social maladjustment, various aspects of neurosis, cognitive ability, employee age and actual job experience would have independent causal effects on accidents, even when risk was partialled out. A social maladjustment scale was constructed from the MMPI, which along with a measure of (neurotic) distractibility was clearly linked to accidents. Both scales, though correlated, demonstrated independent causal relationships to accidents suggesting two major factors at work. The author believes that the central psychological question of psychologists should be changed from 'What personality or cognitive trait is related to accidents?' to 'What is the strength of the causal impact that trait anxiety has on accidents?' He concludes:

> This study demonstrated that some characteristics associated with neurosis and social maladjustment are significantly related to accidents, even when other influential variables such as level of risk and employee age are taken into consideration. In future studies, the global measures of social maladjustment and neurotic distractibility should be decomposed into several measures of individual traits that can then be woven into the refined causal model and tested (p.88).

Finally, Booysen and Erasmus (1989) have done a sterling job in reviewing personality factors associated with accident risk. No less than 43 traits (many of them related) have been examined as regards their relationship to accidents. In a conceptual factor analysis, they suggested that two factors were relevant: recklessness (extraversion, domineering, aggressive, sensation-seeking) and anxiety-depressive. They then administered the 16PF to nearly 200 bus drivers who were divided into three groups depending on their previous involvement in accidents and the degree of seriousness of accidents that they had been involved in. A step-wise multiple regression showed that four factors – dominance, carefreeness, emotional sensitivity and shrewdness – accounted for between 10 per cent and 12 per cent of the variance.

Thus, it seems that there is sufficient evidence that personality variables do relate to all sorts of accidents in all sorts of populations. They appear to be able to account for about 10 per cent of the variance, which is certainly not to be dismissed. The two orthogonal factors that seem to be the best predictors of accidents are clearly extraversion/sensation-seeking/A-type behaviour and neuroticism/anxiety/instability.

Methodological Difficulties

There are a great number of methodological shortcomings of research in this area which prevent the questions of the relationship between personality and accidents being fairly reviewed. These include the following:

• Accident reporting is erratic, biased, inconsistent and done for legal purposes only. Any investigation of industrial (or domestic) accidents is crucially dependent on the quality (and quantity) of accident reporting (Sheehy and Chapman, 1987). Reporting systems might fulfil organizational, medical and legal needs but frequently not those of the ergonomist or the industrial psychologist. Hence, they are investigated as events rather than processes, as most measures do not provide measures of exposure.

- Retrospective studies cannot discriminate between the stress that caused the accident and the stress produced by its occurrence. There is a tremendous shortage of good longitudinal studies in the area.
- Confounding of dependent and independent variables by such practices as explaining causality by post-hoc discrimination between accident and non-accident groups.
- The 'lumping' together of all sorts of accidents as if all accidents were the same. Clearly, one needs a good taxonomy of accidents in order to make prediction more clear. Thus, driving accidents may be seen to be quite different from household accidents; and accidents at work different from accidents at leisure.
- Although there is a welcomed agreement over what personality variables are important in accident research, there does seem to be rather less agreement about which measures to use. Alas, this means that because different measures are used, exact comparisons cannot be made; hence, the corpus of knowledge arising is only at the rather vague conceptual stage.

8.4 PERSONALITY AND STRESS

The work on personality and stress has burgeoned significantly over the past 20 years, no doubt because of the popularity of the concept of stress in both the popular and academic literature (Martocchio and O'Leary, 1989). The voluminous, cross-disciplinary literature has been concerned with the causes (aetiology), consequences and cures of stress, mainly in people at work. However, there is both conceptual and operational confusion in this area which makes the interpretation of data difficult (Newton, 1989). Most of the individual difference literature has looked at both personality correlates of stress directly, and personality correlates of coping strategies which supposedly ameliorate stress.

One of the paradoxes of the literature is that nearly all of the 'models' of occupational stress put the individual – and therefore individual differences – at the centre of the model. Consider first the model of Cooper (1983) which sees individual differences as mediating between job factors and physical and organizational consequences (see Figure 8.2). Motowidlo, Packard and Marning (1986), in contrast, see individual differences as main effects along with job condition rather than moderator variables.

All other models, and there are many (such as that of Hodapp, Neuser and Weiyer 1988), place personality as a major antecedent (predictor, determinant) of stress and hence illness. Most, but not all, emphasize the *interaction* between various personality characteristics and those of the job to produce stress.

What is perhaps most surprising about this literature is the range and choice of individual difference variables selected for examination. While there is general consensus about the dependent variable that is considered (i.e. job satisfaction, minor psychiatric morbidity, blood pressure), there seems to be theoretical consensus as to what type of individual difference variable to consider. However, one variable has been examined extensively, and to the relative neglect of nearly all others – that is, the type A behaviour pattern.

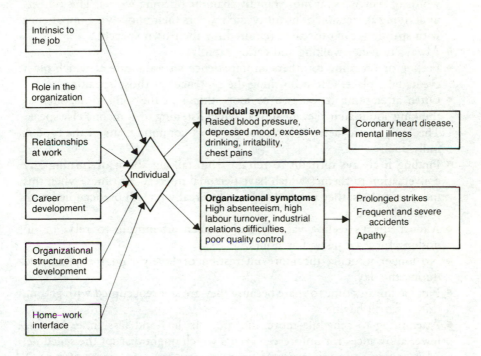

Figure 8.2 Job-related factors that lead to stress
Source: Cooper (1983)

The Type A Behaviour Pattern

The type A behaviour pattern was conceived nearly 25 years ago when it was found that coronary patients under study behaved similarly in many ways – they were extremely competitive, high achieving, aggressive, hasty, impatient and restless. They were characterized by explosive speech patterns, tenseness of facial muscles, and appeared to be under pressure of time and the challenge of responsibility. These individuals were described as 'type A' personality types, as opposed to the more relaxed 'type B', who had a low risk of coronary heart disease. Type As are people having this particular behavioural pattern. They are often deeply involved and committed to their work so that other aspects of their lives are relatively neglected. The original type A researchers, Friedman and Rosenman (1974), identified type A characteristics:

- Possessing the habit of explosively accentuating various key words in ordinary speech without real need and tending to utter the last few words of sentences far more rapidly than the opening words. This reflects underlying aggression or hostility and mirrors their underlying impatience with spending even the time required for their own speech.
- Always moving, walking and eating rapidly.
- Feeling or revealing to others an impatience with the rate at which most events take place. Often finishing the sentences of those speaking.
- Often attempting to do two or more things at the same time, such as thinking about an irrelevant subject when listening to someone else speak. This 'polyphasic' activity is one of the most common traits of the type A individual.
- Finding it always difficult to refrain from talking about or turning any conversation to themes which have personal interest. At times, when this manoeuvre fails, they pretend to listen but really remain preoccupied with personal thoughts.
- Almost always feeling vaguely guilty when attempting to relax or do nothing for even just a few hours.
- No longer noticing the more interesting or lovely things encountered during the day.
- Not having any time to spare because they are so preoccupied with getting things worth having.
- Attempting to schedule more and more in less and less time. Making fewer allowances for unforeseen events which might disrupt the schedule. Also having a chronic sense of time urgency – a core aspect of type A personality.
- Having aggressive, hostile feelings to all type A subjects.
- Resorting to certain characteristic gestures or nervous tics, such as clenching fists or banging a hand on a table for emphasis.
- Becoming increasingly committed to translating and evaluating personal activities and the activities of others in terms of numbers.

Friedman and Rosenman (1974) also outline the following characteristics as indicating type B personality:

- Being completely free of all the habits, and exhibiting none of the traits, of the type A personality.
- Never suffering from time urgency and impatience.
- Harbouring no free-floating hostility and feeling no need to impress others with their achievements or accomplishments unless the situation demands.

- Playing in order to find relaxation and fun, not to demonstrate achievement at any cost.
- Being able to work without agitation, and relax without guilt.

Over the years, the literature on this behaviour pattern has exploded and there are numerous, relatively sophisticated models describing the personal, social and cultural antecedents of the type A pattern through to the environmental, organizational and personal consequences, as well as potentially important moderating effects (Price, 1982).

Recent research on the type A behaviour pattern has demonstrated that type A individuals are more aggressive, more neurotic, more extraverted and more anxious, as well as in greater need for control than B types (Furnham, 1990a). Many studies have shown that type As have feelings of insecurity and self-doubt and feel depressed or anxious about their self-worth (Price, 1982). Furnham, Borovoy and Henley (1986) reported two studies looking at the difference in self-perceptions of type As and Bs. In the first, type As compared to type Bs rated themselves significantly higher on various *negative* traits (complaining, conceited, cruel, dominating, selfish and unkind) and lower on the *positive* traits (patient, reasonable, tolerant and unselfish). This was replicated in a second study where they found that, compared to type Bs, type As believed themselves to be more ambitious, cold, complaining, conceited, cruel, dishonest, dominating, enthusiastic, gloomy, insincere, jealous, malicious, impatient and selfish. They argue that high levels of type A behaviour are associated with a tendency to process information about the self in a fashion that attempts to bolster self-esteem. They note:

> Thus, while type A may have lower self-esteem, and rate themselves more highly on negative traits and less so on positive traits compared to type Bs, they remember more positive traits about themselves. This 'information processing strategy' is an attempt to deny the recognised personal limitations and bolster self-esteem. Whereas neurotics, when presented with both negative and positive information about self, selectively process self-deprecatory rather than self-appreciatory information, A types do the reverse – that is, to a greater extent than most normal subjects (p.371).

More recently, Henley and Furnham (1989) found, as expected, that type As tended toward negative self-ratings and high actual, ideal self-discrepancy scores on a self-evaluation, adjective rating task. They argue that the results do not provide clear evidence that type As have low self-esteem because they appear to value some negative traits as positive and desirable. Yet they note that type As are apparently less satisfied with themselves as they actually are than are type Bs, which is indeed at the heart of the type A syndrome. Although these results concur with other studies in the field (Burke, 1984a), they stress the importance of looking at the association between type A behaviour and beliefs about the self.

Burke (1984a) investigated the beliefs and fears underlying type A behaviour by giving around 150 students the Jenkins Activity Survey as a questionnaire, looking at fears about worthlessness. He found a similar pattern of correlations in that speed and impatience subscale scores correlated significantly in a different direction from the job involvement subscale. Specifically, he found that people scoring highly on speed and impatience tended to have stronger beliefs that one's self-worth is a function of one's accomplishments, that no universal moral principle exists, that things that are worth having are in short supply, personal fears of worthlessness, that justice does not prevail, and a philosophy of revenge. On the other hand, individuals reporting greater job involvement were less likely to report fears of being worthless and getting their fair share of things worth having. Burke (1985) in fact replicated this finding using type A measures of his own devising, by demonstrating that it was predominantly the time urgency of the type A behaviour pattern (rather than say hostility) that is related to feelings of worthlessness and the idea that self-worth is a function of one's accomplishments. Burke also pointed out some implications of these findings:

> If it is assumed that the future research confirms that beliefs and fears examined in this study (and other beliefs and fears as well) are indeed associated with type A behaviour, then these factors would help explain who is likely to display type A behaviour and why this behaviour is difficult to change significantly through behaviour modification approaches. It is not until individuals examine and alter their personal beliefs, thoughts and perceptions about themselves and others, that they can undertake the radical reorientation to themselves and their environment that would be indicated in a shift from type A to type B behaviour. The measures of beliefs and fears thus serve both as useful diagnostic and baseline assessments (p.143).

These studies have demonstrated that certain facets of type A behaviour are associated with specific, negative self-evaluations. The fact that this was particularly true of one particular aspect of A types, namely speed and impatience, helps to explain inconsistencies in the literature.

Type A at Work

Despite the extensive research done on the type A measure, relatively little research has looked at the behaviour of A types at work. Various speculations have been made however. Price (1982) sees the workplace as the key environmental factor influencing type A behaviour. She argues that by modelling or imitating hard-driving, competitive, aggressive behaviour of successful people at work, men in particular learn to be A type. A number of other factors, common in the (American) workplace, lead to (or at least reward) this behaviour pattern. They include the following:

- Peer pressure to work overtime, compete for prizes etc.
- Being outcome or product oriented which confuses the quality/quantity of work with worth.
- Job overload to meet high, often unrealistic, performance standards.
- Setting deadlines that reflect chronic time urgency.
- Crisis generation as a consequence of time management problems.

In short, the workplace for men rewards A type behaviour which leads to considerable personal stress. The type A person is a workaholic with an exaggerated success ethic. Various people have done empirical work in this field (Begley and Boyd, 1985).

Mettlin (1976) looked at 943 white-collar, middle-class males in New York, who came from five different work settings: the administrative staff and professional staff of a state health agency, supervisory personnel from a public service organization, officers from industrial and trade unions, faculty at a major private university, and administrative officers of a large banking corporation. They found that not only was the type A behaviour pattern significantly related to status, as measured by rank, level of occupational prestige and income, but it was also found to be significantly related to rapid career achievement, as indicated by rank and income related to age.

In a review of a number of studies, Chesney and Rosenman (1980) bore out the connection between type A personality and high occupational status: it was found that 'Type As tended to describe their jobs as having more responsibility, longer hours and heavier workloads than do type Bs. Despite these factors, type As in general did not report more job dissatisfaction, anxiety or depression than do type Bs'. Chusmir and Hood (1988) found, as predicted, that in both working men and women type A behaviour patterns were significantly linked to need for achievement, autonomy and power as well as job commitment but not job satisfaction.

Whereas some studies showed that type A is associated positively with productivity and negatively with satisfaction, others have failed to find any relationship (Matteson, Ivancevich and Smith, 1984). Bluen, Barling and Burns (1990), however, found that after partialling out various possibly salient biographical factors, and impatience and irritability, type A did predict policies sold and job satisfaction in insurance salesmen.

The results of various studies lead one to derive fairly plausible and testable hypotheses:

- Type As are more sensitive, and hence responsive, to rewards (Blumenthal et al., 1980).
- Because type As are hurried and time urgent, they will work faster but with more errors than type B workers.

- Type As tend to be aggressive and interpersonally hostile, which makes them difficult to handle, unpredictable and touchy (Hooker, Blumenthal and Siegler, 1987).
- Type As set unrealistically high performance standards of themselves, and others, and hence frequently do not attain them (Ward and Eisler, 1987).
- Type As work harder, suffer more stress, ignore minor ailments (influenza) but when they do become ill suffer major illnesses (Price, 1982).
- Type As tend to be more committed to, and perform better at, organizational goals (Phillips *et al.*, 1990).

These and many other related hypotheses could be tested, all of which suggest that being type A is a mixed blessing in an organizational setting. It certainly suggests that type As are more likely to experience stress and more likely to generate it in others.

Research Problems with the Type A

As one might expect with such a large amount of research work done on this area, a number of conceptual and methodological issues have arisen. Some of the most important of these are as follows:

- The relationship between type A/B and other personality dimensions. Various studies have examined the relationship between type A and other dimensions and found close relationships (i.e. high correlations). For instance, Furnham (1984b) found type A to be positively correlated with extraversion, sensation-seeking and stimulus screening, suggesting that the 'arousal' concept underlies the type A concept. Type A scores are correlated positively with both extraversion and neuroticism, particularly the former. Schiraldi and Beck (1988) also found a number of personality correlates of the A/B pattern, such as the inability to verbalize effect. In addition, a major question concerns what unique variance of the A type construct accounts for a comparison with other, better established, measures.
- The type A behaviour pattern has itself been shown to be multi-dimensional. For instance, the most celebrated and well used measure of the A type, the Jenkins Activity Survey (JAS), has been shown to be multi-dimensional: as well as a total scale score there are three, only moderately correlated, subscale scores: factors J (job involvement), H (hard driving and competitive) and S (speed and impatience). Various studies have shown how various important business-related behaviours are associated with different facets of the A/B type. This suggests that it is no longer feasible to talk about one type (A or B) – perhaps the concept should be broken down into its constituent parts.
- Not only has it been suggested that type A is multi-dimensional, but also that there may be good (adaptive) and bad (maladaptive) A and B types.

Thus, Friedman, Hall and Harris (1985) distinguished between two A types – healthy, charismatic and hostile competitives – and two B types – relaxed, quiet persons and tense, overcontrolled, inhibitors. Thus, only one of the A types was repressed, tense and illness prone while the other was healthy, talkative, in control and charismatic. Hence, before it could be assumed that type A behaviour leads to stress, it is first important to be able to distinguish 'good' and 'bad' A types.

• The measurement of the type A behaviour pattern remains a serious problem as there exist various supposedly valid measures that do not correlate very highly (Eysenck, 1990). The fact that there still remain psychometric problems over the measurement of this syndrome certainly suggests that this is a major cause of the equivocal studies.

Despite lack of agreement about the aetiology, components and psychological processes associated with the type A behaviour pattern, it does seem the case that researchers have identified a personality variable or, more likely, a cluster of factors which are predictive not only of stress at work, but also outside it. For instance, Howard, Cunningham and Rechnitzer (1986) found that whether a particular job characteristic (such as role ambiguity) is stressful depends on whether the person is type A or B, and that intrinsic job satisfaction has the potential to moderate these effects. Generally, type As 'fit' unambiguous environments and find ambiguous environments stressful, while the precise opposite is true for type Bs.

The 'Hardy Personality'

While the type A/B distinction may provide many clues as to stress-prone personality characteristics, many believe that the theory is not adequate to explain why some people suffer ill-health as a result of high stress levels. Kobasa (1979) developed the 'hardy personality' concept and measure to explain the connection between stress and health. The theory states that among persons facing significant work stressors, those high in hardiness will be significantly less likely to fall ill, either mentally or physically, than those who lack hardiness, or who display alienation, powerlessness and threat in face of change. The key attribute – hardiness – is defined as a personality, cognitive or attributional style that expresses commitment, control and challenge. *Commitment* is the ability to believe in the truth, and the importance of who one is and what one is doing and, thereby, the tendency to involve oneself fully in the many situations of life, including work, family, interpersonal relationships and social institutions. Secondly, *control* is defined as the tendency to believe and act as if one can influence the course of events. People with control seek explanations for why something is happening with emphasis on their own responsibility, and not in terms of other actions or fate. This is, of course, internal locus of control. The third aspect of the hardy personality, *challenge*, is based on the individual's belief that change, rather than stability, is the normative mode of life. Thus, with regard to 'challenge', an individual looks for stimulation, change and opportunities with an openness of mind and willingness to experiment.

Kobasa suggests that hardiness leads to a type of coping. Keeping specific stressors in perspective, hardy individuals' basic sense of purpose in life allows them to ground events in an understandable and varied life course. Knowing that one has the resources with which to respond to stressors, hardy individuals' underlying sense of control allows them to appreciate a well exercised coping repertoire. Seeing stressors as potential opportunities for change, enables hardy individuals to see even undesirable events in terms of possibilities rather than threats. Kobasa found evidence to support her theory, namely that executives with high stress but low illness were more hardy and showed stronger commitment to self, and vigorousness toward the environment.

Thus, while the type A literature focused on individuals prone to stress, the hardiness concept focused on individuals who cope well with stress. A problem for the type A literature is that it focuses more on the causes of stress rather than how people cope with it.

8.5 PERSONALITY, HEALTH AND ILLNESS

There is now a good deal of evidence that personality and stress are causally related to various diseases, including cancer and coronary heart disease. The type A/B dichotomy is well known, and there is some evidence linking it with coronary heart disease, although the predictive accuracy of the procedures used to determine type A is far from well established, and it is now widely agreed that only certain traits within the type A group, particularly anger, hostility and aggression, are relevant to coronary heart disease.

Recent research has focused on the main effects of personality on health – that is not moderated through the concept of stress. The idea is not new; for instance, psychosomatic theories have often identified neurotic traits like anxiety, anger and depression with the development, although some have argued that this may simply be a function of symptom reporting.

Currently, there appear to be two highly promising avenues of research into the relationship between individual differences and illness: the one concentrating on *motivational* factors, the other *trait* association. Jemmott (1987) and McClelland (1989) have both reviewed the by-now fairly extensive research on motivational factors in health and illness.

Reviewing psychoneuroimmunological studies on the association between the power motive and the affiliation motive (particularly if these motives are inhibited, challenged or blocked), Jemmott (1987) noted the evidence that whereas the affiliative motive tends to be associated with health, the power motive is associated with illness. It seems that the inhibited power motive is associated with either a chronically activated sympathetic nervous system or a more reactive system, while the affiliative motive is associated with less activity. The tentative, but quite intriguing conclusion, then, is that the affiliative motive, particularly relaxed or unstressed affiliative motivation, has potentially health-protecting effects, whereas the power motive (particularly stressed or inhibited) was seen as increasing risk.

McClelland (1989) has argued that his data showed that a relaxed or easygoing affiliative 'motive syndrome' characterizes insulin-dependent type 1 diabetes and can, if aroused, lead to poorer blood sugar control. Generally though, affiliative trust and a greater sense of agency are associated with better health. A stressed power motive syndrome, on the other hand, is associated with sympathetic activation, release of stress hormones, depressed immune functions, and greater susceptibility to infectious disease. He concluded:

What general conclusions can be drawn from our research experience in the health area?

1. Individual differences in implicit motives or motive syndromes as assessed in associative thought are related to health and various types of illnesses in very specific ways through associated physiological mechanisms.
2. Most probably, the motive syndrome relationships to health are mediated through the chronic activation of emotion centers in the brain and of the autonomic nervous system and through the release of various hormones that affect immune defences or other physiological systems involved in particular diseases.
3. Affiliative trust and implicit agency motivation seem to favour better health. Conversely, affiliative cynicism and a sense of helplessness, either from weakness (low agency) or frustrated agency, are associated with more illness.
4. Motive patterns appear not to be just responses to better or poorer health, but they play a causal role in health outcomes because they predict illness over a 10-year period and because changes in them produced by therapy precede health improvements.
5. Study of the role of personality factors in health and disease represents an exciting new field of great complexity, great difficulty, and great promise. It is of great *complexity* because of the need to study not only psychological variables but also the physiological systems that link them to disease. It involves great *difficulty* because of the complexity of the systems involved and the resistance of the biomedical community to acknowledging the role of psychological variables in disease, and it holds great *promise* because we are in the process of learning through carefully conducted scientific studies just how the mind and body interact in sickness and in health (p.682).

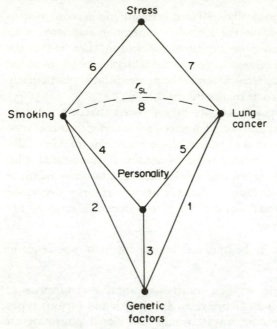

Figure 8.3 Relationships between genetic factors, personality and stress as mediating the correlation between smoking and lung cancer
Source: Eysenck (1985)

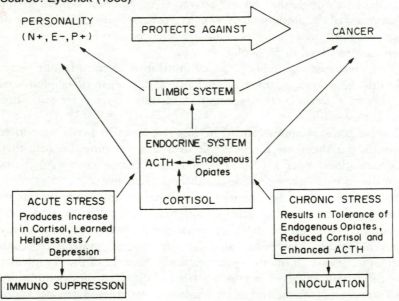

Figure 8.4 Personality-cancer relationship as mediated by stress factors and the endocrine system
Source: Eysenck (1985)

Just as it is no surprise that McClelland believes health and illness are linked with power and affiliation motives (stemming out of his own approach to individual differences), Eysenck (1985) and his colleagues find illness related to his three-dimensional personality theory. Characteristically, Eysenck attempts a theoretically based integration of the material linking personality with both cancer and heart disease. He is, quite rightly, highly critical of the various studies in this area arguing for both methodologically sound prospective and curative studies, which help untangle correlation and cause. For instance, Eysenck claims that the relationship between smoking and cancer is moderated or mediated by three other major factors: personality, genetics and stress. He argues that (see Figures 8.3 and 8.4) genetic factors are part responsible for lung cancer (1) and also for smoking (2); that these genetic factors work through personality traits (3) which in turn is linked (through predispositions) to both smoking (4) and cancer (5). Furthermore, stress is also related to both smoking and cancer. Eysenck is no doubt correct in stating that the link between smoking and cancer is motivated by other factors. He has further developed a model to explain how personality and stress affect the endocrine system, which in turn is correlated with cancer.

More recently, Grossarth-Maticek, Eysenck and Vetter (1988) have developed a typology concerned with people's experiences of, and reactions to, stress that is specifically geared to predict cancer and heart disease. They are as follows:

Type 1: Underestimation. People of this type show a permanent tendency to regard an emotionally highly valued object as the most important condition for their own well-being and happiness. The stress produced by the continued withdrawal or absence of this object is experienced as an emotionally traumatic event. Type 1 individuals fail to distance themselves from the object and remain dependent on it. Thus, individuals of this type do not achieve success in reaching the object, and remain distant and isolated from this highly valued and emotionally important object. Great stress is produced by this failure to achieve nearness to the highly valued person, success in the highly valued occupation, or whatever. The type shows a lack of *autonomy*.

Type 2: Over-arousal. People of this type show a continued tendency to regard an emotionally highly valued object as the most important cause for their particular distress and unhappiness. Rejection by the object (if a person), or failure to reach it (as in the case of occupational success), is experienced as an emotional trauma, but people of this type fail to achieve disengagement from the object; rather, they feel more and more helplessly dependent on the object. Thus, persons of this type remain in constant contact with these negatively valued and emotionally disturbing people and situations, and fail to distance themselves and free themselves from dependence on the disturbing object. Where persons of type 1 keep on seeking nearness to the object of their desires, and experience their failure in terms of hopelessness and helplessness, persons of type 2 fail to disengage themselves from the object and experience a reaction of anger, aggression and arousal.

Type 3: Ambivalence. People of this type show a tendency to shift from the typical reaction of type 1 to the typical reaction of type 2 and back again. This type shows a permanent tendency to regard an emotionally highly valued object alternately as the most important condition for their own well-being, and as the main cause for their own unhappiness. Thus, in individuals of this type, we have an alternation of feelings of hopelessness/helplessness and of anger/arousal.

Type 4: Personal autonomy. The typical reactions of types 1, 2 and 3 indicate a dependence on the highly valued object, and their reactions are characterized by constant contradiction between expected consequences and the actual consequences of their actions. For persons of type 4, there is a strong tendency to regard their own autonomy, and the autonomy of the people with whom they wish to be in contact, as the most important conditions for their own well-being and happiness. This enables people of type 4 to experience realistically the approach or avoidance behaviour of the object of their desires, and thus enables them to accept the autonomy of the object. In other words, persons of type 1 and 2 show a dependence on important objects which engage their emotions, but cannot remain autonomous when these emotional objects withdraw or remain unattainable; it is this that constitutes the stress which, according to the theory, leads to cancer or coronary heart disease. Persons of type 4 are able to deal with the situation by virtue of their autonomy-preserving ability, and thus avoid the stress reaction.

This impressive, extensive research based on prospective data suggests very clearly that type 1s are cancer prone, type 2s are heart attack prone, and types 3 and 4 are essentially healthy. They conclude:

> We may conclude that psychological variables, in particular personality type, are important mediating death from cancer and coronary heart disease; that these personality variables are more influential than physical factors like smoking; and that personality and physical factors interact in a synergistic fashion. These conclusions suggest that current theorizing of the kind: 'Smoking causes lung cancer' is over simplified and unscientific. A progressive research programme demands the inclusion of psychosocial variables of the kind here considered.

These data thus, in a somewhat different way, emphasize both the importance of personality variables (typology) and the synergistic effects of the interaction between organic variables and personality. No analysis of the organic variables can be considered complete which neglects, as most of them have done in the past, the importance of personality variables. This, we believe, is the main conclusion to be drawn from the data of these three large scale prospective studies (p.490).

The Disease-Prone Personality

In an important and scholarly review, Friedman and Booth-Kewley (1987) examine in detail the disease-prone personality, whose traits of depression, anger, hostility and anxiety predict or correlate with classic 'psychosomatic' illnesses like asthma, arthritis, ulcers, headaches and heart disease. They consider a number of causal possibilities:

- Personality processes (that exacerbate disease) are the result of disease.
- Personality predisposes one to unhealthy habits (smoking and drinking).
- Personality affects disease through causal, physiological mechanisms.
- Biological variables (such as hyper-responsive nervous system) determine both personality and disease.
- Personality is linked with illness behaviours but these have no physiological or subjective foundations.

Their meta-analysis involved looking at 229 studies, 101 of which were examined in detail. Five personality variables were examined in detail: anger/-hostility, anger/hostility/aggression, depression, extraversion and anxiety. For the purposes of the analysis, they defined anger as an emotion involving pronounced autonomic arousal (precipitated by some real or perceived wrong); hostility as an enduring attitude involving negative feelings and evaluations of other people; aggression as the actual or intended harmony of others; depression as including neuroticism; extraversion as sociability; and anxiety as both trait and state anxiety. They were related to five illnesses (see Table 8.1).

The authors note:

> Overall, the average magnitude of the relationship between personality problems (depression, anxiety, hostility) and disease appears to be in the range of about .10 to .25 when stated in terms of the correlation coefficient r. Because of unreliabilities in measuring both personality and disease, the true relationship may be somewhat higher. Although the magnitude of this relationship is small when compared to those found in certain realms of experimental psychology, it is moderate or high when compared to other medical risk factors. For example, in the well-known prospective Framingham and Western Collaborative Group studies of heart disease, correlations between cholesterol and CHD, and between smoking and CHD, were all under .15. (Greater amounts of variance explained sometimes results when synergistic interactive effects occur.) (p.548).

Essentially, all five personality dimensions were shown to be associated with these illnesses. Note that extraversion is associated with heart disease

Table 8.1 Results of meta-analysis of personality and disease relationships with assumed effect sizes of zero included

Disease and personality variable	Combined r	No. of articles	No. of samples	z	p	Fail safe N
CHD and anxiety	0.115	14	14	4.90	0.0000005	111
CHD and depression	0.217	13	11	6.06	<0.0000001	139
CHD and anger/hostility/aggression	0.136	21	25	6.78	<0.0000001	400
CHD and anger/hostility	0.162	16	18	7.10	<0.0000001	318
CHD and extraversion	0.067	11	14	2.69	0.0035	24
Asthma and anxiety	0.317	11	15	12.72	<0.0000001	882
Asthma and depression	0.149	7	9	3.73	0.00009	38
Asthma and anger/hostility/aggression	0.201	11	14	5.13	0.0000002	123
Asthma and anger/hostility	0.234	7	10	5.07	0.0000002	85
Asthma and extraversion	−0.095	7	7	−1.59	0.0555	−
Ulcer and anxiety	0.163	8	8	4.41	0.000005	50
Ulcer and depression	0.069	8	8	2.66	0.0039	−
Ulcer and anger/hostility/aggression	−0.027	8	9	−0.09	0.4640	−
Ulcer and anger/hostility	−0.013	7	8	0.14	0.4447	−
Ulcer and extraversion	−0.136	8	9	−2.31	0.01049	9
Arthritis and anxiety	0.200	7	9	5.83	<0.0000001	105
Arthritis and depression	0.137	11	14	6.75	<0.0000001	222
Arthritis and anger/hostility/aggression	0.111	3	4	2.82	0.0024	8
Arthritis and anger/hostility	0.158	2	3	3.77	0.00008	13
Arthritis and extraversion	−0.103	8	9	−2.10	0.0180	6
Headache and anxiety	0.205	3	5	3.89	0.00005	23
Headache and depression	0.180	8	11	5.54	<0.0000001	114
Headache and anger/hostility/aggression	0.052	1	2	0.52	0.3016	−
Headache and anger/hostility	−0.13	1	2	−0.13	0.4502	−
Headache and extraversion	0.063	8	12	1.39	0.0828	−

CHD: coronary heart disease
Source: Friedman and Booth–Kewley (1987)

and headaches, while introversion is associated with asthma, ulcers and arthritis. The authors even admit the possibility of an illness-specific disease personality, such as the 'arthritic personality' or the 'headache-prone personality', but at present the existing evidence does not support this. While the evidence for the link between personality and illness is not totally consistent, nor does it provide evidence of causality, one cannot dismiss it as 'folklore'. With better longitudinal studies, using comprehensive and psychometrically validated personality inventories, and sensitive measures of disease, the exclusive mechanisms to explain the no doubt extant relationship between personality and illness might be forthcoming.

8.6 PERSONALITY AND SUBSTANCE ABUSE

Alcohol

A comprehensive study of 928 adults in London (Edwards, Chandler and Hensman, 1972) showed a strong relationship between extraversion and drinking behaviour in the normal population. Subjects were questioned about the frequency and quantity of use of 15 alcoholic beverages during a one-year period. For both sexes, extraversion scores increased linearly from abstainers to heavy drinkers with the greatest differences appearing between the abstainers and occasional drinkers, and between the frequent light drinkers and the moderate-to-heavy drinkers. Thus, extraversion scores differentiated both between abstainers and drinkers, and between different groups of drinkers, based on the combined quantity–frequency index. Edwards *et al.* also asked the same subjects to complete a 25-item scale concerning troubles with drinking or the adverse consequences of drinking. They found that troubles with drinking were unrelated to extraversion. This latter finding is the conclusion drawn from a review of literature conducted by Braught, *et al.* Brakarsh, Follingstad, and Berry (1973), that problem drinkers among the college population show aggressive and impulsive characteristics in combination with some basic neurotic tendencies. The studies by Edwards *et al.* found no relationship between neuroticism and alcohol use.

Although extraversion is probably positively related to alcohol use in the normal population, clinical groups of alcoholics may be different from non-alcoholics. Ayers, Ruff and Templer (1976) compared a group of 94 male alcoholics with 43 male psychiatric patients whose problems were not associated with alcohol, and found that the alcoholics had higher extraversion than other patients. Similarly, using 160 newly admitted psychiatric patients representing a wide range of alcohol use and abuse, abstainers excluded, Overall and Patrick (1972) administered a 135-item inventory of alcohol abuse and related behaviours. Factor analysis revealed only one major factor that indicated that alcohol abuse involves a collection of related problems arranged along a single continuum. Scores on the 42 items that best reflected the content of the major factor were related to MMPI items in order to determine the personality correlates of alcohol abuse. About one-third of the items that related positively to alcohol abuse could be considered an extraversion item, from the social introversion, hypomania and psychopathic deviate scales, although the neurotic–anxiety–depression component was much more prominent.

Narcotics

Two additional studies agree that alcoholics are higher in neuroticism and anxiety than heroin addicts, with no differences in extraversion. Lorefice *et al.* (1976) compared extraversion and neuroticism scores of 25 outpatient alcoholics and 25 outpatient addicts, and Ciotola and Peterson (1976) compared the 16PF profiles of 68 alcoholics, 79 'mixed street drugs' users and 50 heroin addicts. Although there were no differences on the Eysenck scale or on the second-order extraversion factor of the 16PF, the heroin addicts were higher in venturesomeness (impulsivity), one of the primary scales that loads on the extraversion factor.

Gossop and Kristjansson (1977), and Gossop (1978) actually found that drug-dependent outpatients in England were lower in Eysenck Personality Questionnaire (EPQ) extraversion but higher in neuroticism and psychoticism than published norms. There were subtle differences in the Gossop and Kristjansson study which shed some light on the subject. The most introverted subjects were those with no convictions, who were completely voluntary outpatients; they were also lower in neuroticism, psychoticism and criminality (a special collection of EPQ items). Of the convicted offenders in the sample, those with drug convictions only were less extraverted than those with both drug and violence convictions.

It appears that narcotics-only users are characterized by social introversion; that is, they are low in the sociability component of extraversion. Effective treatment programmes have a marked effect on this aspect of their lifestyle. However, they are not typically low in the impulsiveness component of extraversion and may in fact be high on this variable as well, a quite atypical combination. When narcotic use is seen in combination with criminal lifestyles, social introversion is no longer a crucial differentiating variable, but rather impulsiveness takes on increased importance.

Marijuana and Soft Drugs

Soft-drug users among clinical groups have been shown to be generally introverted. In the normal population, however, users of soft drugs and marijuana had shown to be either no different from controls, or slightly extraverted. Khavari, Mabry and Humes (1977) paid 298 adults from local labour unions to complete a battery of tests, including the Eysenck Personality Inventory, Zuckerman's Sensation-Seeking Scale and the Wisconsin Substance Use Inventory, which assesses past and current use of 19 substances. Their study focused on the use of marijuana, hashish, LSD and other psychedelics. There was a slight positive correlation of drug use with extraversion and a stronger one with sensation-seeking, especially experience seeking. The latter subscale was related to the use of all these drugs but particularly to marijuana. When correlates of marijuana use and of other hallucinogens were separated via canonical analysis, extraversion and general social stimulation seeking were more closely related to the latter.

Several studies have found no differences in extraversion among groups differing in the use of marijuana. Skinner (1974) found no differences between self-reported users and non-users, even though users were perceived by non-users to be higher in extraversion. Marin (1976) administered a questionnaire about alcohol, tobacco, marijuana and other drugs in 2142 college students in South America and found no relationship to extraversion. In a study conducted in Scotland (Wells and Stacey, 1976a, 1976b), significant differences were found for anxiety, neuroticism and psychoticism but not for extraversion. There were 352 female users and 123 male users divided into graduated groups on the basis of extent of drug use. Studies in Jamaica (Beaubrun and Knight, 1973) and in India (Mendhiratta, Wig and Verma, 1978), where marijuana usage is widespread and generally accepted, likewise failed to find differences between chronic users and controls on modified extraversion scales. Finally, it is possible that some groups of users are more extraverted and others more introverted.

8.7 CONCLUSION

This chapter concentrated on the possible links between personality traits and various work-related issues like absenteeism, accidents and illnesses. For some, the much sought after Holy Grail has been to discover evidence for the absenteeism, accident or illness-prone 'personality'; that is, to seek out, describe and explain the link between these phenomena and personality.

Although personality factors have been shown to play a part in absenteeism, these are frequently 'washed out' by powerful organizational factors that are the primary determinant of absenteeism. A variety of sociological and organizational factors combined to affect absenteeism levels. While personality factors do play a small part, these probably only operate in very loose or unrule-bound organizations. Alas, however, the fact that individual difference factors seem less important has meant that there has been comparatively little research in this area.

The concept of accident-prone personality, despite conceptual and statistical problems associated with it, has refused to go away, no doubt because of the accumulating evidence that such a phenomenon exists. There are both good theoretical reasons and a substantial literature to suggest that extraversion (and related arousal concepts like sensation-seeking) and neuroticism are closely tied to accidents of all kinds. Although some of the best work has been done on road accidents, there is little reason to suspect that these traits are predictive of minor and major accidents at work.

Finally, the relationship between personality and health, stress and illness has attracted considerable interest, research money and the development of theoretical models. There appears to be accumulating evidence of personality traits like anger, depression and anxiety being productive of highly specific illnesses. While the 'mechanisms' are not always clear, there exist some plausible and testable models/theories that link personality-determined social behaviour with endocrinal and immunological changes that relate directly to stress, and hence illness.

There is, then, no doubt that various personality traits are implicated in this fairly wide variety of work-related problems.

Chapter 9

Personality, leisure, sport, unemployment and retirement

There can be no high civilization where there is not ample leisure.

H.W. Beedner

I must confess that I am interested in leisure in the same way that a poor man is interested in money.

Prince Philip

Serious sport has nothing to do with fair play ... it is war minus the shooting.

George Orwell

It is a general truth that those persons who are good at games are good at nothing else. Generally speaking, good players are but miserable and useless persons.

Thomas Tegg

It is almost impossible to remember how tragic a place the world is when one is playing golf.

Robert Lynd

It seems to me that the main contact the bulk of English have with sport consists in looking on, and betting.

G. Renier

Retirement means twice as much husband on half as much money.

Anon

One of the many pleasures of old age is giving things up.

Malcolm Muggeridge

It's a recession when your neighbour loses his job; it's a depression when you lose your own.

H. Truman

A man willing to work, and unable to find work, is perhaps the saddest sight that fortune's inequality exhibits under the sun.

Thomas Carlyle

There are hazards in anything one does, but there are greater hazards in doing nothing.

Shirley Williams

9.1 INTRODUCTON

This chapter is concerned with the relationship between individual differences (personality) and non-occupational behaviours, i.e. behaviours outside of work. There are various typologies which have attempted to set out the precise relationship between work and non-work, usually leisure (Furnham, 1990b). A general assumption is that some individual difference factors (needs, traits, motives) determine the choice of, and satisfaction in, work but that when work is not being done (through retirement, unemployment) these factors also influence the choice of activities after work. Naturally, some areas have attracted more and better research than others. It is probably true to say, however, that personality theorists have in general paid remarkably little attention to the three dependent variables examined in this chapter.

Theoretically, the problems are first definitional, second epistemological and third interpretational. The definition of both sport and/or leisure remains highly problematic. Neulinger (1978) has contrasted the classical and twentieth century definition of leisure, and attempted a denotative and connotative definition of leisure which stressed such things as discretionary time and activity as well as a state of mind being the essential characteristics of leisure. Although a number of definitions exist, they are somewhat vague, contradictory and nebulous. Yet as Stockdale (1986) has noted, it is difficult to develop a coherent theoretical framework or body of knowledge if no clear, consensually held definition of leisure exists. She writes:

> Some researchers take the easy way out; they pay lip service to the definitional problems and focus on easily measurable aspects, such as frequency of participation in activities which the majority regard as leisure. This frequently leads to a focus on more formal leisure activities and the neglect of informal, private or inactive pursuits. However, it perseverates an implicit view of leisure as defined by researchers rather than by the individual consumer (p.7).

Thus, as we have seen before, the definition and hence measurement of the dependent variable is highly problematic, which could easily, of itself, account for equivocal results. The same problem occurs with unemployment, but less so with retirement.

Like leisure, the concept of sport remains definitionally unclear. Almost all forms of activity can, and do get, regarded as sport by certain individuals. The Olympics committee is frequently lobbied by enthusiasts eager to have their particular 'sport' recognized formally. Given the diversity of sports from 'blood sports', which may or may not involve the pursuit and killing of wild animals, to highly physically inactive sports like bridge or chess, it seems highly unlikely that any useful definition of sport could ever arise. As a consequence, reviews have attempted to isolate various fundamental dimensions useful for categorizing sport. These may include: physical vs cognitive; individualistic vs team; predominantly male vs female; ball based vs non-ball based; touch vs non-touch; use of machinery/tools; dangerous vs non-dangerous etc. The usefulness of these and other dimensions used to describe or categorize sports can be tested empirically through multi-variate statistics, although repeated attempts have not resulted in an agreed taxonomy.

The reason why definitions and categorizations are important (Eysenck, Nias and Cox, 1982; Dowd and Innes, 1981) is because both personality and sport (as well as unemployment or retirement activities) are multi-faceted and it is quite possible that some dimensions of the former are related to some, but by no means all, of the latter. Eysenck *et al.* (1982) make two basic distinctions regarding sport: individualistic vs team sport and outstanding vs average performance. Various other dimensions are possible: ball vs non-ball sport; amount of physical contact; extent to which endurance is important; the nature of the skill involved (i.e. perceptual motor vs cognitive). However, just as there is considerable disagreement regarding how to classify or taxonomize personality and individual differences, so there appears to be considerable disagreement about how to group sports. Thus, to examine the personality of say cricketers or swimmers is meaningless unless one knows their preferred position or style (batsmen vs bowlers), their level of skill or, indeed, their history of success and failure.

Two related but quite common problems occur when researchers from different traditions or theoretical backgrounds attempt to examine the relationship between two areas: firstly, that though they are highly skilled in measuring one variable (from their area of expertise), they are frequently naïve and unsophisticated in measuring the other. Hence, sport scientists may choose psychometrically weak and theoretically unsound personality questionnaires based on shaky, even non-existent foundations, while personality theorists' choice of sports performance measures is unrepresentative, unreliable, and confuses or confounds serious and important performance differences. A second problem of concern is which is the dependent and which the independent variable. Personality theorists tend to see personality as the independent variable and sports performance as the dependent variable, while the opposite is true of sports scientists. The implicit assumption of the former is that sports preference and performance is a consequence of personality functioning, while the latter assumes that personality can be shaped by sporting computations and exercise. Both are probably correct and necessitate a reciprocal determinism model being employed.

Nearly all researchers and reviewers in the area have pointed out the serious methodological shortcomings in the area. This is to be lamented yet remains true, and it makes conclusions in the area difficult to assess. Essentially, two reasons clearly exist for this disappointing research. Most such research is weak in both conception and design. Conceptually, the research strategy governing much of the personality and performance research effort is, as Ryan (1968) noted:

> ... of the shotgun variety. By that I mean the investigator grabbed the nearest and most convenient personality test, and the closest sports group, and with little or no theoretical basis for their selection, fired into the air to see what they could bring down. It isn't surprising; that firing into the air at different times and at different places, and using different ammunition, should result in different findings. In fact, it would be surprising if the results weren't contradictory and confusing (p.17).

Experimental design weaknesses in this body of research appear to be unusually plentiful. They include the following:

1. Inadequately defined and operationalized variables, for example, focus on abnormality and deficiency rather than personality strengths.
2. Poor sampling procedures, for example, what defines 'an athlete'.
3. Inappropriate selection of measures, for example, 'choice by scale title', poor validity and reliability, response sets.
4. Investigator expectancy effects, for example, investigator expectancies influencing subject responses.
5. Inappropriate statistical analyses, for example, use of multiple t tests.
6. Interpretive errors in explaining results, for example, levelling, ignoring non-differences, non-criticalness, implying causation from correlation, inadequate social validity.

Kroll (1968) has also pointed out that the *meaning* of the correlations involved is that a person with certain personality traits selects and excels in particular sports. High positive correlations between one or more traits and outstanding performance might, alternatively, reflect situations in which (a) players in a sport share no common personality characteristics at first, but through personality modification of those remaining in the sport and attrition of those who don't, those who remain are homogeneously high on the trait(s), or (b) there are common personality characteristics among novices, but through personality modification and attrition, veterans possess very different personality traits. In either instance, a strong, positive correlation of personality trait and performance would be of no value for the recruitment, selection, assignment and training purposes noted earlier as lying at the heart of the applied interest in this subarea of sports psychology. Thus, we can broadly conclude that personality–performance research, its extensiveness notwithstanding, has thus far yielded exceedingly little pay-off for either applied researcher or the athletic practitioner. It is hoped that its recent move toward an interactionist, person–time–situation perspective will enhance its future applied value for both.

9.2 PERSONALITY, SPORT AND LEISURE

Personality Preferences Within and Between Sports

Why do some people prefer tennis to cricket, golf to rugby, marathon running to motocross racing? Clearly, participation in sport is a complex, multi-determined social activity with a variety of intrinsic and extrinsic rewards. The question remains to what extent does personality play a part in determining preference (let alone performance).

Many early studies assumed simple trait determinants of preference and performance. For instance, Schendel (1968) compared high-school athletes and non-participants on the CPI over a three-year period and found minor differences. Similarly, in a multi-variate personality profile analysis of four athlete groups, Kroll and Crenshaw (1968) compared the profiles of footballers, wrestlers, karate specialists and gymnasts. Rushall (1968) argues that knowing a sports person's personality one could predict performance; eliminate situations that produce undesirable behaviours; improve coach-player interactions; differentiate between players of equal skill; evaluate change more efficiently. In a more recent study, Dowd and Innes (1981) found significant differences on the 16PF between squash and volleyball players and between high- and average-level competitors. They note:

> The present analysis showed differences at high levels of participation which suggest that those who by special enthusiasm, drive, and ability have graduated to positions of success may be identifiable as having a common constellation of personality characteristics (p.87).

Investigators have also attempted to understand sport preferences by examining the sources of satisfaction that people get from participating in different sports. For instance, Wankel and Kreisel (1985) found that intrinsic motivations, like excitement of the sport, personal accomplishment and improving one's skills, were rated more highly than extrinsic factors, like pleasing others, winning rewards and winning the game.

Studies using arousal concepts like extraversion, impulsivity and sensation-seeking have proved more useful in understanding sport preferences. For instance, Rowland, Franken and Harrison (1986) found high sensation-seeking males preferred pool, snooker, water skiing and racquetball, whereas low sensation-seeking males preferred running/jogging, weight-lifting and hiking. Females high in sensation-seeking preferred white-water rafting, windsurfing and kayaking, while those who scored low preferred sailing, handball and ballet. Similarly, Svebak and Kerr (1989) looked at the role of impulsivity in sports preference, and found clear and predictable differences supporting the idea that impulsivity is associated with preference for explosive and 'paratelic' as opposed to endurance sports.

Two other areas of research should be mentioned. The first concerns a self-presentation analysis of sports preference, the idea being that participation in sport is part of an ongoing process of self-definition and that different sports define dimensions of social identity. Sadella, Linder and Jenkins (1988) showed that stereotypes concerning the participants in each sport are widely shared, and that specific identity dimensions are associated with each sport:

> A self-presentational analysis suggests the hypothesis that sport preference can be used to modify or enhance the impression created by less malleable personal characteristics. The actor can choose not to reveal a sport preference if anticipating a negative reaction from a specific observer. And the actor can modify statements about expertise and depth of involvement to achieve self-presentational ends (p.221).

Finally, there is increasing interest in sex–role correlates of sports/leisure preference and satisfaction (Henderson, Staknaker and Taylor, 1988). Recently, Csizma, Whitting and Schur (1988) have reviewed the extant literature on sports stereotypes and gender. A few studies have actually examined the relationship between sex–role and leisure activities. Gentry and Doering (1979) in their study of sex–role orientation and leisure in American college students found that males are significantly more likely to go to car races, go fishing and hunting, watch sports shown on television, and read sex-orientated magazines. Similarly, they found that females were significantly more likely to watch ballet, to knit, read the society page in newspapers, and read womens' and home-orientated magazines. Androgynous individuals, more than the masculine and feminine, were more likely to watch ballet, ride bicycles, go to car races, go to movies, and swim. These findings tend to suggest that stereotype sex–roles still pervade in many leisure activities. It was also found that actual gender explained more of the differences in the use of leisure time than the related sex–role (masculinity–femininity). As measured, however, this study had several limitations. Firstly, Gentry and Doering only included ten leisure activities in their survey. Thus, their conjecture that androgynous individuals tend to be more active recreationally is based on a very small number of leisure pursuits. While it remains virtually impossible to include all recreations in any leisure time, it would seem sensible to include as many as possible so that results may be generalizable to a wide variety of pursuits. Secondly, their choice of independent measures to measure sex–role – the CPI, FC scale and the Personal Attributes Questionnaire – seem strange, both because two (not necessarily compatible) measures were used while the Bem Sex–Role Inventory (Bem, 1974), certainly the most extensive, psychometrized (and criticized) measure, was ignored. Furthermore, the authors divided subjects into four depending on their combined high/low scores and masculine/feminine score, but have no way of checking the validity or comparability of their classification. Finally, although they made 'a conscious effort . . . include a wide range of activities in terms of their stereotyped sexual orientation' (p.104), the authors have little empirical evidence of this.

Gruber (1980) has, however, set about empirically determining the sex typing of leisure activities. The results showed that seven of the 24 skilled sports activities were reliably sex typed as masculine (wrestling, pool, chess, fencing, auto-racing, pole-vaulting, handball and sky-diving) and six were sex typed as feminine (cooking, interior decorating, ballet, sewing, knitting, embroidery). He also suggested that men and women continue to have preferences for activities not stereotypically associated with the opposite sex. Another interesting aspect of Gruber's study was that the male and female sample (the majority of whom were college students) rated the masculinity–femininity of each activity with remarkably strong agreement. The study also lends support to Kagan and Moss's (1962) suggestion that activities which have an emphasis on achievement, like games and sport, and which are traditionally identified with the masculine sex, are essential to the development of the masculine role.

Nearly all of the studies on sports preference are correlational and, thus, cause cannot be inferred. Worse, personality variables may be powerful mediating variables but do not have a direct influence on sports preference, yet this idea appears to have occurred to very few researchers.

The Effects of Sport and Leisure on Personality

Whereas personality has nearly always been treated as the independent variable in sport psychology by examining personality differences in preference for, or effectiveness at, specific sports, some research work has considered personality as the dependent variable. Depending on the personality theory or model adhered to, it is possible that various physical and social consequences that occur in sport and leisure could change certain aspects of personality functioning.

Dienstbier (1984) has proposed four possible mechanisms for personality change as a function of sport exercise:

- *Physiological changes*. Sport exercise can effect many physiological systems, including hormonal, which are known to have influential effects on mood and emotions:

  If we define temperament as a long-term tendency toward certain moods or emotional dispositions, it is apparent that we should expect to see some effect upon which such measure after extreme training. Thus there seems a strong probability that changes in depression, anxiety, and positive moods and emotions should follow directly (with no additional mediators) from physiological changes induced through running (p.250).

- *Self-perception of changes.* There appear to be potential, positive self-concept and self-esteem consequences of sports that reduce body fat, redistribute weight, increase energy levels, and lead to a more youthful appearance.

The amazing distances a healthy individual may be able to run after only a few months of training therefore can lead to an increased sense of one's ability to master challenges and to attain goals that seemed remote only months earlier. One's entire belief system about the degree to which one's life is self-determined or internal (versus other or fate-determined, or external) may be influenced by such significant successes (p.257).

- *Socialising and lifestyle changes.* Dedication to a particular sport or leisure activity brings with it lifestyle changes in such things as eating, drinking, smoking, sleeping and resting; in short, lifestyle. Lifestyle changes mean different interaction patterns with different individuals who may have a substantial effect on personality functioning.
- *Expectations.* Expectations and values may change as a function of being exposed to peers and coaches who share a quite different pattern of expectation about health, diet and exercise. Gradually, these new values and expectations are associated so as to change personality functioning.

Although all of these effects are possible, they are far from easy to demonstrate. Research evidence is patchy and problematic. Dienstbier has listed six control features that one would need to set in place in order to demonstrate some causal relationship between exercise, sport (leisure pattern) and personality: studies need to be longitudinal so as to tease out cause and effect; non-sport control groups must be involved in the before–after design; the control group should be engaged in some systematic activity capable of giving some of the same psychological benefits of the sport (i.e. achievement); the control group needs to be involved in a socially engaging activity; changes in lifestyle need to be co-varied out in analysis to ensure that this is not the cause of change; the control group needs to be given similar expectations of personality change. It is only when these various criteria are met that it is in any way possible actually to demonstrate personality change as a function of sport leisure.

This means that the extant literature is difficult to evaluate. For instance, Folkins and Sime (1981) concluded that there are no global changes on personality test scores after fitness training. However, others have reported more favourable results. For instance, Janoksi and Holmes (1981) used the 16PF to demonstrate that subjects became more imaginative, less shy, and more apprehensive after a 15-week aerobic training programme. Dienstbier (1984) reviewed four major studies using the 16PF and concluded:

> . . . there is so little agreement on specific dimensions that one could make quite different conclusions for each study if they were reviewed singly . . . Overall, of the eleven changes noted in the four studies, four are in predicted directions on two of the three strongest anxiety dimensions (p.267–8).

A major problem with this research area, like so many in the area of sport and personality, is theoretical naïvety. For instance, few researchers appear to have considered personality theory, or indeed theories, and evaluated them (and the instruments to measure personality) in terms of validity, veridicality and reliability. Once this has been done, a judicious rather than a random choice of test and theory may be made, and more robust findings shown. Secondly, it seems fairly naïve to expect changes to occur too soon after 'short, sharp, shock' exposure to sport and exercise. Whether changes are physiological or cognitive, they are likely to take place over fairly lengthy periods of time and then only minimally. Whether sporting activity changes the sympathetic nervous system functioning, or expectations and values, these occur slowly and gradually, and would presumably decay or revert to previous functioning once the activity ceased. If one takes a psychobiological view of personality, or even a genetic view, it is not at all clear how (when, where or why) something as relatively untraumatic as sport could have any major or long lasting effects on personality functioning.

A Review of Reviews

Over the years there has been a number of reviews of the area. They have differed on a whole range of dimension, so to give some flavour of these, five have been chosen.

Iso-Ahola (1976) argued that the literature can easily be categorized along two quite different approaches: the *trait* approach, which insists that personality exists in the individual being observed, and the *attributional* approach, which believes that personality is in the eye of the beholder. Despite the volume of research from the trait position, Iso-Ahola seemed highly sensitive to interactionist critiques of the trait concept and under-represents the volume of studies available. The attributional approach is seen to have various components: the process by which people attribute personality factors to others on the basis of their knowledge of their sport/leisure preferences; attribution errors in the perception of the amount of freedom that people have to choose their leisure; how participants explain the causes of success and failure in their own and others' leisure behaviour. Thus, while the trait approach is predominantly biological in conception, the attributional approach is essentially cognitive.

In their highly comprehensive, critical and thoughtful review of the relationship between sport and personality, Eysenck, Nias and Cox (1982) list a number of important conclusions. Based around the three well-defined dimensions of personality – extraversion, neuroticism and psychoticism – a number of findings are apparent: both average and superior sports people tend to be extraverted, no doubt because of their higher pain thresholds, sensation-seeking, assertiveness, competitiveness and speed of reaction. On the other hand, sports people tend to be low on neuroticism (with its attendant anxiety) but high on psychoticism, no doubt because of the aggressiveness, egocentricity and competitiveness associated with tough-mindedness. Also, body type (most frequently mesomorphic) is related both to personality and sports performance. They also conclude that the effects of sport and competition on personality are not known. State, as well as trait, measures of mood are good correlates of sporting behaviour. They note that competence in sport has a strong genetic component, accounting for between 70 per cent and 90 per cent of the variance, and that behaviour modification and therapy could be of considerable importance in leading to greater achievement in sport. They note:

> We may conclude that there are undoubtedly fairly close relationships between personality, on the one hand, and sporting activity on the other. These relationships must always be qualified by the *level of activity* reached by the competitor, by the particular *type of sport* indulged in, and even by *particular parameters* within a given sport . . . putting these approaches together, the whole field is ready and hope for research of an altogether higher quality than has been characteristic of the past two or three decades. There is already enough evidence available to show that the rewards will be considerable (p.49).

Because of the comprehensiveness of their review and the critical way in which they handled the material available to them, it is probably worth quoting all 20 concluding points of Eysenck *et al*.

1. Sportsmen and sportswomen tend to be characterized by an *extraverted* temperament. This seems equally true of outstanding performers as of average performers, physical education students, and others who are at a much lower level than Olympic participants or champions in various sports.
2. There are many different trains of argument leading from the low levels of cortical arousal level experienced by the extravert to the superior sporting performance characteristic of such individuals. Among these are: high pain thresholds, sensation-seeking, assertiveness and competitiveness, and generally a lack of cortical control and inhibition of ongoing behaviour and immediate reactions.
3. There is a tendency for athletes, particularly outstanding ones, to

be *low on neuroticism*, and to suffer less from anxiety than do non-sportsmen and women. The findings do not support this conclusion universally, but the trend is definitely in this direction, particularly with outstanding sportsmen.

4. The reaction for the negative relationship between the excellence in sport and anxiety–neuroticism lies probably in the *drive stimulus qualities* of anxiety, which distract the athlete from his appointed task. The situation is complicated because of the curvilinear relationship between anxiety as a drive, and performance; the Yerkes-Dodson law is often invoked in this connection.

5. There are few direct studies of the psychoticism–superego variable, but in general very successful athletes seem to have *higher scores on P(sychoticism)* than do less successful sportsmen or non-sporting persons. Unfortunately, less work has been done with this variable than with E and N, but the results seem fairly well established.

6. The reasons for the relationship between P and success with sport probably lies in the aggressiveness of the high P scorer, his egocentricity, and his general competitiveness. It is possible that these qualities may be less apparent in team sports, where co-operation is necessary, than in individual sports, but there are no data to support this hypothesis as yet.

7. The body-build of the typical successful athlete is *mesomorphic*, a type of physique usually associated with *extraverted* personality types. The relationship appears stronger with the physical than with the personality type.

8. *Ectomorphic* body types can also be found among successful sportsmen, although not as frequently as mesomorphic body types, and never in extreme form.

9. *Endomorphic* body forms are practically never found among successful sportsmen and women, with the exception of swimmers. Even there the endomorphic component is not likely to be strong.

10. Body type is quite markedly related to *type of sport*, with long-distance runners being relatively ectomorphic and wrestlers and weight-lifters being strongly mesomorphic. Short-distance runners seem to be intermediate between the other two groups.

11. The effects of sporting activities on personality are not really known, although there are many theories in this connection. It is often suggested that sporting activities may have a beneficial effect on personality, particularly in reducing depression and anxiety, but the evidence does not support such a view.

12. The effects of competition on personality are also not known, although here too there are many theories equally unsupported by good evidence.

13. Driving a car may be regarded as a sporting activity, and is quite

definitely related to personality, in the sense that both *extraversion and neuroticism* are positively related to accident proneness. The combination of high-N and high-E is uniquely favourable for the occurrence of driving accidents.

14. Sexual activity too may be regarded as partaking of the characteristics of a sport, these activities being carried out in many cases for amusement, and being physical in nature. Here too *extraversion* has been found to be the personality component most commonly correlated with different types of sexual activity, such as early sexual activity, activity involving many different partners, activity indulged in frequently, etc. *Neuroticism* appears to have a negative influence on sexual activity, being associated with frigidity, impotence, lack of orgasmic capacity, and other disorders.

15. *State measures* of mood may correlate even more highly with athletic performance and sporting activity generally than do traits. Anxiety in particular has been found to be so related when state rather than trait measures are taken. The same is true of feelings of energy, competitiveness, and other similar states. This is a promising area which has not been investigated sufficiently.

16. Most investigations use groups which are too heterogeneous to give clear-cut results. It has been found that even in apparently homogeneous groups, such as shooters, different types of shooting are correlated with quite different personality traits, by depending on such things as time allowed for reaction to the stimulus, etc. Where little time is allowed, *extraverts* excel but where much time is allowed, *introverts* do quite well. Such finer distinctions should always be looked at in future research.

17. Physical skills learning, and the strategies which are being developed, are also related to personality, and this type of study has been done almost exclusively in the laboratory. An integration of this experimental approach with the study of sport-type situations could be of considerable importance in throwing a new light on the relation between sport and personality.

18. Genetic factors are known to determine to a large extent both personality and physique; it has also been shown that competence in many different sporting activities has a strong genetic component, accounting for between seventy and ninety per cent of the total variance. This finding does not suggest that training cannot help people to improve their performance, but it does suggest that selection for sport in general, and for specific types of sport in particular, should take account both of personality and physique.

19. Behaviour modification, i.e. the application of psychological principles to learning and improvement in sport, could be of considerable importance in leading to greater achievement in sport. The possibility

of these methods has not yet been explored sufficiently to make any more definite statement.

20.   The technique of behaviour therapy (desensitization, flooding, modelling) could be of considerable use in reducing anxiety insofar as this interferes with optimum performance. Here the evidence for the general usefulness of these methods is very much stronger than in the case of the methods of behaviour modification, but little has been written about their application to sportsmen and women in particular. This illustrates the relative isolation of psychology from sport, and suggests that we already have methods of training and treatment which could with advantage be applied in this field (p.47–8).

Nias (1985), who examined the relationship between personality and recreational behaviour, stressed the importance of classifying interests, not all of which are usually described in sports. Various taxonomies are available depending largely on the nature (number, detail, type) of items selected for analysis *and* the statistical method chosen. After reviewing half a dozen or so studies he concludes:

> . . . personality has been shown to be related to interest preferences, but at a rather low level. Perhaps because of the specific nature of interest factors, it is expecting too much for general personality dimensions to show anything other than tenuous relationships to them. A more fruitful approach might be to relate specific personality traits to the interest factors (p.285).

Nias was clearly influenced by need theory and concerned with the motives that people have for pursuing specific interests. He also points out both a genetic component to interest preference as well as the notion of family influence on interest development. Finally, he points out that the current state of the literature does not allow for accurate 'leisure guidance' along the lines of vocational guidance, but that work is moving in that direction.

Davies (1989) argues quite rightly that myths and over-simplistic viewpoints exist in the area of psychological factors and performance in competitive sport. Many factors like technical ability and skill, speed of movement, physical fitness, persistence, anticipation, concentration and temperament combine to determine excellence at sport. He lists, somewhat arbitrarily, and discusses eight 'psychological' factors that are thought to influence sporting behaviour, personality and adjustment: past experience of tournament play; availability of psychological support and counselling; social pressures; persistence; confidence and concentration; mental preparation; and motivation. Davies believes that all self-report measures of personality have problems because of dissimulation and because people are not always able to report accurately on their needs. However, he is convinced both of the importance of extraversion and neuroticism in predicting and explaining sports performance:

> It does seem to be the case that on balance sportsmen who compete at international level are extroverted and emotionally stable. They tend to be dominant, tough-minded, self-assured, self-confident, and with a high capacity to endure the pressures of competitive sport. They are temperamentally robust ... Research also shows that extraverts are less adversely affected by distracting stimuli such as, for example, the noise and movement of the crowd and tend to enjoy performing in the company of others rather than in seclusion. On the other hand, however, extraverts are likely to be at a disadvantage in sports in which the emphasis is on accuracy ... For such sports as rifle-shooting and archery which call for calm, slow, and deliberate preparation the quick impulsive nature of the extravert is therefore likely to be a handicap (p.145–6).

Finally, Vealey (1989) has updated a review by Martens (1975) of the sport and personology literature published between 1950 and 1970. Martens categorized the literature as experimental (10 per cent), correlational (89 per cent) and clinical (1 per cent), and found evidence of methodological problems (poor operationalization of variables, poor sampling, inappropriate instrumentation, and biased statistical analysis) as well as interpretive errors (improper inferences to causal relationships from correlational data, unsupported generalization, and improper prediction of sports success from clinical personality assessment). Vealey's review update has four aims: the examination of paradigmatic trends from 1974 to 1989; to examine predominant methodologies; to identify the primary objectives of sport personality research; to identify what we know about the role of personality in sport-based research. The methodology involved a content analysis of 11 prominent journals carrying personality and sport research. He found that 68 per cent of the studies were correlational, 28 per cent experimental and 4 per cent clinical. The research settings varied between survey methodology (26 per cent); field studies (25 per cent); laboratory experiments (23 per cent); field survey (15 per cent) and field experiments (11 per cent). A statistical analysis of the content analysis showed that the trait approach decreased markedly from 1974 to 1981 whereas the cognitive approach showed a marked increase during this time. Also, the trait–state approach increased from the early 1970s but this approach never demonstrated great popularity.

Seventy-four per cent of the studies in the trait–state paradigm and 67 per cent of those in the cognitive paradigm were theoretical whereas 70 per cent of the studies in the trait paradigm were atheoretical. In terms of method, it was interesting that the trait (80 per cent) and trait-state (68 per cent) paradigms primarily used correlational methods whereas the cognitive paradigm (51 per cent correlational, 42 per cent experimental,

7 per cent clinical) demonstrated more of the methodological balance
... The areas that demonstrated the highest proportions of theoretical
research were attributions (97 per cent), self-confidence (77 per cent),
anxiety (74 per cent), and motivation (74 per cent). The areas that
demonstrated the highest proportions of atheoretical research were
personality profiles (87 per cent), self-concept/self-esteem (84 per cent),
and cognitive strategies (82 per cent) (p.224).

Vealey answered his four major questions thus:

- Classic trait approaches have declined in favour of a trait–state fit such
  that individuals with different dispositions are seen to react to situations
  with state responses that contribute to their behavioural responses.
- Methodologically, the field has become more balanced with fewer correlational and more experimental studies, yet there remain serious problems:
  uni-variate as opposed to multi-variate designs and analyses, and the misuse
  of psychological theories and measures.
- Research remains equally divided into questions about structure (description) and dynamics (prediction) with a small percentage interested in
  modification (intervention).
- Most progress has been in areas characterized by established theoretical
  bases in attribution research, self-confidence, anxiety and modification.

Future Research in Sport and Personality

Feltz (1987) argued for three different but related approaches to expanding
a framework for understanding in sports psychology: first, more expan-
sive process-orientated conceptualizations and idea manipulation; second,
more systematic consideration of the influence of context on interpersonal
characteristics; and, thirdly, a multi-variate research approach that focuses
on planned and systematic programs that emphasize multi-variate causal
models.

Many researchers agree that the standard of research in sports psychology
has been poor. A number of factors have been consistently mentioned: poor
choice of theories or alternatively a-theoretical, dustbowl-empirical research;
poor measurement (unreliable and invalid) of both the independent and
dependent variable; poor sampling of subjects; simplistic and sometimes
erroneous statistical analysis; going beyond the information given by over-
interpreting results; and few, if any, longitudinal studies. The recognition of
these shortcomings may go a long way to eliminate them, to make sports
and leisure psychological research truly scientific.

The search for sport and leisure correlates of personality has yielded
modest results given nearly 30 years of effort. Neither studies using
personality/individual difference variables as the independent or dependent

variable have shown up many robust, powerful or theoretically surprising results. This is despite a sustained, if naïve, research effort and, more importantly, despite the personal experience that the personality of people playing different sports, or those good vs bad at a given sport, is noticeably different.

There are eight possible reasons why this is the case. Firstly, weak, invalid or inappropriate personality theories have been selected to investigate the area. Secondly, the measurement techniques (rather than the theory on which it is based) have been unreliable, invalid, too open to dissimulation, or uni-variate rather than multi-variate. Thirdly, it could be that the personality traits selected, although appropriately conceived and measured, simply do not relate to or predict the sporting behaviour specified.

On the other hand, the problem might lie with the measurement of the sport or leisure behaviour. This could be either because the behavioural measure needs to be aggregated into a reliable and robust measure; or because the measure is open to some systematic error. Fifthly, the sport or leisure-related behaviour may be shaped or constrained by other more powerful factors than personality-like ability. Sixthly, personality may be more of a moderator variable than a direct predictor of sport-related behaviour, and thus its force depends on a wide range of other variables being present and specified. Seventh, poor unrepresentative samples have 'washed out' or suppressed (or, indeed, in some cases exaggerated) the relationship between sport and personality for practical reasons. Finally, through self-selection and selection by others, people with inappropriate traits for the sport leave or are not invited to continue, thus reducing the possibility of finding an effect.

Thus, for both theoretical and methodological reasons, it remains difficult to evaluate the evidence for the relationship between sport (leisure) and personality. But the evidence of this and other reviews points to a guarded optimism where the quality of research is on the rise and hence the question central to this review can be answered.

9.3 PERSONALITY AND UNEMPLOYMENT

Are some personalities more likely to find themselves unemployed than others? How well do people with different personalities cope with unemployment? Recent research on individual difference (including personality) correlates of unemployment have considered personality both as the dependent *and* independent variable, but the vast majority of research studies in this area have looked at the effect of unemployment on personality functioning, rather than how personality differences relate to job seeking and maintenance.

In essence, three types of individual difference variable have been looked at in this area:

- Measures of mental health, particularly *minor psychiatric morbidity* as measured by instruments such as the General Health Questionnaire (GHQ), *depression* (often measured by the Beck Depression Inventory or BDI), *anxiety* and *neuroticism*, as well as psychoticism.
- Measures of *self-esteem*, *life satisfaction*, and other measures of *well-being*.
- Measures of *attributional style*, particularly *locus of control*, but also the standard attributional dimensions like stability and globality.

There are many ways of categorizing research in this area:

- *Type of study*. Most studies have been cross-sectional but some have been longitudinal, the latter having the significant advantage of being clearer about direction of causality.
- *Subjects involved*. These have included young vs old; professional vs unskilled; men vs women; school-leavers vs the young unemployed. Results have not been very inconsistent, suggesting some general patterns of findings.
- *Variable measures*. As set out above, these have been numerous, which makes issues of comparison difficult.

The most common type of psychological study has concentrated exclusively on the mental/physical health and psychological *well-being* of unemployed people, examining individual differences as the dependent variable. This usually involves the administration of a self-report on minor psychiatric morbidity (usually the GHQ or Langner 22 index). These tests have been found to be valid, reliable, predictive and discriminatory measures of mental health. Banks, Clegg and Jackson (1982) compared the mental health (as measured by the GHQ) of employees in an engineering firm, recent school-leavers and a group of unemployed men. They found, as predicted, that the unemployed group, and women more than men, had scores indicating lower mental health but that these scores were unrelated to age, job level or marital status.

Furnham (1983) looked at the mental health (as measured on the Langner index) of five groups depending on their employment status: full-time employed; part-time employed; unemployed; retired; and students. Although there were no age or sex differences in the total mental health score, there was a significant difference between the five employment groups' total score with the full-time employed having the lowest (best adjusted) score, the retired and students having moderately high scores, and the unemployed and the part-time employed having the highest scores. The part-time employed people's score was almost as high as, and not significantly different from, that of the unemployed. There could be many reasons for this. Firstly, people seeking full-time work may take a part-time job which they do not like, and which is not well paid, simply as an interim measure. Secondly, people with other commitments, such as a family and handicapped relatives, may only be able to take a part-time job which, because of travelling and other stress, is too much for them and leads to mental distress. Thirdly, some part-time work is very casual in that it is for very short periods only; thus, instead of giving the benefits of work, it does the precise opposite. Certainly, future study on the part-time employed would do well to tease apart these various hypotheses by getting subjects to stipulate clearly why they have chosen part-time employment, how long they intend to be in the job, and what the hours are. With the prospect of increased job sharing, the importance of part-time employment is likely to rise.

Swinburne (1981) also attempted to look at the psychological impact of unemployment on managers and professional staff. In the interview study, she questioned subjects on their feelings about being unemployed, the problems of structuring time, and their job search process. She found that although the experience of unemployment varied according to individual circumstances, certain trends were apparent. Many (50 per cent) reported initial shock and fear/uncertainty about the future, but as few as 10 per cent reported shame, and loss of status and self-respect. Although the negativity of their initial reactions appeared less than reported elsewhere, they appeared to pass through the various hypothetical stages much more slowly.

Not all studies on unemployment have been retrospective. Jenkins et al. (1982) carried out a prospective study to examine the effects of the threat of journalists' promised redundancy on minor psychiatric morbidity. Each subject was tested three times: two months prior to closure (one month after receiving notice of redundancy), immediately after redundancy notices were revoked and work continued under a new proprietor, and then three months after the threat of redundancy had been removed. Despite various methodological problems, it was unambiguously demonstrated that subsequent to the withdrawal of redundancy notices, there was a considerable reduction in minor symptomatology.

Hepworth (1980) looked at moderating factors in the relationship between unemployment and mental health. She found that length of unemployment was inversely correlated with mental health and well-being; semi-skilled and unskilled men were less well adjusted than those of higher occupational status; and that the best predictor of the unemployed's mental health was whether or not they felt that their time was occupied. In a re-analysis of this data, Brenner and Bartell (1983) found that with the passage of time a reciprocal process takes place in which mental health affects subjective well-being and the proportion of time occupied. The authors suggest that there may well be a 'critical period' immediately following job loss in which time adaptation may or may not occur. Poor adaptation leads to a vicious circle which results in increased negative effects with time. More recently, time-budgeting studies have attempted to investigate this relationship between time structuring and adaptation.

It has been argued that the self-concept is a schema which locates the individual within the social environment and shapes his/her interactions with it. Hence, becoming unemployed causes psychological dislocation and disorientation which induces a modification of the self-concept. Tiffany, Cowan and Tiffany (1970) administered the Tennessee Self-concept Scale to two comparable groups, one in work and one not, and found that the profile of the unemployed group reflected a lower level of self-esteem. The unemployed had significantly less faith or confidence in themselves, and saw themselves as less desirable, doubted their worth more, and felt more anxious, depressed and unhappy than the employed group. This pattern has been studied by Allerhand *et al.* (1969), Hodgson and Brenner (1968), and Teahan (1969); all of them found lower self-esteem in the previously unemployed compared to the previously employed. Briar (1977) has also noted a desire for secrecy and a distancing in the unemployed which appears to be a means of protecting themselves against being labelled failures and 'welfare dependent'.

In Canada, Burke (1984) was concerned with the correlates of well-being 16 months after a work force of 177 were made redundant. He found that individuals who found less favourable, less well paid, or temporary jobs reported less life satisfaction, as did those who were currently unemployed. Also, individuals earning low hourly pay rates reported more psychosomatic symptoms, and individuals unemployed for more weeks in the intervening 16-month period reported less general satisfaction and greater alcohol consumption. Although the results were consistent with previous studies, the psychological effect of job loss was modest.

Of course, a familiar problem plagues the self-esteem and unemployment literature – that is, correlation and cause. It is possible that those with low self-esteem and poor self-concept are more susceptible to unemployment rather than unemployment reducing self-esteem. However, what is more probable is that both occur together, only exacerbating each other.

Another important source of data on the relationship between unemployment and *health* concerns studying the characteristics of unemployed people admitted to mental hospitals, because this helps to unravel the direction of causality. Fruensgaard *et al.* (1983a) investigated the psychosomatic characteristics of a group of unemployed patients consecutively admitted to a psychiatric emergency clinic in Denmark. They found that alcohol abuse was registered in two-thirds of their sample of 70, and about half were found to be habitual neurotics with a tendency to anti-social behaviour while intoxicated. However, only 4 per cent had never suffered from a mental disorder requiring treatment prior to their unemployment; indeed, 41 per cent had previously been admitted to a mental hospital and 60 per cent were on sick leave prior to dismissal from unemployment. Despite the fact that this sample was hardly typical or representative, and that there were other potential causal factors giving rise to mental disease as well as unemployment, it was noted that anxiety, depression, and neurasthenic and psychotic illness were accentuated by, or commenced with, unemployment. In a follow-up study, Fruensgaard *et al.* (1983b) found that in most of the sample there had been a drop in alcohol and drug abuse and an improvement in mental health. Most importantly, they found that those who had succeeded in getting work and/or those who had favourable employment experiences were 'stronger' than those who did not get employment, and had a significantly lower frequency of previous admission to the psychiatric department and of sick leave prior to unemployment. Thus, it seems that the relationship between mental health and unemployment is bi-directional. The mentally unstable are less likely to find employment than the mentally stable, but lack of employment accentuates the problem, whereas employment does the opposite.

However, there are some studies that have looked at the relationship between personality and reactions to unemployment using recognizable and well-known personality questionnaires.

Evans (1981) hypothesized that high psychoticism scorers may actually generate their own stress, and found business adjustment, change in financial state, change in responsibility, trouble with boss, among others, to be stressors to which people were particularly vulnerable. The addition of an environmental stress component may aggravate genetic predisposition with regard to psychology. Furnham (1987b) found that the unemployed were less stable (i.e. more neurotic) than the employed, although cause and correlation are unclear. Lewis (1935) and Shanthamani (1973) commented on the higher levels of neurosis among the unemployed. Fineman (1983) found, using the N scale of the EPI, that 64 unemployed managers differed significantly from the general population, and professional and managerial norms as provided by the EPI manual. The problem with these studies is, of course, that one is unable to draw unequivocal results regarding causality, though Fineman concluded that the higher N scores in the unemployed may have been the cause of their job loss, suggesting a degree of social Darwinism. Ormel (1983), using three neuroticism inventories, suggested a complex interaction between personality, life events, difficulties and a person's well-being, and Cherry (1976) found that N and E, or their interaction, as measured by a short version of the MPI, have predictive power for men, concerning problems as a result of frequent job changing.

Wunderlich (1934), Eisenberg and Lazarsfeld (1938), and Bakke (1940) all reported decreased social participation and a more introverted outlook on life for their unemployed subjects. Furnham (1987b) found the unemployed, when compared to the full-time employed, to be more introverted. Clearly, the shy, retiring, reserved manner of the introvert could account for their inability to secure work, when the more adventurous, social and optimistic extravert might more easily acquire employment in times of high unemployment.

It is possible that the personality differences between the employed and unemployed are even greater than those between holders of different jobs. MacLean (1977) administered Cattell's 16 Personality Factor Questionnaire to unemployed married men between the ages of 25 and 40 who had at least average intelligence and education, and no physical disability. These men were more neurotic, psychotic and introverted than matched controls, especially when they had been without work for a long time. There is some doubt about causality here, since their inadequate personalities may have rendered them unemployable, or the degradation of unemployment may have affected their personality, or both.

Fineman (1979a) has looked specifically at psychological stress induced by managerial unemployment. He interviewed 25 unemployed managers and also gave them a battery of tests. Predictably, they had high GHQ scores, indicating psychological disturbance almost twice the national average, yet their *16PF* scores fell within the normal range. Whereas some managers seemed highly stressed by unemployment, others seemed to enjoy it. What appeared to characterize the high stress group was prior high personal involvement in the job, belief in personal competence, domestic problems, failure in job applications, and learned helplessness. Low-stress cases, on the other hand, perceived their problem in low-threat terms, had previous low job involvement, strong belief in personal worth, and a direct, confronting (as opposed to avoidance, passive) approach to problems. From his rich but unquantifiable data, Fineman draws a number of conclusions. Stress in unemployment arises from the interaction of four factors: an individual's perception of the environment, personality, experienced threat, and behaviour in response to threat. Direct confrontation is the only form of behaviour which can involve mastering the problem of stress; a stressed person needs to be encouraged to examine his/her perception of environmental demands.

Perhaps the kind of study which is most needed but is fairly rare is the path analytic study of Lynn, Hampson and Magee (1984) who tried to determine which variables predicted unemployment in young people. They used the EPQ to attempt to increase the explanatory power of the model by including personality traits. It was found that home background, intelligence, personality, school type and educational attainments all had significant effects on unemployment. For instance, home background exerts a direct influence on unemployment, but it is also indirect through its effects on intelligence, school type, educational attainment, psychoticism and status aspiration. Personality and motivational variables did not discriminate between the employed and unemployed, but multiple regressional analysis showed that psychoticism was predictive and that unemployed males were lower than employed young males or those in further education. They note:

This may be a surprising result in view of the association of psychoticism with mental disorders and psychopathy, which might lead to the expectation that the unemployed would be higher in psychoticism rather than lower. Possibly the explanation may be in the assertiveness component of psychoticism, motivating young men to seek and obtain the status and financial advantages of employment, either immediately or eventually after further education. The result indicates that psychoticism may be a socially useful trait to have at moderate values (p.556).

The path model is presented in Figure 9.1.

Layton and Eysenck (1985) gave the EPQ to 186 male school-leavers, and 101 male skilled and semi-skilled workers facing redundancy. Whereas extraversion and neuroticism showed no significant difference, the unemployed group had higher psychoticism scores (see Table 9.1). They note:

Immature, irresponsible, troublesome, solitary, hostile, anti-authoritarian, independent, non-conformist, querulous and generally difficult to handle are not exactly characteristics, though of course the question is one of degree, that enhance employment selection. It may be that such high scorers lack the necessary social skills required to present themselves in

Predictors of unemployment in young people

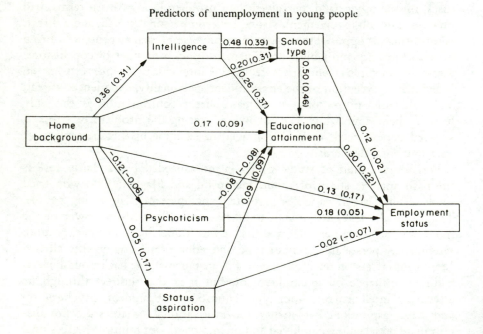

Figure 9.1 Path model for employment status for males and females (in parentheses)
Source: Lynn, Hampson and Magee (1984)

a favourable light with prospective employers. However, it seems likely that such individuals might not be so inclined to look for work (p.388).

Table 9.1 One-way ANOVA on E, N, P and L by work status, contrasting the gainfully employed with the unemployed: school group

	Employed (N = 77)		Unemployed (N = 29)		Further Education (N = 80)				Contrast	
	x	SD	x	SD	x	SD	F	P	t	p
E	14.67	4.20	14.03	4.78	15.11	4.55	0.66	0.52	0.93	0.35
N	9.10	4.30	8.62	4.83	7.77	4.85	1.64	0.20	0.19	0.85
P	4.90	3.47	7.10	4.78	3.30	2.59	14.21	0.0001	4.39	0.001
L	8.62	3.90	7.79	3.72	7.76	4.21	1.02	0.36	0.49	0.62

Source: Layton and Eysenck (1985)

It should be pointed out that the above two studies yielded contradictory findings. There may well be methodological explanations for this: comparability; representativeness of samples; measurement skill and unreliability. Both researcher groups had, however, no difficulty in finding explanations for their results.

In a more recent, and methodologically more sophisticated, longitudinal study, Payne (1988) tested 75 unemployed men on three occasions over a period of two years. At time three in the study, neuroticism was measured using the EPI to test the hypothesis that large inter-correlations among the negatively termed scales (of anxiety, depression, psychometric morbidity)

Table 9.2 Correlations between extraversion and neuroticism and the main variables for employed and unemployed samples[a]

	Extraversion		Neuroticism	
Variable	Unemployed	Employed	Unemployed	Employed
GHQ-12	−0.06	−0.04	0.65	0.34
Anxiety	0.01	−0.11	0.76	0.69
Depression	0.02	−0.23	0.46	0.57
Yesterday's strain	0.08	−0.06	0.36	0.36
Yesterday's pleasure	−0.17	0.16	−0.21	−0.34
Externality	−0.01	−0.08	0.50	0.45
Employment commitment	0.04	0.20	0.32	0.09
Financial worries	0.07	0.25	0.48	0.28
Problems	0.03	−0.11	0.63	0.64
Support and constraints	0.01	[b]	0.01	[b]

[a]For extraversion, N = 92 (unemployed), 31 (employed)
[b]Not measured.
Source: Payne (1988)

were the result of trait neuroticism. The results are shown in Table 9.2. Whereas extraversion showed low, non-significant correlations, neuroticism was correlated very highly with all of the measures except 'yesterday's pleasure'.

Payne notes that the results suggest that reactions to unemployment are heavily affected by an individual's tendency to experience anxiety. He also wonders if the stability in measures like GHQ and the perceived environment variables (that he found) were largely due to the fact that they both have a close relationship with the (by definition, stable trait of) neuroticism. The issue is an important one and concerns the possibility that personality variables are moderator variables.

Traditional personality traits have been rather neglected in the unemployment literature which appears to have been a major omission. It seems, however, that whereas extraversion is not a very important correlate and determinant of unemployment, neuroticism and psychoticism are.

One personality variable that has attracted a great deal of attention in this area is attributional style, particularly locus of control (Feather, 1986; O'Brien and Kabanoff, 1979; Hesketh, 1984). For instance, Ostell and Divers (1987) tested the hypotheses that people with an internal attributional style will experience poor mental health if they make characterological attributions about unemployment and its consequences, but not if they make behavioural (or external) attributions. They confirmed those hypotheses and thus saw attributional style a major coping mechanism. Winefield, Tiggeman and Smith (1987) tested a similar thesis on employed and unemployed young people and found limited support for the hypotheses. Specifically, the kind of causal attributions made for bad outcomes proved better predictors than attributions for good outcomes for the unemployed, but the reverse for the employed.

The employed who made internal attributions for good outcomes displayed both higher self-esteem and lower depressive effect than those giving external attributions. Similarly, in the unemployed, the girls giving unstable attributions for bad outcomes were higher in self-esteem than those giving stable attributions for bad outcomes and boys giving unstable attributions were lower in depressive effect than those giving stable attributions. The employed girls who gave unstable attributions for bad outcomes were also lower in depressive effect than those giving stable attributions.

For the unemployed girls, an earlier tendency to attribute bad outcomes to external causes was associated with lower depressive effect; in the employed boys, an earlier tendency to attribute good outcomes to internal causes was associated with higher self-esteem; and in the employed girls, an earlier tendency to attribute good outcomes to stable causes was also associated with higher self-esteem. There was no relation between earlier causal attributions for good outcomes and current measures of self-esteem and depressive effect in the unemployed, neither was there any relation between earlier causal attributions for bad outcomes and current measures of self-esteem and depressive effect in the employed.

The Work Ethic and the Unemployed

Furnham (1990b) entertained a number of hypotheses concerning the Protestant work ethic (PWE) of the unemployed:

- Unemployed people with strong PWE beliefs would become more depressed, anxious and apathetic than unemployed people who did not believe in the PWE.
- Unemployed people with strong PWE beliefs would participate more frequently in a greater range of non-work (but work-like or work-substitute) activities than people who did not believe in the PWE.
- Unemployed people with strong PWE beliefs would persevere with more effort and over a longer period to get a job than unemployed people who did not believe in the PWE.
- Belief in the PWE would gradually decrease the longer a person remained unemployed.

He also reviewed studies which threw light on the above.

Shamir (1985) examined over 400 adults in Israel, all of whom had been employed. Contrary to his hypothesis, however, he found that individuals with a high PWE turn to non-work activities more frequently while unemployed and derive more psychological benefit from such activities than individuals low on PWE beliefs. Thus, it appears that PWE beliefs contribute to, rather than hinder, coping strategies useful while unemployed. There may be some sort of 'spill-over' principle where stable, intellectual and motivational coping styles associated with the PWE in the occupational role get transferred to non-work activities:

> In summary, the results of this study raise some doubts concerning the claim that a reduction in the PWE would automatically lead to coping better with unemployment. In fact, the opposite might be true. Rather than fighting the Protestant work ethic, a more realistic strategy would be to harness it and channel it to non-employment related work and to other non-work activities which have the potential for answering individuals' needs for activity structure, social meaning and intellectual stimulation (p.344).

In a related study, Shamir (1986) tested various hypotheses about the psychological well-being of unemployed individuals, focusing on the moderating effects of the PWE. Contrary to predictions, the PWE did not moderate the relationship between employment status and psychological state, although various methodological problems could account for them. Thus, Shamir (1986) concludes:

> There is also no evidence in our study that the Protestant work ethic hinders the processes of coping with unemployment in any way or that individuals who 'free' themselves of the ethic find unemployment easier to bear (p.36).

Furthermore, using the same data, Shamir (1987) was able to demonstrate that people's belief in, and adherence to, the PWE is *not* influenced by their change in work status in and out of work. This implies both that the PWE is a relatively stable dispositional factor, but also that the experience of unemployment does not lead to work inhibitions.

Shamir's work would appear to indicate that PWE beliefs do not adversely affect people who are unemployed; indeed, they may even make adjustment to worklessness better. However, it should be pointed out that these results are based on a limited sample of middle-class Israelis. It is quite probable that variables than other than the PWE mediate between unemployment and psychological reactions such as class, self-esteem, attributional style, coping strategies etc. In fact, the studies on young people – school-leavers – have tended to examine those other factors and, as a result, come up with a rather different set of findings concerning the moderator effects of the PWE.

Some studies, both cross-sectional and longitudinal, have looked at the PWE and other moderators between unemployment and psychological well-being in young people (Lynn *et al.*, 1984). Feather (1982), in a cross-sectional study, showed that unemployed young males had lower PWE scores than employed male subjects, and that active pursuit of employment tended to be more frequent among those with higher self-esteem, stronger PWE values, and lower apathy. However, it is only by longitudinal studies that it is possible to separate cause from correlation. Feather and O'Brien (1986a,b) in fact reported on a longitudinal study of nearly 3000 Australian school-leavers. They found that those young people who did not find work, compared to those who did, tend to see themselves as less competent, pleasant and active; to report more stress and depressive effect but less satisfaction with life; to have lower PWE scores; and to rate their need for a job as less important. But the PWE scores did not change in time such that the high scores of the employed remained much the same and significantly higher than the unemployed at both time periods. However, Feather and O'Brien (1986b) showed that for those who changed their status there were significant changes: those who were employed and then became unemployed tended to show a decrease in their PWE score, while those who went from unemployment into employment showed a significant increase in their PWE score. They also found that PWE beliefs in both the employed and unemployed were correlated with feelings that one needed a job, the perceived attractiveness of work, self-perceptions of competence and life satisfaction, and the perception that the unemployed lack motivation. More recently, in a study of 320 young unemployed people, Feather and O'Brien (1987) found that their perceived desirability of being employed was positively related to their endorsement of the PWE.

Longitudinal Studies on Unemployment

The importance of longitudinal studies in disentangling causes and correlation has already been mentioned.

In a study of the effect of *social support* in moderating the health consequences of unemployment, Gore (1978) interviewed 100 married men who previously had been stably employed but had suddenly been made redundant. The men were interviewed five times over a two-year period. She was particularly interested in the effect of supportive and affiliative relations with wife, friends and relatives on the unemployed man's illness symptoms. She found that the rural unemployed, because of the ethnic ties and concern in a small community, had a higher level of support than the urban unemployed. In addition, the unsupported unemployed had significantly greater levels of cholesterol illness symptoms and emotional response than did the supported. The author argued that these results demonstrated not so much that support buffers the effects of life stress, but rather a low sense/level of social support exacerbates life stress. Unemployment, in large part, means the inability to make instrumental accomplishments. Thus, it might be interpreted that this loss in the absence of a continuing sense of self-worth maintained through supportive relationships contributes to negative health responses. In this research, it is impossible to point to specific behaviours of others which ameliorated life stress. It thus makes more sense to explain the more negative responses of some terminees as the exacerbation of the unemployment experience by a low sense of social support.

Warr, Jackson and Banks (1982) have attempted a longitudinal study looking at the duration of unemployment and psychological well-being in young men and women. The importance of longitudinal studies cannot be ignored. To establish a relationship between unemployment and psychological distress tells one nothing of causation, merely correlation. It is possible that the less psychologically adjusted are prone to unemployment, or are indeed unemployable! In all, two cohorts of recent school-leavers were interviewed over a two-year period, but measures of psychological stress and self-esteem were found to be uncorrelated with the duration of unemployment for young men. In fact, in one cohort, the women appeared to be better adjusted the longer they were unemployed, apparently because of their reduced commitment to the labour market along with a stronger personal involvement in family matters. The authors offer two (compatible) explanations for their puzzling findings. The association between well-being and length of unemployment may differ between age groups (older people with more commitments may experience greater distress). Also, it may only be that longer periods of unemployment than those studied here lead to distress.

Banks *et al.* (1982) interviewed two age cohorts of young people up to two and a half years after leaving school to investigate the association between unemployment and risk of minor psychiatric morbidity. They found a positive relationship between unemployment and morbidity after controlling for sex, ethnic group and educational qualifications. Furthermore, longitudinal analyses showed that the experience of unemployment was more likely to create increased psychological symptoms, rather than the reverse. Jackson *et al.* (1983) studied longitudinally two cohorts of young people in the first three years of their working lives. They found, as predicted, that psychological distress is higher for the unemployed than for the employed and that changes in employment status lead to changes in distress score.

More recently, Stokes and Cochrane (1984) completed a longitudinal investigation of the psychological consequences of redundancy and unemployment, looking at general symptomatology, hostility, social attitudes and life satisfaction. The results showed that the redundant workers who remained without work for at least six months had significantly more psychological symptoms; total hostility (including criticism of other, paranoid hostility and guilt); reduced self-satisfaction and acceptance by others. They failed to confirm previous stage models of unemployment but felt that this may have been due to the exceptionally good redundancy arrangement for this group which facilitated a lengthy period of constructive adjustment and optimism.

9.4 PERSONALITY AND ADJUSTMENT TO RETIREMENT

While the unemployed and the retired are both out of work, and experience an often sizeable drop in income, the latter appear much happier. But are some retired people happier than others? Why do some people opt for early retirement while others plead to stay at work even to an advanced age? Which personality factors relate to retirement satisfaction and which to retirement activities?

Argyle (1989) has noted various factors which relate to retirement satisfaction:

1. *Health* has been found to predict satisfaction in all studies, although the effect is modest, typically 0.2 to 0.3.
2. *Finance* is a predictor in most studies but had no effect in a study of retired American managers.
3. *Purpose in life*, life interest and self-esteem, was the strongest predictor in a study of retired British managers.
4. *Having strong interests*, old or new, is important, as is belonging to

educational, leisure or other organizations. The main predictors of satisfaction were the amount of social interaction and the number of different activities, not the use of skills.

5. *Education and social class* can predict satisfaction in retirement. Although middle-class people are giving up more interesting jobs, they have more resources and leisure interests with which to replace work. Managers find it difficult to accept the loss of responsibility, professionals can keep up their skills and interests more.

6. Satisfaction can be predicted when retirement is *voluntary and planned*. However, the effects of pre-retirement courses are found to be negligible.

7. *Married women* have the least difficulty in adjusting to retirement (p.303–4).

He was also concerned with delineating the experience of being unemployed vs retired:

> What is the explanation for these dramatic differences between the welfare of the unemployed and the retired? It must be because retirement is an accepted and honourable social status, while unemployment is not. Retirement is seen as a proper reward for a hard life's work, while unemployment has the implication of failure, being unwanted, a scrounger, living on charity (p.306).

Research in the area has, however, produced some fairly consistent findings:

- Most workers look forward to retirement and have a positive attitude toward it.
- Those with positive attitudes toward retirement tend to be: younger, with higher education, having had fewer episodes of unemployment; have a higher expected retirement income; and tend to be in better health.
- The relationship of retirement attitudes to occupational status appears curvilinear in that those at both ends of the spectrum have more negative attitudes.
- Specific work role variables appear to have a limited influence; neither work commitment nor job satisfaction appear to have a major association with attitude toward retirement, although it is possible that some specific component is of some significance to retirement.
- The transition from before to after retirement is not associated with any immediate reliable major health status changes.
- There seems a slight tendency for unskilled workers to show a mild improvement in health status and for the other groups to show a mild decline.
- Comparisons of retirees with those continuing to work showed that in both groups a little over 40 per cent were classified as 'no change';

among those changing, there was a slight excess of improvements in the retirees and slight excess of decrements in health among those continuing to work.

Kasl (1980) in a lengthy and scholarly review came to the following six-point conclusion:

1. The evidence does not suggest that the transition from work to retirement is accompanied by an adverse impact – on the average – on physical health of the person. This conclusion is based on results from a variety of studies using different designs and assessing mortality, morbidity, and self-reported health status. The consistency of the findings is difficult to dismiss, even though each study by itself is vulnerable to criticism. A few studies suggest an improvement in health status following retirement, but they all depend on self-assessed health status. And there is every reason to suspect that with the removal of work-role demands following retirement, the whole subjective framework for self-evaluation of health changes.

2. Similarly, the evidence does not suggest that retirement has an adverse impact – on the average – on mental health and well-being. Differences between employed and retired tend to wash out when one adjusts for age, health status, income, and functional disability. Evidence for probable adverse impact does exist but it is very rare and reflects only a narrow domain of functioning or well-being, such as lowered perceived usefulness.

3. Variations in post-retirement outcomes are most convincingly seen as reflecting continuities of pre-retirement status, particularly in the areas of physical health, social and leisure activities, and general well-being and satisfaction.

4. Certain predictors of outcome, such as prior attitudes toward the process of retirement and expectations about post-retirement outcomes, appear to make their contribution primarily via their association with underlying variables, such as prior health status and financial aspects of retirement. Consequently, they do not indicate the differential impact of retirement but rather reflect, once again, the continuities noted in the previous point.

5. Variables reflecting aspects of the work-role (such as job satisfaction, work commitment) do not appear to be powerful or consistent predictors of outcomes. This conclusion may be viewed as somewhat of a surprise and those who do not wish to accept it can rightfully argue that the cumulative evidence is not yet very compelling. Nevertheless, should future studies support it, it may be necessary to reconceptualize the process and the status of retirement and reduce the prominence of work-role dimensions.

6. Financial considerations dominate the entire picture and represent the

most obvious target for ameliorating the condition of retired elderly. However, adaptation to reduced income is a poorly understood process, and the effects of changes in income on health status and medical care utilization may be small (p.176).

Studies on retirement have been longitudinal (following people through the latter years of work to retiring) or cross-sectional (comparing pre-retired and retired people of comparable age, sex, class etc). The latter cross-sectional studies are cheaper and hence more common. For instance, Gigy (1985) compared pre-retired and retired white-collar women and found no difference in marital adjustment or self-esteem. However, she does note that retirement does not directly affect psychological functioning but leads to a change in coping strategies. Longitudinal studies are thought preferable but are difficult and expensive. Problems include the unrepresentativeness of sampling due to self-selection and selected drop-out; the difficulty of determining and then measuring a robust, sensitive and salient set of variables for the dependent measure; and, as always, taking into account the numerous mediating and confounding variables between personality and retirement satisfaction and activity.

There are various 'theories' of the nature of the retirement process outlined by Kasl (1980) but nearly all tend to neglect personality variables, preferring to concentrate on demographic characteristics. If personality factors play a major role in determining occupation choice, productivity and satisfaction (see Chapters 3, 4 and 5), do they not play an equally important role in retirement? Kremer and Harpaz (1982) tested two hypotheses: the compensatory hypothesis that retired people engage in new areas of interest and become deeply involved in leisure activities; and the spill-over hypothesis that there is no difference in the variety and frequency of non-work interests and activities after retirement. They found strong evidence in their sample for the spill-over hypothesis, a result which has been replicated. Thus, if a person has passive, solitary, leisure behaviour before retirement this is likely to continue. This suggests that the sort of lifestyle that people maintain while working will not be very much affected by retirement. Thus, outgoing extraverts will maintain numerous social contacts in retirement (through clubs etc) while quiet introverts may become even more inward looking and solitary after retirement.

Pre-retirement attitudes and behaviour seem to influence retirement activities and satisfaction in retirement. However, as Dobson and Morrow (1984) have found, work commitment was negatively related to retirement attitudes, whereas job satisfaction and work ethic endorsement was positively related in a group of university dons. The question, of course, remains why do people have strong work commitment which seems negatively associated with attitudes to, and subsequent adjustment in, retirement.

All individuals face the crises of old age from the standpoint of their own perceptions: the retirement experience that rejuvenates one, ages another. Personality is a more important determinant of physical activity than age. Among retired men with a median age of 65 years, relatively greater current involvement with physical activity was associated with characteristics such as greater orientation toward helping professions, altruistic interests and greater extroversion, but not with age. Greater involvement with cultural events related to a theoretical orientation and extraversion (Rogers, 1984).

Far-sighted and flexible people often enjoy the challenge posed by their new role, and probably make a good adjustment. The internally controlled, who believe that personal rewards depend on their own behaviours and attitudes, differ sharply from the externally oriented, who feel that rewards are controlled by forces outside themselves. Retirement does not constitute a special crisis for the internally oriented. Self-directed individuals quickly reorganize their lifestyles and progress to non-career-related activities and goals. For externally oriented people, retirement can create adjustment problems, since they ordinarily look to others for guidance and find self-direction difficult. On the other hand, self-assured, internally-oriented individuals may be more depressed after the death of a spouse because now they must deal with factors over which they have no control. In the same instance, externally oriented individuals may lean on others for help. People also differ in the way that they organize their time, and how much organization means to them. Some of the elderly find it hard to structure their time. By contrast, younger and middle-aged persons' time is usually structured for them. Some older people become disturbed at finding the days slipping away aimlessly. Others enjoy unstructured time and spend it in casual activities.

A number of studies have examined the relationship between locus of control and retirement adjustment. As predicted, Reid, Kleiman and Travis (1977) found instrumentalists (those with internal locus of control) reported more contentment and happiness than fatalists. This was more true of males than females and independent of the health of the retired. O'Brien (1981) noted that it is possible that the relationship between locus of control and satisfaction depends on the particular aspect of life in retirement which the respondent is asked to evaluate. In his own study of 301 Australian retirees, O'Brien used partial correlations and showed that locus of control was significantly related to a number of dimensions of satisfaction, including satisfaction with retirement activities, satisfaction with people, health satisfaction, satisfaction with finance, life satisfaction and skill utilization. Again, the results were stronger in males than females. He admits that the results do not indicate exactly why internals are more adapted, although it could all be due to the fact that they use environmental resources more wisely and maintain better goal-directed activity.

Fillenbaum and Maddox (1974) listed a number of potentially important factors that predict retirement adjustment:

- Negative attitudes to retirement.
- Inappropriate or no plans for retirement.
- Amount of intrinsic vs extrinsic work commitment.
- Personality factors such as need for achievement.
- The influence of peers.

They found that all of these factors, but least of all the personality dimensions that were measured, were direct predictors of work after retirement. Continued working appears to be a function of personal dislike of retirement, and the presence of younger friends who are themselves working.

How do PWE beliefs relate to work after retirement states/active with retirement etc? Clearly, PWE beliefs are related to leisure and non-work, hence it is possible to entertain a number of testable hypotheses such as the following: High as opposed to low PWE believers will:

- Tend to resist early retirement and opt for delayed retirement.
- Tend, if possible, to continue working at the same job.
- Find alternative employment if available.
- Report lower retirement satisfaction if unable to work.
- Adapt a lifestyle, particularly in terms of time keeping, closely akin to that of working people.

Hooker and Ventis (1984) in fact examined the relationship between PWE beliefs, retirement satisfaction and the daily activities of those who were retired. They found, as predicted, that PWE beliefs were inversely related to satisfaction in retirement. This may have been because high PWE scorers tended to have fewer non-work-related activities which are usually related to work satisfaction, but are in any case under-valued being leisure. Least satisfied retirees were those with high PWE beliefs who did not perceive their activities as useful, and vice versa. The authors feel that pre-retirement counselling should be aimed at helping to relinquish the strong work orientation of some people, but that work-like activities remain a source of satisfaction for high PWE scorers.

Retirement is a major transition from the world of work where most people spend their entire adult lives. The workplace provides well-defined roles and specific interpersonal relationships, and these are lost on retirement. Hence, retirement has been seen as something of a psychosocial crisis of disengagement, replacement of roles, and readjustment of social life. Yet retirement will, of necessity, have different meanings for different individuals. Factors that relate to the perceived meaning of, attitudes to, and satisfaction with retirement include the following:

- Attitudes to work and leisure.
- Employment pressures and changes.
- Family and social relationships.
- Health and the impact of physical aging.

- Life events, especially bereavement.
- Individual differences in personality functioning.

Health and financial changes are important stressors for the newly retired. But to a large extent, certain individual differences moderate the negative effects of retirement.

McGoldrick (1987) has concentrated on the two important factors related to retirement adaptation: coping mechanisms and social support. But she laments the paucity of research in this area.

> Nonetheless, not all individuals view retirement positively and for the minority adaption problems may be severe, especially in respect of financial problems and health decline. The experience of early retirement has so far received little research attention, with most studies focusing instead on factors in the decisions to retire, presumably as a result of its importance at governmental and organizational levels. If it is to remain a viable manpower planning tool, however, we need to examine subsequent satisfaction, lifestyles and problems more extensively. Schemes will ultimately be discredited if those opting for them become disillusioned. In relation to the retirement decision, an area where evidence is weak is reaction to job stresses and work problems. In the study of retirement generally, attention to personality factors and coping mechanisms has been neglected. Little is known of the support of partner and family, since the majority of studies focus only on the retiree. We should also be looking at the feasibility of other alternative approaches to retirement, which would more effectively enable individuals to cope with the transition. These include gradual or phased retirement, re-training, skills up-grading and job re-design to suit older workers' needs. In addition, literature in respect of women and retirement is still slow growing. Nor have studies tended to take a 'family' perspective on the subject, which is surprising, since retirement can mean a re-establishment of the couple's joint activities and the partner may be an important support resource or may, in fact, increase the pressures experienced (p.112).

One way to derive some sensible hypotheses about personality and retirement is to examine what people actually do when retired. Once a robust and comprehensive taxonomy is produced, it becomes possible to derive various hypotheses about the personality correlates of preferred retirement activity. Thus, active socially oriented individuals are probably extraverts etc.

Most studies in this area have not looked at personality variables, preferring to concentrate on demographic or attitudinal factors, many of which are shown to be powerful correlates of retirement satisfaction (Szinovacz, 1987). However, the importance of psychological factors is readily admitted. Holloway and Youngblood (1985) discovered that people's survival after retirement is bi-modal: a group died (on average) 16$\frac{1}{2}$ years after retirement, while the other survived on average 19 years. They noted that even after controlling for factors such as age, sex, type of job and location, differences in survival beyond retirement were still observed. They believe that personality, intelligence, pre-retirement attitudes, work-related attitudes, health practices and socio-economic characteristics would help to account for the large unexplained variation in the longevity index.

Clearly, more systematic, theory-driven work needs to be done looking at which personality variables effect which retirement behaviours. There is no doubt that there are powerful demographic and occupational factors that moderate this relationship; and also that there is some reciprocal effect between retirement 'situation' and personality. Yet to ignore the variance accounted for by personality is to ignore a major influence on retirement adjustment, activities and satisfaction.

9.5 CONCLUSION

This chapter focused on the effect of personality on 'after-work' behaviours both in the sense of at the end of the working day/week, and at the end of the working life. A number of consistent themes emerged from the literature: firstly, the paucity of good research studies; secondly, the general neglect of personality variables; and, thirdly, problems in the measurement of the variables.

The literature on the relationship between personality and sport/leisure seem to suggest that personality variables, particularly extraversion (sensation–seeking) and to some extent neuroticism, were important in the choice of sport, the choice of position (i.e. forward vs back), style etc and indeed competence at that sport/leisure activity. The literature on personality and the effects on unemployment suggest that neuroticism (low self-esteem, anxiety, psychosomatic illnesses), psychoticism, attributional style (locus of control) and work-related beliefs (the PWE) were all important determinants both of getting a job *and* reacting to unemployment. As yet, few studies have examined personality factors in the coping styles of retired persons, but there is currently enough research in this field to generate sensible and testable hypotheses.

Chapter 10

Implications for selection, training and reward structure

If you think education is expensive, try ignorance.

D. Bok

Never learn to do anything. If you don't learn, you will always find someone else to do it for you.

Mark Twain

If you have great talents, industry will improve them: if you have but moderate abilities, industries will supply their deficiency.

Joshua Reynold

Management is now where the medical profession was when it decided that working in a drug store was not sufficient training to become a doctor.

L.A. Appley

Training is everything. The peach was once a bitter almond; cauliflower is nothing but cabbage with a college education.

Mark Twain

Personally I'm always ready to learn, although I do not always like being taught.

Winston Churchill

10.1 INTRODUCTION

If it is the case that personality and other individual difference variables are correlated with a whole range of job-related beliefs and behaviours, it makes sense that these factors should be taken into consideration in selection, training and rewarding personnel. As regards selection, what is clearly important is that the most able, capable and organizationally compatible individuals are selected. Where necessary, these individuals have to be trained to reach a minimum level of competence. Good employees, then, need to be retained by equitable and appealing reward packages.

Various personnel and human-resource professionals use personality tests in selection. Their reasons for doing so are various. Some use tests in the belief that it aids their selection validity by selecting *in* desirable candidates and *out* undesirable candidates. Others attempt to match profiles to some pre-established profile of the ideal candidate. Others are more concerned that people fit in, not so much with the job as with the other people in the organization. Still others use tests for impression management reasons, because they are under the illusion that candidates will be impressed by the scientific rigour that they are applying to the whole procedure. Most people naïvely assume that personnel selection is done because it can be demonstrated that appropriate selection and productivity are closely linked. Yet, as Cook (1988) has pointed out, this very simple assumption has never really been tested.

There are a number of criteria that one might apply to the various ways of assessing personality. Cook (1988) provides the following table (see Table 10.1) by which different selection methods are judged by five criteria. While not everyone would agree either with the criteria or the rating, what the table does illustrate is the variety of methods available, and the extent to which they vary according to various criteria.

Table 10.1 Summary assessment of ten selection tests by five criteria

Test	Criteria				
	Validity	Cost	Practicality	Generality	Legality
Interview	Low	Medium/high	High	High	Untested
References	Moderate	Very low	High	High	A few doubts
Peer ratings	High	Very low	Very limited	Military only	Untested
Biodata	High	Medium	High	High	Some doubts
Ability	High	Low	High	High	Major doubts
Personality	Low	Low	Fair	?White-collar only	Untested
Assessment centre	High	Very high	Fair	Fairly high	No problems
Work sample	High	High	High	Blue-collar only	No problems
Job knowledge	High	Low	High	Blue-collar only	Some doubts
Education	Low	Low	High	High	Major doubts

Source: Cook (1988)

Not everyone would agree with Cook's criteria. Supervisor/peer assessments, assessment centres, biodata and general mental ability are usually regarded as the best of the remaining methods. References, interviews, personality, and assessment and interest inventories provide low but positive validity coefficients, although this is not always the case. Predictably, recent evidence from meta-analytic studies, on the validity of interviews, suggests that different types of interview may have different validities. Self-assessments and handwriting do not provide much support for their use as a predictor of work performance.

For most of the selection methods, the range of validities reported in different studies is relatively narrow. It is worth noting that for cognitive (and personality) tests there is a somewhat larger variation in the range of coefficients reported. Ghiselli (1973) reported average validity coefficients of between 0.25 and 0.30 for intelligence and aptitude tests. Schmitt *et al.* (1984) produced similar results, whereas Hunter and Hunter (1984) reported a mean validity coefficient of 0.45 with job proficiency as the criterion being predicted. The source of this variation is based on whether or not investigators using meta-analysis techniques have corrected for error of measurement and restriction of range, and the precise studies reviewed.

Validity is a crucial factor when considering the value of personnel selection methods. As noted above, however, other facets of selection methods are important. Fairness is the topic of another section in this book and will not be discussed in detail further here. It is worth noting, however, that for several methods (e.g. references) only very limited information is available. The idea of selection is very simple: select in the good candidates and select out the bad ones. Also, poor or weak candidates are sometimes chosen which selectors learn about to their cost, while sometimes good candidates are rejected yet selectors never know about this group. A simple selection model is set out thus:

Step 1: *Examination of the job(s) having vacancies.* This step consists of job analysis. Job analysis is a most critical and basic problem area in occupational psychology and is, or should be, the foundation of any testing. A thorough knowledge and understanding of a job is of paramount importance and must precede the use of any test in the selection and placement of workers. Rarely is this step done, yet it must be the first.

Step 2: *Selection of criterion and predictor.* The second step involves two parts – choosing an indicator criterion which measures the extent of how 'good' or successful a worker is, and choosing a particular measure that can be used to predict how successful a worker will be on the job. Criterion selection is a complicated but basic statistical problem; the solution decides how job success is defined and/or measured. There are a wide variety of potentially useful devices which can be successful in discriminating between 'good' and 'poor' workers. Often used are such predictors as tests, interviews, application blanks and letters of recommendation among others. Personality tests appear to be being used with greater frequency.

Step 3: *Measurement of performance.* Once the criterion and the predictor have been selected, it is necessary to obtain measures on both from a sample of workers on the job.

One can simultaneously obtain criterion measures, or give the predictor to new employees and wait a specified time before obtaining the criterion measures (thus allowing enough time for the new employees to establish themselves as successful or unsuccessful). Both methods are used, and each has its advantages and disadvantages.

Step 4: *Relating predictor to criterion*. The fourth step in the selection process involves determining whether a true and meaningful relationship exists between the employee score on the predictor and the criterion. Only if such a relationship exists can the selection process be considered successful. Establishing the existence of such a relationship is called *assessing the validity* of a predictor. This is usually a statistical process.

Step 5: *Deciding on the utility of the selection device*. Making the final decision as to whether to use the predictor to select new job hires depends not only on the size of the relationship found (in Step 4) and its significance, but also on many other conditions: the number of applicants, number of job openings, proportion of present employees considered successful (the *base rate*), and respective variances of the successful and unsuccessful worker groups.

Step 6: *Re-evaluation*. The fact that the predictive situation is a dynamic, ever-changing one should never be forgotten. What makes for good selection today may not be at all appropriate tomorrow: applicants change, jobs change, and employment conditions change. Thus, any good selection programme should be re-evaluated periodically to make certain it is doing the job for which it has been designed.

Despite the relative simplicity of this model, a considerable effort is required to do it well. Possibly because of lack of competence, but also because of costs, not all of the steps are done. Yet there is more and more interest in calculating the cost/benefit of selection.

This in fact goes back to Brogden (1950). He argues that the amount an employer can save, per employee recruited, per year, is: VALIDITY of the test *times* CALIBRE of recruits *times* SD, *minus* COST of selection *divided by* PROPORTION of applicants selected. Brogden's equation in fact states:

$$\text{Saving per employee per year} = (r \times \text{SD}, \times Z) - (C/P),$$

where r is the validity of the selection procedure (expressed as a correlation coefficient), SD is the standard deviation of employee productivity in pounds/dollars, Z is the calibre of recruits (expressed as their standard score on the selection test used), C is the cost of selection per applicant and P is the proportion of applicants selected.

Cook (1988) provides a work example:

1. The employer is recruiting in the salary range £20,000 p.a., so SD can be estimated – by the 70 per cent 'rule of thumb' – at £14,000. (Or SD can be measured by *rational estimate* or *superior equivalents* techniques.)
2. The employer is using a test of high level mental ability whose proven validity is 0.45, so r is 0.45.
3. The people recruited score on average 1 SD above the mean for the ability test, so Z is 1. This assumes the employer succeeds in recruiting high-calibre people.
4. The employer uses a consultancy, who charge £480 per candidate.
5. Of ten applicants, four are appointed, so P is 0.40.

The saving per employee per year is

$$(0.45 \times £14,000 \times 1) \text{ minus } (£480/0.40) = £6300$$
$$\text{minus } £1200 = £5100$$

Each employee selected is worth over £5000 a year more to the employer than one recruited at random. The four employees recruited will be worth in all £20,400 more to the employer, *each year*. The larger the organization, the greater the total sum that can be saved by effective selection, hence the estimate of $18 million for the Philadelphia police force, with 5000 employees. Selection pays off better:

(a) when CALIBRE of recruits is high,
(b) where employees differ a lot in worth to the organization, i.e., when SD$_y$ is high,
(c) where SELECTION procedure has low validity.

> In the worked example, even using a fairly expensive selection procedure, the cost per employee selected is only a fifth of the increased value per employee per year, giving the lie to the oft-heard claim that elaborate selection methods, or psychological assessment, aren't worthwhile. In this example selection pays for itself six times over in the first year. Failure to select the right employee, by contrast, goes on costing the employer money, *year after year* (p. 243).

Again, this area is frequently debated and not everyone would agree with the above, rather simplistic analysis. Yet few would disagree with the remark that the costs of selecting and hiring the wrong person can be very high indeed.

10.2 PERSONALITY AND SELECTION
The Selection Interview

Many interviewers see it as their task to assess the interviewees' personality (as well as their ability, intelligence and suitability in the organization). However, comparatively few studies have actually related candidates' personality characteristics to interview assessments. Keenan (1982) found that machiavellians were rated differently from non-machiavellians, but that measures of social difficulty and locus of control had no effect. Fletcher (1987) measured self-monitoring, extraversion, neuroticism and state–trait anxiety of university applicants and related these to seven ratings of such things as emotional stability, drive and motivation to do the degree. Neither self-monitoring nor trait anxiety showed significant correlations, and extraversion correlated positively with overall acceptability. Interestingly, neuroticism was positively correlated with favourable assessments of motivation, verbal expression, emotional stability, anxiety in the interview, and the overall rating. Fletcher gives no explanation for the counter-intuitive findings nor for possibly serious methodological flaws in the study, such as the poor reliability between interviewers.

In a similar study, Fletcher (1990) gave student applicants measures of machiavellianism, extraversion, neuroticism and locus of control, and a 14-item rating scale looking at how they behave in interviews. Again, there were few significant correlations and evidence that although interviewers seem influenced by the self-presentation strategies of subjects, they do not reflect personality differences in a consistent way.

These studies do not, of course, mean either that interviewers (trained or not) can accurately rate an interviewee's personality (as that has not been their task), or that their personality traits do not predict behaviour. These studies have to be faulted on a number of criteria: the convenient, rather homogeneous sample of university students; interviewer differences which were not considered systematically; the rather a-theoretical choice of personality measures; and the vague, non-behavioural nature of many of the dependent ratings. Nevertheless, research of this kind is clearly important.

The employment interview continues to be widely used. While many psychologists are well aware of its very limited reliability and validity, few advocate not interviewing candidates for jobs in their own organizations (even if it is to select out rather than in). Thus, research on the interview continues and will continue as long as it is a widely used technique.

Outside the narrow and occasionally blinkered world of I/O psychology, other researchers have come up with powerful findings relevant to the employment interview. Perhaps the two most salient areas are the following:

1. *Attribution theory.* The employment interview and the evaluation judgements made by interviewers is a function of the many attributions that they make about interviewees. Attribution theory suggests that interviewers

judge the success or failure of interviewees, and attribute such success or failure in turn to internal factors associated with interviewees or to external factors beyond the control of the interviewee. All attribution models differentiate between factors which are assumed to be stable (e.g. ability, difficulty of task) or relatively unstable (e.g. effort, luck). Interviewers clearly form judgements about interviewees according to the attributions that they make about the causes of the candidate's past achievements.

2. *Impression formation and management.* There is a rich database on the way that individuals form impressions and how impressions may be managed: for example, studies investigating whether interviewers use and weigh information differently from one another in the interview. Thus, interviewers might give different weights to academic standing and job experience factors in evaluating applicants than undergraduate students serving as raters.

The business of selection, however, is by no means easy or straightforward. Arvey and Campion (1984) grouped 23 separate factors that can, and do affect, the interview outcome under three headings: applicant, situation and interviewer (see Figure 10.1). Clearly, all of these factors (and their interactions) can in part determine whether candidates are accepted or rejected. What is perhaps most interesting is that the non-applicant factors outweigh the applicant factors. That is, factors not specifically to do with the candidate may be (and frequently are) more important factors in determining candidate selection than actual features (personality, abilities etc) of the candidate!

Leadership Traits

There have been various approaches to the study and identification of leadership traits (Yukl, 1989).

The trait approach emphasizes the personal attributes of leaders. Early leadership theories attributed success to possession of extraordinary abilities, such as tireless energy, penetrating intuition, uncanny foresight and irresistible persuasive powers. Hundreds of trait studies were conducted during the 1930s and 1940s to discover these elusive qualities, but the considerable research effort failed to find any traits that would guarantee leadership success. Nevertheless, with recent evidence from better designed research and new research methods, trait research is slowly designing how traits relate to leadership behaviour and effectiveness. The focus of much of the recent trait research has been on managerial motivation and specific skills, whereas earlier research focused more on personality traits and general intelligence. Some researchers now attempt to relate traits to specific role requirements for different types of managerial position.

The search for traits relevant for effective leadership has continued over the years, and some different methodologies have been employed in recent years.

For example, Boyatzis (1982) used 'behaviour event interviews', a variation of the critical incident method, to infer traits and skills from incidents reported by managers. Various studies found a fairly consistent pattern of results. Traits that relate most consistently to managerial effectiveness or advancement include high self-confidence, energy, initiative, emotional maturity, stress tolerance, and belief in internal locus of control. With respect to interests and values, successful managers tend to be pragmatic and results oriented, and they enjoy persuasive activities requiring initiative and challenge (Yukl, 1989).

Managerial motivation is one of the most promising predictors of effectiveness. A programme of research on managerial motivation conducted over the years by Miner and his colleagues (Berman and Miner, 1985) found that the most relevant component was interaction with peers, and a positive attitude toward authority figures. Research by McClelland (1987) and other investigators found evidence that effective leaders in large hierarchical organizations tend to have a strong need for power, a fairly strong need for achievement, and a relatively weaker need for affiliation. Effective managers have a socialized power orientation due to high emotional maturity. They are more interested in building up the organization and empowering others than in personal aggrandizement or domination of others. The optimal pattern of managerial motivation is somewhat different for entrepreneurs, who tend to have a dominant need for achievement, and a strong need for independence.

Skills are another promising predictor of leader effectiveness. Technical

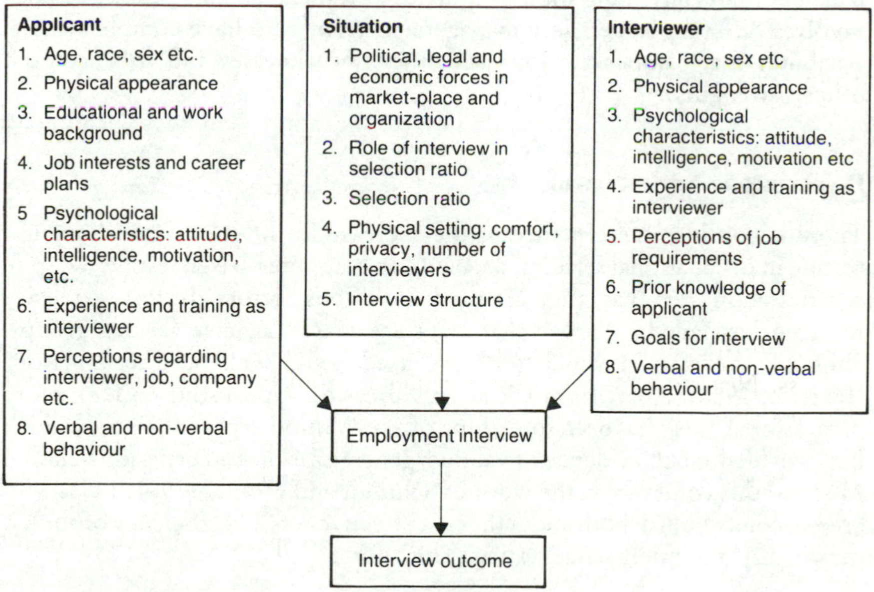

Applicant	Situation	Interviewer
1. Age, race, sex etc.	1. Political, legal and economic forces in market-place and organization	1. Age, race, sex etc
2. Physical appearance		2. Physical appearance
3. Educational and work background		3. Psychological characteristics: attitude, intelligence, motivation etc
4. Job interests and career plans	2. Role of interview in selection ratio	
5 Psychological characteristics: attitude, intelligence, motivation, etc.	3. Selection ratio	4. Experience and training as interviewer
	4. Physical setting: comfort, privacy, number of interviewers	5. Perceptions of job requirements
6. Experience and training as interviewer	5. Interview structure	6. Prior knowledge of applicant
7. Perceptions regarding interviewer, job, company etc.		7. Goals for interview
8. Verbal and non-verbal behaviour		8. Verbal and non-verbal behaviour

Employment interview

Interview outcome

Figure 10.1 Factors affecting selection
Source: Arvey and Campion (1984)

skills, conceptual skills and interpersonal skills are necessary for most leadership roles, but the relative importance of the three types of skills varies greatly from situation to situation. In addition, the optimal mix of specific component skills and the nature of technical expertise required by a leader vary greatly from one type of organization to another. Even for the same type of organization, the optimal pattern of traits and skills may vary depending on the prevailing business strategy. Some specific skills, such as analytical ability, persuasiveness, speaking ability, memory for details, empathy, tact and charm, are probably useful in all leadership positions but how, why and when remains unclear.

One of the key findings coming out of the trait approach is the idea of balance or optimal amounts. In some instances, balance means a moderate amount of some trait, such as need for achievement, need for affiliation, self-confidence, risk taking, initiative, decisiveness and assertiveness, rather than either a very low or very high amount of the trait. Balance also means tempering one trait with another, such as tempering a high need for power with the emotional maturity required to ensure that subordinates are empowered rather than dominated. Balance must be achieved between competing values: concern for the task must be balanced against concern for people; concern for a leader's own needs must be balanced against concern for organizational needs; concern for the needs of subordinates must be balanced against concern for the needs of peers, superiors and clients; desire for change and innovation must be balanced against need for continuity and predictability. Finally, balance is not only a question of individual leaders. In some cases, balance involves different leaders in a management team who have complementary attributes that compensate for each other's weaknesses and enhance each other's strengths.

Psychometric Advancement

There is considerable evidence of the increase in the use of psychometric testing in occupational settings, particularly computer-based testing. Despite worries about test bias, they are used in various sectors. In fact, extensive research has failed to prove that tests are biased against various groups, although the way in which tests are used could well be discriminatory (Herriot, 1988). Apart from social pressures to adapt testing to look more professional, there has been something of a revolution in psychometrics which has provided much evidence of validity generalization and criterion validity. Much of this comes from the work of Schmidt and Hunter (1981, 1983) who are extremely bullish both about the cost effectiveness and efficiency of ability, personality and intelligence testing. They note:

> This article contains two messages: a substantive message and a methodological message. The substantive message is this: (a) professionally

developed cognitive ability tests are valid predictors of performance on the job and in training for all jobs in all settings; (b) cognitive ability tests are equally valid for minority and majority applicants and are fair to minority applicants in that they do not underestimate the expected job performance of minority groups; and (c) the use of cognitive ability tests for selection in hiring can produce large labour cost savings, ranging from $18 million per year for small employers such as the Philadelphia police department to $16 billion per year for large employers such as the federal government (4,000,000 employees).

The methodological message is this: in the last 10 years the field of personnel selection has undergone a transformation in viewpoint resulting from the introduction of improved methods of cumulating findings across studies. Use of these methods has shown that most of the conflicting results across studies were the result of sampling error that was not perceived by reviewers relying on statistical significance tests to evaluate single studies. Reviews in our field were also subject to systematic distortion because reviewers failed to take into account the systematic effects of error of measurement in range in the samples studied. The real meaning of 70 years of cumulative research on employment testing was not apparent until state-of-the-art meta-analytic procedures were applied. These methods not only cumulate results across studies but correct variance across studies for the effect of sampling error and correct both mean and variance for the distorting effects of systematic artifacts such as unreliability and restriction of range (p.120).

They then set about showing how various popularly held theories were *false*:

- The theory of low utility – the idea that employee selection methods have little impact on the performance and productivity of the resultant work force.
- The theory of subgroup validity differences – the idea that because of cultural difference, cognitive tests have lower validity for minority than for majority groups.
- The theory of test unfairness – the idea that even if validity coefficients are equal for minority/majority groups, a test is unlikely to be fair if the average test score is lower for minorities.
- The theory of test validity – the idea that test validity is situationally specific (test validity for a job in one organization/setting may be invalid *for the same job* in another organization) or job specific (a cognitive test valid for one job may be invalid in another).
- The theory that criteria of success in training are insufficient – the idea that a test valid for predicting success in training programmes may be invalid for predicting performance on the job because the two are unrelated.

It is because Schmidt and Hunter have been so persuasive that there is a renewed interest and vigour in the field. Their conclusions have, of course, not met with total agreement in all sectors, however, and research continues. This can only be healthy for the field as a whole.

Evaluating Personality in Assessment Centres

There has been a marked increase in interest expressed in assessment centres for evaluating ability, competency, intelligence and personality. Assessment centres grew out of army and civil service selection and have extensive growth. They come in different forms but have various common features:

• They tend to assess individuals as they work in group (as well as individual) exercises.
• Their behaviour is observed and recorded by (trained) assessors.
• Assessment uses a variety of methods and tasks, and the centre may take as little as four hours but more like one to two days.
• Most candidates are rated on a set of pre-ordinated criteria (called competencies, dispositions or traits) usually concerned with problem-solving skills or interpersonal skills.

Personality tests have more uses than just as actuarial devices for use in selection, auditing organizational skills, and dealing with issues of succession and promotion. They are also used in assessment centres and courses aimed at individual development.

Campbell and Van Velsor (1985) who use tests in management development programmes, and show how they can discriminate between people doing well and poorly on leadership courses, note nine other reasons for using tests (like the FIRO-B, CPI, Myers–Briggs):

1. To demonstrate, describe and explain various psychological principles and processes.
2. To help the individual to understand his/her strengths, limitations and coping strategies more efficiently and effectively.
3. To help people understand the behaviour of others that they work with.
4. To help the individual plan a course of action around career planning.
5. To emphasize the wide range of psychological diversity in groups.
6. To emphasize the unique individuality of each person so as to encourage people not to treat others all the same.
7. To increase the scientific credibility of training programmes, although this is no doubt utterly dependent on the selection and use of tests.
8. To provide enjoyment, because the feedback from tests is frequently inherently interesting.

9. For research purposes to investigate the validity of tests.

Woodruffe (1990) described both advantages and disadvantages of such a system. More importantly, he attempts to define the 'competencies' that observers hope to measure in these centres. These are made up of attitudes, traits, values and experience, although it is rather unclear how they interact. It is not surprising therefore that organizations come up with such a 'rag-bag' of pretty unoperationalized sets of competencies such as team membership, strategic thinking, productivity or impact. However, the idea is that once a set of competencies (criteria) are decided on, candidates are rated while undertaking various tasks, such as written exercises, in-tray tasks, one-to-one or group exercises etc. Woodruffe does point out some of the major problems of this approach, particularly the weak and equivocal data on criterion or productive validity. He also points out the occurrence of the 'exercise effect' which shows that there is more in common between ratings of different dimensions within each exercise than there is between ratings of the same dimension across exercises. In other words, heterotrait, monomethod correlations are higher than monotrait, heteromethod correlations. Assessment centres lacked convergent validity (ratings of the same traits/competencies in different exercises do not converge on the same answer) *and* divergent validity (ratings of different traits within an exercise do not diverge from one another). This error could be due to a number of problems, such as the vague non-behaviour specifications of the rated behaviour; the fact that raters are not trained; the halo effect; the poor design of the exercises; or a combination of all three.

However, meta-analysis of assessment centres suggests that they show both validity generalization and situational specificity. Gaugler *et al.* (1987) found that the validities were higher under specific conditions: when the percentage of female assessees was high; when several evaluation devices were used; when the assessors were psychologists rather than managers; when peer evaluation was also used; and where the study was valid.

Do self-report personality tests correlate with assessment ratings? Crowley, Pinder and Herriot (1990) set out to determine whether personality test scores or aptitude test scores were better predictors of various assessment centre ratings. Using two assessment centres, and four well-known and often used tests like the Occupational Personality Questionnaire (OPQ), Myers–Briggs and FIRO-B, they found few and weak correlations between traits and dimensions like stress, tolerance, delegation, business awareness etc. The ability tests, on the other hand, showed consistent and high correlations. But the authors are well aware of the shortcomings of such an approach. These include: the possibility that the personality tests were less psychometrically sound than the ability tests; the fact that the psychometric tests were ipsative; the validity of the ratings were not checked. They end:

The general implication for assessment centre design is to cast further doubt on the use of the 'sign' as opposed to the 'sample' rationale. In other words, the inferential sequence should not be from job analysis to task areas to dimensions to exercises designed to assess those dimensions. Rather, it should be from job analysis to job sample exercises with content validity. More specifically, the research also suggests ways in which the psychometric tests which are often administered during assessment centres might more profitably be used. If assesssees are low on these personality attributes (e.g. assertiveness, extraversion) which permit expression of desirable assessment centre behaviours, more attention should be paid to the results of tests of intellectual aptitude, and less to their assessment centre ratings. The danger of misinterpreting poor situation-specific performance as a general lack of competence might be avoided. Future research could profitably investigate whether certain personality attributes moderate the validity of assessment centre dimensions (p.215).

Certainly, if salient and psychometrically sound personality measures are chosen, there is every reason to expect that they will be able to predict robust, reliable, job-related criteria.

However, not all self-assessment questionnaires are equally valid. Mihal and Graumenz (1984) compare self-assessment on specific job dimensions and 'expert' assessment centre ratings. Significant discrepancies were found on ten of the 13 dimensions. Subjects tended to be lenient on themselves, giving themselves much higher ratings on ambition, motivation and sensitivity. Disagreement is lower when behaviours were concrete, and higher where dimensions are more abstract and/or potentially damaging to an individual's self-esteem. Of course, it is not clear whether the 'bias' was in the eye of the beholder (rater) or the subject (Furnham and Henderson, 1983). Yet the authors do make some valuable points with respect to some self-assessment devices, many with little or no psychometric validity, which attempt to provide a person with insight into their vocational and suitability for specific careers:

1. Self-assessment of potential for career decision making has a high probability of leading to an unrealistically high rating of ability for a wide range of job dimensions.
2. Standardized tests, inventories, and exercises combined with feedback from trained assessors are desirable for effective career decision making.
3. Career counsellors should be aware of potential bias in self-assessments when dealing with counsellees and should attempt to validate self-assessments whenever possible.
4. 'Self-help' type literature should warn users concerning potential bias and advise them to make an effort to obtain professional assistance (p.253)

10.3 PERSONALITY AND TRAINING

Many organisations invest a great deal of money in developing various skills through training. Employees at all levels are sent on courses varying in length, topic and teaching style in order to ensure that they can perform more efficiently and effectively. Apart from the more difficult questions to answer, there is a central problem concerning whether training works. A major issue concerns individual differences in learning styles. As was noted in Chapter 2, Kolb (1976) and others have argued that people have preferred quite different learning styles. Presumably, people learn more efficiently and effectively when taught in their preferred way. However, the evidence linking personality and preferred learning style is not clear.

Recent studies have shown that aptitude batteries predict success in training moderately well. For instance, Dunbar and Novick (1988) found that abilities like arithmetic reasoning and word knowledge were predictive of nine quite different training criteria, although they did find considerable evidence of sex differences.

There is, however, an extensive literature in cognitive psychology showing how individual differences in such things as neuroticism and extraversion are related to learning through differences in verbal learning, memory and performance. For instance, Eysenck (1981) has noted the following:

1. Reward enhances the performance of extraverts more than introverts, whereas punishment impairs the performance of introverts more than extraverts.
2. Introverts are more susceptible than extraverts to distraction.
3. Introverts are more affected than extraverts by response competition.
4. Introverts take longer than extraverts to retrieve information from long-term or permanent storage, especially non-dominant information.
5. Introverts have higher response criteria than extraverts.
6. Extraverts show better retention-test performance than introverts at short retention intervals, but the opposite happens at long retention intervals (p.204).

There is general agreement about how to develop and evaluate a training programme:

Step 1. Define training objectives.
Step 2. Develop criterion measures for evaluating training.
Step 3. Derive training content.
Step 4. Design methods and training materials.
Step 5. Integrate training programme and trainees.
Step 6. Compare graduates to criteria standards set in step 2.
Step 7. Modify steps 3 and 4 based on results of step 6.

There is close agreement in terms of the sort of criteria that managers have for training programmes. These include:

1. Better quality and quantity of production.
2. Increase in the number of operators able to meet job standards.
3. Reduction in time required to do specific job.
4. Decrease in breakable supplies or tools.
5. Increase in customer orders.
6. Reduction in operational costs.
7. Better performance on personnel tools, such as tests, rating scales and attitude surveys.

However, there is little agreement about the following five questions:

1. How are training needs determined?
2. What are the relative merits of different training methods?
3. What are the relative merits of different training aids?
4. What has training accomplished?
5. How are different measures appropriate to the needs of different individuals?

Of course, training is only one solution to one problem as the typical managerial decision tree in Figure 10.2 suggests.

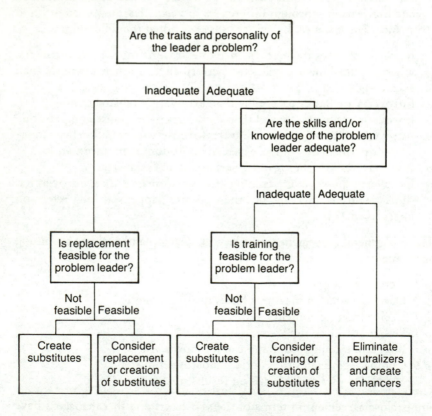

Figure 10.2 Whether or not training is necessary

A major objection to all training programmes is that they fail due to lack of generalization or maintenance of the acquired skills. This is illustrated in Figure 10.3. Whereas the solid line indicates the desired result, the dotted line indicates the more common result. It is argued that this lack of transference of training is due to little or poor organizational reinforcement which fails to do the following:

- Help participants diagnose problems to determine if new skills are needed.
- Discuss possible alternatives for handling specific situations.
- Act as a coach to help the participants apply the skills.
- Encourage participants to use the skills frequently.
- Serve as a role model for the proper use of the skills.
- Give positive rewards to participants when the skills are unsuccessfully used.

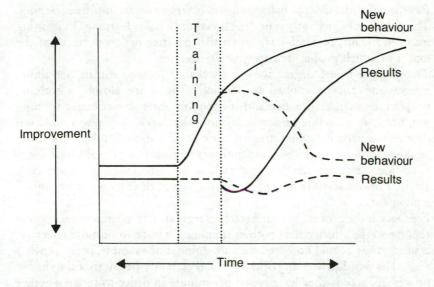

Figure 10.3 On-the-job improvement (—) or lack of it (- - -) in performance resulting from new behaviour

Essentially, what post-training programmes need to do is to pinpoint the desired level, quantity or quality of occupational behaviour; perform a thorough and reliable post-training course baseline audit; define a criterion standard or level to aim at; select an individually salient reinforcer of the desired behaviour and selectively reward that behaviour. This is rarely done, nor are important individual difference factors taken into account.

There are, however, various fairly well established principles of effective training. The aim of any training programme is to get trainees to perform at the desired level (i.e. to reach the stated behavioural objective) as quickly as possible. Although different skills are acquired at different rates and follow different patterns, a typical learning curve shows that learning may, at first, be very rapid, and then level off, or plateau. Then, after repeated training over time, the rate of learning will rise again. The aim of training is to get the trainee's performance up to the desired level as quickly as possible. Four major principles are most relevant:

1. *Participation* occurs when trainees are actually personally involved with the desired skills. People learn more quickly, and tend to retain the learned skills, when they actively participate in learning. For example, students who actively participate in class may be more effective learners than those who just sit passively. Individual differences in values, abilities and personality no doubt determine the degree of participation and hence learning.
2. *Repetition* of the desired behaviour has been shown to improve learning. The process of constantly repeating it certainly helps learning. In learning many job skills, research has shown that practice makes perfect but the extent to which people are happy to do it varies.
3. *Transference* is the degree to which what is learned during a training programme can be applied to the job. The more closely a training programme matches the demands of the job, the more effective training will be. It is with this principle in mind that very elaborate simulation devices are used in the training of various jobs such as pilots. By using sophisticated computer-based techniques to simulate carefully real flight conditions, trainees can learn what it is like to manipulate their craft safely, without actually having to risk the loss of their lives and expensive equipment.
4. *Feedback* is the process of giving trainees regular, active, thorough progress reports on the effectiveness of their training. To learn to be more effective, trainees must be told how well they are doing. For example, persons being trained as word-processing operators will certainly find it useful to know how many words they have typed per minute in order to judge whether they have improved.

A major omission in the whole area of training is considering how systematic individual differences affect preferences for training methods, efficacy and transference of training.

10.4 PERSONALITY, FINANCIAL COMPENSATION AND REWARD

Chapter 4 has already considered individual differences in motivation and reward in some detail. However, a few additional points need to be made. There are various theories of the role of money in stimulating, regulating or indeed suppressing job effort and motivation. As well as various job and task variables, Opsahl and Dunnette (1966) have looked at various individual difference factors that play a part, such as personality, ability, values, beliefs and preferences. Perhaps more than any other theory, expectancy and equity theory recognize the potential importance of individual beliefs, which include the following:

1. His/her beliefs concerning the degree to which he/she possesses various characteristics.
2. His/her convictions concerning the degree to which these characteristics should result in the attainment of rewarding outcomes from his/her job, i.e. their value as inputs.
3. His/her beliefs concerning the degree to which he/she receives these rewarding outcomes from his/her job.
4. His/her beliefs concerning the degree to which others possess these characteristics.
5. His/her beliefs concerning the degree to which others receive rewarding outcomes from their jobs.
6. The extent to which he/she compares himself/herself with these others.

Expectancy and equity theory both suggest that to understand how, which and why a source of reward (e.g. money) does or does not work to 'motivate' an employee in terms of productivity, systematic individual differences need to be considered. In short, reward structures or systems are sensitive to individual differences.

But how do rewards differ? Over the years, researchers in this area have been able to make a number of distinctions given the nature of rewards that employees may seek or value. These include the following:

- *Self-administered vs other-administered*. Self-administered rewards (and punishments) arise from appraisals that employees themselves make when comparing their performance with their personal goals and standards. Other-administered rewards result from attaining goals set by other people in the organization. Clearly, the latter are more common and considered less biased, more objective etc. Some combination of the two is of course possible.
- *Personal value or significance of the rewards*. Just as one man's meat is another's poison, so rewards and compensation packages differ from individual to individual. The declining marginal utility of money suggests that as the supply of money in the shape of salary increases, so other factors like free time become relatively more valuable. Personal values and trait-dependent preferences no doubt influence this strongly.
- *Contingent and non-contingent rewards*. Typically, non-contingent rewards are fringe benefits, basic pay, seniority awards, job security, flexible hours, good equipment, pleasant surroundings etc, while contingent rewards are merit pay raises, promotion and recognition. The former do not imply equity, namely individual effort and ability will be rewarded, while the latter

does. Performance management systems are built exclusively on contingent rewards.

- *Difficulty of attainment*. Some rewards seem relatively easy to attain, others are difficult. Some depend on effort, others on ability. Ideally, rewards should be attainable but with some considerable effort; they should be relatively exclusive; and personally valuable. These factors seem to imply that they are most valuable.
- *Tangible and intangible*. The former refers to such things as contingent pay, time off based on performance, and increased job title, while the latter is as intangible as praise. Some individuals are content to know personally that they are rewarded, others need to be able to flaunt these rewards.

Although studies done on preferred reward systems show some degree of consensus, there are sufficient individual and group differences to suggest that they are highly salient. Clearly, the effectiveness and efficacy of the reward system in motivating employees is utterly dependent on its relative personal attractiveness.

10.5 CONCLUSION

The fact that individual differences in personality beliefs and abilities relate specifically to occupational success has obvious and immediate implications. The first is that people with traits and predispositions that are correlated with success should be selected for certain jobs. Equally, those scoring low on these traits or high on traits correlated with occupational failure should be rejected. The task of selecting people with particular traits is by no means easy or straightforward. Whereas there is some agreement on the standard procedure to use to validate the association between personality traits and occupational success criteria, there is much less agreement on: calculating the costs of good vs poor selection; sources of error and bias in the selection interview; how good personality and ability tests are at measuring personality; and the benefit of assessment centre methods.

Because of historical, legal and other constructs, selecting ideal or optimal candidates may be impossible. The next best thing to do is to train people selectively to reach certain standards. Despite the work done by personality and cognitive psychologists, there seems to be much less interest by training specialists on adapting training programmes to suit individual preferences and differences. Recent work on learning preference inventories, however, has helped progress work in this field.

Finally, the way in which people are rewarded/compensated at work, too, has not always taken into consideration systematic, yet very important, individual differences. Given the many types of possible rewards available, it seems obvious to match the reward with the values and preferences of the employee.

Chapter 11

Conclusion

Today's businessman must have the genius of Einstein, the memory of an elephant and the education of a lawyer, scientist, and educator all wrapped in one.

R. Long

One man, no matter how brilliant, can't be a successful corporation. A successful corporation is a group effort. The man at the top can help shape and define the company's goals; he can create an environment that gets people working together creatively; and he can act as umpire. He might know it all, but can't run it all alone.

H. Gleason

Businesses aren't run by geniuses. It is a matter of putting one foot after another in a logical fashion. The trick is in knowing in what direction you want to go.

J. Barker

11.1 INTRODUCTION

It seems completely self-evident to the layperson that people have 'stable' personalities and that personality variables correlate with, and hence predict, occupational behaviour. This book has attempted to review systematically the literature on personality correlates of such things as vocational preference, work motivation, productivity, satisfaction, absenteeism and accidents. The research in this whole area is highly patchy: some topics have been relatively ignored, others thoroughly investigated; some topics and areas are highly dominated by particular theoretical or methodological approaches; some research is of a highly scientific standard, other studies are poorly executed for a number of reasons. The first chapter discussed the reasons for the lack of *rapprochement* between personality and occupational psychology.

The balkanization of the discipline of psychology has meant that various branches have had progressively less and less contact with one another. Personality psychology and organizational behaviour are good examples.

Whereas few personality and individual difference theorists have paid much attention to the role of personality differences in work productivity, satisfaction and motivation, so few researchers in organizational behaviour in turn have done more than acknowledge personality traits in occupational behaviour.

Some would agree that 'organizational behaviour' as a field of study has done little more than acknowledge personality factors, although it may have done more to look at other individual differences (in terms of preferences, values, beliefs). This is perhaps not surprising, as the sociological–organizational perspective arose in part as a reaction to an over-emphasis on the individual as the unit of analysis in occupational psychology. Indeed, sociologists still argue that much of the literature in the field of occupational psychology is dominated by individual difference literature.

Organizational behaviour is a term that is primarily used by teachers and writers operating in a business school/management department context. It draws largely (although not exclusively) on psychological concepts and research for its standard fare. Typical topics include job satisfaction, motivation, commitment, leadership, decision making, group behaviour, conflict etc. In other words, its foci of interest are largely at the individual and group level.

Organizational behaviour tends to have very strong points of affinity with the social psychology of organizations, but with a more managerial and applied focus; this is scarcely surprising as the majority of organizational behaviour practitioners are trained psychologists.

Organization theory is largely concerned with organizations as objects of study. It is much more concerned with the nature and source of organizational structures, power in organizations, the role of the environment etc. Like organizational behaviour, the field of organization theory derives from a business school context, but the former tends to be found more frequently than the latter. Of course, there are areas in which the two streams of thought and research converge, such as when researchers focus on the effects of attributes of organizational structure on individuals' work experiences. However, the two strands are distinct in researchers' minds.

However, outside the academic world, managers in the workplace have begun not only to acknowledge the great importance of individual differences, but also to seek out, in ever-increasing numbers, consultants who 'profile' or test people in assessment centres in order to determine their strengths and weaknesses. Unfortunately, many of the consultants use tests and methods of poor psychometric quality and make invalid claims for their tests.

11.2 PERSONALITY VERSUS ORGANIZATIONAL INTERACTION

The 1970s and 1980s saw personality psychology racked by the person-situation debate which saw the emergence of three camps:

- *Trait theorists* argued that a person's behaviour was cross-situationally consistent and that in the same situation predictable differences in social behaviour occurred. Supporters of this position would no doubt argue that organizational behaviour was a function of the stable traits and abilities of people in the organization.
- *Situationists* believed that behaviour varied considerably from situation to situation and that in 'strong' situations (rule bound, formal, goal oriented) few major differences occurred. Thus, they would argue that organizational behaviour was primarily a function of the organizational culture and climate, and the everyday social situation that it prescribes and proscribes.
- *Interactionists*, which held a compromise or synthetic position, argued that social behaviour was the function of a continuous process of multi-directional interaction between the person and the situation. Hence, supporters would argue from a personality theory *and* social psychological perspective that organizational behaviour was a function of the interaction between traits and organizational culture.

The debate, often acrimonious and repetitive, hinged around a number of supposedly robust and replicated findings such as:

- The fact that personality tests appeared pretty poor at predicting any sort of behaviour (within or outside organizations).
- The average correlation between the same types of behaviour in different situations was always about 0.3.
- Neither trait nor situational variables on their own appeared to account for more than 10 per cent of the total variance.

The traditional or dispositional model came under severe attack because it was argued that, quite simply, there was little or no empirical evidence to suggest that traits were consistent over situations, stable over time, or, indeed, little more than features in the eye of the beholder. There are various summaries of this debate. For instance, Pervin (1984) has argued that after 15 years of research in this field we can be sure about what we do and what we don't know. What we do know is:

- There is evidence of both personality and situational determinants of behaviour. No one doubts that there is evidence for person consistency and situational variability in social behaviour.
- Some people are more consistent than others.
- Some situations have more powerful influences than others in reducing or maximizing the role of individual differences in personality.

- The amount of evidence for consistency of behaviour across situations and time depends on who is being studied, where, the personality variables being studied, and the measures used.
- People observe their own behaviour as well as that of others and have systematic errors in reporting their, and others', behaviour.

Many researchers have taken a quite specific person–situation orientation. For instance, Mehrabian and West (1977) examined the desire to work at a task as a function of the psychological properties of the setting (the situation and task pleasantness and arousing qualities) and the individual (screening or not screening external data). They argued that a worker's arousal level is a direct function of the information rate in the situation where he/she performs a task plus the information rate of the task he/she performs. For instance, arousal levels are expected to be higher when: (a) other workers are present compared to when the worker is alone; (b) the worker is required to move about and be physically active compared to when he/she is confined to the same position, the same location or the same routine movement sequences; (c) the work setting is colourful and changeable compared to when it is monochromatic and static; (d) the task itself is novel, complex, difficult or unpredictable compared to being familiar, simple, easy or predictable. In short, the conception of information rate together with the information rate–arousal hypothesis allows one easily to conceptualize the effects of a myriad of situational and task variables on the worker's arousal level.

Mehrabian and West performed regression analysis. The three regression analyses explored the main and interactive effects of the following on the desire to work: (a) situational pleasantness, situation-arousing quality and stimulus screening; (b) task pleasantness, task-arousing quality and stimulus screening; and (c) situation–task pleasantness, situation–task-arousing quality and stimulus screening. The 0.01 level significant effects obtained from the three regressions are summarized in the following three equations which have been written for standardized variables:

Work = 0.36 situational pleasantness −0.11 situation-arousing quality +0.08 stimulus screening +0.08 situational pleasantness × situation-arousing quality −0.07 situational pleasantness × stimulus screening

Work = 0.09 task pleasantness + (0.5 stimulus screening) + (0.05 task pleasantness × task-arousing quality)

Work = 0.37 Situation–task pleasantness −0.10 situation–task-arousing quality + 0.06 stimulus screening + 0.09 situation–task pleasantness × situation–task-arousing quality −0.09 situation–task pleasantness × stimulus screening

Perhaps the most thoughtful review of this controversy, however, has been that of Kenrick and Funder (1988) who note that nearly all of the arguments

against personality traits as determinants of social behaviour have turned out
to be specious, and yet we have not come full circle to the reacceptance of
traits as they were understood 20 years ago. Current wisdom is summed up
as follows:

> Other practical lessons have emerged from this controversy. The research
> now indicates quite clearly that anyone who seeks predictive validity from
> trait ratings will do better to use (a) raters who are thoroughly familiar
> with the person being rated; (b) multiple behavioural observations; (c)
> multiple observers; (d) dimensions that are publicly observable; and
> (e) behaviours that are relevant to the dimension in question. On the
> other hand, one should not expect great accuracy when predicting (a)
> behaviour in 'powerful' and clearly normatively scripted situations from
> trait ratings and (b) single behavioural instance from another single
> behavioural instance (p.31).

Various studies have been done in the person–situation tradition in the
organizational behaviour area. For instance, Newton and Keenan (1983)
asked if work involvement was an attribute or the person or the environment,
and concluded that it was predominantly the latter. A revival in interest and
research in the dispositional determinants of organizational behaviour (Weiss
and Adler, 1984) has met with various criticisms. Davis-Blake and Pfeffer
(1989) have rehearsed some of the person–situation debate but this time
conceiving of it in terms of the person–organization debate. Their argument
is essentially thus:

- Organizations are strong settings that have a powerful effect on individual
  beliefs and behaviours. Therefore, dispositions are likely to have only
  limited effects on individual reactions in organizations. Such factors
  as well-defined organizational roles and strong corporate systems all
  minimize individual differences.
- To argue that individuals do not change and adapt requires an explanation
  (and evidence), as yet not forthcoming, as to why that is the case. Indeed,
  they argued that all of the evidence suggests that individuals are frequently
  affected by organizational structure and information.

Furthermore, they point out the problems associated with the current empirical evidence for the dispositional approach. These include the following:

- Problems associated with interpreting correlations over time: firstly, that
  stability does not necessarily require the trait concept for explanation;
  secondly, correlations provide only evidence of relative ranking and do
  not discount the possibility of large situational differences. A true test of
  the predictive validity of a measured trait needs to be done.
- No research attempts a causal model of job attitudes, or attitude changes,
  over time. A major problem, according to these authors, is that their

moderating and confounding variables are neither modelled nor measured in person–organization research so invalidating interpretation of the model.

They believe that person–organization dispositional research requires, at minimum, four steps:

1. Dispositional factors need to be properly measured, and data stability over time must not be used to infer both the existence and effects of a trait.
2. Non-dispositional factors (features of work itself) need to be measured as well as traits.
3. The relative importance (i.e. variance accounted for) needs to be considered so that test models can simultaneously examine the effects of both dispositions and organizational situations.
4. Researchers must develop some testable ideas about the sources and stability of dispositions.

It is important to consider the various reasons why this debate, now for all purposes settled in social and personality psychology, should be so powerfully discussed in the organizational behaviour literature. This could be argued on sociological as well as psychological grounds. Firstly, the idea that disposition predicts organizational behaviour reduces, for the most part, organizational behaviour theory and research to personality theory and psychometrics, something management scientists have a vested interest in not letting happen. Secondly, the organizational behaviour literature seems to have neglected the dispositional approach for a longer period of time than the clinical literature, hence the sudden and belated level of the topic. Thirdly, if the dispositional determinants' position is true, it makes organizational change more difficult, something organizational behaviour specialists might not like to admit.

• Why is it OB (organizational behaviour) and not OS (organizational science)?
• What is (and isn't) an organization?
• Is organizational behaviour different from non-organizational behaviour?
• Is organizational theory derivative of other core disciplines? If so, which?
• Are there any theories unique to OB?
• Organizations influence individual behaviour but individuals also influence the behaviour of organizations.

Organizations can only influence the behaviour of individuals within them if they are very powerful. This is either because of loyalty to organization values, roles and norms of behaviour, or because organizations demand strong conformity (like armies or total institutions) and individuals are strongly pressured into a homogenous, 'corporate culture', behavioural repertoire. Organizations can equally reward individuality, eccentricity and polymorphous perversity (like universities) so that, in a paradoxical way, they can also strongly shape the behaviour of individuals in them by stressing individuality. It could be argued that the major concerns (topic areas, problems, agendas) of a discipline can be ascertained from the chapter headings and references of standard textbooks.

11.3 WHY PERSONALITY TRAITS DO NOT PREDICT BEHAVIOUR AT WORK

To both lay person and trait theorist alike, it is self-evident that personality traits are correlates, indicators or predictors of social behaviour in the workplace or elsewhere. But it is equally true that the diverse and patchy literature is highly equivocal about that relationship, with as many studies indicating a statistically significant relationship as not. Where a theoretically meaningful and statistically significant relationship is found, researchers usually rejoice. But what does one do with no significant findings? Why do personality traits *not* predict occupational behaviour?

The following explanations are not mutually exclusive or rank ordered, but they may explain non-significant findings:

- There are problems with the theoretical formulation in the first place in that the personality theory or system has been poorly or inaccurately conceived.
- The measurement of the personality trait is poor for a variety of reasons:

    (a) It measures a single trait which is actually multi-dimensional.
    (b) The measure has poor reliabilities (e.g. Cronbach's alpha) or is not a valid measure of what is being tested.
    (c) Various systematic errors involved with self-report, such as attributional errors or dissimulators, render the scores meaningless.

- Although the personality measures and theory are satisfactory, there is no reason to suppose that the trait(s) selected actually predicts the occupational behaviour specified. That is, the dependent variable is quite simply, and for good theoretical reasons, not related to the independent variable.
- The measurement of the occupational behaviour (i.e. absenteeism, productivity) is poor for a number of reasons:

    (a) Only one or very few measures have been taken, so threatening the reliability of the measure (i.e. no good aggregate measure is used).

(b) The occupational behaviour measure is subject to systematic error whether it is derived by observation, test data or self-report.

• The occupational behaviour is shaped and constrained by other more powerful factors than personality traits. That is, although there is a coherent and consistent relationship between personality and occupational behaviour, such as union agreements, unalterable working conditions or incentive schemes (usually the lack of), these suppress or diminish the relationship which actually exists.

• Personality is a moderator variable rather than a direct predictor of occupational behaviour and, thus, its force depends on a wide range of other variables being present.

• Sampling problems have 'washed' out or suppressed the relationship for a number of reasons:

(a) Because of self-selection, or indeed rigorous recruitment to too many jobs, people in them are too homogeneous in terms of their personality to show strong findings.

(b) For practical reasons, it is impossible to sample the occupational behaviour unconstrained by other factors, hence the range is limited and related to other factors.

• Through resignation, sacking and self-selection, people with particular traits inappropriate to a job producing a specific occupational behaviour actually leave, thus reducing the possibility of finding an effect.

Butcher (1985) outlined eight factors that influence (often adversely) the validity of psychological assessment in industrial settings:

a. Invalid response patterns may occur as a result of an individual's fear that management will use the test results against him or her.

b. The attitudes of local labour organizations may affect the psychological evaluation. The union may actively protest the evaluation, encourage assessments beneficial to the employee, take a more positive, neutral, or negative position, any of which might affect the validity of the evaluation through psychological assessment methods.

c. For example, it may wish to eliminate candidates for promotion who may not remain in the position long. Factors other than personality variables, such as better pay elsewhere or unpleasant working conditions, may be more powerful determinants of job tenure.

d. The psychological tests selected should be the most valid available measures of the attributes in question.

e. Management may have been 'oversold' on psychological techniques, and may expect easy categorical answers to complex or unanswerable questions.

f. The assessment questions may be inappropriate. I was once asked whether it would be possible to use psychological tests to detect the sexual preference of male candidates who would be applying for positions as airline stewards. The managers wanted to reject homosexuals, who, they believed, would 'harass the male customers'. Clearly, this is an inappropriate (and in many jurisdictions, unlawful) use of personality assessment.

g. Some aspects of the evaluation may be unwarranted violation of the individual's right to privacy. There must be valid psychological reasons for having the particular information sought in making the assessment.

h. The report or the recommendations from the assessment must be used properly (p.280–1).

Individual differences have long been claimed to be powerful *moderator* variables between job characteristics (like job scope) and employee reactions (like job satisfaction). In a review article, White (1978) lists six psychological variables (authoritarianism, need for independence, alienation, Protestant ethic, higher-order need strength, and locus of control) and two demographic variables (urban/rural, education). He lists a significant number of studies on this topic and lists various critical issues:

1. Cross-sectional studies mean that cause and correlation cannot be disentangled: i.e. intrinsically motivated people seek out, or are selected for, high quality jobs, or jobs of certain types make people happy.
2. Subject and treatment may be confounded such that, for instance, high performing employees may distort their reports of job characteristics.
3. It is not certain if job enrichment or job structure change is more motivating. Thus, quite a different set of personality characteristics might moderate the effectiveness of the enrichment process as opposed to make rating reactions to existing job conditions.
4. The magnitude of the mediating effect is not clear. That is, the results do not indicate the power of the moderator effect.
5. Most importantly, neither duplicative nor replicative results show consistency.

Because of these results, White is rather sceptical about research in the area. He concludes:

It appears that the only chance to identify reproducible moderators is for very narrowly defined constructs and very specific samples and situations. Of what significance would such research be?

There seems to be little reason for pursuing this line of research, given that: (a) often no moderating effects are found; (b) moderators which are found tend to be modest and inconsistent; (c) the real situation is probably worse than indicated because studies that found no or inconsistent effects were probably less likely to be accepted for publication; (d) at best, moderators can be expected to hold up only for narrowly defined constructs and specific samples and situations; and (e) even when there are moderating effects all groups tend to respond in the same direction. Nineteen years of theory building and empirical research have not provided much hope in finding generalizable individual difference moderators of the relationship between job quality and worker responses. Why continue? (p.279).

11.4 ARE SOME BEHAVIOURS OR SOME PEOPLE EASIER TO PREDICT?

Some (occupational) behaviours and some people seem easier to predict than others. Criterion behaviours certainly seem easier to predict if they are more reliable; multiple acts, aggregated over time and prototypes. More importantly, what kinds of people are difficult to predict? Hogan (1990) appears to have come up with three kinds:

• Those who always describe their behaviour as dependent on the situation. Those with external locus of control who believe luck or powerful others shape their behaviour are difficult to predict because they are controlled from without, not within.
• Those who are defensive and conscious of the socially desirable thing to do, or be. Their behaviour is thus determined not by what their natural preferences are, but rather what they believe will get most approval. High self-monitors who try to act in a way appropriate to the particular setting are also difficult to predict.
• Those with well-developed self-presentational skills are more predictable because they are able to present an inherently good performance in a variety of settings.

There is also a question of whether occupational behaviour is easier to predict in some situations rather than others. As Buss (1989) has noted, traits become better predictors (than situational factors) of occupational behaviour when:

• The social content is familiar, informal and private (rather than novel, formal and public).
• When instructions are general or don't really exist (as opposed to detailed and complete).
• When there is considerable choice of behaviours.
• When the duration of social behaviour is extensive rather than brief.
• When responses are broad rather than narrow based.

Many people in business say that through the joint factors of selection (by the individual *and* the organization) and socialization, people in the same department (or part of the organization) tend to have the same sort of traits, preferences and abilities. Thus, the accounts department is full of numerically talented introverts and marketing creative extraverts.

Table 11.1 shows a hypothetical 'map' of the relationship between personality and occupational roles. This is intuitively appealing but suffers from a number of drawbacks:

- This table represents hypotheses only, as programmatic work of this kind has really not been done. Whether this is true or not represents an empirical question.
- It assumes, possibly falsely, a homogeneity of types/traits with occupational roles, which is unlikely to occur.
- It assumes that these relationships are valid across all industries and businesses, which may not be true. That is, the relationship between personality and occupational role may be revised in two highly disparate organizations.
- One cannot be sure whether the homogeneity in group roles occurred by self-selection, organizational selection, or strong or weak socialization.
- It is unlikely that organizationally defined groups would work well if they were all too similar (Belbin, 1981).
- The relationship ignores the fact of hierarchies within groups and the real possibility that 'leaders' (elected or emerged) are probably different from those who do not move upward.

It would be most attractive if Table 11.1 was true; the results were generalized across industries and valid within groups; and that the relationship was functional. Alas, there is no evidence that this is indeed the case.

Whereas some have argued that personality factors are crucial in determining job performance (satisfaction, motivation, productivity), others have agreed that performance is a function of the characteristics of the job. O'Brien (1982) has argued that five characteristics are central: skill variety, test identity, task significance, autonomy and feedback. But he does argue that the need for psychological growth does moderate the relationship between job characteristics and growth. His argument is that the five job characteristics lead to various psychological states, like experienced meaninglessness of work, responsibility for outcome, knowledge of results which have direct effects on the outcomes. Overall, his review reveals equivocal and weak support for the approach. No doubt one reason for this is that crucially important individual difference factors are ignored.

Others have stressed the moderator variable approach. For instance, Lysonski and Andrews (1990) looked at role autonomy, need for affiliation, and tolerance of ambiguity as moderators between job role and outcome. Tolerance of ambiguity did not show any effect but the other variables did. Role autonomy moderated between ambiguity and job satisfaction,

Table 11.1 A possible grid looking at the relationship between personality variables and organizational roles

Personal profile	1 Marketing and sales	2 Accounts and finance	3 Research and development	4 Human resources (personnel)	5 Manufacturing and production	6 Computing and systems	7 Strategic planning
Extraversion	++	--	--	+	-	-	+
Neuroticism	+	-	++	++	-	-	-
Instrumentalism	-	++	++	++	++	++	++
Conservatism	-	++	++	-	++	++	++
Intelligence	+	+	++	+	++	+	++

++ High probability of an association (i.e. marketing and sales are extraverts)
+ Medium probability of an association
- Medium probability of inverse association (i.e. accounts and finance are introverts)
-- High probability of inverse association

while need for affiliation moderated between role conflict and perceived performance. Hence, they conclude that a judicious selection of product managers in terms of the two traits already identified will have important benefits for company productivity.

11.5 IS OCCUPATIONAL SUCCESS INHERITED?

The very idea that individuals may be genetically programmed to varying degrees to strive for, and attain, occupational success has been considered anathema for certain psychologists. Many assume that organizational, structural and sociological factors are primary determinants of occupational success.

Contrary to the assumption that individuals do not inherently vary in their tendencies to strive for, and attain, occupational goals, several research studies conducted over the past two decades have suggested that genetic factors, in fact, are involved. For example, both twin and adoption studies have found evidence that genetic factors make significant contributions to variations in educational achievement (Willerman, Horn and Loehlin, 1977), even in specific subject areas (Vandenberg, 1969; Scarr and Weinberg, 1983). Also, one twin study indicated that 'need for achievement' appeared to be genetically influenced (Vandenberg, 1969). Regarding earnings, a comparison of identical and fraternal twins led researchers to conclude that substantial variance in earnings by adult males was attributable to genetic factors (Behrman *et al.*, 1980). Finally, various studies based on twin data (Vandenberg and Kelly, 1964; Vandenberg and Stafford, 1967; Loehlin and Nichols 1976) and one based on adoption data (Grotevant, Scarr and Weinberg, 1978) indicated that fairly specific career interests and choices are genetically influenced. Probably the most convincing evidence that vocational interests (and thereby the occupational success and earnings typical of those vocations) are genetically influenced has come from recent studies of identical twins reared apart (Bouchard, Moloney and Segal, 1989).

11.6 THE STUDY OF 'HIGH-FLYERS'

One fairly obvious, although frequently flawed, way of attempting to understand the link between personality (traits, beliefs and behaviours) is to study those already successful. This 'known groups' method, however, seldom looks at the correlates of failure, preferring to examine (in detail) those of success.

The sort of issues examined are pretty obvious and predictable. Thus, Cox and Cooper (1988) examined family background, education, career pattern, orientation to work, philosophy of life, and personality. They found evidence of early childhood feelings of independence and self-reliance, frequently through loss and separation. Another self-evident finding is that parental expectations (attainable but high) relate to later success. The 'high-flyers' seem ambitious, determined, restless and change oriented. They seem intrinsically motivated and felt management, by and large, was interesting, enjoyable and worthwhile. Their values place high importance on achievement, ambition, relationships and integrity. Based on as much previous literature as empirical data, Cox and Cooper seem to believe that three abilities are crucial: problem solving/decision making, 'people skills' and 'vision'.

In order to investigate personality determinants of 'high-flyers', they gave the 16PF, the Kirton Scale and the A/B type measure. No very clear rationale is provided for this rather obvious and uninformed collection of

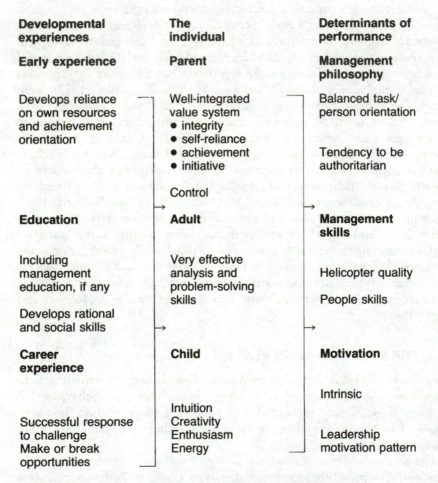

Figure 11.1 Factors contributing to high-flyer performance
Source: Cox and Cooper (1988)

questionnaires. However, from simply the mean 'profiles' of the group, they concluded:

> The managing directors in this study showed very varied personalities but with some key traits in common. It is not really very surprising that chief executives of large companies have powerful personalities and are *assertive* and *outgoing*. They also tend to be *emotionally stable, trusting, imaginative, experimenting, self-sufficient* and *shrewd*. They are very *innovative*; that is, they are prepared, if necessary, to challenge and change the existing system and not be constrained by conventional assumptions and beliefs. This characteristic stems from having a high *internal locus of control* and *self-confidence*, coupled with *originality* and *low conformity*, when occasion demands, to rules and group norms. They score very highly on type A behaviour, showing themselves to be *hard driving, aggressive, time-conscious* and *heavily involved in work*. This puts them at risk from coronary heart disease and other stress-related illnesses, but their attention to their own health and their generally healthy lifestyle outside working hours probably mitigate the worst effects of this aspect of their lives. Life is not always smooth for the 'top man' in any organization, and chief executives develop effective strategies for coping with adversity – treating setbacks as challenges to be overcome and opportunities for learning. All in all, theirs is a very positive approach to life (p.154–5).

In their final analysis, 16 characteristics of managerial success were suggested. These include: determination; learning from adversity; seizing chances when presented; achievement orientation; internal locus of control; well-integrated value system; effective management of risk; clear objectives; high dedication to the job; intrinsic motivation; well-organized life; pragmatic approach; sound, analytic and problem-solving skills; high level of 'people skills'; high level of innovation; type A personality. They offered a pictorial version of their understanding of how these factors related to one another (see Figure 11.1).

Manz *et al.* (1988) completed a most interesting attribution-like study of over 1500 managers – divided into higher and lower performing groups – who rank ordered typical hindrances. They were interested in identifying whether there were managerial thought patterns that show a higher awareness of performance hindrances that are associated with higher vs lower performing managers. They were asked to indicate to what extent each of 33 managerial hindrances negatively affected organizational culture. As ever, a major problem of this sort of research concerns the validity and sensitivity by which managers are classified as high or low. Various validity checks were put in place to ensure that the classification was sensitive and fair before the data was analysed. The results showed an interesting and interpretable pattern (see Table 11.2). While no apparent difference occurred between the number of hindrances perceived to occur, higher performing managers focused on

Table 11.2 Analysis of differences between higher and lower performance management groups on proportions identifying specific hindrance as important

Items	Higher performance managers (%)[a]	Lower performance managers (%)[b]	t	p<
Items with significant differences in direction of higher performers				
Little or no opportunity for advancement	33.2	14.7	12.88	0.001
Non-performance-based evaluations (degrees emphasized over performance, who rather than what you know, political nature of system and people outside division making selection/promotions)	17.5	8.3	8.0	0.001
Being too valuable for a product line or project to be developed or get promoted	9.0	3.4	6.69	0.001
Being direct/outspoken and disagreeing with management	14.4	10.3	3.66	0.001
Authoritarian management/closed climate/no risk taking	15.0	12.4	2.26	0.024
Societal conditions outside of (company's name) including the business climate	6.3	3.3	4.00	0.001
Age discrimination	3.6	1.9	2.99	0.003
Not being considered valuable enough to be developed	8.0	5.4	2.97	0.003
Items with significant difference in direction of lower performers				
My own lack of people-managing and communication skills	6.0	12.5	−6.80	0.001
My not being able to give up control of the technical decision-making process	4.2	9.6	−6.43	0.001
Lack of technical skills	5.1	8.5	−4.15	0.001
Inability to handle stress	1.0	3.0	−4.32	0.001
Not enough initial orientation on job	6.8	15.8	−8.77	0.001
Lack of time for development because of other job demands	20.8	27.8	−4.91	0.001
Being promoted too quickly	0.3	2.0	−4.90	0.001
Lack of feedback about your performance	16.8	19.6	−2.22	0.027
Poor health	0.3	0.8	−2.22	0.026
Not assertive enough	14.9	17.0	−1.17	0.077

Items with no significant differences at the $p < 0.10$ level

	$N = 1534$[a]	$N = 2048$[b]		
No inter-divisional or inter-functional experience	7.9	6.5	1.65	0.10
Lack of motivation or interest on my part	3.4	4.4	-1.48	0.139
Negative consequences associated with development, i.e. cost of retraining and cost of replacement	3.0	2.1	1.57	0.116
Business mistake/project failure	2.8	2.0	1.42	0.156
Working for a climber	4.6	3.7	1.42	0.154
Working for someone who others do not respect	13.2	11.8	1.21	0.23
Race discrimination	0.2	0.4	-1.09	0.274
Sex discrimination	1.3	0.9	1.05	0.295
Management's emphasis on short-term results	25.4	24.1	0.85	0.396
Physical handicap (including hearing, speech and/or vision)	0.7	0.4	0.84	0.400
Organization's lack of emphasis on establishing training goals and carrying them out	12.8	12.2	0.55	0.58
Too many subordinates	4.3	4.7	-0.55	0.583
Personal conflicts outside of work	2.8	3.0	-0.39	0.694
Being delegated responsibility without being given adequate amount of authority	17.0	16.5	0.39	0.695
Negative consequences for trying to develop myself, i.e. peer pressure and kidding about being a climber	1.6	1.7	-0.07	0.944

[a]$N = 1534$
[b]$N = 2048$
Source: Manz et al. (1988)

structural and procedural deficits (like few promotion opportunities, poor performance-based evaluations), while lower performing managers focused more on personal skill deficits (like lack of people-managing/communication skills, lack of technical skills etc). In line with many of the findings from attributional research, the results seem to indicate that dwelling on personal shortcomings in one's performance capabilities may decrease the probability of being a higher performer:

> While lower performers appear to be much more sensitive to limitations in their own performance capabilities, higher performers appear to be better insulated from damage to their self-perceptions stemming from achievement shortfalls e.g., negative evaluations are attributed to a lack of relationship with performance in the appraisal process, unsatisfactory advancement is viewed as stemming from being too important to be promoted, etc. (p.461).

The following are among the frequent problems of the 'high-flyers' method:

- *Definition*. What is a high-flyer? Cox and Cooper (1988) chose at random the Chief Executive Officer (CEO) from companies with a successful financial record. This will not do – companies succeed and fail through many other factors than the ability of their CEO. A monopoly, a major international crisis, or a highly able and dedicated work force may all lead to a company succeeding. Clearly, one needs a clear, multi-dimensional, operationalizable definition of a high-flyer before beginning.
- *Sampling*. Using samples of convenience rather than those chosen by theory. Predictably, many 'high-flyers' are too busy flying high to undertake interviews or fill out long questionnaires. Hence, those that self-select and in some way volunteer may be exceptionally unusual or simply unrepresentative. It is important, for any understanding of the subtle and complex causes of occupational success, that researchers choose carefully sampled groups.
- *Contrast groups*. It is quite pointless attempting to understand the factors that lead to somebody becoming a high-flyer, unless one can show that they are unique to high-flyers. This requires some contrast with those who are less successful but similar in other ways. That is, unless contrast or control groups are employed, it becomes impossible to ascertain how unique factors are in leading a person to becoming a high-flyer or not.
- *Memory effects*. Many studies of successful people request and require them to recall childhood and early adult experiences that are implicated in their success. This of course means that various memorial biases may occur, so threatening the reliability of this information. This is all the more likely when one knows that high-flyers are fairly frequently asked to reflect on their childhood, and that therefore stories may get modified and more and more fabricated on the re-telling.
- *Tests and hypotheses*. Few, if any, of these studies have any clear hypotheses

or theories to test. Hence, there is rarely a sensitive, judicious choice of psychometric test to give high-flyers. The whole exercise thus becomes something of a fishing expedition in the deep and murky waters of invalid personality tests and common-sense suppositions that yield nothing but trivialities.

● *Cause and effect*. Of course, showing that high-flyers have a particular personality or belief system does not mean that in some sense this leads to them being successful. Correlation does not infer cause. Only longitudinal research can show quite clearly how psychological factors impinge on success and vice versa. It is entirely misleading to believe that there is no feedback mechanism whereby the reward of success has no effects on beliefs and behaviour.

● *Stability of predictors*. It is often supposed that those factors which relate to (predict, correlate with) occupational success, leading to a person being a high-flyer, are fairly stable over time. However, in a rapidly changing economic climate, factors that correlated with yesterday's high-flyer might not do so today. Indeed, the correlations might easily change from significantly positive to significantly negative. That is, correlates of current success need not be correlates of future success.

11.7 SELF-ESTEEM AT WORK

Since the work of Korman (1970), the concept of self-esteem at work as a motivating variable has attracted attention. For instance, Terborg, Richardson and Pritchard (1980) found that self-esteem was significantly correlated with effort and the quality and quantity of output. Ellis and Taylor (1983) found that self-esteem was related to the job search process, including the sources that individuals used to find jobs; interview evaluations received from organizational recruiters; satisfaction with job search; number of offers received; and acceptance of a job before graduation. Hollenbeck and Whitener (1988) illustrated their point that personality traits can and do predict occupational behaviour by focusing specifically on self-esteem. They argue, following various theoretical tenets, that with ability held constant, self-esteem would be related to work motivation and performance only in those situations characterized by high job involvement. They then review a number of studies which confirm their thesis.

However, there are other, more general studies on self-esteem and employee behaviour. Sullivan (1989) has reviewed the area and suggested that two paradigms govern all self-theories: self as active agent; self as self-concept under which all theories of motivation can be subsumed. The self as agent related to many other psychological theories, like need, balance, equity and expectancy theory, while the self as process involves various other theories, like self-reinforcement, self-schematic and self-efficacy. Sullivan argues that different motivation theories are predictive for the initiation, direction, intensity, persistence and termination of work behaviour, so rejecting the possibility of a grand theory. Equally, however, he sees self-theories as essential explanation.

Brockner (1988) argued that employees bring to their work different levels of self-esteem which correlate with how they act, feel and think while on the job. All individuals need to feel good about themselves, and much of what they do and believe is concerned with enhancing, preserving and restoring their self-esteem. Brockner notes that compared to those workers low in self-esteem, those high in self-esteem are:

- more apt to work harder in response to negative feedback;
- less likely to imitate the managerial style of their supervisors;
- less likely to perform deferentially as a function of the supportiveness of their work group;
- less negatively affected by chronic stressors, such as role ambiguity and conflict, and acute stressors – stress and lay-offs;
- more likely to be productive in quality circles.

Brockner recognizes that self-esteem may be both global and specific, and that there is a whole range of related concepts, self-confidence and self-assurance. His review of the literature is both comprehensive and fascinating. For instance, self-esteem has been shown to be related to occupational choice. Those high in self-esteem believe that their career is likely to satisfy their desires and that they possess more of the ability in order to succeed than those low in self-esteem. Because people act and think in ways consistent with their self-esteem, those with more self-esteem are more ambitious. Furthermore, the way in which they search for jobs is likely to have a more successful outcome.

Brockner notes the research on the relationship between such things as self-esteem and performance, job attitudes and the performance–satisfaction relationship:

> Many studies have failed to document a relationship between self-esteem and work attitudes and behaviours; however, this should not be taken to mean that self-esteem is not an important determinant or predictor of work attitudes – and behaviours. Rather, investigators typically have explored self-esteem in the organizational context in ways that may have masked its potential influence (p.20).

He offers a theory of behavioural plasticity, as it relates to self-esteem. Behavioural plasticity refers to the extent to which an individual's actions are susceptible to influence, by external and social cues. People low in self-esteem are usually more susceptible to influence by organizational events than their high self-esteem counterparts. This is because low self-esteem people:

- relate to social comparisons and uncertainty concerning the correctness of one's beliefs and behaviours;
- have a greater need for social approval and dependency on others to provide them with positive evaluations;
- have a greater susceptibility to the influence of negative feedback.

Plasticity is related to employee performance in a number of ways: prior to performance (low self-esteem people are more influenced by expectations), during performance (low self-esteem people are more susceptible to external cues) and after performance (low self-esteem people have a pessimistic attributional style). Brockner notes:

> To illustrate how the cognitions may interrelate and provide further evidence on the plasticity hypothesis, consider the effect of success versus failure feedback on the subsequent performance of low and high SEs. Several studies have shown that individuals generally perform better following success than failure. Why might this be so, and especially for low SEs?
>
> 1. Expectancies. The effect of the success–failure variable may be to alter workers' expectations for their performance at a subsequent task, such that they approach it far more optimistically following success than failure.
> 2. Attentional focus. It is possible that failure induces self-focused attention (whereas success may elicit task-focused attention). Thus, following failure, workers may be more self-focused than subsequent to success, accounting for better performance in the latter than the former condition.
> 3. Goal setting. Related to attentional focus above, it is possible that success causes individuals to focus on the task in ways that facilitate performance. For example, prior success may 'psychologically free up' the worker to think about strategies for effective performance, which is believed to be one of the mediators of goal-setting effects (Brockner *et al.* 1981). Said differently, failure and its resultant self-focused attention probably interferes with workers' abilities to set goals or contemplate strategies to achieve goals.
> 4. Attribution. It may not merely be the outcome, but rather the attribution for that outcome that influences subsequent performance. Thus, failure coupled with pessimistic attributions for the failure may cause workers to perform worse than following success.

Any or all of these cognitive mechanisms could mediate the impact of feed-back on subsequent performance. Moreover, the plasticity hypothesis posits that such performance-relevant cognitions are more manipulable among low than high SEs, suggesting that success versus failure feedback may have a greater effect on the subsequent performance of the former than the latter group (p.77).

Research findings tend to support the original theory, namely that workers low in self-esteem tend to be more affected by all sorts of organizational stimuli, including peer-group interactions, evaluation feedback, socialization practices, leadership behaviours etc. More importantly perhaps, self-esteem has been seen to moderate between such things as lay-offs and performance. The functional value of plasticity was also discussed.

Brockner also reviewed the by-now, fairly extensive literature which has examined the relationship between self-esteem (global and work specific) and both intrinsic (e.g. autonomy, role ambiguity, job complexity) and extrinsic (pay, job level) job characteristics:

> The discussion here suggests that global and specific self-esteem may combine interactively to affect employee behaviour. A related question to be addressed by future research is the interaction between global and specific self-esteem, as they affect one another. For example, at what point, or how, does change in specific self-esteem become change in global self-esteem? Two of the factors that may moderate the impact of specific self-esteem on global self-esteem are the importance and frequency of the situations-specific domain. Change in specific self-esteem may translate into change in global self-esteem if the domain is important and/or frequently encountered. Both moderator variables may help explain why work conditions affect personality, including global self-esteem. For many adults, work is an important specific domain in their lives. Furthermore, the conditions in their work worlds are those to which they are frequently exposed. So powerful is the effect of work on personality, argue Kohn and Schooler, that work-produced change in personality often generalizes to the nonwork areas in individuals' lives. For example, if working conditions provide employees with self-direction, they come to value self-direction in their work as well as nonwork activities. Future research needs to delineate the workplace factors that moderate the relationship between specific and global self-esteem.

> Finally, a central theme in the field of organizational behaviour is that effectiveness – whether measured at the individual group, or organizational levels of analysis – is a function of the degree of fit or congruence between the various component parts of the organization (that is, the people, the nature of the work, and informal and formal organizational arrangements). If managers do try to influence their subordinates' self-esteem – in the service of increasing effectiveness – then they must be certain that such self-esteem change is in synchrony with any changes produced in other component parts of the organization. For

example, suppose the managers aspire to raise subordinates' self-esteem. If so, they should also try to ensure that the organization provides the kind of environment in which high SEs function more effectively. Since high SEs respond well to challenging tasks, then the key of managerial effectiveness in this example is not only to raise subordinates' self-esteem, but also to ensure that their work is challenging. In short, it should not be forgotten that even a dimension as fundamental as self-esteem must be treated within the context of (that is, in interaction with) a wide range of organizational events, factors, and processes (p.158).

Finally, Brockner considers how workers act, and sometimes at cost to both them and their organization, to maintain and enhance self-esteem needs. Three examples of the negative effects of people attempting to fulfil self-esteem needs are as follows:

- Workers' reluctance to seek assistance which if actually acquired is beneficial.
- Decision makers' reluctance to withdraw commitment and a U-turn from a previously advocated and publicly failing commitment.
- Workers not performing at optimal levels, to fulfil the inappropriate expectations and values of stress.

A major theme of Brockner's work is that, to a large extent, a manager's ability to influence his/her subordinates' self-esteem, in a positive direction, is the key to effective management. Managers, he believes, can:

- reduce workers' self-esteem needs to decrease the negative impact that such needs have on their work behaviour;
- channel workers' self-esteem needs into a constructive rather than destructive course of action;
- increase workers' self-esteem, although many factors may combine to determine this.

The importance of Brockner's work is three-fold: he highlighted a fundamentally important personality variable frequently ignored; he offered a sophisticated, parsimonious account of how self-esteem needs relate to occupational behaviour; and he reviewed the literature comprehensively. More importantly, he offered a sound methodological critique of the various studies in the literature which has yielded such contradictory findings.

Not everyone will go along with Brockner in his analysis, arguing that self-esteem is either epiphenomena or a consequence of more important and fundamental personality processes. Nevertheless, it is certainly true that self-esteem can be shown to be systematically, and theoretically coherently, related to occupational behaviour.

11.8 INDIVIDUAL DIFFERENCES IN REACTIONS TO TIME

Yet another neglected area is the relationship between personality and time. The way in which people at work perceive, estimate, feel threatened by or liberate time has long been a concern of psychologists. Clearly, the concern with time management courses in the 1980s indicates the extent to which managers are interested in the way that individuals understand the passing of time. Although the scattered and diffuse literature has concentrated on various psychological aspects of time, comparatively little has focused on individual differences. Serendipitously, however, a number of rather diffuse areas of research have looked at time. These include the following:

• Individual difference measures all related to *arousal* (especially type A), many of which are concerned with people's attitude to time, preference for pace, and stimulation.
• Postponement of gratification, future time orientation and the experience of time by different groups.
• Chronobiology and the consequences of being a morning- or evening-type person for social and work-related behaviour at various times of the day.
• Obsessionality about time passing.
• Procrastination and the reasons for, and types of, people that *postpone* doing things.
• Time at work – a consideration of some of the issues concerned with how time is organized (and preferred) in the workplace, such as flexitime etc.

Individual Differences, Especially A Type and Arousal

There are a number of individual difference variables in psychology that show considerable overlap: extraversion/introversion; high/low sensation-seeking; screeners vs non-screeners; augmenters/reducers; type A/B. Nearly all are based on the idea of arousal which can be traced back to Pavlovian ideas of the excitatory strength of the nervous system. Low-reactive individuals (extraverts, type As) seek stimulation, while high-reactive individuals (introverts, type Bs) reduce stimulation to maintain or restore a genetically fixed optimal level of arousal. Low-reactive individuals tend to be more time-sensitive.

Extensive work on vigilance, attention and memory suggests that extraverts need more stimulation in the sense of greater variety or more intense stimuli than introverts. Thus, they should have shorter, more varied meetings. Extraverts could operate in high arousal situations (trains, open-planned offices) better than introverts.

Type A people are always in a hurry, doing too much and frequently taking on too much. In a sense, they may be particularly productive, but under certain circumstances they are precisely the opposite. Time urgency has been thoroughly investigated in the type A literature, as has psychological entrapment with respect to time investment (Strube, Denchmann and Kickham, 1989).

Postponement of Gratification and Time Perspectives

There is a long tradition of research into time perspectives. A number of different themes run through this literature, but one of the most common is the idea of postponement of gratification: two contrasting patterns of delay and impulsivity have been conceptualized as extreme poles. On one end is the individual who predominantly chooses larger, delayed rewards or goals for which he/she must either wait or work. This person is more likely to be oriented toward the future and to plan carefully for distant goals. He/she is also apt to have high scores on 'ego control' measures, high achievement motivation, to be more trusting and socially responsible, to have a high level of aspiration, and to show less uncontrolled impulsivity. This extreme pattern resembles what has been called the 'puritan character structure'. Socioculturally, this pattern tends to be found most often in middle and upper (in contrast to lower) socio-economic classes, and in highly achievement-oriented ('Protestant ethic') cultures. This pattern of high ego-strength is also related to a relatively high level of competence, as revealed by higher intelligence, more mature cognitive development, and a greater capacity for sustained attention.

At the opposite extreme is the individual who predominantly prefers immediate gratification and declines the alternative of waiting or working for larger, delayed goals. Correlated with this is a greater concern with the immediate present than with the future, and great impulsivity. Socioculturally, this pattern is correlated with the membership in the lower socio-economic classes, with membership in cultures in which the achievement orientation is low, and with indices of lesser social and cognitive competence.

In other words, this dimension is concerned with the planning, and receiving, of rewards from short-, middle- and long-term goals. Clearly, those people who show difficulty in postponing their gratification will show a preference for short-term goals which are not always appropriate. The ability to delay gratification is associated with future time perspective. There are some 'four-legs-good, two-legs bad' suggestions in this work, suggesting that ability to postpone gratification is always a good thing, although this is far from the case. Furthermore, it is possible that people have both personal- and work-related patterns of postponement, the one 'compensating' for the other.

Chronobiology: Morning and Evening Types

The idea of chronobiology arises out of the work on circadian variations of oral temperature. The work in this area falls under many titles: time-of-day effects, morningness–eveningness, chronobiology and circadian rhythms. There are significant variations over the day in the subjective arousal that people experience, and in the speed and accuracy that they perform motor and cognitive tasks. All sorts of bodily measures (blood, urine, oral temperature) can be shown to vary over the day, and these are related to the duration, speed and accuracy with which people are able to perform various tasks.

It is suggested that people differ in these rhythms and that one can distinguish between morning, intermediate and evening people depending on the peak in body temperature and efficiency curves over the day. In this sense, one could talk about larks and owls, but this term could become fairly confusing since these are comparative terms. Larks or morningness people do not reach their peak during the morning, but they are significantly more aroused than eveningness people who reach their peak later in the day. In fact, the peak time for both groups is in the early evening only about an hour apart. But there are noticeable differences between the two groups in their sleeping patterns – bed and rising time, and sleep length. Thus:

- Evening types prefer to go to bed later than morning types (by as much as two hours).
- Evening types prefer to get up later than morning types (by as much as two hours).
- There is a significant difference during the day between the two types which is most apparent during the early morning when both types are relatively cold and under-aroused.

Two important points should be noted here. First, these types are related to other important variables like introversion–extraversion, and traits associated with psychopathology (Matthews, 1988). More importantly, people attempt to change their arousal levels by simple, but relatively powerful things such as caffeine. Thus, an evening person may improve his/her performance in the morning by taking a lot of caffeine, while reducing arousal in the evening by taking alcohol. Recent work on the measurement of circadian rhythms has taken place (Smith, Reilly and Midkiff, 1989).

Obsessionality and Order

One very important aspect of individual differences with respect to time is need for order. This may simply be a very high need or may be pathological obsessionality. In order to describe this, Freud identified three main traits associated with people who had fixated at the anal stage – orderliness, parsimony and obstinacy, with associated qualities of cleanliness, conscientiousness, trustworthiness, defiance and revengefulness.

If a child is traumatized by the experience of toilet training, he/she tends to retain ways of coping and behaving during this phase. The way in which a miser hoards money is seen as symbolic of a child's refusal to eliminate faeces in the face of parental demands. The spendthrift, on the other hand, recalls the approval and affection that resulted from submission to parental authority to defecate. Thus, some people equate elimination/spending with receiving affection and hence feel more inclined to spend when feeling insecure, unloved or in need of affection. Attitudes to money are then bi-modal – either they are extremely positive or extremely negative.

There are different types of anal characteristics – associated with holding on and letting go (accumulative vs expulsive) – many of which are relevant to time keeping: need for regularity to the point of rigidity; concern with order of all facets of behaviour; frugality in all things; concern with time keeping; the idea that time is a precious resource. To some extent, the opposite of the anal personality is the oral character, but to a larger extent there is no opposite – either one is non-anal or anal to some degree. Like nearly every other concept, anality has both good and bad points, and there are jobs well suited to and highly appropriate for the anal type: quality controller, proof reader, record keeper.

Procrastination

Procrastination is the tendency to postpone that which is necessary to reach a goal. It appears that the tendency to procrastinate can occur for a number of reasons. These include:

- Neurotic disorganization – being so disorganized that certain goals have to be postponed because they cannot be faced or achieved.
- Low self-esteem and high anxiety, which means never achieving a goal (such as taking a test), which means that one cannot fail it. In other words, doubt about one's ability leads to procrastination.
- Low energy levels, which means that people attempt to cope by spacing out various activities so that there is sufficient energy for each occasion.

It is quite possible that procrastination is a coping strategy, but it may also be associated with other traits and work-related behaviours. Lay (1986) has argued that procrastinators do not draw well from past experience in accurately estimating how long it will take them to complete a task. This includes not only those things that they ought to be doing, but also the secondary tasks that they attend to while avoiding what they ought to be doing. Procrastinators underestimate the duration of time needed to complete such tasks and are, then, unrealistic and irrational. This tendency in procrastinators to underestimate will occur when they are under pressure, under pressure of time to some deadline, and under pressure of enticing alternatives to working on the task at hand. It is this pressure factor that is important in this proposal. Well before deadlines, procrastinators may be equally accurate.

Part of the irrationality of procrastinators may be in their failure to maintain priorities over a series of ongoing and upcoming tasks and goals. The procrastinator may be as likely as the non-procrastinator to make plans in conjunction with the importance of tasks in one's life, and in conjunction with time considerations about those tasks. That is, they may equally be able to prioritize ongoing tasks on a day-to-day basis. On the other hand, during periods of the wait stage, they may be less able to keep these priorities sorted and cognitively available to them through the course of the day and the week. Or they may actively engage in behaviour which does not correspond to their priorities. This link between priorities and goal-associated behaviour may be viewed as an inherent part of the defining of procrastinator behaviour.

Time at Work: Structure and Flexitime

Work fulfils a number of functions, one of the most important of which is that it structures time. Researchers who have been interested in unemployment have been particularly interested in this function (Bond and Feather, 1988). It determines at what time people have to get out of bed, how long they will be away from home, and how they will spend their time during the day. It also provides structure over longer periods. It differentiates weekends and holidays from working days, and provides many with a timetable for progressing through a career. As mentioned elsewhere in this book, many of the people we talked to found that loss of work was very disorienting because it undermined the way that they structured their lives. Jahoda (1979) illustrates this by describing what happened in an Austrian village in the 1930s when a factory closed down. She found that unemployed men lost their sense of time. When asked at the end of a day what they had done during it, they seemed unable to describe their activities. 'Real' time only appeared to enter their descriptions at the biologically incisive points – getting up, eating, going to bed – but the rest was vague and nebulous. She found that activities such as fetching wood from the shed, which could not have consumed more than a few minutes, were recorded as if they had filled the whole morning.

None the less, women complained that their menfolk were unpunctual for meals.

A great deal of work has gone into flexitime. This gives people the opportunity to choose their hours of work. However, the term is misleading in one sense. Although it is possible to change their hours of work on a day-to-day basis (as long as they are there between say 11.00 and 15.00 *and* work the requisite hours during the day), people simply choose a time structure (in early–home early vs in late–home late) that suits them and they stick to it. However, people appear to enjoy this system and work better within it.

11.9 INDIVIDUALS, TEAMS AND OCCUPATIONAL SUCCESS

Most major decisions in business organizations are made by teams. Team building is considered an essential part of occupational behaviour, as teams open up a wider range of experience and abilities. There is considerable literature on whether teams produce, qualitatively and quantitatively, better ideas and solutions than individuals working apart. Essentially, it seems that two factors are important in determining whether 'too many cooks spoil the broth' or 'many hands make light work': the nature of the task (structured vs creative) and the ability of the individuals (high vs low). Whatever the research results show, most senior management occurs in teams, and many managers see themselves akin to sports captains (or coaches) who select, train and lead teams (to win the game).

There is a surprising paucity of psychological and sociological studies that focus on individual difference reactions in teams, or role preferences in teams. This is reflected by the fact that so few measures exist to determine team-role behaviour. Very few tests attempt to ascertain how people characteristically behave in work teams. Personality tests supposedly measure behaviours in a wide variety of settings (both in and out of teams), while occupational-based measures of work-related behaviours frequently ignore the social dimensions of work-related behaviour. Managers, aware that just as the right mix of people in terms of ability, preferences and predispositions create efficient, effective and contented teams so the opposite (the wrong mix) can have potentially disastrous results, have long attempted to design or develop optimal teams in terms of the composition of members.

There is considerable literature on the creation of teams, the way in which they function, and the consequences of their make-up. Most of the work in this field is proscriptive and prescriptive, based on various case studies (Handy, 1985). There does, however, appear to be little empirical evidence to support the various theories in this area. There are at least two major problems that have contributed to this relatively sorry state of affairs. The first is the extreme difficulty in measuring salient, ecologically valid and reliable team-dependent outcome variables in order to establish some criterion of team success. Unless one has a reasonable measure of team performance, it is difficult to discover how individual difference factors in constituting a team differ. Secondly, and perhaps equally importantly, is the lack of psychometrically valid measures of how people behave in teams. Although there are innumerable measures of personality, coping and attributional styles, there are very few measures which explicitly set out to examine how people behave in work teams.

A recent study aimed to examine, quite specifically, the psychometric properties of one such measure: the Belbin Team-Role Self-perception Inventory (BTRSPI). This measure is used extensively in applied settings, especially selecting, counselling and developing management teams (Hogg, 1990) but has received comparatively little psychometric assessment or validation. Belbin's measure, however, is not the only measure attempting to assess team-role behaviour. McCann and Margerison (1989) have also developed a team-role measure which also has 8 types: explorer–promoter; assessor–developer; thruster–organizer; concluder–producer; checker–inspector; upholder–maintainer; reporter–advisor; creator–innovator. This measure appears to be heavily influenced by the Jungian theories developed in the Myers–Briggs test (Myers and McCaulley, 1985). It not only has norms but evidence of internal reliability and concurrent validity; however, there appears to be little or no evidence of the factorial structure of the measure (to confirm the classification/taxonomic scheme), nor any evidence of the predictive or construct validity of the test. Furthermore, the test is ipsative, which presents various problems, but more importantly and ironically it provides no evidence that any one mix of 'team types' is any more efficient than any other.

Belbin's (1981) Self-Perception Inventory first appeared in his frequently reprinted book *Management Teams*. It outlines the 'theory' which suggests eight quite distinct team-role types (see Table 11.3). Although norms based on a very limited $N = 78$ were provided, little evidence of the psychometric properties of the test are offered. Thus, we know little of the test's reliability (test–retest, split-half, internal), validity (concurrent, content, predictive, construct) or of its dimensionability. The same appears to be true of the second extended version. The BTRSPI questionnaire is unusual and problematic for a number of reasons. Firstly, it is an ipsative test where subjects are required to read seven hypothetical situations, and then rate either 8 (version 1) or ten (version 2) behaviour statements relating to that situation and 'distribute a total of ten points among the sentences which you think most accurately describe your behaviour'. Recently, Johnson, Wood and Blinkhorn (1988) pointed out five uncontroversial drawbacks of such ipsative tests:

1. They cannot be used for comparing individuals on a scale by scale basis;
2. Correlations amongst ipsative scales cannot legitimately be factor analysed in the usual way;
3. Reliabilities of ipsative tests overestimate, sometimes severely, the actual reliability of the scales: in fact, the whole idea of error is problematical;
4. For the same reason, other validates of ipsative tests overestimate their utility;
5. Means, standard deviations, and correlations derived from ipsative test scales are not independent and cannot be interpreted and further utilised in the usual way (p.154).

They are highly critical of ipsative tests in general, particularly those used in occupational settings. A second problem of the Belbin BTRSPI concerns the way in which the questions are asked. Both versions are arranged such that for each of the seven sections, subjects are required to specify their typical behaviour. Thus, for instance, one reads: 'When involved in a project with other people . . .' or 'I gain satisfaction in a job because . . .'. These situations are vague, inconsistent, and do nothing to let the subject know about crucial aspects of the nature of the group/team that they are involved with. This could easily lead to poor reliability (Argyle, Furnham and Graham, 1981).

A third problem concerns the fact that the measure is entirely a-theoretical. As he explained in his book, Belbin (1981) used standard psychometrically validated measures like the 16PF and the EPI, but developed his typology not on theoretically deductive, but by observatory and inductive means. A major problem with this approach lies in the fact that previously well documented and theoretically important traits, like neuroticism, tend to get overlooked. Frequently, poorly psychometrized tests marketed for human-resource training appear to neglect 'negative' personality traits like neuroticism.

Despite the lack of psychometric evidence for his test, Belbin (1981) has made some interesting findings which require replication. Excellent teams tend to have the following characteristics which can be described in terms of the team members' roles in the team:

• The leader should have attributes similar to the 'chairman' type profile, described above. He should be a patient but commanding figure who generates trust and who knows how to use the spread of abilities in the team effectively.
• Excellent teams often include a person who generates creative and original solutions to problems (a plant).
• There should be a spread of mental abilities. If everyone in the team is *very* bright then the team will spend most of its time arguing and won't agree on any effective solutions to problems.

Table 11.3 A description of the eight 'key team roles'

Type	Symbol	Typical features	Positive qualities	Allowable weaknesses	Observed contributions
1. Team leaders					
a. Chairman	CH	Calm, self-confident, controlled	A capacity for treating and welcoming all potential contributors on their merits without prejudice – a strong sense of objectives	No more than ordinary in terms of intellect, creative ability	1. Clarifying the goals, objectives 2. Selecting the problems on which decisions have to be made, and establishing their priorities 3. Helping establish roles, responsibilities and work boundaries within the group 4. Summing up the feelings and achievements of the group, and articulating group verdicts
b. Shaper	SH	Highly strung, outgoing, dynamic	Drive and a readiness to challenge inertia, ineffectiveness, complacency	Proneness to provocation, irritation and impatience	1. Shaping roles, boundaries, responsibilities, tasks and objectives 2. Seeking to find pattern in group discussion 3. Pushing the group towards agreement on policy and action towards making decisions
2. Creative thinkers					
a. Plant	PL	Individualistic, serious-minded, unorthodox	Genius, imagination, intellect, knowledge	Up in the clouds, inclined to disregard practical details or protocol	1. Advancing proposals 2. Making criticisms that lead up counter-suggestions. 3. Offering new insights on lines action already agreed
b. Monitor evaluator	ME	Sober, unemotional	Judgement, discretion, hard-headedness	Lack inspiration or the ability to motivate others	1. Analysing problems and situations 2. Interpreting complex written

material and clarifying obscurities

3. Assessing the judgements and contributions of others

3. Negotiators

Role		Typical features	Positive qualities	Allowable weaknesses	Contribution
a. Resource investigator	RI	Extroverted, enthusiastic, curious, communicative	A capacity for contacting people and exploring anything new. An ability to respond to challenge	Liable to lose interest once the initial fascination has passed	1. Introducing ideas and development of external origin 2. Contacting other individuals or groups of own volition 3. Engaging in negotiation-type activities
b. Team worker	TW	Socially, orientated, rather mild	An ability to respond to people and to situations, and to promote team spirit	Indecisiveness at moments of crisis	1. Emphasizing the need for task completion, meeting targets and schedules and generally promoting a sense of urgency 2. Looking for and spotting errors, omissions and oversights 3. Galvanizing others into activity

4. Company workers

Role		Typical features	Positive qualities	Allowable weaknesses	Contribution
a. Company workers	CW	Conservative, dutiful, predictable	Organizing ability, practical common sense, hard-working, self-discipline	Lack of flexibility, unresponsiveness to unproven ideas.	1. Transforming talk and ideas into practical steps 2. Considering what is feasible 3. Trimming suggestions to make them fit into agreed plans and established systems
b. Completer Finisher	CF	Painstaking, orderly, conscientious, anxious	A capacity for follow through. Perfectionism	A tendency to worry about small things. A reluctance to 'let go'	1. Giving personal support and help to others 2. Building on to or seconding a member's ideas and suggestions 3. Drawing the reticient into discussion 4. Taking steps to avert or overcome disruption of the team

Source: (Belbin, 1981).

- Teams which excel have a wide spread of abilities which include, in particular, one completer (to finish the work) and one company worker (to organise the team). A winning team often contains people with a wider spread of team roles than other less successful groups.
- Another mark of excellent teams is that the team members often have team roles to which they are most suited; they perform a role which best fits their personal characteristics and abilities. In less successful teams this may not be the case – people may be given a role just because they have done it before, and no account is taken of how well they performed in that role last time.
- An excellent team can sense its own faults and do something about them by *compensating* for its team role weaknesses. One way in which it can compensate is by allocating appropriate members of the team to cover the missing role. The greater the spread of abilities in the team, the easier it is to do this. An excellent team is also sensitive to competition for particular roles because where such a situation exists, there may be a 'personality clash'. Two team members may work against one another and may have a damaging effect on the team's overall performance. Being aware of this possibility, the team can work out how the role could be shared or, alternatively, how to allocate one person to another role.

11.10 SOME NEGLECTED TOPICS

Some other potentially important research topics in this area appear to have been relatively neglected. They include the following:

- Personality and organizational climate. Patsfall and Feimer (1985) conceived of the PE fit idea in terms of the relationship between personality and the perceived organizational climate. However interesting the idea, they lament the current dearth of literature on the topic. There are various different definitions and models of climate but some evidence that personality variables are related to preference for, perception of, and satisfaction with organizational outcome such as performance. Hence, the concept of *fit* between personality and organizational climate. For instance, Pritchard and Karasick (1973) predicted that employees' performance and satisfaction would be highest when managers high in needs for achievement, order and dominance perceived climates to be high in achievement motivation, structure and status polarization. There was a significant interaction between the climate dimension of status polarization and the need for dominance, with managers high in need for dominance showing greater satisfaction and performance in a climate of low status polarization. This was interpreted to suggest that the number of managers who perceived their opportunity for relative power and dominance would be greater in a climate where there was less differentiation between managerial levels. There was also a significant interaction between the managers' need for autonomy and the climate dimension of decision centralization. For subjects low in need for autonomy, performance was higher when decision centralization was low. It is interesting that there was no main effect due to personality (needs) on performance or satisfaction. There was a main effect for the climate dimension of status polarization on performance, and the climate dimensions of achievement, social relations, status polarization and decision centralization were significantly related to job satisfaction.

More recently, Witt (1989) showed clear evidence of the interaction of locus of control with organizational climate factors.

- Less attractive personality traits. Some studies have concentrated on 'darker', less attractive personality traits and how they relate to behaviour at work. Two traits that have been fairly extensively studied are *machiavellianism* (the willingness and ability to manipulate other people for one's own purposes, deceitfulness and opportunism) and *social desirability* (the need to obtain the approval of others). For instance, Graus and Rogers (1990) found that individuals loading high on these traits used quite different tactics to influence colleagues. Thus, machiavellians used indirect, non-rational tactics like deceit, but also appealed to emotions to try to plant their ideas in the needs of their targets. High-need-for-approval workers used indirect, rational strategies like dropping hints, compromising and bargaining. Clearly, if personality is linked to influence tactics, and if the latter can lead to resistance, resentment and retaliation, it becomes all the more important to assess personality at work.

- Personality and impression management at work. Some studies have shown how personality differences relate to how people arrange their offices, specifically desk placement and visitor-chair arrangements. McElroy, Morrow and Ackerman (1983) found that locus of control related to office design such that internals had more 'open' designs than extraverts. They note that this research has two implications: designing working environments that enhance individual satisfaction and work efficiency; and learning something about the personality of individuals as a function of their preferred design.

- Personality and career change. Some people make major and frequent career changes, others stick in the same job for long periods of time – indeed all their working life. While there are no doubt certain job-related factors which determine this, there must also be certain individual difference characteristics that determine frequency of job move.

- The examination of pencil-and-paper predictors of employee theft, lying etc. Sackett and Harris (1985) have done a critical and comprehensive review of these measures and lament the general lack of interest in the area. This is an area of increased concern to business people, yet for obvious reasons, to do with dissimulation, psychometric development has been mediocre.

• Personality and behaviour in groups. How personality factors determine group roles chosen and the total effect on groups has been neglected. George (1990) believes that personality factors – positive vs negative affectivity – can have powerful effects on group behaviour.

11.11 CONCLUSION

The role of personality testing in the business world has been both good and bad for research. Sceptics have quite correctly pointed out that the proliferation and aggressive marketing of poorly psychometrized tests has frequently overstated and wrongly assessed their predictive value. Blinkhorn and Johnson (1990) note:

> We are not suggesting that personality tests have no uses, or that there are no stable underlying aspects of temperament which are important in the determination of behaviour. Indeed, for counselling purposes, or in other situations where self perception is as important as the truth, they may be invaluable. But we see precious little evidence that even the best personality tests predict job performance, and a good deal of evidence of poorly understood statistical methods being pressed into service to buttress shaky claims. If this is done for the most reputable tests in the hands of specialists, one may imagine what travesties are committed further down market. But we leave this as an exercise for the reader (p.672).

But these authors have not done their homework. Despite the factors mentioned in Section 11.3, there is, indeed, considerable evidence that personality factors are related to various occupational behaviours (see Chapter 2). For instance, in a recent extensive meta-analytic review of personality measure predictors of a job performance, Tett *et all.* (1991) concluded: 'Contrary to conclusions of certain past reviews, the present findings provide some grounds for optimism concerning the use of personality measures in employee selection' (p.703). They are, however, correct about poor research and (even worse) the specious claims of many management consultants who are less interested in the truth than clients' needs. Hopefully, there will be a growing *rapprochement* between occupational and personality psychology, and that well designed and executed research will reveal not only *which* personality factors relate to various occupational behaviours, but *why they do so!*

References

Abramson, L., Seligman, M. and Teasdale, J. (1978). Learned helplessness in humans: Critique and reformulation. *Journal of Abnormal Psychology*, **87**, 32–48.

Adams, J. (1965). Inequity in social exchange. In L. Berkowitz (Ed.) *Advances in Experimental Social Psychology*. Vol. 2. New York: Academic Press.

Adler, S. and Weiss, H. (1988). Recent developments in the study of personality and organizational behaviour. In C. Cooper and I. Robertson (Eds) *International Review of Industrial and Organizational Psychology*. Chichester: Wiley.

Ahmed, S. (1985). *n*Ach, risk taking propensity, locus of control and entrepreneurship. *Personality and Individual Differences*, **6**, 781–782.

Alderfer, C. (1972). *Existence, Relatedness and Growth*. New York: Free Press.

Allerhand, M., Friedlander, J., Marlone, H., Meadow, H. and Rosenberg, M. (1969). *A Study of the Impact and Effectiveness of the Comprehensive Manpower Project of Cleveland*. Washington, DC: Department of Labour.

Allison, C. and Hayes, J. (1988). The learning styles questionnaire: An alternative to Kolb's theory? *Journal of Management Studies*, **25**, 269–281.

Allodi, F. and Montgomery, R. (1979). Psychosocial aspects of occupational injury. *Social Psychology*, **14**, 25–29.

Amos, W. (1987). Just do it. *Journal of Creative Behaviour*, **22**, 155–161.

Anderson, C. (1976). *The Relationship between Locus of Control, Decision Behaviours, and Performance in a Stress Setting*. Proceedings of the Academy of Management.

Anderson, C. (1977). Locus of control, coping behaviours, and performance in a stress setting: A longitudinal study. *Journal of Applied Psychology*, **62**, 446–451.

Andrisani, P. and Nestel, G. (1976). Internal–external control as contributor to and outcome of work experience. *Journal of Applied Psychology*, **61**, 156–165.

Anthony, W. (1973). The development of extraversion, of ability, and of the relation between them. *British Journal of Educational Psychology*, **43**, 223–227.

Argyle, M. (1989). *The Social Psychology of Work*. Harmondsworth: Penguin.

Argyle, M., Furnham, A. and Graham, J. (1981). *Social Situations*. Cambridge: CUP.

Arnett, J. (1990). Drunk driving, sensation seeking, and egocentrism among adolescents. *Personality and Individual Differences*, **11**, 541–546.

Arsenault, A. and Dolan, S. (1983). The role of personality, occupation and organization in understanding the relationship between job stress, performance and absenteeism. *Journal of Occupational Behaviour*, **56**, 227–240.

Arvey, R. and Campion, J. (1984). Person perception in the employment interview. In M. J. Cook (ed.) *Issues in Person Perception*. London: Methuen.

Arvey, R., Bouchard, T., Segal, N. and Abraham, L. (1989). Job satisfaction:

Environmental and genetic components. *Journal of Applied Psychology*, **74**, 187–192.

Atkinson, J. (1968). *An Introduction to Motivation*. New Jersey: Van Nostrand.

Atkinson, G. (1988). Reliability of the Learning Style Inventory. *Psychological Reports*, **62**, 775–778.

Atkinson, G. (1989). Kolb's Learning Style Inventory. *Psychological Reports*, **64**, 991–995.

Ayers, J., Ruff, C. and Templer, D. (1976). Alcoholism, cigarette smoking, coffee drinking and extraversion. *Journal of Studies on Alcohol*, **37**, 983–985.

Babu, P. (1978). *A Study of the Sociological Characteristics of Small Scale Industries*. Kerala University Doctorate.

Baehr, M. and Williams, G. (1968). Prediction of sales success from factorially determined dimensions of personal background data. *Journal of Applied Psychology*, **52**, 98–103.

Bailey, J. (1986). Learning styles of successful entrepreneurs. In R. Ronstadt, J. Hornaday, R. Peterson and K. Vesper (Eds) *Frontiers of Entrepreneurship Research*. Wesley: Babson College.

Bakke, E. (1940). *Citizens without Work*. New Haven: Yale University Press.

Balch, R. (1972). The police personality: Fact or fiction. *Journal of Criminal Law, Criminology and Police Science*, **63**, 106–109.

Balch, R. (1977). *Personality Trait Differences between Successful and Non-successful Police Recruits at a Typical Police Academy and Veteran Police Officers*. PhD Thesis: United States International University.

Banks, O. and Finlayson, D. (1973). *Success and Failure in the Secondary School*. London: Methuen.

Banks, M., Clegg, C. and Jackson, P. (1982). Unemployment and risk of minor psychiatric disorder in young people. *Psychological Medicine*, **12**, 789–798.

Baran, P. (1957). *The Political Economy of Growth*. New York: Monthly Review Press.

Barbarik, L. (1968). Abnormal driving behaviour. *Ergonomics*, **3**, 111–117.

Baron, R. and Greenberg, J. (1990). *Behaviour in Organizations*. Boston: Allyn & Bacon.

Barrett, G. and Thorton, C. (1968). Relationship between perceptual style and driver reaction to an emergency situation. *Journal of Applied Psychology*, **52**, 169–176.

Bartnick, L., Kappelman, M., Berger, J. and Sigman, B. (1985). The value of the California Psychological Inventory in predicting medical students' career choice. *Medical Education*, **19**, 143–147.

Bartol, K. (1976). Expectancy theory as a predictor of female occupational choice and attitude toward business. *Academy of Management Journal*, **102**, 101–107.

Bartram, D. and Dale, H. (1982). The Eysenck Personality Inventory as a selection test for military pilots. *Journal of Occupational Psychology*, **55**, 287–296.

Bates, G., Parker, H. and McCoy, J. (1970). Vocational rehabilitants, personality and work adjustment: A test for Holland's theory of vocational choice. *Psychological Reports*, **26**, 511–516.

Beaton, R. (1975). Use of tests in a national retail company. In K. Miller (Ed.) *Psychological Testing in Personnel Assessment*, p.137–148. New York: Wiley.

Beaubrun, M. and Knight, F. (1973). Psychiatric assessment of 30 chronic users of cannabis and 30 matched controls. *American Journal of Psychiatry*, **130**, 309–11.

Becker, B. and Krzytofiak, F. (1982). The influence of labour market discrimination on locus of control. *Journal of Vocational Behaviour*, **21**, 60–70.

Begley, T. and Boyd, D. (1985). The relationship of the Jenkins Activity Survey to type A behaviour among business executives. *Journal of Vocational Behaviour*, **27**, 316–328.

Begley, T. and Boyd, D. (1986). Psychological characteristics associated with entrepreneurial performance. In R. Ronstadt, J. Hornaday, R. Peterson and K. Vesper (Eds) *Frontiers of Entrepreneurship Research*. Wesley: Babson College.

Begley, T. and Boyd, D. (1987a). A comparison of entrepreneurs and managers of small firms. *Journal of Management*, **13**, 99–108.

Begley, T. and Boyd, D. (1987b). Psychological characteristics associated with performance in entrepreneurial firms and smaller businesses. *Journal of Business Venturing*, **2**, 79–93.

Behrman, J., Hrubec, Z., Taubman, P. and Wales, T. (1980). *Socioeconomic Success: A Study of the Effects of Genetic Endowments, Family Environment and Schooling*. Amsterdam: North Holland.

Belbin, M. (1981). *Management Teams*. London: Heinemann.

Bem, S. (1974). The measurement of psychological androgyny. *Journal of Clinical and Consulting Psychology*, **42**, 153–162.

Bendig, A. (1963). The relationship of temperament traits of social extraversion and emotionality to vocational interests. *Journal of General Psychology*, **69**, 311–318.

Benge, E. (1944). How to learn what workers think of job and boss. *Factory Management Maintenance*, **102**, 101–104.

Bennett, S. and Youngman, M. (1973). Personality and behaviour in school. *British Journal of Educational Psychology*, **43**, 228–233.

Bentz, V. (1985a). Research findings from personality assessment of executives. In H. Bernardin and S. Bownas (Eds) *Personality Assessment in Organizations*; p.82–144. New York: Praeger.

Bentz, V. (1985b). *A View from the Top: A 30 Year Perspective of Research Devoted to the Discovery, Description, and Prediction of Executive Behaviour*. Los Angeles: APA Annual Meeting.

Berman, F. and Miner, J. (1985). Motivation to manage at the top executive level. *Personnel Psychology*, **38**, 377–391.

Bernardin, H. (1977). The relationship of personality variables to organizational withdrawal. *Personnel Psychology*, **30**, 17–27.

Bernardin, H. and Beatty, R. (1984). *Performance Appraisal: Assessing Human Behaviour at Work*. Boston: Kent.

Biberman, G. (1985). Personality and characteristic work attitudes of persons with high, moderate and low political tendencies. *Psychological Reports*, **57**, 1303–1310.

Biesheuvel, S. (1984). *Work Motivation and Compensation*. Johannesburg: McGraw-Hill.

Birley, S. and Watson, L. (1988). *The British Entrepreneur 1988: A Study of the Top 100 Owner-managers*. Cranfield Occasional Paper.

Bishop, D. and Jean Renaud, G. (1976). End-of-day mood on work and leisure days in relation to extraversion, neuroticism, and amount of change in daily activities. *Canadian Journal of Behavioural Science*, **8**, 388–400.

Blau, G. (1987). Locus of control as a potential moderator of the turnover process. *Journal of Occupational Psychology*, **60**, 21–29.

Blaylock, B. and Winkofsky, E. (1983). An explanation of R&D decision processes through individual information processing preferences. *R&D Management*, **13**, 129–141.

Blinkhorn, S. and Johnson, C. (1990). The insignificance of personality testing. *Nature*, **348**, 671–672.

Block, T. (1980). Sex differences in interest measurement. *Journal of Occupational Psychology*, **53**, 181–186.

Bluen, S., Barling, J. and Burns, W. (1990). Predicting sales performance, job satisfaction, and depression using the achievement striving and impatient-irritability dimensions of type A behaviour. *Journal of Applied Psychology*, **75**, 212–216.

Blum, R. (Ed.) (1964). *Police Selection*. Springfield: C. C. Thomas.

Blumenthal, J., Mckee, D., Haney, T. and Williams, R. (1980). Task incentives, type A behaviour pattern, and verbal problem solving performance. *Journal of Applied Social Psychology*, **10**, 101–114.

Blunt, P. (1978). Personality characteristics of a group of white South African managers. *International Journal of Psychology*, **13**, 139–146.

Boddy, J., Carver, A. and Rowley, K. (1986). Effects of positive and negative verbal reinforcement on performance as a function of extraversion–introversion: Some tests of Gray's theory. *Personality and Individual Differences*, **7**, 81–88.

Bond, M. and Feather, N. (1988). Some correlates of structure and purpose in the use of time. *Journal of Personality and Social Psychology*, **55**, 321–329.

Booysen, A. and Erasmus, J. (1989). Die verband tussen enkele persoonlik – hendfaktore en belsing risiks. *South African Journal of Psychology*, **19**, 144–152.

Borgen, W. and Young, R. (1982). Career perceptions of children and adolescents. *Journal of Vocational Behaviour*, **21**, 37–49.

Borislow, B. (1958). The Edwards Personal Preference Schedule and fakability. *Journal of Applied Psychology*, **42**, 22–27.

Borland, C. (1975). *Locus of Control, Need for Achievement and Entrepreneurship*. University of Texas doctorate.

Bouchard, T., Moloney, D. and Segal, N. (1989). *Genetic Similarity in Vocational Interests*. Paper at the ISSID meeting: Heidelberg, West Germany.

Boyatzis, R. (1982). *The Competent Manager*. New York: Wiley.

Boyd, D. and Begley, T. (1987). Assessing the type A behaviour pattern with the Jenkins Activity Survey. *British Journal of Medical Psychology*, **60**, 155–161.

Bradley, C., Brewin, C., Gamsu, D. and Moses, J. (1984). Development of scales to measure perceived control of diabetes mellitus and diabetes related health beliefs, *Diabetic Medicine*, **1**, 213–218.

Bragg, J. and Andrews, I. (1973). Participative decision-making: An experimental study in a hospital. *Journal of Applied Behavioural Science*, **9**, 727–736.

Brand, C. (1973). The personality of the motoring offender. In T.Willett (Ed.) *Drivers after Sentence*. London: Academic Press.

Braught, G., Brakarsh, D., Follingstad, D. and Berry, R. (1973). Deviant drug use in adolescents. *Psychological Bulletin*, **79**, 92–106.

Brenner, S. and Bartell, R. (1983). The psychological impact of unemployment: A structural analysis of cross-sectional data. *Journal of Occupational Behaviour*, **56**, 129–136.

Brewin, C. (1988). *Cognitive Foundations of Clinical Psychology*. London: Lawrence Erlbaum.

Brewin, C. and Shapiro, D. (1984). Beyond locus of control: Attribution of responsibility for positive and negative outcomes. *British Journal of Psychology*, **15**, 43–50.

Briar, R. (1977). The effect of long-term unemployment on workers and their families. *Dissertation Abstracts International*, **37**, 6062.

Bridges, J. (1988). Sex differences in occupational performance expectations. *Psychology of Women Quarterly*, **12**, 75–90.

Bridges, J. (1989). Sex differences in occupational values. *Sex Roles*, **20**, 205–211.

Bridgman, C. and Hollenbeck, G. (1961). Effect of simulated applicant status on

Kinder Form D occupational interest scores. *Journal of Applied Psychology*, **45**, 237–239.

Brief, A. and Aldag, R. (1976). Correlates of role indices. *Journal of Applied Psychology*, **61**, 466–472.

Brief, A. and Oliver, R. (1976). Male–female differences in work attitudes among retail sales managers. *Journal of Applied Psychology*, **61**, 526–528.

Brief, A., Rose, G. and Aldag, R. (1977). Sex differences in preferences for job attributes revisited. *Journal of Applied Psychology*, **62**, 645–646.

Brockhaus, R. (1977). *Locus of Control and Risk-taking Propensity as Entrepreneurial Characteristics*. Washington University Doctorate.

Brockhaus, R. (1982a). The psychology of the entrepreneur. In C. Kent, D. Sexton and K. Vesper (Eds) *Encyclopaedia of Entrepreneurship*. New Jersey: Prentice Hall.

Brockhaus, R. (1982b). *Psychological and Environmental Factors which Distinguish the Successful from the Unsuccessful Entrepreneur*. Unpublished Report.

Brockner, J. (1988). *Self-esteem at Work: Research, Theory and Practice*. Lexington: Lexington Books.

Brockner, J., Rubin, J. and Lang, E. (1981) Face-saving and entrapment. *Journal of Experimental Social Psychology*, **17**, 68-79.

Broedling, L. (1975). Relationship of internal–external control to work motivation and performance in an expectancy model. *Journal of Applied Psychology*, **60**, 65–70.

Brogden, H. (1950). When testing pays off. *Personnel Psychology*, **2**, 171–183.

Brooks, L. and Betz, N. (1990). Utility of expectancy theory in predicting occupational choices in college students. *Journal of Counselling Psychology*, **37**, 57–64.

Brousseau, K. (1978). Personality and job experience. *Organization Behaviour and Human Performance*, **22**, 235–252.

Brownell, P. (1982). The effects of personality–situation congruence in a managerial context. *Journal of Personality and Social Psychology*, **42**, 753–763.

Buchholz, R. (1976). Measurement of beliefs. *Human Relations*, **29**, 1177–1188.

Budd, R. and Paltiel, R.L. (1989). A review of the Occupational Personality Questionnaire. *Guidance and Assessment Review*, **5**, 5–7.

Buel, W. (1964). Voluntary female clerical turnover: The concurrent and predictive validity of a weighted application blank. *Journal of Applied Psychology*, **48**, 180–182.

Burbeck, E. and Furnham, A. (1984). Personality and police selection: Trait differences in successful and non-successful applicants to the Metropolitan police. *Personality and Individual Differences*, **5**, 257–263.

Burbeck, E. and Furnham, A. (1985). Police officer selection: A critical review of the literature. *Journal of Police Science and Administration*, **13**, 58–69.

Burch, J. (1986). Profiling the entrepreneur. *Business Horizons*. Sept-October, 13–16.

Burgess, E. (1955). Personality factors of over- and under-achievers in engineering. *Journal of Educational Psychology*, **29**, 89–99.

Burke, R. (1984a). Beliefs and fears underlying type A behaviour. *Psychological Reports*, **54**, 655–662.

Burke, R. (1984b). The closing at Canadian Admiral: Correlates of individual well-being sixteen months after shutdown. *Psychological Reports*, **55**, 91–98.

Burke, R. (1985). Beliefs and fears underlying type A behaviour: Correlates of time urgency and hostility. *Journal of General Psychology*, **112**, 133–145.

Burke, J. and Wilcox, D. (1972). Absenteeism and turnover among female telephone operators. *Personnel Psychology*, **25**, 639–648.

Buss, A. (1989). Personality as traits. *American Psychologist*, **44**, 1378–1388.

Butcher, J. (1985). Personality assessment in industry: Theoretical issues and illustrations. In H. Bernardin and D. Bownas (Eds) *Personality Assessment in Organizations*, p.277–309. New York: Praeger.

Butler, M. and Jones, A. (1979). Perceived leader behaviour, individual characteristics, and injury occurrence in hazardous work environments. *Journal of Applied Psychology*, **64**, 299–304.

Campbell, D. and Van Velsor, E. (1985). The use of personality measures in a management development programme. In H. Bernardin and D. Bownas (Eds) *Personality Assessment in Organizations*, p.193–214. New York: Praeger.

Caplan, R. (1983). Person–environment fit: Past, present and future. In C.L. Cooper (Ed) *Stress Research Issues for the Eighties*. Chichester: Wiley.

Caplan, R., Cobb, S., French, J., Harrison, R. and Pinneau, S. (1980). *Job Demands and Worker Health*. Ann Arbor: Institute for Social Research.

Carland, J., Hoy, F., Boulton, W. and Carland, J. (1984). Differentiating entrepreneurs from small business owners: A conceptualisation. *Academy of Management Review*, **9**, 354–359.

Carlson, R. (1980). Studies of Jungian typology II. Representation of the personal world. *Journal of Personality and Social Psychology*, **38**, 801–810.

Carlson, J. (1985). Recent assessment of the Myers–Briggs Type Indicator. *Journal of Personality Assessment*, **49**, 356–365.

Carsrud, A. and Johnson, R. (1989). Entrepreneurship: A social psychological perspective. *Entrepreneurship and Regional Development*, **1**, 21–31.

Carter, H. (1932). Twin similarities in occupation interests. *Journal of Educational Psychology*, **23**, 641–655.

Cascio, W. (1976). Turnover biographical data, and fair employment practice. *Journal of Applied Psychology*, **61**, 576–580.

Caston, R. and Branto, R. (1985). The worker-to-job 'fit' hypothesis. *Work and Occupation*, **12**, 269–284.

Cattell, R. (1971). *The Scientific Analysis of Personality*. Baltimore: Penguin.

Cattell, R. (1986). The 16PF personality structure and Dr Eysenck. *Journal of Social Behaviour and Personality*, **1**, 153–160.

Cattell, R. and Butcher, H. (1968). *The Prediction of Achievement and Creativity*. New York: Bobbs-Merrill.

Cattell, R. and Drevdahl, J. (1955). A comparison of the Personality Profile (16PF) of eminent researchers with that of eminent teachers and administrators, and of the general population. *British Journal of Psychology*, **46**, 248–261.

Cattell, R. and Warburton, F. (1961). A cross-cultural comparison of patterns of extraversion and anxiety. *British Journal of Psychology*, **52**, 3–15.

Cattell, R., Eber, H. and Tatsuoka, M. (1970). *Handbook for the 16PF Questionnaire*. Champaign: IPAT.

Chadwick-Jones, J., Brown, C., Nicholson, N. and Sheppard, C. (1977). Absence measures: Their reliability and stability in an industrial setting. *Personnel Psychology*, **24**, 463–470.

Chase, F. (1951). Factors for satisfaction in teaching. *Phi Delta Kappa*, **33**, 127–132.

Chatman, H. (1989). Improving international organizational research: A model of person–organization fit. *Academy of Management Review*, **14**, 333–349.

Chell, E. (1985). The entrepreneurial personality: A few ghosts laid to rest. *International Small Business Journal*, **3**, 43–54.

Chell, E. and Haworth, J. (1987). *Entrepreneurship and the Entrepreneurial Personality*. Unpublished Report from the University of Salford.

Chell, E. and Haworth, J. (1988). *Explorations of the Entrepreneurial Personality: A Latent Class Analysis*. Paper to EIASM, Vienna, December.

Cheloha, R. and Farr, J. (1980). Absenteeism, job involvement, and job satisfaction in an organizational setting. *Journal of Applied Psychology*, **65**, 467–473.

Cherry, N. (1976). Persistent job changing – is it a problem? *Journal of Occupational Psychology*, **49**, 203–221.

Chesney, M. and Rosenman, R. (1980). Type A behaviour in the work setting. In C. Cooper and R. Payne (Eds) *Current Concerns in Occupational Stress*. Chichester: John Wiley.

Childs, A. and Klimoski, R. (1986). Successfully predicting career success: An application of the biographical inventory. *Journal of Applied Psychology*, **71**, 3–8.

Christie, M. and Venables, P. (1973). Mood changes in reaction to age, EPI, scores, time and day. *British Journal of Social and Clinical Psychology*, **12**, 61–72.

Chusmir, L. and Hood, J. (1988). Predictive characteristics of type A behaviour among working men and women. *Journal of Applied Social Psychology*, **18**, 688–698.

Ciotola, P. and Peterson, J. (1976). Personality characteristics of alcoholics and drug addicts in a merged treatment program. *Journal of Studies on Alcohol*, **37**, 1229–35.

Cole, A. (1946). An approach to the study of entrepreneurship. *Journal of Economic Psychology*, **6**, 1–15.

Cole, R. (1940). A survey of employee attitudes. *Public Opinion Quarterly*, **4**, 497–506.

Collins, O., Moore, D. and Unwalla, D. (1964). The enterprising man. *MSU Business Studies*, **241**, 243–244.

Colman, A. and Gorman, L. (1982). Conservation, dogmatism and authoritarianism in British police officers. *Sociology*, **16**, 1–11.

Cook, J., Hepworth, S., Wall, T. and Warr, P. (1981). *The Experience of Work*. London: Academic Press.

Cook, M. (1988). *Personnel Selection and Productivity*. Chichester: Wiley.

Cooke, R. (1989). Assessing managerial skills with the 'Management Effectiveness Profile System'. *Educational and Psychological Measurement*, **49**, 723–732.

Cooper, C. (1983). Identifying stressors at work: Recent research developments. *Journal of Psychosomatic Research*, **27**, 369–376.

Cooper, R. and Payne, R. (1967). Extraversion and some aspects of work behaviour. *Personnel Psychology*, **20**, 45–47.

Cooper, A., Woo, C. and Dunkelberg, W. (1988). Entrepreneurs' perceived chances for success. *Journal of Business Venturing*, **3**, 97–108.

Copeland, J. (1975). Selecting engineers in an electronics firm. In K. Miller (Ed.) *Psychological Testing in Personnel Assessment*, p.91–107. New York: Wiley.

Costa, P. and McCrae, R. (1990). Neuroticism, somatic complaints, and disease: Is the bark worse than the bite? *Journal of Personality*, **58**, 143–156.

Costa, P., McCrae, R. and Holland, J. (1984). Personality and vocational interests in an adult sample. *Journal of Applied Psychology*, **69**, 390–400.

Cowan, D. (1989). An alternative to the dichotomous interpretation of Jung's psychological functions. *Journal of Personality Assessment*, **53**, 459–472.

Cox, C. and Cooper, L. (1988). *High Flyers: An Anatomy of Managerial Success*. Oxford: Blackwell.

Coyne, J. (1987). Software entrepreneurship: Lessons learned. *Journal of Creative Behaviour*, **22**, 203–215.

Craske, S. (1968). A study of the relation between personality and accident history. *British Journal of Medical Psychology*, **41**, 399–404.

Cromie, S. (1987). Motivations of aspiring male and female entrepreneurs. *Journal of Occupational Behaviour*, **8**, 251–261.

Cromie, S. and Johns, S. (1983). Irish entrepreneurs: Some personal characteristics. *Journal of Occupational Behaviour*, 4, 317–324.

Crowley, J. and Shapiro, D. (1982). Aspirations and expectations of youth in the United States. *Youth and Society*, 13, 391–422.

Crowley, B., Pinder, R. and Herriot, P. (1990). Assessment centre dimensions, personality and aptitudes. *Journal of Occupational Psychology*, 63, 211–216.

Csizma, K., Whitting, A. and Schur, K. (1988). Sport stereotypes and gender. *Journal of Sport and Exercise Psychology*, 10, 75–80.

Dahlback, D. (1991). Accident-proneness and risk-taking. *Personality and Individual Differences*, 12, 79–83.

Danziger, P., Larsen, J. and Connors, V. (1989). Myers–Briggs type and keeping appointments for an experiment on problem-solving. *Psychological Reports*, 65, 322.

Davidsson, P. (1989). Entrepreneurship – and after? A study of growth willingness in small firms. *Journal of Business Venturing*, 4, 211–226.

Davies, D. (1989). *Psychological Factors in Competitive Sports*. London: Falmer Press.

Davis-Blake, A. and Pfeffer, J. (1989). Just a mirage: The search for dispositional effects in organizational research. *Academy of Management Review*, 14, 385–400.

Day, D. and Silverman, S. (1989). Personality and job performance: Evidence of incremental validity. *Personnel Psychology*, 42, 25–36.

Deivasenapathy, P. (1986). Entrepreneurial success: Influence of certain personal variables. *Indian Journal of Social Work*, 46, 547–555.

Devito, A. (1985). A review of the Myers–Briggs Type Indicator. In J. Mitchell (Ed.) *Ninth Mental Measurements Yearbook*. Lincoln: University of Nebraska Press.

Dienstbier, R. (1984). The effects of exercise on personality. In M. Sachs and G. Buffore (Eds) *Running as Therapy*. Lincoln: University of Nebraska Press.

Dobson, C. and Morrow, P. (1984). Effects of career orientation on retirement attitudes and retirement planning. *Journal of Vocational Behaviour*, 24, 73–83.

Dodd, W., Wollowick, H. and McNamara, W. (1970). Task difficulty as a moderator of long-term prediction. *Journal of Applied Psychology*, 54, 265–270.

Donovan, A. and Oddy, M. (1982). Psychosocial aspects of unemployment. *Journal of Adolescence*, 5, 15–30.

Dore, R. and Meacham, M. (1973). Self-concepts and interests related to job satisfaction of managers. *Personnel Psychology*, 26, 49–59.

Dowd, R. and Innes, J. (1981). Sport and personality: Effects of type of sport and level of competition. *Perception and Motor Skills*, 53, 79–89.

Druker, P. (1985). *Innovation and Entrepreneurship*. New York: Harper & Row.

Dunbar, S. and Novick, M. (1988). On predicting success in training for men and women: Example from marine corps clerical specialists. *Journal of Applied Psychology*, 73, 545–550.

Dunkelberg, W. and Cooper, A. (1982). Entrepreneurial typologies: An empirical study. In K. Vesper (Ed.) *Frontiers of Entrepreneurial Research*. Wellesley: Babson Centre for Entrepreneurial Studies.

Dunnette, S. and S. Maetzold (1955). Use of a weighted application blank in hiring seasonal employees. *Journal of Applied Psychology*, 39, 308–310.

Durand, D. (1972). *Black Entrepreneurial Training*. Washington University Doctorate.

Durand, D. and Shea, D. (1978). Entrepreneurial activity as a function of achievement motivation and reinforcement control. *Journal of Psychology*, 88, 57–63.

Dyer, E. (1987). Can university success and first-year job performance be predicted from academic achievement, vocational interest, personality and biographical measures. *Psychological Reports*, **61**, 655–671.

Eberhardt, B. and Muchinsky, P. (1982). An empirical investigation of the factor stability of Owen's biographical questionnaire. *Journal of Applied Psychology*, **67**, 130–145.

Edwards, R. (1977). Personal traits and 'success' in schooling and work. *Educational and Psychological Measurement*, **37**, 125–138.

Edwards, G., Chandler, C. and Hensman, C. (1972). Drinking in a London pub. I. Correlates of normal drinking. *Journal of Studies on Alcohol*, **33**, 69.

Eisenberg, P. and Lazarsfeld, P. (1938). The psychological effects of unemployment. *Psychological Bulletin*, **35**, 358–378.

Elliott, C. (1972). Noise tolerance and extraversion in children. *British Journal of Psychology*, **62**, 375–380.

Ellis, R. and Taylor, M. (1983). Role of self-esteem within the job search process. *Journal of Applied Psychology*, **68**, 632–640.

Elton, C. and Rose, H. (1973). Relationship between variety of work experience and personality. *Journal of Applied Psychology*, **58**, 134–136.

Elton, C. and Smart, J. (1988). Extrinsic job satisfaction and person–environment congruence. *Journal of Vocational Behaviour*, **32**, 226–238.

England, P., Chassic, M. and McCormack, L. (1982). Skill demands and earnings in female and male occupations. *Sociology and Social Research*, **66**, 147–168.

Entwistle, N. (1972). Personality and academic attainment. *British Journal of Educational Psychology*, **42**, 137–151.

Entwistle, N., Nisbet, J., Entwistle, D. and Cowell, M. (1972). The academic performance of students. *British Journal of Educational Psychology*, **42**, 258–265.

Erdle, S., Murray, H. and Rushton, J. (1985). Personality, classroom behaviour, and student ratings of college teaching effectiveness. *Journal of Educational Psychology*, **77**, 394–407.

Erkut, S. (1983). Exploring sex differences in expectancy, attribution, and academic achievement. *Sex Roles*, **9**, 217–231.

Erwee, R. (1986). An attempt to arouse the achievement motivation of young women by experimental interaction. *South African Journal of Psychology*, **16**, 8–14.

Evans, W. (1981). Stress and psychoticism. *Personality and Individual Differences*, **2**, 21–24.

Evans, G., Palsane, M. and Carrere, S. (1987). Type A behaviour and occupational stress: A cross-cultural study of blue-collar workers. *Journal of Personality and Social Psychology*, **52**, 1002–1007.

Eysenck, H. (1967a). *The Biological Basis of Personality*. Springfield: Thomas.

Eysenck, H. (1967b). Personality patterns in various groups of businessmen. *Occupational Psychology*, **41**, 249–250.

Eysenck, H. (1981). Learning, memory and personality. In H.J. Eysenck (Ed.) *A Model for Personality*. Heidelberg: Springer.

Eysenck, H. (1985a). Can personality study ever be scientific. *Journal of Social Behaviour and Personality*, **1**, 3–19.

Eysenck, H. (1985b). Personality, cancer, and cardiovascular disease: A causal analysis. *Personality and Individual Differences*, **6**, 535–556.

Eysenck, H. (1990). Type A behaviour and coronary heart disease: The third stage. *Journal of Social Behaviour and Personality*, **5**, 25–44.

Eysenck, H. and Eysenck, M. (1975). *Personality and Individual Differences: A Natural Science Approach*. London: Plenum.

Eysenck, H., Nias, D. and Cox, D. (1982). Sport and personality. *Advances in Behaviour Therapy*, **4**, 1–56.

Fagerström, K. and Lisper, H. (1977). Effects of listening to car radio, experience, and personality of the driver on subsidiary reaction time and heart rate in a long-term driving task. In R. Machie (Ed.) *Vigilance*. New York: Plenum.

Farkas, A. and Tetrick, L. (1989). A three-wave longitudinal analysis of the causal ordering of satisfaction and commitment on turnover decisions. *Journal of Applied Psychology*, **74**, 855–868.

Farmer, H. (1985). Model of career and achievement motivation for women and men. *Journal of Counselling Psychology*, **32**, 363–390.

Farrell, D. and Petersen, J. (1984). Commitment, absenteeism, and turnover of new employees: A longitudinal study. *Human Relations*, **37**, 681–692.

Feather, N. (1982). Unemployment and its psychological correlates. *Australian Journal of Psychology*, **34**, 309–323.

Feather, N. (1985). Attitudes, values and attributions: Explanations of unemployment. *Journal of Personality and Social Psychology*, **48**, 876–889.

Feather, N. (1986). Employment importance and helplessness about potential unemployment among students in secondary schools. *Australian Journal of Psychology*, **38**, 33–44.

Feather, N. and Bond, M. (1983). Time structure and purposeful activity among employed and unemployed university graduates. *Journal of Occupational Psychology*, **56**, 241–254.

Feather, N. and O'Brien, G. (1986a). A longitudinal study of the effects of employment and unemployment on school-leavers. *Journal of Occupational Psychology*, **59**, 121–144.

Feather, N. and O'Brien, G. (1986b). A longitudinal analysis of the effects of different patterns of employment and unemployment on school-leavers. *British Journal of Psychology*, **77**, 459–479.

Feather, N. and O'Brien, G. (1987). Looking for employment: An expectancy–valence analysis of job-seeking behaviour among young people. *British Journal of Psychology*, **78**, 251–272.

Feldman, J. (1974). Race, economic class and the intention to work: Some normative and attitudinal correlates. *Journal of Applied Psychology*, **59**, 179–186.

Feltz, D. (1987). Advancing knowledge in sport psychology. *Quest*, **39**, 243–254.

Fernald, L. (1987). The underlying relationship between creativity, innovation and entrepreneurship. *Journal of Creative Behaviour*, **22**, 196–202.

Ferris, G., Youngblood, S. and Yates, V. (1985). Personality, training performance, and withdrawal. *Journal of Vocational Behaviour*, **27**, 377–388.

Ferris, G., Bergin, T. and Wayne, S. (1988). Personal characteristics, job performance, and absenteeism of public school teachers. *Journal of Applied Social Psychology*, **18**, 552–563.

Fichman, M. (1989). Attendance makes the heart grow fonder: A hazard approach to modelling attendance. *Journal of Applied Psychology*, **74**, 325–335.

Fillebaum, G. and Maddox, G. (1974). Work after retirement: An investigation into some psychologically relevant variables. *The Gerontologist*, **8**, 418–424.

Fine, B. (1963). Introversion–extraversion and motor vehicle driver behaviour. *Perceptual and Motor Skills*, **12**, 95–100.

Fineman, S. (1979a). A psychological model of stress and its application to managerial unemployment. *Human Relations*, **32**, 323–345.

Fineman, S. (1979b). The achievement motive construct and its measurement: Where are we now? *British Journal of Psychology*, **68**, 1–22.

Fineman, S. (1983). *White Collar Unemployment: Impact and Stress*. London: Wiley.

Fiorentine, R. (1988). Sex differences in success expectancies and causal attributions. *Social Psychology Quarterly*, **51**, 236–249.

Fishman, D. and Zimet, C. (1967). Speciality choice and beliefs about specialities among freshman medical students. *Journal of Medical Education*, **55**, 682–691.

Fletcher, C. (1987). Candidate personality as an influence on selection interview assessments. *Applied Psychology*, **36**, 157–162.

Fletcher, C. (1990). The relationship between candidate personality, self-presentation strategies, and interviewer assessments in selection interviews. *Human Relations*, **43**, 739–749.

Folkins, C. and Sime, W. (1981). Physical fitness training and mental health. *American Psychologist*, **36**, 373–389.

Forgionne, G. and Peeters, V. (1982). Differences in job motivations and satisfaction among male and female managers. *Human Relations*, **35**, 101–118.

Fraboni, M. and Saltstone, R. (1990). First and second generation entrepreneur typologies: Dimensions of personality. *Journal of Social Behaviour and Personality*, **5**, 105–113.

Frank, H., Llaschka, G. and Roessel, D. (1989). Planning behaviour of successful and non-successful founders of new ventures. *Entrepreneurship and Regional Development*, **1**, 191–206.

Frantz, R. (1980). Internal–external locus of control and labour market performance: Empirical evidence using longitudinal survey data. *Psychology: Quarterly Journal of Human Behaviour*, **17**, 23–29.

Fretz, B. and Leong, F. (1982). Vocational behaviour and career development, 1981: A review. *Journal of Vocational Behaviour*, **21**, 123–163.

Friedman, M. and Booth-Kewley, S. (1987). *The 'Disease-Prone Personality'*. New York: Knopf.

Friedman, M. and Rosenman, R. (1974). *Type A Behaviour and Your Heart*. New York: Knopf.

Friedman, H., Hall, J. and Harris, M. (1985). Type A, nonverbal expressive style, and health. *Journal of Personality and Social Psychology*, **48**, 1299–1315.

Fruensgaard, K., Benjaminsen, S., Joensen, S. and Helstrup, K. (1983a). Psychosocial characteristics of a group of unemployment patients consecutively admitted to a psychiatric emergency department. *Social Psychiatry*, **18**, 137–144.

Fruensgaard, K., Benjaminsen, S., Joensen, J. and Helstrup, K. (1983b). Follow up of a group of unemployment patients consecutively admitted to a psychiatric emergency department. *Social Psychiatry*, **18**, 129–135.

Fryer, D. (1986). Employment deprivation and personal agency during unemployment. *Social Behaviour*, **1**, 3–23.

Furnham, A. (1981). Personality and activity preference. *British Journal of Social Psychology*, **20**, 57–60.

Furnham, A. (1983). Mental health and employment status. *British Journal of Counselling and Guidance*, **11**, 199–210.

Furnham, A. (1984a). Personality and values. *Personality and Individual Differences*, **5**, 483–485.

Furnham, A. (1984b). Extraversion, sensation seeking, stimulus screening and type 'A' behaviour pattern: The relationship between various measures of arousal. *Personality and Individual Differences*, **5**, 133–140.

Furnham, A. (1986a). Economic locus of control. *Human Relations*, **39**, 29–43.

Furnham, A. (1986b). Career attitudes of preclinical medical specialities. *Medical Education*, **20**, 286–300.

Furnham, A. (1986c). Attitudes to the medical specialities. *Social Science and Medicine*, **23**, 587–594.

Furnham, A. (1987a). The social psychology of working situations. In A. Gale and B. Christie (Eds) *Psychophysiology and the Electronic Workplace*, p.89–111. Chichester: Wiley.

Furnham, A. (1987b). Work related beliefs and human values. *Personality and Individual Differences*, **8**, 627–637.

Furnham, A. (1990a). The type A behaviour pattern and the perception of self. *Personality and Individual Differences*, **11**, 841–851.

Furnham, A. (1990b). *The Protestant Work Ethic*. London: Routledge.

Furnham, A. (1991). Personality and occupational success: 16PF correlates of cabin crew performance. *Personality and Individual Differences*. **12**, 87–90.

Furnham, A. (1992). Personality and learning style: A study of the instruments. *Personality and Individual Differences*. **13**, 429–38.

Furnham, A. and Goddard, L. (1986). Sex differences in job satisfaction. *Psychologia*, **29**, 132–146.

Furnham, A. and Henderson, M. (1983). The mote in thy brother's eyes, the beam in their own: Predicting one's own and other's personality test scores. *British Journal of Psychology*, **74**, 381–389.

Furnham, A. and Koritsas, E. (1990). The protestant work ethic and vocational preference. *Journal of Organizational Behaviour*, **11**, 43–55.

Furnham, A. and Procter, E. (1989). Belief in a just world: Review and critique of the individual difference literature. *British Journal of Social Psychology*, **28**, 365–384.

Furnham, A. and Schaeffer, R. (1984). Person–environment fit, job satisfaction, and mental health. *Journal of Occupational Psychology*, **57**, 295–307.

Furnham, A. and Walsh, J. (1991). The consequences of person–environment incongruence: Absenteeism, frustration, and stress. *Journal of Social Psychology*, **131**, 187–204.

Furnham, A., Sadka, V. and Brewin, C. (1992). The development of an occupational attributional style questionnaire. *Journal of Occupational Behaviour*. **13**, 27–39.

Furnham, A. and Zacherl, M. (1986). Personality and job satisfaction. *Personality and Individual Differences*, **7**, 453–459.

Furnham, A., Borovoy, A. and Henley, S. (1986). Type A behaviour pattern: The recall of positive personality and self-evaluation. *British Journal of Medical Psychology*, **59**, 365–374.

Garrison, K. and Muchinsky, R. (1977). Attitudinal and biographical predictors of incidental absenteeism. *Journal of Vocational Behaviour*, **10**, 221–230.

Gaudet, F. (1963). *Solving the Problems of Employee Absence*. New York: AMA.

Gaudet, F. and Carli, A. (1957). Why executives fail. *Personnel Psychology*, **10**, 1.

Gaugler, B., Rosenthal, D., Thornton, G. and Bentson, C. (1987). Meta-analysis of assessment centre validity. *Journal of Applied Psychology*, **72**, 493–511.

Gentry, F. and Doering, M. (1979). Sex role orientation and leisure. *Journal of Leisure Research*, **11**, 102–111.

George, J. (1989). Mood and absence. *Journal of Applied Psychology*, **74**, 317–324.

George, J. (1990). Personality, affect, and behaviour in groups. *Journal of Applied Psychology*, **75**, 107–116.

Gerhart, B. (1987). How important are dispositional factors as determinants of job satisfaction? *Journal of Applied Psychology*, **72**, 366–373.

Ghiselli, E. (1955). *The Measurement of Occupational Aptitude*. Berkeley: University of California Press.

Ghiselli, E. (1973). The validity of aptitude tests in personnel selection. *Personnel Psychology*, **26**, 461–477.

Ghiselli, E. and Barthol, R. (1953). The validity of personality inventions in the selection of employees. *Journal of Applied Psychology*, **37**, 18–20.

Ghiselli, E. and Brown, C. (1955). *Personnel and Industrial Psychology*. New York: McGraw Hill.

Gibb, A. and Ritchie, J. (1981). *Influences on Entrepreneurship: A Study over Time*. London: Polytechnic of Central London.

Gibson, J. (1982). Square pegs in square holes. *Police Review*, **90**, 1702–1707.

Gigy, L. (1985). Pre-retired and retired women's attitudes toward retirement. *International Journal of Aging and Human Development*, **22**, 31–45.

Ginsberg, A. and Buchholz, A. (1989). Are entrepreneurs a breed apart? A look at the evidence. *Journal of General Management*, **15**, 32–40.

Goh, D. and Moore, C. (1978). Personality and academic achievement in three educational levels. *Psychological Reports*, **43**, 71–79.

Goldsmith, D. (1922). The use of the personal history blank as a salemanship test. *Journal of Applied Psychology*, **6**, 149–155.

Goodenough, D. (1976). A review of individual differences in field dependence as a factor in auto safety. *Human Factors*, **18**, 53–62.

Goodstein, L. and Schroder, W. (1963). An empirically derived managerial key for the California Psychological Inventory. *Journal of Applied Psychology*, **47**, 42–45.

Gordon, M. and Fitzgibbons, W. (1982). Empirical test of the validity of seniority as a factor in staffing decisions, *Journal of Applied Psychology*, **67**, 311–319.

Gore, S. (1978). The effect of social support in moderating the health consequences of unemployment. *Journal of Health and Social Behaviour*, **19**, 157–165.

Gossop, M. and Kristjansson, I. (1977). Crime and personality. A comparison of convicted and non-convicted drug-dependent males. *British Journal of Criminology*, **17**, 264–73.

Gottfredson, L. (1978). An analytic description of employment according to race, sex, prestige at Holland's types of work. *Journal of Vocational Psychology*, **13**, 210–221.

Gotz, K. and Gotz, K. (1973). Introversion–extraversion and neuroticism in gifted and ungifted art students. *Perceptual and Motor Skills*, **36**, 675–678.

Gough, H. (1968). College attendance among high aptitude students as predicted from the CPI. *Journal of Counselling Psychology*, **69**, 269–278.

Gough, H. (1984). A managerial potential scale for the California Psychological Inventory. *Journal of Applied Psychology*, **69**, 233–240.

Gough, H. (1985) A work orientation scale for the California Psychological Inventory. *Journal of Applied Psychology*, **70**, 505–513.

Gough, H. (1989). The California Psychological Inventory. In C. Niemark (Ed.) *Major Psychological Assessment Instruments*, p.67–98. Boston: Allyn & Bacon.

Gratton, L. (1987). How can we predict management potential in research scientists? *R&D Management*, **17**, 87–97.

Graus, W. and Rogers, R. (1990). Power and personality: Effects of machiavellianism, need for approval, and motivation on use of influence tactics. *Journal of General Psychology*, **117**, 71–82.

Gray, J. (1973). Causal theories of personality and how to test them. In J.R. Royce (Ed.) *Multivariate Analysis and Psychological Theory*. New York: Academic Press.

Greenhaus, J. and Parasuraman, S. (1986). Vocational and organizational behaviour, 1985: A review. *Journal of Vocational Behaviour*, **29**, 115–176.

Gross, P., Cattell, R. and Butcher, H. (1967). The personality pattern of creative artists. *British Journal of Educational Psychology*, **41**, 292–299.

Grossarth-Maticek, R., Eysenck, H. and Vetter, H. (1988). Personality type, smoking habit and that interaction as predictors of cancer and coronary heart disease. *Personality and Individual Differences*, **9**, 479–495.

Grotevant, H., Scarr, S. and Weinberg, R. (1978). Are career interests inherited? *Psychology Today*, **11**, 88–90.

Gruber, J. (1980). Sex-typing of leisure activities: A current appraisal. *Psychological Reports*, **46**, 259–265.

Gudjonsson, G. and Adlam, K. (1983). Personality patterns of British police officers. *Personality and Individual Differences*, **4**, 507–512.

Guilford, J., Zimmerman, W. and Guilford, J. (1976). *The Guilford–Zimmerman Temperament Survey Handbook*, San Diego: Edits.

Guion, R. and Gottier, R. (1965). Validity of personality measures in personnel selection. *Personnel Psychology*, **18**, 135–165.

Gupta, B. (1976). Extraversion and reinforcement in verbal operant conditioning. *British Journal of Psychology*, **67**, 47–52.

Gurney, R. (1980a). The effects of unemployment on the psychological development of school-leavers. *Journal of Occupational Behaviour*, **53**, 205–213.

Gurney, R. (1980b). Does unemployment affect the self-esteem of school-leavers? *Australian Journal of Psychology*, **32**, 175–182.

Hackett, R. and Guion, R. (1985). A re-evaluation of the absenteeism, job satisfaction relationship. *Organizational Behaviour and Human Decision Processes*, **35**, 340–381.

Hackman, J. and Lawler, E. (1971). Employee reaction to job characteristics. *Journal of Applied Psychology Monograph*, **55**, 259–286.

Hagen, E. (1962). *On the Theory of Social Change: How Economic Growth Begins*. Homewood: Dorsey Press.

Haley, U. and Stumpf, J. (1989). Cognitive traits in strategic decision-making: Linking theories of personalities and cognition. *Journal of Management Studies*, **26**, 477–497.

Hameed, K. (1974). *Enterprise-industrial Entrepreneurship in Development*. London: Sage.

Hammer, T. and Vardi, Y. (1981). Locus of control and career self-management among non supervisory employees in industrial settings. *Journal of Vocational Behaviour*, **18**, 13–29.

Handy, C. (1985). *Understanding Organizations*. Harmondsworth: Penguin.

Hansen, C. (1989). A causal model of the relationship among accidents, biodata, personality, and cognitive factors. *Journal of Applied Psychology*, **74**, 81–90.

Hanson, B. and Harrell, T. (1985). Predictors of business success over two decades: An MBA longitudinal study. *Stanford Business School*, No. 788.

Harano, R. (1969). *The Relationship between Field Dependence and Motor Vehicle Accident Involvement*. Washington: APA No.065B.

Harmon, L. and Farmer, H. (1983). Current theoretical issues in vocational psychology. In W. Walsh and S. Osipow (Eds) *Handbook of Vocational Psychology*, Vol.1, p.39–75. Hillsdale, NJ: Lawrence Erlbaum.

Harré, R. (1979). *Social Being*. Oxford: Blackwell.

Harrell, T. and Harrell, M. (1984). *Stanford MBA Careers: A 20 Year Longitudinal Study*. Grad. School of Business, Research Paper 723.

Harrell, M., Harrell, T., McIntyre, S. and Weinberg, C. (1977). Predicting compensation among MBA graduate five and years after graduation. *Journal of Applied Psychology*, **62**, 636–640.

Harrison, R. (1978). Person–environment fit and job stress. In C. Cooper and R. Payee (Eds) *Stress at Work*. Chichester: Wiley.

Hearn, J. and Parkin, W. (1987). *'Sex' at 'Work': The Power and Paradox of Organizational Sexuality*. Chatham: Harvester.

Heaven, P. (1990). Suggestions for reducing unemployment. A study of Protestant work ethic and economic locus of control beliefs. *British Journal of Social Psychology*, **29**, 55–65.

Hébert, R. and Link, A. (1982). *The Entrepreneurs: Mainstream Views and Radical Critique*. New York: Praeger.

Heckhausen, H., Schmalt, H. and Scneider, K. (1985). *Achievement Motivation in Perspective*. Orlando: Academic Press.

Heesacker, M., Elliott, T. and Howe, L. (1988). Does the Holland code predict job satisfaction and productivity in clothing factory workers? *Journal of Counselling Psychology*, **35**, 144–148.

Helmes, E. (1989). Evaluating the internal structure of the Eysenck Personality Questionnaire: Objective criteria. *Multivariate Behavioural Research*, **24**, 353–364.

Henderson, J. and Nutt, P. (1980). The influence of decision style on decision making behaviour. *Managerial Science*, **26**, 371–386.

Henderson, K., Staknaker, D. and Taylor, G. (1988). The relationship between barriers to recreation and gender-role personality traits for women. *Journal of Leisure Research*, **20**, 69–80.

Hendrix, W. and Spencer, B. (1989). Development and test of a multivariate model of absenteeism. *Psychological Reports*, **64**, 923–938.

Henley, S. and Furnham, A. (1989). The type A behaviour pattern and self-evaluation. *British Journal of Medical Psychology*, **62**, 51–59.

Henry, P. (1989). Relationship between academic achievement and measured career interest. *Psychological Reports*, **64**, 35–40.

Hepworth, S. (1980). Moderating factors of the psychological impact of unemployment. *Journal of Occupational Psychology*, **53**, 139–145.

Herriot, P. (1988). Selection at the crossroads. *The Psychologist*, **10**, 388–392.

Herzberg, F., Mausner, B. and Snyderman, B. (1959). *The Motivation to Work*. New York: Wiley.

Herzberg, F., Mausner, B., Petersen, O. and Capwell, D. (1957). *Job Attitudes: Review of Research and Opinion*. Pittsburgh: Psychological Services of Pittsburgh.

Hesketh, B. (1984). Attribution theory and unemployment: Kelly's covariation model, self-esteem, and locus of control. *Journal of Vocational Behaviour*, **24**, 44–109.

Hicks, L. (1984). Conceptual and empirical analysis of some assumptions of an explicitly typological theory. *Journal of Personality and Social Psychology*, **46**, 1118–1131.

Hill, A. (1975). Extraversion and variety-seeking in a monotonous task. *British Journal of Psychology*, **66**, 9–13.

Hinrichs, J. (1978). An eight-year follow-up of a management assessment centre. *Journal of Applied Psychology*, **63**, 596–601.

Hirsh, S. and Kummerow, J. (1989). *Life Types*. New York: Warner.

Hobert, R. and Dunnette, M. (1967). Development of moderator variables to enhance the prediction of managerial effectiveness. *Journal of Applied Psychology*, **51**, 50–64.

Hodapp, V., Neuser, K. and Weyer, G. (1988). Job stress, emotion, and work environment: Toward a causal model. *Personality and Individual Differences*, **9**, 851–859.

Hodgson, J. and Brenner, M. (1968). Successful experience: Training hard-core unemployed. *Harvard Business Review*, **46**, 148–156.

Hofstede, G. (1984). *Culture's Consequences*. New York: Sage.

Hogan, R. (1990). Personality and personality measurement. In M. Dunnette (Ed.) *Handbook of Industrial Organizational Psychology*. Palo Alto, California: Consulting Psychologists Press.

Hogan, R., Carpenter, B., Briggs, S. and Hansson, R. (1985). Personality assessment and personnel selection. In H. Bernadin and D. Bownas (Eds) *Personality–Assessment in Organizations*. New York: Praeger.

Hogg, C. (1990). Team building. *Personnel Management: Factsheet*, **34**.

Holland, J. (1973). *Making Vocational Choices: A Theory of Careers*. Englewood Cliffs, NJ: Prentice Hall.

Holland, J. (1985). *The Self-directed Search – Professional Manual*. P.A.R. Florida.

Hollenbeck, J. and Whitener, E. (1988). Reclaiming personality traits for personnel selection: Self-esteem as an illustrative case. *Journal of Management*, **14**, 81–91.

Hollenbeck, J., Ilgen, D., Ostroff, C. and Vancouver, J. (1987). Sex differences in occupational choice, pay, and worth. *Personnel Psychology*, **40**, 715–743.

Holloway, C. and Youngblood, S. (1985). Survival after retirement. *International Journal of Aging and Human Development*, **22**, 45–54.

Honess, T. and Kline, P. (1974). Extraversion, neuroticism and academic attainment in Uganda. *British Journal of Educational Psychology*, **44**, 74–75.

Honey, P. and Mumford, A. (1982). *The Manual of Learning Styles*. Maidenhead: Honey.

Hooker, K. and Ventis, D. (1984). Work ethic, daily activities, and retirement satisfaction. *Journal of Gerontology*, **39**, 478–484.

Hooker, K., Blumenthal, J. and Siegler, I. (1987). Relationship between motivation and hostility among type A and type B middle-aged men. *Journal of Research and Personality*, **21**, 103–113.

Hoppock, R. (1935). *Job Satisfaction*. New York: Harper & Row.

Hornaday, J. and Aboud, J. (1971). Characteristics of successful entrepreneurs. *Personnel Psychology*, **24**, 141–153.

Hornaday, J. and Knutzen, P. (1986). Some psychological characteristics of successful Norwegian entrepreneurs. In R. Ronstadt, J. Hornaday, R. Peterson and K. Vesper (Eds) *Frontiers of Entrepreneurship Research*. Wesley: Babson College.

Hough, L., Eaton, N., Dunnette, M., Kaye, J. and McCloy, R. (1990). Criterion-related validities of personality constructs and the effect of response distortion on those validities. *Journal of Applied Psychology*, **75**, 581–595.

Howard, A. and Bray, D. (1988). *Managerial Lives in Transition: Advancing Age and Changing Times*. New York: Guilford Press.

Howard, J., Cunningham, D. and Rechnitzer, P. (1986). Role ambiguity, type A behaviour, and job satisfaction. *Journal of Applied Psychology*, **71**, 95–101.

Hrebiniak, L. and Roteman, R. (1973) A study of the relationship between need satisfaction and absenteeism among managerial personnel. *Journal of Applied Psychology*, **58**, 381–3.

Hulin, C. and Blood, M. (1968). Job enlargement, individual differences, and worker responses. *Psychological Bulletin*, **69**, 41–55.

Hulin, C. and Smith, P. (1964). Sex differences in job satisfaction. *Journal of Applied Psychology*, **48**, 88–92.

Hull, D., Bosley, J. and Udell, G. (1980). Renewing the hunt for a heffalump: Identifying potential entrepreneurs by personality characteristics. *Journal of Small Business*, **18**, 11–18.

Hunter, J. (1986). Cognitive ability, cognitive aptitude, job knowledge, and job performance. *Journal of Vocational Behaviour*, **29**, 340–362.

Hunter, J. and Hunter, R. (1984). Validity and utility of alternate predictors of job performance. *Psychological Bulletin*, **96**, 72–98.

Hunter, J., Schmidt, F. and Judiesch, M. (1990). Individual differences in output variability as a function of job complexity. *Journal of Applied Psychology*, **75**, 28–42.

Huse, E., and Taylor, E. (1962). The reliability of absence measures. *Journal of Applied Psychology*, **46**, 159–160.

Igen, D. and Hodenbeck, J. (1977). The role of job satisfaction in absence behaviour. *Organizational Behaviour and Human Performance*, **19**, 148–161.

Ingham, G. (1970). *Size of Industrial Organization and Worker Behaviour*. Cambridge: CUP.

Ingleton, C. (1975). Graduate selection. In K. Miller (Ed.) *Psychological Testing in Personnel Assessment*, p.61–71. New York: Wiley.

Inwald, R. (1988). Five-year follow-up study of departmental terminators as predicted by 16 pre-employment psychological indicators. *Journal of Applied Psychology*, **73**, 1–8.

Iso–Ahola, S. (1976). On the theoretical link between personality and leisure. *Psychological Reports*, **39**, 3–10.

Jablonsky, S. and De Vries, D. (1972). Operant conditioning principles extrapolated to the theory of management. *Organizational Behaviour and Human Performance*, **14**, 340–358.

Jackson, P., Stafford, M., Banks, M. and Warr, P. (1983). Unemployment and psychological distress in young people. *Journal of Applied Psychology*, **68**, 525–535.

Jahoda, M. (1979). The impact of unemployment in the 1930s and the 1980s. *Bulletin of the British Psychological Society*, **32**, 309–314.

Jahoda, M. (1982). *Employment and Unemployment: A Social-psychological Analysis*. Cambridge: CUP.

Janoksi, M. and Holmes, D. (1981). Influence of initial aerobic fitness, aerobic training, and changes in aerobic fitness of personality functioning. *Journal of Psychosomatic Research*, **25**, 553–556.

Jemmott, J. (1987). Social motives and susceptibility to disease: Stalking individual differences in health risks. *Journal of Personality*, **55**, 267–278.

Jenkins, R., MacDonald, A., Murray, J. and Strathdee, G. (1982). Minor psychiatric morbidity and the threat of redundancy in a professional group. *Psychological Medicine*, **12**, 799–807.

Jensen, A. (1973). Personality and scholastic achievement in three ethnic groups. *British Journal of Educational Psychology*, **43**, 115–123.

Jessup, G. and Jessup, H. (1971). Validity of the Eysenck Personality Inventory in pilot selection. *Occupational Psychology*, **45**, 111–123.

Johnson, C., Messé, L. and Crano, W. (1984). Predicting job performance of low income workers: The work opinion questionnaire. *Personnel Psychology*, **37**, 291–299.

Johnson, C., Wood, R. and Blinkhorn, S. (1988). Spiriouser and spiriouser: The use of ipsative personality tests. *Journal of Occupational Psychology*, **61**, 153–161.

Jones, J. and Wuebker, L. (1985). Development and validation of the safety locus of control scale. *Perceptual and Motor Skills*, **61**, 151–161.

Jones, H., Sasek, J. and Wakefield, J. (1976). Maslow's need hierarchy and Cattell's 16PF. *Journal of Clinical Psychology*, **32**, 74–76.

Joyce, W. (1982). Person–situation interaction: Competing models of fit. *Journal of Occupational Behaviour*, **3**, 265–280.

Jung, C. (1953). *The Integration of Personality*. New York: Farrar & Ruchart.

Kagan, J. and Moss, H. (1962). *Birth to Maturity*. New York: Wiley.

Kahana, E., Liang, J. and Felton, B. (1980). Alternative models of person–environment fit: Prediction of morale in three homes for the aged. *Journal of Gerontology*, **35**, 584–595.

Kanter, R. (1986). *The Change Masters: Corporate: Entrepreneurs at Work*. London: Unwin.

Karson, S. and O'Dell, J. (1970). *A Guide to the Clinical Use of the 16PF*. Illinois: IPAT.

Kasl, S. (1973). Mental health and the work environment: An examination of the evidence. *Journal of Occupational Medicine*, **15**, 509–518.

Kasl, S. (1980). The impact of retirement. In C. Cooper and R. Payne (Eds) *Current Concerns in Occupational Stress*. Chichester: Wiley.

Katz, A. (1984). Creative styles: Relating tests of creativity to the work patterns of scientists. *Personality and Individual Differences*, **5**, 281–292.

Kay, H. (1981). Accidents: Some facts and theories. In P. Warr (Ed) *Psychology at Work*. Harmondsworth: Penguin.

Keenan, A. (1982). Candidates, personality and performance in selection interviews. *Personnel Review*, **11**, 20–22.

Keinan, G., Friedland, N., Yitzhaky, J. and Moran, A. (1981). Biographical, physiological, and personality variables as predictors of performance under sickness-inducing motion. *Journal of Applied Psychology*, **66**, 233–241.

Keller, R. (1983). Predicting absenteeism from prior absenteeism, attitudinal factors, and non attitudinal factors. *Journal of Applied Psychology*, **68**, 536–540.

Kennedy, R. (1958). *The Prediction of Achievement and Creativity*. New York: Bobbs-Merrill.

Kenrick, D. and Funder, D. (1988). Profiting from controversy: Lessons from the person–situation debate. *American Psychologist*, **43**, 23–34.

Kets de Vries, M. (1977). The entrepreneurial personality: A person at the crossroads. *Journal of Management Studies*, **14**, 34–57.

Kets de Vries, M. (1985). The dark side of entrepreneurship. *Harvard Business Review*, Nov, 160–167.

Khavari, K., Mabry, E. and Humes, M. (1977). Personality correlates of hallucinogenic use. *Journal of Abnormal Psychology*, **86**, 172–8.

Kim, J. (1980). Relationships of personality to perceptual and behavioural responses in stimulating and non stimulating tasks. *Academy of Management Journal*, **23**, 307–319.

King, A. (1985). Self-analysis and assessment of entrepreneurial potential. *Stimulation and Games*, **16**, 399–416.

Kirchner, W. (1961). 'Real-life' faking on the Strong Vocational Interest Blank by sales applicants. *Journal of Applied Psychology*, **45**, 273–276.

Kirchner, W. (1962). 'Real-life' faking on the Edwards Personal Preference Schedule by sales applicants. *Journal of Applied Psychology*, **46**, 128–130.

Kirkcaldy, B. (1985). Sex and personality differences in occupational interests. *Personality and Individual Differences*, **9**, 7–13.

Kirton, M. and Mulligan, G. (1973). Correlates of managers' attitudes toward change. *Journal of Applied Psychology*, **58**, 101–107.

Kirton, M. and Pender, S. (1982). The adaption–innovation continuum, occupational type, and course selection. *Psychological Reports*, **51**, 883–886.

Kirzner, J. (1973). *Competition and Entrepreneurship*. Chicago: University of Chicago Press.

Kline, P. (1975). *The Psychology of Vocational Guidance*. London: Batsford.

Kline, P. (1978). *OOQ and OPQ Personality Tests*. Windsor: NFER.

Kline, P. (1983). *Personality Measurement and Theory*. London: Hutchinson.

Kobasa, S. (1979). Stressful life events, personality, health: An enquiring into hardiness. *Journal of Personality and Social Psychology*, **37**, 1–11.

Kohn, M. and Schooler, C. (1982). Job conditions and personality: A longitudinal assessment of their reciprocal effects. *American Journal of Sociology*, **87**, 1257–1286.

Kolb, D. (1976). *Learning Style Inventory: Technical Manual*. Boston, Massachusetts.

Kolb, D. (1984). *Experimental Learning*. Englewood Cliffs, NJ: Prentice Hall.

Komives, J. (1972). *A Preliminary Study of Personal Values of High Technical Entrepreneurs*. Milwaukee: Centre for Venture Management.

Korman, A. (1970). Toward a hypothesis of work behaviour. *Journal of Applied Psychology*, **54**, 31–41.

Kremer, Y. and Harpaz, I. (1982). Leisure patterns among retired workers: Spillover and compensating trends. *Journal of Vocational Behaviour*, **21**, 183–195.

Kriedt, P. and Gadel, M. (1953). Prediction of turnover among clerical workers. *Journal of Applied Psychology*, **37**, 338–340.

Kroll, W. and Crenshaw, W. (1968). Multivariate personality profile analysis of four athletic groups. In S. Kenyon (Ed.) *Contemporary Psychology of Sport*, p.97–106, Chicago: ISSP.

Kuder, F. (1970). *General Interest Survey: Manual*. Chicago: Science Research.

Landy, F. (1985). *Psychology of Work Behaviour*. Illinois: Dorsey Press.

Landy, F. and Farr, J. (1983). *The Measurement of Work Performance: Methods, Theory, and Applications*. New York: Academic Press.

Lautenschlager, G. and Shaffer, G. (1987). Re-examining the components stability of Owen's biographical questionnaire. *Journal of Applied Psychology*, **72**, 149–152.

Lawler, E. (1971). *Pay and Organizational Effectiveness: A Psychological View*. New York: McGraw Hill.

Lawler, E. (1973). *Motivation in Work Organizations*. Pacific Grove: Brooks/Cole.

Lay, C. (1986). At last, my research article on procrastination. *Journal of Research in Personality*, **20**, 474–495.

Layton, C. and Eysenck, S. (1985). Psychoticism and unemployment. *Personality and Individual Differences*, **6**, 387–390.

Lefkowitz, J. (1975). Psychological attributes of policemen: A review of research and opinion. *Journal of Social Issues*, **31**, 3–26.

Leibenstein, H. (1966). Allocation efficiency vs x-efficiency. *American Economic Review*, **58**, 72–83.

Leibenstein, H. (1979). The general x-efficiency paradigm and the role of the entrepreneur. In M. Rizzo (Ed.) *Time, Uncertainty and Disequilibrium*. Lexington: Heath.

Lester, D. (1983). The selection of police officers: An argument for simplicity. *Police Journal*, **56**, 53–55.

Lester, D. and Purgrave, C. (1980). Predicting graduation from a police academy with the Kuder Occupational Interest Survey. *Psychological Reports*, **47**, 78.

Lester, D. and Ferguson, R. (1989). Predicting performance of the state police from scores on psychological tests. *Perceptual and Motor Skills*, **69**, 626.

Levin, I. and Stokes, J. (1989). Dispositional approach to job satisfaction: Role of negative effectivity. *Journal of Applied Psychology*, **74**, 752–758.

Levy, R. (1967). Predicting police failures. *Journal of Criminal Law, Criminology and Police Science*, **58**, 265–276.

Levy, D., Kaler, S. and Schall, M. (1988). An empirical investigation of role schemata: Occupations, and personality characteristics. *Psychological Reports*, **63**, 3–14.

Lewis, A. (1935). Neurosis and unemployment. *Lancet*, **I**, 293–296.

Lim, C. (1977). Small industry in Malaysia: A socio-economic profile of entrepreneurs. *Social Action*, **27**, 2.

Linden, W. (1987). On the impending death of type A construct: Or is there a phoenix rising from the ashes? *Canadian Journal of Behavioural Science*, **19**, 178–190.

Ling, T. and Putti, J. (1987). Is personality a determinant of leadership style? *Human Resources Journal*, **2**, 29–36.

Lipper, A. (1987). Defining the win and thereby lessening the losses for successful entrepreneurs. *Journal of Creative Behaviour*, 22, 172–177.

Llorente, M. (1986). Neuroticism, extraversion and the type A behaviour pattern. *Personality and Individual Differences*, 7, 427–429.

Locke, E. (1969). What is job satisfaction? *Organizational Behaviour and Human Performance*, 4, 309–336.

Locke, E. (1976). The nature and causes of job satisfaction. In M. Dunnette (Ed.) *Handbook of Industrial and Organizational Psychology*, p.1297–1349. Chicago: Rand McNally & Co.

Locke, E. (1984). Job Satisfaction. In M. Gruneberg and T. Wall (Eds) *Social Psychology and Organizational Behaviour*, p.93–117. Chichester: Wiley.

Locke, E. and Latham, G. (1990). Work motivation and satisfaction. *Psychological Science*, 1, 240–246.

Loehlin, J. and Nichols, R. (1976). *Heredity, Environment, and Personality: A Study of 850 Twins*. Austin: University of Texas Press.

Lombardo, M. and McCall, T. (1984). The Boss. *Psychology Today*, Jan, 45–48.

Loo, R. (1979). Role of primary personality factors in the perception of traffic signs and driver violations and accidents. *Accident Analysis and Prevention*, 11, 125–127.

Lorefice, L., Steer, R., Fine, E. and Schut, J. (1976). Personality traits and moods of alcoholics and heroin addicts. *Journal of Studies on Alcohol*, 37, 687–9.

Loucks, S., Kobos, J., Stanton, B., Burstein, A. and Lawlis, G. (1979). Sex-related psychological characteristics of medical students. *Journal of Psychology*, 102, 119–123.

Low, M. and MacMillan, I. (1988). Entrepreneurship: Past research and future challenges. *Journal of Management*, 14, 139–158.

Lynn, R., Hampson, S. and Magee, M. (1984). Home background, intelligence, personality and education as predictors of unemployment in young people. *Personality and Individual Differences*, 5, 549–557.

Lyons, T. (1972). Turnover and absenteeism: A review of relationships and shared correlates. *Personnel Psychology*, 25, 271–281.

Lyonski, S. and Andrews, C. (1990). Effects of moderating variables on product managers' behaviour. *Psychological Reports*, 66, 295–306.

MacLean, M. (1977). Chronic welfare dependency: A multivariate analysis of personality factors. *Multivariate Experimental and Clinical Research*, 3, 83–93.

Males, S. (1983). *Police Management on Division and Subdivision*. Police Research Services Unit.

Mancuso, J. (1973). *Funds and Guts: The Entrepreneur's Philosophy*. Boston, MA: Addison-Wesley.

Mancuso, J. and Mascolo, M. (1987). Recognising achievement motivation. *Motivation and Emotion*, 11, 323–330.

Manz, C., Adsit, D., Campbell, S. and Mathison-Hance, M. (1988). Managerial thought patterns and performance: A study of perceptual patterns of performance hindrance for higher and lower performing managers. *Human Relations*, 41, 447–465.

Marcia, D., Aiuppa, T. and Watson, J. (1989). Personality type, organizational norms and self-esteem. *Psychological Reports*, 65, 915–919.

Marhardt, P. (1972). Job orientation of male and female college graduates in business. *Personnel Psychology*, 25, 361–368.

Marin, E. (1976). Social psychological correlates of drug use among Columbian university students. *International Journal of Addiction*. 11, 199–207.

Martens, R. (1975). The paradigmatic crisis in American sport personology. *Sportwissenschaft*, 1, 9–24.

Martocchio, J. and O'Leary, A. (1989). Sex differences in occupational stress: A meta-analytic review. *Journal of Applied Psychology*, **74**, 495–501.

Maslow, A. (1954). *Motivation and Personality*. New York: Harper & Row.

Matteson, M., Ivancevich, J. and Smith, S. (1984). Relation of type A behaviour to performance and satisfaction among sales personnel. *Journal of Vocational Behaviour*, **25**, 203–214.

Matthews, G. (1988). Morningness–eveningness as a dimension of personality: Trait, state and psychophysiology correlates. *European Journal of Personality*, **2**, 277–293.

Matthews, G., Stanton, N., Graham, N. and Brimelow, C. (1990). A factor analysis of the scales of occupational personality questionnaire. *Personality and Individual Differences*, **11**, 591–596.

McBer & Co. (1986). *Entrepreneurship and Small Enterprise Development*. Second Annual Report to USAID.

McCall, M. and Lombard, M. (1983). What makes a top executive. *Psychology Today*, Feb, 26–31.

McCann, R. and Margerison, C. (1989). Managing high-performing teams. *Training and Development Journal*, **11**, 53–60.

McClelland, D. (1962). Business drive and national achievement. *Harvard Business Review*, **40**, 99–101.

McClelland, D. (1965). Achievement motivation can be developed. *Harvard Business Review*, **43**, 99.

McClelland, D. (1987). Characteristics of successful entrepreneurs. *Journal of Creative Behaviour*, **21**, 219–233.

McClelland, D. (1989). Motivational factors in health and disease. *American Psychology*, **44**, 675–683.

McClelland, D. and Winter, D. (1969). *Motivating Economic Development*. New York: Free Press.

McClelland, D., Atkinson, J., Clark, R. and Lowell, E. (1953). *The Achievement Motive*. New York: Appleton–Century–Crofts.

McCord, R. and Wakefield, J. (1981). Arithmetic achievement as a function of introversion–extraversion and teacher-presented reward and punishment. *Personality and Individual Differences*, **2**, 145–152.

McCrae, R. and Costa, P. (1988). Reinterpreting the Myers–Briggs Type Indicator from the perspective of the five-factor model of personality. *Journal of Personality*, **57**, 17–40.

McDaniel, M. (1989). Biographical constructs for predicting employee suitability. *Journal of Applied Psychology*, **74**, 964–970.

McElroy, J., Morrow, P. and Ackerman, R. (1983). Personality and interior office design: Exploring the accuracy of visitor attributes. *Journal of Applied Psychology*, **68**, 541–544.

McGoldrick, A. (1973). *Early Retirement: A New Leisure Opportunity?* Polytechnic of Central London. Unpublished Report.

McGoldrick, A. (1987). Stress, early retirement and health. In K. Markides and C. Cooper (Eds) *Aging, Stress and Health*. Chichester: Wiley.

McGuire, F. (1956). The safe-driver inventory. *US Armed Forces Medical Journal*, **7**, 1249–1264.

McKenzie, J. (1989). Neuroticism and academic achievement: The Furneaux Factor. *Personality and Individual Differences*, **10**, 509–515.

McLoughlin, C., Friedson, D. and Murray, J. (1983). Personality profiles of recently terminated executives. *Personnel and Guidance Journal*, **61**, 226–229.

Mehrabian, A. and West, S. (1987). Emotional impact of task and its setting on work performance of screeners and nonscreeners. *Perceptual and Motor Skills*, **45**, 895–909.

Mehryar, A., Khajavi, F., Razavich, A. and Hosseini, A. (1973). Some personality correlates of intelligence and educational attainment in Iran. *British Journal of Educational Psychology*, **43**, 8–16.

Melamed, S., Najenson, T., Jucha, E. and Green, M. (1989). Ergometric stress levels, personal characteristics, accidents reoccurrence and sickness absence among factory workers. *Ergometrics*, **32**, 1101–1110.

Mendhiratta, S., Wig, N. and Verma, S. (1978). Some psychological correlates of long-term heavy cannabis users. *British Journal of Psychiatry*, **132**, 482–486.

Meredith, G., Nelson, R. and Neck, P. (1982). *The Practice of Entrepreneurship*. Geneva: International Labour Office.

Mescon, T. and Montanari, J. (1982). *The Personality of Independent and Franchise Entrepreneurs*, p.413–417. Proceedings of the Academy of Management.

Metcalfe, B. (1987). Male and female managers: An analysis of biographical and self-concept data. *Work and Stress*, **1**, 207–219.

Mettlin, C. (1976). Occupational careers and the prevention of coronary prone behaviour. *Social Science and Medicine*, **10**, 367–372.

Mihal, W. and Graumenz, J. (1984). An assessment of the accuracy of self-assessment for career decision making. *Journal of Vocational Behaviour*, **25**, 245–253.

Miller, K. (1975a). *Psychological Testing in Personnel Assessment*. New York: Wiley.

Miller, K. (1975b). Choosing tests for clerical selection. In K. Miller (Ed.) *Psychological Testing in Personnel Assessment*, p.109–121. New York: Wiley.

Miller, D. (1983). The correlates of entrepreneurship in three types of firms. *Management Science*, **29**, 770–791.

Miller, D. and Friesen, P. (1982). Innovation in conservative and entrepreneurial firms: Two models of strategic momentum. *Strategic Management Journal*, **3**, 1–25.

Miller, D., Kets de Vries, M. and Toulouse, J.-M. (1982). Top executive locus of control and its relationship to strategy-making, structure and environment. *Academy of Management Journal*, **25**, 237–253.

Mills, C. and Bohannon, W. (1980). Personality characteristics of effective state police officers. *Journal of Applied Psychology*, **65**, 680–684.

Miner, J., Smith, N. and Bracker, J. (1989). Role of entrepreneurial task motivation in the growth of technologically innovative firms. *Journal of Applied Psychology*, **74**, 554–560.

Mitchell, T. and Klimoski, R. (1982). Is it rational to be empirical? A test of methods for scoring biographical data. *Journal of Applied Psychology*, **67**, 411–458.

Mitchell, V. and Mowdgill, P. (1976). Measurement of Maslow's need hierarchy. *Organizational Behaviour and Human Performance*, **16**, 334–349.

Mobley, W. and Locke, E. (1970). The relationship of value importance to satisfaction. *Organizational Behaviour and Human Performance*, **5**, 463–483.

Montag, I. and Comrey, A. (1987). Internality and externality as correlates of involvement in fatal driving accidents. *Journal of Applied Psychology*, **72**, 339–343.

Moore, T. (1987). Personality tests are back. *Fortune*, 30 March, 74–82.

Moore, R. and Stewart, R. (1989). Evaluating employee integrity. *Employee Responsibility and Rights Journal*, **2**, 203–218.

Morgenstern, F., Hodgson, R. and Law, L. (1974). Work efficiency and personality: A comparison of introverted and extraverted subjects exposed to conditions of distraction and distortion of stimulus in a learning task. *Ergonomics*, **17**, 211–220.

Morse, J. (1975). Person–job congruence and individual adjustment and development. *Human Relations*, 28, 841–861.

Morse, J. and Caldwell, D. (1979). Effects of personality and perception of the environment on satisfaction with task group. *Journal of Psychology*, 103, 183–192.

Mortimer, J., Lorence, J. and Kumka, D. (1986). *Work, Family, and Personality: Transition to Adulthood*. Norwood, NJ: Ablex.

Mosel, J. (1952). Prediction of department stores sales performance from personal data. *Journal of Applied Psychology*, 36, 8–10.

Motowidlo, S., Packard, J. and Marning, M. (1986). Occupational stress: Its causes and consequences for job performance. *Journal of Applied Psychology*, 71, 618–629.

Mount, M. and Muchinsky, P. (1978). Person–environment congruence and employee job satisfaction: A test of Holland's theory. *Journal of Vocational Behaviour*, 13, 84–100.

Mowday, R. and Spencer, D. (1981). The influence of task and personality characteristics on employee turnover and absenteeism. *Academy of Management Journal*, 24, 634–642.

Muchinsky, P. (1977). Employee absenteeism: A review of the literature. *Journal of Vocational Behaviour*, 10, 316–340.

Murray, H. (1938). *Explorations in Personality*. New York: Oxford University Press.

Myers, J. and McCaulley, M. (1985). *Manual: A Guide to the Development and Use of the Myers–Briggs Type Indicator*. Palo Alto: CP Press.

Naylor, J. and Vincent, N. (1959). Predicting female absenteeism. *Personnel Psychology*, 12, 81–84.

Naylor, F., Care, E. and Mount, T. (1986). The identification of Holland categories and occupational classification by the Vocational Preference Inventory and the Strong–Campbell Interest Inventory. *Australian Journal of Psychology*, 38, 161–167.

Neel, R. and Dunn, R. (1960). Predicting success in supervisory training programs by the use of psychological tests. *Journal of Applied Psychology*, 44, 358–360.

Neiner, A. and Owens, W. (1982). Relationships between two sets of biodata with 7 years separation. *Journal of Applied Psychology*, 67, 146–150.

Nelson, R. (1963). Knowledge and interests concerning sixteen occupations among elementary and secondary school students. *Educational and Psychological Measurement*, 23, 741–754.

Neulinger, J. (1978). *The Psychology of Leisure*. Springfield: C.C. Thomas.

Nevo, B. (1976). Using biographical information to predict success of men and women in the army. *Journal of Applied Psychology*, 61, 106–108.

Newton, T. (1989). Occupational stress and coping with stress: A critique. *Human Relations*, 42, 441–461.

Newton, T. and Keenan, A. (1983). Is work involvement an attribute of the person or the environment? *Journal of Occupational Behaviour*, 4, 169–178.

Nias, D. (1985). Personality and recreational behaviour. In B. Kirkcaldy (Ed.) *Individual Differences in Movement*. Lancaster: MTP Press.

Nicholson, N., Brown, C. and Chadwick-Jones, K. (1977). Absence from work and personal characteristics. *Journal of Applied Psychology*, 62, 319–327.

Nutt, P. (1986a). Decision style and strategic decisions of top executives. *Technological Forecasting and Social Change*, 30, 39–62.

Nutt, P. (1986b). Decision style and its impact on managers and management. *Technological Forecasting and Social Change*, 29, 341–366.

Nutt, P. (1986c). The effects of culture on decision making. *OMEGA: International Journal of Management Science*, 16, 553–567.

Nutt, P. (1989). Uncertainty and culture in bank loan decisions. *OMEGA: International Journal of Management Science*, **17**, 297–308.

Nutt, P. (1990). Strategic decisions made by top executives and middle managers with data and process dominant styles. *Journal of Management Studies*, **27**, 173–194.

O'Brien, G. (1981). Locus of control, previous occupation and satisfaction with retirement. *Australian Journal of Psychology*, **33**, 305–318.

O'Brien, G. (1982). Evaluation of job characteristics theory of work attitudes and performance. *Australian Journal of Psychology*, **34**, 383–401.

O'Brien, G. (1984). Locus of control, work and retirement. In H. Lefcourt (Ed.) *Research with the Locus of Control Construct*. Vol. 3, p.7–72. New York: Academic Press.

O'Brien, G. and Kabanoff, B. (1979). Comparison of unemployed and employed workers on work values, locus of control and health variables. *Australian Psychologist*, **14**, 143–154.

Okaue, M., Nakamura, M. and Niura, K. (1977). Personality characteristics of pilots on EPPS, MPI, and DOSEFU. *Reports of Aeromedical Laboratory*, **18**, 83–93.

Olson, P. and Bosserman, D. (1984). Attributes of the entrepreneurial type. *Business Horizons*, **27**, 53–56.

Opsahl, R. and Dunnette, M. (1966). The role of financial compensation in industrial motivation. *Psychological Bulletin*, **66**, 94–116.

O'Reilly, C. (1977). Personality–job fit: Implications for individual attitudes and performance. *Organizational Behaviour and Human Performance*, **18**, 36–46.

O'Reilly, C. and Caldwell, D. (1979). Informational influence as a determinant of perceived task characteristics and job satisfaction. *Journal of Applied Psychology*, **64**, 157–165.

Organ, D. (1975a). Extraversion, locus of control, and individual differences in conditionability in organizations. *Journal of Applied Psychology*, **60**, 401–404.

Organ, D. (1975b). Effects of pressure and individual neuroticism on emotional responses to task-role ambiguity. *Journal of Applied Psychology*, **60**, 397–400.

Ormel, J. (1983). Neuroticism and well-being inventories: Measuring traits or states *Psychological Medicine*, **13**, 165–176.

Orpen, C. (1976). Personality and academic attainment: A cross-cultural study. *British Journal of Educational Psychology*, **46**, 220–222.

Orpen, C. (1983). Note on prediction of managerial effectiveness from the Californian Psychological Inventory. *Psychological Reports*, **53**, 622.

Ostell, A. and Divers, P. (1987). Attributional style, unemployment and mental health. *Journal of Occupational Psychology*, **60**, 333–337.

Overall, J. and Patrick, J. (1972). Unitary alcoholism factor and its personality correlates. *Journal of Abnormal Psychology*, **79**, 303–9.

Owens, W. (1976). Background data. In M. Dunnette (Ed.) *Handbook of Industrial and Organizational Psychology*. Chicago: Rand McNally.

Owens, D. and Schoenfeldt, L. (1979). Toward a classification of persons. *Journal of Applied Psychology*, **64**, 569–607.

Palmer, M. (1971). The application of psychological testing to entrepreneurship potential. *California Management Review*, **13**, 32–38.

Palmer, W. (1974). Management effectiveness as a function of personality traits of the manager. *Personality Psychology*, **27**, 283–295.

Pandey, J. and Tewary, N. (1979). Locus of control and achievement of entrepreneurs. *Journal of Occupational Behaviour*, **52**, 107–111.

Papanek, G. (1971). The industrial entrepreneurs – education, occupation, background, and finance. In W. Folcon and G. Papanek (Eds) *Development Policy*. Cambridge: Harvard University Press.

Paramesh, C. (1976). Dimensions of personality and achievement in scholastic subjects. *Indian Journal of Psychology*, **51**, 302–306.

Patterson, C., Kosson, D. and Newman, J. (1987). Reaction to punishment, reflectivity, and passive avoidance learning in extraverts. *Journal of Personality and Social Psychology*, **52**, 565–575.

Patsfall, M. and Feimer, N. (1985). The role of person–environment fit in job performance and satisfaction. In J. Bernardin and D. Bownas (Eds) *Personality Assessment in Organization*, p.53–81. New York: Praeger.

Payne, R. (1987). Individual differences and performance among R and O personnel. *R&O Management*, **17**, 153–161.

Payne, R. (1988). A longitudinal study of the psychological well-being of unemployed men and the mediating effect of neuroticism. *Human Relations*, **41**, 119–138.

Perairo, M. and Willerman, L. (1983). Personality correlates of occupational status according to Holland's types. *Journal of Vocational Behaviour*, **22**, 268–277.

Perone, M., De Waard, R. and Baron, A. (1979). Satisfaction with real and simulated jobs in relation to personality variables and drug use. *Journal of Applied Psychology*, **64**, 660–668.

Perry, A. (1986). Type A behaviour pattern and motor vehicle drivers' behaviour. *Perceptual and Motor Skills*, **63**, 875–878.

Pervin, L. (1967). *Personality: Theory and Research*. New York: Wiley.

Pervin, L. (1984). *Current Controversies and Issues in Personality*. New York: Wiley.

Peterson, R. (1980). Entrepreneurship and organization. In R. Ronstadt (Ed.) *Frontiers of Entrepreneurial Research*. Babson College: Babson.

Peterson, C. Semmel, A., Von Baeyer, C., Abramson, L, Metalsky, G. and Seligman, M. (1982). The Attributional Style Questionnaire. *Cognitive Research and Therapy*, **6**, 281–30.

Phillips, J., Freedman, S., Ivancevich, J. and Mateson, M. (1990). Type A behaviour, self-appraisals, and goal setting: A framework for future research. *Journal of Social Behaviour and Personality*, **5**, 59–76.

Pillai, P. (1975). A study of factors related to the disparity between occupational aspirations and value choices of high school students. *Indian Journal of Social Work*, **36**, 61–73.

Porter, C. and Corlett, E. (1989). Performance differences of individuals classified by questionnaire as accident prone or non-accident prone. *Ergometrics*, **32**, 317–333.

Porter, W. and Steers, R. (1973). Organizational work and personal factors in employee turnover and absenteeism. *Psychological Bulletin*, **80**, 151–171.

Power, C. (1977). Effects of student characteristics and level of teacher–student interaction on achievement and attitudes. *Contemporary Educational Psychology*, **2**, 265–274.

Prediger, D. (1989). Ability differences across occupations: More than g. *Journal of Vocational Behaviour*, **34**, 1–27.

Price, V. (1982). *Type A Behaviour Pattern: A Model for Research and Practice*. London: Academic Press.

Pritchard, R. and Karasick, B. (1973). The effects of organizational job performance and job satisfaction. *Organizational Behaviour and Human Performance*, **9**, 126–146.

Pritchard, R., Dunnette, M. and Jorgenson, D. (1972). Effects of perceptions of equity and inequity on worker performance and satisfaction. *Journal of Applied Psychology*, **57**, 75–94.

Quenalt, S. (1968). *Driver-behaviour – Safe and Unsafe Drivers II*. Report LR146 to the Ministry of Transport.

Quinn, R., Staines, G. and McCullough, M. (1974). *Job Satisfaction? Is there a Trend?* Washington DC: US Dept.

Rabinowitz, S., Hall, D. and Goodale, J. (1977). Job scope and individual differences as predictors of job involvement: Independent or interactive. *Academy of Management Journal*, **20**, 273–281.

Rahim, A. (1981). Job satisfaction as a function of personality–job congruence: A study with Jungian psychological types. *Psychological Reports*, **49**, 496–498.

Ramsey, J. (1978) *Ergonomic Support of Consumer Product Safety*. Paper to the AIHA Conference. May.

Randle, C. (1956). How to identify promotable executives. *Harvard Business Review*, **34**, 122–134.

Raphael, K. and Gorman, B. (1986). College women's Holland-theme congruence: Effects of self-knowledge and subjective occupational structure. *Journal of Counselling Psychology*, **33**, 143–147.

Rawls, D. and Rawls, J. (1968). Personality characteristics and personal history data of successful and less successful executives. *Psychological Reports*, **23**, 1032–1034.

Ray, D. and Trupin, D. (1989). Crossnational comparison of entrepreneurs' perceptions of success. *Entrepreneurship and Regional Development*, **1**, 113–127.

Reid, P., Kleiman, L. and Travis, C. (1977). Attribution and sex differences in the employment interview. *Journal of Social Psychology*, **126**, 205–212.

Reif, W. and Luthans, F. (1972). Does job enrichment really pay off? *California Management Review*, **14**, 30–37.

Reilly, R. and Chao, G. (1982). Validity and fairness of some alternative employee selection procedures. *Personnel Psychology*, **32**, 83–90.

Reinhardt, R. (1970). The outstanding jet pilot. *American Journal of Psychiatry*, **127**, 732–736.

Rice, G. and Lindecamp, D. (1989). Personality types and business success of small retailers. *Journal of Occupational Psychology*, **62**, 177–182.

Richards, J. (1983). Validity of locus of control and self-esteem measures in a national longitudinal study. *Educational and Psychological Measurements*, **43**, 897–905.

Rim, Y. (1961). Dimensions of job incentives and personality. *Acta Psychologia*, **18**, 332–336.

Rim, Y. (1977). Significance of work and personality. *Journal of Occupational Psychology*, **50**, 135–138.

Robertson, I. (1978). Relationships between learning strategy, attention deployment and personality. *British Journal of Educational Psychology*, **48**, 86–91.

Robertson, I. and Makin, P. (1986). Management selection in Britain: A survey and critique. *Journal of Occupational Psychology*, **59**, 45–57.

Robertson, I. and Smith, M. (1989). Personnel selection methods. In M. Smith and I. Robertson (Eds) *Advances in Selection and Assessment*. Chichester: Wiley.

Robinson, H. and Hoppock, R. (1952). Job satisfaction résumé of 1951. *Occupations*, **30**, 594–598.

Rogers, D. (1984). *The Adult Years*. Englewood Cliffs, NJ: Prentice Hall.

Rokeach, M. (1973). *The Nature of Human Values*. New York: Free Press.

Rothstein, H., Schmidt, F., Erwin, F., Owens, W. and Sparks, C. (1990). Biographical data in employment selection: Can validities be made generalizable? *Journal of Applied Psychology*, **75**, 175–184.

Rotter, J. (1966). Generalized expectancies for internal versus external control of reinforcement. *Psychological Monographs*, **80**, 609.

Rotter, J. (1982). *The Development and Application of Social Learning Theory*, New York: Praeger.

Rowell, J. and Renner, V. (1975). Personality, mode of assessment and student achievement. *British Journal of Educational Psychology*, **45**, 232–238.

Rowland, G., Franken, R. and Harrison, K. (1986). Sensation seeking and participation in sporting activity. *Journal of Sport Psychology*, **8**, 212–220.

Rushall, B. (1968). Some practical applications of personality information to athletics. In S. Kenyon (Ed.) *Contemporary Psychology of Sport*, p.167–173. Chicago: ISSP.

Rushton, J., Murray, H. and Paunonen, S. (1983). Personality, research creativity and teaching effectiveness in university professors. *Scientometrics*, **5**, 93–116.

Russell, C. (1990). Selecting top corporate leaders: An example of biographical information. *Journal of Management*, **16**, 73–86.

Russell, C., Mattson, J., Devlin, S. and Atwater, D. (1990). Predictive validity of biodata items generated from retrospective life experience essays. *Journal of Applied Psychology*, **75**, 569–580.

Russell, D. (1982). The causal dimension scale: A measure of how individuals perceive causes. *Journal of Personality and Social Psychology*, **42**, 1137–1145.

Russell, J. and Mehrabian, A. (1975). Task, setting, and personality variables affecting the desire to work. *Journal of Applied Psychology*, **60**, 518–520.

Sackett, P. and Harris, M. (1985). Honesty testing for personnel selection: A review and critique. In H. Bernardin and D. Bownes (Eds) *Personality Assessment in Organizations*, p.236–276. New York: Praeger.

Sackett, P., Burns, L. and Callahan, C. (1989). Integrity testing for personnel selection: *Personnel Psychology*, **42**, 491–530.

Sadella, E., Linder, D. and Jenkins, B. (1988). Sports preference: A self-presentational analysis. *Journal of Sport and Exercise Psychology*, **10**, 214–222.

Saleh, S. and Lalljee, M. (1969). Sex and job satisfaction. *Personnel Psychology*, **22**, 465–471.

Sauser, W. and York, M. (1978). Sex differences in job satisfaction: A re-examination. *Personnel Psychology*, **31**, 537–547.

Savage, R. and Stewart, R. (1972). Personality and the success of card-punch operators in training. *British Journal of Psychology*, **63**, 445–450.

Savickas, M. (1984). Construction and validation of a physician career development inventory. *Journal of Vocational Behaviour*, **25**, 106–123.

Saxe, S. and Reiser, M. (1976). A comparison of three police applicant groups using the MMPI. *Journal of Police Science and Administration*, **47**, 419–425.

Scanlan, T. (1979). *Self-employment as a Career Option*. University of Illinois doctorate.

Scarr, S. and Weinberg, R. (1983). The Minnesota Adoption Studies: Genetic differences and malleability. *Child Development*, **54**, 260–267.

Schacter, S. and Singer, J. (1962). Cognitive, social and physiological determinants of emotional state. *Psychological Review*, **69**, 379–399.

Schendel, R. (1968). Some practical applications of personality information to athletics. In S. Kenyon (Ed.) *Contemporary Psychology of Sport*; p.79–96. Chicago :ISSP.

Schenk, J. and Rausche, A. (1979). The personality of accident prone drivers. *Psychologie und Praxis*, **23**, 241–247.

Scherer, R., Adams, J. and Wiebe, F. (1989). Developing entrepreneurial behaviour: A social learning theory perspective. *Journal of Organizational Change Management*, **2**, 16–27.

Schiraldi, G. and Beck, K. (1988). Personality correlates of the Jenkins Activity Survey. *Social Behaviour and Personality*, 16, 109–115.

Schmidt, F. (1988). The problem of group differences in ability test scores in employment selection. *Journal of Vocational Behaviour*, 33, 272–292.

Schmidt, F. and Hunter, J. (1981). Employment testing: Old theories and new research findings. *American Psychologist*, 36, 1128–1137.

Schmidt, F. and Hunter, J. (1983). Individual differences in productivity: An empirical test of estimates derived from studies of selection procedure utility. *Journal of Applied Psychology*, 68, 407–414.

Schmidt, F., Mack, M., and Hunter, J. (1984). Selection utility in the occupation of US park ranger for three modes of test use. *Journal of Applied Psychology*, 68, 590–601.

Schuler, R. (1975). Sex, organizational level and outcome importance: Where the differences are. *Personnel Psychology*, 31, 537–593.

Schurr, K., Ruble, V. and Henriksen, L. (1988). Relationships of Myers–Briggs Type Indicator personality characteristics and self-reported academic problems and skill ratings with scholastic aptitude test scores. *Educational and Psychological Measurement*, 48, 187–196.

Schwartz, R., Andiappan, P. and Nelson, M. (1986). Reconsidering the support for Holland's congruence–achievement hypothesis. *Journal of Counselling Psychology*, 33, 425–428.

Scott, R. and Johnson, R. (1967). Use of the weighted application blank in selecting unskilled employees. *Journal of Applied Psychology*, 51, 393–395.

Seddon, G. (1975). The effects of chronological age on the relationship of intelligence and academic achievement with extraversion and neuroticism. *British Journal of Psychology*, 66, 493–500.

Seddon, G. (1977). The effects of chronological age on the relationship of academic achievement with extraversion and neuroticism. *British Journal of Educational Psychology*, 47, 187–192.

Seligman, M. (1975). *Helplessness: On Depression, Development, and Death*. San Francisco: W.H. Freeman.

Seligman, M. and Schulman, P. (1986). Explanatory style as a predictor of productivity and quitting among life insurance sales agents. *Journal of Personality and Social Psychology*, 50, 832–883.

Sexton, D. (1987). Advancing small business research: Utilizing research from other areas. *American Journal of Small Business*, 11, 25–30.

Sexton, D. and Bowman, N. (1986). Validation of a personality index: Comparative psychological characteristics analysis of female entrepreneurs, managers, entrepreneurship students and business students. In R. Petersen and K. Vesper (Eds) *Frontiers of Entrepreneurship Research*. Wesley: Babson College.

Shackleton, V. and Newell, S. (1991). Management selection: A comparative study of methods used in top British and French companies. *Journal of Occupational Psychology*, 64, 23–36.

Shadbolt, D. (1978). Interactive relationships between measured personality and teaching strategy variables. *British Journal of Educational Psychology*, 48, 227–231.

Shamir, B. (1985a). Unemployment and 'free time.' *Leisure Studies*, 4, 333–345.

Shamir, B. (1985b). Sex differences in psychological adjustment to unemployment and reemployment: A question of commitment, alternatives or finances. *Social Problems*, 33, 67–79.

Shamir, B. (1986). Protestant work ethic, work involvement, and the psychological impact of unemployment. *Journal of Occupational Behaviour*, 7, 25–38.

Shamir, B. (1987). *The Stability of Protestant Work Ethic and Work Involvement*. Unpublished paper.

Shanthamani, V. (1973). Unemployment and neuroticism. *Indian Journal of Social Work*, **34**, 43–45.

Shapiro, D. and Stern, L. (1975). Job satisfaction: Male and female, professional and non-professional. *Personnel Journal*, **21**, 388–406.

Shaw, L. and Sichel, H. (1970). *Accident Proneness*. Oxford: Pergamon.

Sheehy, N. and Chapman, A. (1987). Industrial Accidents. In C. Cooper and I. Robertson (Eds) *International Review of Industrial and Organizational Review*, p.201–227. Chichester: Wiley.

Schneidman, E. (1984). Personality and 'success' among a selected group of lawyers. *Journal of Personality Assessment*, **48**, 609–616.

Sims, R. and Veses, J. (1987a). Person–job match: Some alternative models. *International Journal of Management*, **4**, 156–165.

Sims, R. and Veres, J. (1987b). A person–job match (congruence) model: Toward improving organizational effectiveness. *International Journal of Management*, **4**, 98–104.

Skinner, N. (1974). Personality characteristics of heavy smokers and abstainers as a function of perceived predispositions towards marijuana use. *Social Behaviour and Personality* **2**, 157–60.

Slocum, J. (1978). Does cognitive style affect diagnosis and intervention strategies of change agents. *Group and Organizational Studies*, **3**, 199–210.

Smart, J. (1985). Holland environments as reinforcement systems. *Research in Higher Education*, **23**, 279–292.

Smart, J. (1987). Student satisfaction with graduate education. *Journal of College Student Personnel*, **5**, 218–222.

Smart, J., Elton, C. and McLaughlin, G. (1986). Person–environment congruence and job satisfaction. *Journal of Vocational Behaviour*, **29**, 216–225.

Smernou, L. and Lautenschlager, G. (1991). Autobiographical antecedents and correlates of neuroticism and extraverts. *Personality and Individual Differences*, **12**, 49–53.

Smith, C., Reilly, C. and Midkiff, K. (1989). Evaluation of three circadian rhythm questionnaires with suggestions for an improved measure of morningness. *Journal of Applied Psychology*, **74**, 728–738.

Smith, P. (1976). Behaviours results, and organizational effectiveness: The problem of criteria. In M. Dunnette (Ed.) *Handbook of Industrial and Organizational Psychology*. Chicago: Rand.

Smith, W., Albright, L., Glennon, J. and Owens, W. (1961). The prediction of research competence and creativity from personal history. *Journal of Applied Psychology*, **45**, 59–62.

Smulder, P. (1980). Comments on employee absence/attendance as a dependent variable in organizational research. *Journal of Applied Psychology*, **62**, 319–327.

Snyder, M. (1974). Self-monitoring of expressive behaviour. *Journal of Personality and Social Psychology*, **30**, 526–537.

Snyder, M. (1988). *Public Appearances; Private Realities*. New York: Freeman.

Soloman, G. and Winslow, E. (1987). Toward a descriptive profile of the entrepreneur. *Journal of Creative Behaviour*, **22**, 162–171.

Sparks, C. (1983). Paper and pencil measures of potential. In G. Dreher and P. Sackett (Eds) *Perspectives on Employee Staffing and Selection*. Homewood: Irwin.

Spector, P. (1982). Behaviour in organizations as a function of employee's locus of control. *Psychological Bulletin*, **91**, 482–497.

Spector, P. (1986). Perceived control by employees: A meta-analysis of studies concerning autonomy and participation at work. *Human Relations*, **11**, 1005–1016.

Spector, P. (1988). Development of the Work Locus of Control Scale. *Journal of Occupational Psychology*, **61**, 335–340.

Spence, J. and Helmreich, R. (1978). *Masculinity and Femininity: Their Psychological Dimensions, Correlates and Antecedents*. Austin: University of Texas.

Spielberger, C. (1979). *Police Selection and Evaluation: Issues and Techniques*. New York: Praeger.

Spitzer, M. and McNamara, W. (1964). A managerial selection study. *Personnel Psychology*, **17**, 19–40.

Staw, B. and Ross, J. (1985). Stability in the midst of change: A dispositional approach to job attitudes. *Journal of Applied Psychology*, **70**, 469–480.

Staw, B., Bell, N. and Clausen, J. (1986). The dispositional approach to job attitudes: A lifetime longitudinal test. *Administrative Science Quarterly*, **31**, 56–77.

Steers, R. (1977). Antecedents and outcomes of reorganizational commitment. *Administrative Science Quarterly*, **22**, 46–56.

Steers, R. and Rhodes, S. (1978). Major influences on employee attendance: A process model. *Journal of Applied Psychology*, **63**, 391–407.

Sterns, L., Alexander, R., Barrett, G. and Dambrot, F. (1983). The relationship of extraversion and neuroticism with job preference and job satisfaction for clerical employees. *Journal of Occupational Psychology*, **56**, 145–155.

Stevens, G., Hemstreet, A. and Gardner, S. (1989). Fit to lead: Predictions of success in a military academy through use of personality profile. *Psychological Reports*, **64**, 227–235.

Stockdale, J. (1986). *What is Leisure*? Sports Council/ESRC Special Report.

Stockford, L. and Kunze, K. (1950). Psychology and the pay check. *Personnel*, **27**, 129–143.

Stokes, G. and Cochrane, R. (1984). A study of the psychological effects of redundancy and unemployment. *Journal of Occupational Psychology*, **57**, 309–322.

Stone, R. (1988). Personality tests in management selection. *Human Resources Journal*, **3**, 51–55.

Storms, P. and Spector, P. (1987). Relationships of organizational frustration with reported behavioural reactions: The moderating effects of locus of control. *Journal of Occupational Behaviour*, **60**, 2–9.

Strelau, J. (1981). *Temperament, Personality, Activity*. London: Academic Press.

Streufert, S. and Nogami, G. (1989). Cognitive style and complexity: Implications for I/O Psychology. In C. Cooper and I. Robertson (Eds) *International Review of Industrial and Organizational Psychology*, p.93–143. Chichester: Wiley.

Stricker, L. and Ross, J. (1964). Some correlates of a Jungian Personality Inventory. *Psychological Reports*, **14**, 623–643.

Strong, E. (1951). Interest scores while in college of occupations engaged in 20 years later. *Educational and Psychological Measurement*, **11**, 335–348.

Strube, M., Denchmann, A. and Kickham, T. (1989). Time urgency and the type A behaviour pattern: Time investment as a function of cue salience. *Journal of Research in Personality*, **23**, 287–301.

Stuart, J. and Brown, B. (1981). The relationship of stress and coping ability to the incidence of disease and accidents. *Journal of Psychosomatic Research*, **25**, 255–260.

Sullivan, J. (1989). Self-theories and employee motivation. *Journal of Management*, **15**, 345–363.

Super, D. (1953). A theory of vocational development. *American Psychologist*, **8**, 186–195.

Susbauer, J. (1969). *The Technical Company Formation Process*. University of Texas Doctorate.

Svebak, S. and Kerr, J. (1989). The role of impulsivity in preference for sport. *Personality and Individual Differences*, **10**, 51–58.

Swaney, K. and Prediger, D. (1985). The relationship between interest–occupation congruence and job satisfaction. *Journal of Vocational Behaviour*, **26**, 13–24.

Swinburne, P. (1981). The psychological impact of unemployment on managers and professional staff. *Journal of Occupatioanal Psychology*, **54**, 47–64.

Szilagiji, A. and Sims, H. (1975). Locus of control and expectancies across multiple occupational levels. *Journal of Applied Psychology*, **60**, 638–640.

Szinovacz, M. (1987). Preferred retirement timing and retirement satisfaction in women. *International Journal of Aging and Human Development*, **24**, 301–316.

Szymanski, D. and Churchill, G. (1990). Client evaluation cues: A comparison of successful and unsuccessful sales people. *Journal of Marketing Research*, **27**, 163–174.

Tannenbaum, A. and Kuleck, W. (1978). The effect on organization members of discrepancy between perceived and preferred rewards implicit in work. *Human Relations*, **21**, 809–822.

Taylor, M. (1985). The roles of occupational knowledge and vocational self-concept crystallization in students' school-to-work transaction. *Journal of Counselling Psychology*, **32**, 539–550.

Taylor, E. and Nevis, E. (1957). The use of projective techniques in management selection. *Personnel*, **33**, 462–474.

Taylor, K., Kelso, G., Cox, G., Alloway, W. and Matthews, J. (1979). Applying Holland's vocational categories to leisure activities. *Journal of Occupational Psychology*, **52**, 199–207.

Taylor, C., Smith, W., Ghiselin, B. and Ellison, R. (1961). *Explorations in the Measurement and Prediction of Contributions of One Sample of Scientists*. ASO-TR-61–96. Lachland Airbase.

Teahan, J. (1969). *Future Time Perspective and Job Success*. Washington, DC: Department of Labour.

Terborg, J., Richardson, P. and Pritchard, R. (1980). Person–situation effects in the prediction of performance: An investigation of ability, self-esteem, and reward contingencies. *Journal of Applied Psychology*, **65**, 574–583.

Tett, R. and Jackson, D. (1990). Organization and personality correlates of participative behaviours using an in-basket exercise. *Journal of Occupational Behaviour*, **63**, 175–188.

Tett, R., Jackson, D. and Rothstein, M. (1991) Personality measures as predictors of job performance: a meta-analytic review. *Personnel Psychology*, **44**, 703–35.

Tiffany, D., Cowan, J. and Tiffany, P. (1970). *The Unemployed: A Social-psychological Portrait*. Englewood Cliffs, NJ: Prentice Hall.

Timmons, J., Smollen, L. and Dingee, A. (1977). *New Venture Creation: A Guide to Small Business Development*. Homewood: Irwin.

Timmons, J., Smollen, L. and Dingee, A. (1985). *New Venture Creation* (2nd Edition). Homewood: Irwin.

Toole, D., Gavin, J. Murdy, L. and Sells, S. (1972). The different validity of personality, personal history, and aptitude data for minority and non minority employees. *Personnel Psychology*, **25**, 661–672.

Torrubia, R. and Tobena, A. (1984). A scale for the assessment of 'susceptibility to punishment' as a measure of anxiety: Preliminary results. *Personality and Individual Differences*, **5**, 371–375.

Tremaine, L., Schau, C. and Busch, J. (1982). Children's occupational sex-typing. *Sex Roles*, **8**, 691–710.

Trice, A., Haire, J. and Elliott, K. (1989). A career locus of control scale for undergraduate students. *Perceptual and Motor Skills*, **69**, 555–561.

Tripathi, D. (1985). An integrated view of entrepreneurship. *Economic and Political Weekly*, **20**, 30–38.

Turnbull, A. (1976). Selling and the salesman: Prediction of success and personality change. *Psychological Reports*, **38**, 1175–1180.

Tversky, A. and Kahneman, D. (1982). Judgement under uncertainty. In D. Kahneman, P. Slovic and A. Tversky (Eds) *Judgements Under Uncertainty: Heuristic and Biases*, p.3–20. New York: Cambridge University Press.

Van Daalen, H. (1989). *Individual Characteristics and Third World Entrepreneurial Success*. Pretoria: U. Of Pretoria PhD thesis.

Van Daalen, H. and van Niekerk, E. (1989a). Achievement motivation and third world entrepreneurship. *Southern African Journal for Entrepreneurship and Small Business*, **1**, 12–19.

Van Daalen, H. and van Niekerk, E. (1989b). Locus of control and third world entrepreneurship. *South African Journal of Entrepreneurship and Small Business*, **1**, 41–46.

Van Daalen, H., van Niekerk, E. and Pottas, C. (1987). The validation of Furnham's locus of control scale for a black South African group. *Journal of Industrial Psychology*, **15**, 12–21.

Vandenberg, S. (1969). A twin study of spatial ability. *Multivariate Behavioural Research*, **4**, 273–294.

Vandenberg, S. and Kelly, L. (1964). Hereditary components in vocational preferences. *Acta Geneticae Medicae et Gemellogiae*, **23**, 266–277.

Vandenberg, S. and Stafford, R. (1967). Hereditary influence on vocational preferences as shown by scores of twins on the Minnesota Vocational Interest Inventory. *Journal of Applied Psychology*, **51**, 17–19.

Vealey, R. (1989). Sport personology: A paradigmatic and methodological analysis. *Journal of Sport and Exercise Psychology*, **11**, 216–235.

Vecchio, R. (1981). Workers' beliefs in internal versus external determinants of success. *Journal of Social Psychology*, **114**, 199–207.

Venables, P. (1956) Car driving consistency and measures of personality. *Journal of Applied Psychology*. **40**, 21–24.

Venkatapathy, R. (1983). Biographical characteristics of first generation and second generation entrepreneurs. *Journal of Small Enterprise Development in Management*, **10**, 15–24.

Venkatapathy, R. (1984). Holland personality model among entrepreneurs. *Personality Study and Group Behaviour*, **4**, 86–93.

Venkataphy, R. (1985). Perception of self among first- and second-generation entrepreneurs. *Perceptual and Motor Skills*, **60**, 858.

Vondracek, F., Lerner, R., and Schulenberg, J. (1986). *Career Development: A Life-Span Development Approach*. Hillsdale, NJ: Lawrence Erlbaum.

Vroom, V. (1964). *Work and Motivation*. New York: Wiley.

Vroom, V. (1960). *Some Personality Determinants of the Effects of Participation*. Englewood Cliffs, NJ: Prentice Hall.

Wagner, E. (1960). Predicting success for young executives from objective test scores and personal data. *Personnel Psychology*, **13**, 181–186.

Wainer, H. and Rubin, I. (1969). Motivation of research and development entrepreneurs. *Journal of Applied Psychology*, **53**, 178–184.

Wakefield, J. (1979) *Using Personality to Individualize Instruction*. San Francisco: Edits.

Wall, T. and Payne, R. (1973). Are deficiency scores deficient? *Journal of Applied Psychology*, **58**, 322–326.

Walsh, W. and Osipow, S. (Eds) (1986). *Advances in Vocational Psychology*. Hillsdale, NJ: Lawrence Erlbaum.

Walsh, W., Bingham, R. and Sheffey, M. (1986). Holland's theory and college educated working black men and women. *Journal of Vocational Behaviour*, **29**, 194–200.

Walther, R. (1961). Self-description as a predictor of success or failure in foreign service clerical jobs. *Journal of Applied Psychology*, **45**, 16–21.

Wankel, L. and Kreisel, P. (1985). Factors underlying enjoyment of youth sports: Sports and age group comparisons. *Journal of Sports Psychology*, **7**, 51–64.

Wankowski, J. (1973). *Temperament, Motivation and Academic Achievement*. University of Birmingham: Unpublished report.

Wanous, J. and Lawler, E. (1972). Measurement and meaning of job satisfaction. *Journal of Applied Psychology*, **56**, 95–105.

Wanous, J., Keon, T. and Latack, J. (1983). Expectancy theory and occupational/organizational choices: A review and test. *Organizational Behaviour and Human Performance*, **32**, 66–86.

Ward, C. and Eisler, R. (1987). Type A behaviour, achievement striving, and a dysfunctional self-evaluation system. *Journal of Personality and Social Psychology*, **53**, 318–326.

Warr, P. (1987). *Work, Unemployment and Mental Health*. Oxford: Clarendon Press.

Warr, P., Jackson, P. and Banks, M. (1982). Duration of unemployment and psychological well-being in young men and women. *Current Psychological Research*, **2**, 207–214.

Weaver, K. (1987). Developing and implementing entrepreneurial cultures. *Journal of Creative Behaviour*, **22**, 184–195.

Weiner, N. (1980). Determinants and behavioural consequences of pay satisfaction: A comparison of two models. *Personnel Psychology*, **33**, 741–757.

Weiss, H. (1978). Social learning of work values in organization. *Journal of Applied Psychology*, **63**, 711–718.

Weiss, H. and Adler, S. (1984). Personality and organizational behaviour. *Research in Organizational Behaviour*, **4**, 1–50.

Weiss, H. and Shaw, A. (1979). Social influences on judgements about tasks. *Organizational Behaviour and Human Performance*, **24**, 126–140.

Wells, B. and Stacey, B. (1976a). A further comparison of cannabis (marijuana) users and non-users. *British Journal of Addiction*, **71**, 161–5.

Wells, B. and Stacey, B. (1976b). Social and psychological features of young drug misusers. *British Journal of Addiction*, **71**, 243–51.

Wheeler, K. (1981). Sex differences in perceptions of desired rewards, availability of rewards, and abilities in relation to occupational selection. *Journal of Occupational Psychology*, **54**, 141–148.

White, J. (1978). Individual differences and job quality–worker response relationship: Review, integration, and comments. *Academy of Management Review*, **21**, 267–279.

Whiting, B. (1987). Creativity and entrepreneurship: How do they relate? *Journal of Creative Behaviour*, **22**, 178–183.

Whitlock, G., Clouse, R. and Spencer, W. (1963). Predicting accident proneness. *Personality Psychology*, **16**, 35–44.

Whyte, W. (1963). Culture, industrial relations, and economic development: The case of Peru. *Industrial and Labour Relations Review*, July. 14–24.

Wiener, T. and Vaitenas, R. (1977): Personality correlates of voluntary mid career change in enterprising occupations. *Journal of Applied Psychology*, **62**, 706–712.

Wiggins, J., Lederer, D., Salkowe, A. and Rys, G. (1983). Job satisfaction related to tested congruence and differentiation. *Journal of Vocational Behaviour*, **23**, 112–121.

Wigington, J. (1983). The applicability of Holland's typology to clients. *Journal of Vocational Behaviour*, 23, 286–293.

Willerman, L., Horn, J. and Loehlin, J. (1977). The aptitude-achievement test distinction: A study of unrelated children reared together. *Behaviour Genetics*, 7, 465–470.

Wilson, D. (1975). Use of tests in United Biscuits. In K. Miller (Ed.) *Psychological Testing in Personnel Assessment*, p.45–60. New York: Wiley.

Wilson, D. (1986). An investigation of the properties of Kolb's Learning Style Inventory. *Leadership and Organizational Development Journal*, 7, 3–15.

Wilson, G. (1973). *The Psychology of Conservatism*. London: Academic Press.

Wilson, G., Tunstall, O. and Eysenck, H. (1972). Measurement of motivation in predicting industrial performance: A study of apprentice gas fitters. *Occupational Psychology*, 46, 15–24.

Wilson, G., Barrett, P. and Gray, J. (1989). Human reactions to reward and punishment: A questionnaire examination of Gray's personality theory. *British Journal of Psychology*, 80, 509–515.

Winefield, A., Tiggeman, M. and Smith, S. (1987). Unemployment, attributional style, and psychological well-being. *Personality and Individual Differences*, 8, 659–665.

Witt, L. (1989). Person–situation effects in the explanation of self-presentation on the job: Locus of control and psychological climate. *Journal of Social Behaviour and Personality*, 4, 521–530.

Woodruffe, C. (1990). *Assessment Centres: Identifying and Developing Competence*. London: IPM.

Wortman, M. (1987). Entrepreneurship: An ingrating typology and evaluation of the empirical research in the field. *Journal of Management*, 13, 259–279.

Wright, L. (1988). Type A behaviour pattern and coronary artery disease. *American Psychologist*, 43, 2–14.

Wunderlich, F. (1934). New aspects of unemployment in Germany. *Social Review*, 1, 97–110.

Yanico, B. and Mihlbauer, T. (1983). Students' self-estimated and actual knowledge of gender traditional and non-traditional occupations. *Journal of Vocational Behaviour*, 22, 278–287.

Yukl, G. (1989). Managerial leadership: A review of theory and research. *Journal of Management*, 15, 251–289.

Zedeck, S. (1977). An information processing model and approach to the study of motivation. *Organizational Behaviour and Human Performance*, 18, 47–77.

Zeldow, P., Clark, D., Daugherty, S. and Eckerfels, E. (1985). Personality indicators of psychosocial adjustment in first-year medical students. *Social Science and Medicine*, 20, 95–100.

Zuckerman, M. (1979). *Sensation Seeking: Beyond the Optimal Level of Arousal*. London: Wiley.

Name index

Aboud, J. 178
Abramson, L. 160–1
Adams, J. 209
Adlam, K. 112
Adler, S. 17–18, 343
Ahmed, S. 86, 191
Aldag, R. 245
Alderfer, C. 131–2
Allerhand, M. 303
Allison, C. 89
Allodi, F. 261
Amos, W. 185
Anderson, C. 21, 194
Andrews, C. 349, 351
Andrews, I. 256
Andrisani, P. 153
Anthony, W. 117–18
Argyle, M. 98, 312–14, 369
Arnett, J. 264
Arsenault, A. 257
Arvey, R. 214–15, 239, 326, 327
Atkinson, G. 89
Atkinson, J. 189
Ayers, J. 281

Babu, P. 187
Baehr, M. 233, 234, 235
Bailey, J. 186
Bakke, E. 304
Balch, R. 114, 115
Banks, M. 301, 312
Banks, O. 118
Baran, P. 171
Barbarik, L. 261
Barrett, G. 260
Bartell, R. 302
Barthol, R. 45–6, 122–3

Bartnick, L. 116
Bartol, K. 246, 248
Bartram, D. 74–5
Bates, G. 101
Beaton, R. 56
Beatty, R. 17
Beaubrun, M. 283
Beck, K. 272
Becker, B. 153–4
Begley, T. 186, 187, 188, 191–2, 195, 271
Behrman, J. 351
Belbin, M. 349, 368–71
Bem, S. 247, 290–1
Bendig, A. 70–1, 73
Benge, E. 245
Bennett, S. 117
Bentz, V. 56–8, 83
Berman, F. 327
Bernardin, H. 17, 257
Betz, N. 108
Biberman, G. 86
Biesheuvel, S. 192
Birley, S. 182
Bishop, D. 76
Blau, G. 155
Blaycock, B. 67
Blinkhorn, S. 374
Block, T. 245
Bluen, S. 271
Blum, R. 115
Blumenthal, J. 271
Blunt, P. 74
Boddy, J. 219
Bohannon, W. 84
Bond, M. 136, 366
Booth-Kewley, S. 279–80

Subject index

ability 12; and success 222–31
ability tests 223–6; *see also* intelligence
   tests
absenteeism 72, 105; causes of 255–6;
   measuring and defining 250–5; and
   personality 257–8
academic performance: and neuroticism
   216; and personality 117–22
accident proneness 77, 262–3
accident repetitiveness 260
accidents 258–66; and individual
   differences 260–2; and personality
   263–6
achievement motivation: of
   entrepreneurs 189–93
activity: work as 137
adjustment, personal 28–32
adolescents *see* young people
advancement, career 26–32
affiliation motive 274–5
age: and accidents 261; as biographical
   pointer 239; of entrepreneurs 187
alcohol abuse: and personality 281; and
   unemployment 303–4
Alderfer's ERG needs theory 131–2
alpha press 135
ambition 26, 27, 28
aptitude tests 42–3, 223–6
Armed Forces Questionnaire Test
   (AFQT) 225
Armed Services Vocational
   Aptitude Battery (ASVB)
   225–6
arousal levels 110, 211–12, 289–90, 342,
   362–3, 364
artists: introversion of 121
assessment centres 330–2

attainment, occupational: social
   factors 23–5
attentional focus 359
attitude questionnaires 87–8
attributional style 160–4; and
   interviews 325–6; and job
   satisfaction 211–12; and sport
   293; and success 359; and
   unemployment 308–9
Attributional Style Questionnaire
   (ASQ) 161
Australia 316

balance: of traits 328
Behaviour Check Questionnaire 191
behaviour *see* occupational behaviour;
   organizational behaviour
behaviour event interview 327
behaviour potential 193
behavioural plasticity 358–60
Belbin Team-Role Self-Perception
   Inventory (BTRSPI) 368–72
beliefs, work 141–5
Bernreuter Personality Inventory 87
beta press 135
bias: in early personality tests 51–3
biodata 235–42; compared to
   personality tests 237–8
biography 9–10; of entrepreneurs
   186–9; of managers 84; as predictor
   of success 231–42
biographical questionnaires 236–7
biotechnology 178, 180
body type: and sport 295
businessmen: personality
   tests 71; *see also* managers;
   salespeople